Coulomb AND THE EVOLUTION OF PHYSICS AND ENGINEERING IN EIGHTEENTH-CENTURY FRANCE

Charles Augustin Coulomb, in the dark blue coat with red piping and brass buttons of the *Corps royal du génie*. He is wearing the *Croix de Saint Louis* and holding his torsion balance and a paper artificially entitled *"Traité de phisique* [sic] *et magnétisme."* The medal awarded him by the *Legion d'honneur* rests on the table. The portrait was probably painted between 1803 and the year of his death, 1806; the artist is unknown.

C. Stewart Gillmor

Coulomb AND THE EVOLUTION
OF PHYSICS AND ENGINEERING
IN EIGHTEENTH-CENTURY FRANCE

Princeton University Press
Princeton, New Jersey, 1971

Printed in the United States of America
by Princeton University Press, Princeton, New Jersey

This book has been composed in Linotype Times Roman

Publication of this book has been aided by a grant from
the Louis A. Robb Fund of
Princeton University Press

To E.N.G.
and to the memory
of C.S.G.

Preface

Charles Augustin Coulomb was a physicist and engineer of the first rank. Beyond this he held important positions of service to the French government both before the Revolution and in the first years of the Empire. Coulomb is known for his work in electricity and magnetism. His engineering studies, his personal life, and his career as a public servant are much less familiar to historians of science and to the general reader. This biography intends to give a full account of his life and to present as well a rather complete analysis of his work in engineering mechanics and in physics. It is hoped that this will be of use to those engineers and physicists who share with me an interest in the historical development of these disciplines. In addition, historians may profit from the discussions here of the relations between science and government in eighteenth-century France.

The body of this study consists of six chapters. Of these, the first two are devoted to Coulomb's biography and the last four to his studies in engineering and in physics. Engineering developed rapidly in early eighteenth-century France, and by mid-century there were well-established groups of men in several engineering disciplines. Even so, Coulomb's mathematical training at the *Collège de France* and at the *Ecole du génie* at Mézières provided him with the means to approach many basic engineering problems in new ways. Mathematics alone did not make him an engineer. Following his graduation from Mézières, he entered into a period of twenty years of engineering in the field, separated from Paris and most of the scientific activity of his day. It was during this time that he gained the experience which, coupled with his use of rational analysis, allowed him to conceive of attacking engineering problems through a "mélange du calcul et de la physique." Chapter I presents this part of his biography.

Chapter II discusses Coulomb's life and career after he turned to physics. He entered the French Academy of Sciences in 1781 but he was elected on his reputation as engineer rather than physicist.

His engineering, which had benefited from his early work in mathematics, now contributed to his development as a physicist. Biot said that one owes to Borda and to Coulomb the renaissance of exact physics in France. Delambre saw Coulomb's contributions to physics in the same way. Both men meant by this "physics" not rational mechanics but the emerging fields of heat, light, crystallography, electricity and magnetism. Coulomb's physics was colored by his conception of experiment. He brought to physical experimentation not only his instrumental ability but also a sense of significance and reality gained from his work in engineering.

Coulomb's twenty-five years as member of the Academy of Sciences and of its successor, the Institute, were filled with other duties in addition to those of Academician and physicist. He participated in the administration of waters and fountains, the reform of hospitals and the system of weights and measures, and after the Revolution, in the reorganization of French education.

Discussions of Coulomb's technical studies occupy their proper chronological place in the two biographical chapters, but separate, detailed examinations of these comprise the last four chapters of this book. Chapters III and IV examine his work in strength of materials, soil mechanics, structural design and friction. General questions of mechanics and of the nature of close-acting forces in friction and cohesion carry over into his later work in physics. Chapter V discusses Coulomb's work in the physics of torsion and its applications to research in other areas of physics. Chapter VI explores both his experimental work and his theories in electricity and magnetism. The work as well as the life of a biographical subject must be seen in the context of his times. Coulomb's lesser known works in engineering and applied mechanics are examined in terms of the history of certain problems or disciplines and thus Chapters III and IV, particularly, treat of seventeenth- and earlier eighteenth-century events in some detail. Finally, Coulomb's activities in his last years are presented in an Epilogue.

Beyond the life and career of Coulomb, this book considers the general development of certain fields in physics and in engineering. It has come to be acknowledged that the various sciences were affected differently in the scientific revolution. The physics of the early eighteenth century was not merely a less mathematized version as Clerk Maxwell knew it or as we know it today. Some have chosen to see the evolution of physics in terms of the mathematization of the natural philosophy: analysis as first applied to mechan-

ics eventually ordering heat and light and electricity and magnetism by the turn of the nineteenth century. These latter fields did
not join with mechanics to form what we call physics quite so
easily. They did, however, emerge from that somewhat disordered
realm the French called *la physique générale* during the lifetime of
men like Coulomb, Borda, and Lazare Carnot.

This biography is not a history of classical physics, but one of
its themes is that engineering, particularly as it evolved in France,
played a significant role in the emergence of physics. Coulomb's
studies in physics were strongly influenced by his earlier work in
applied mechanics and engineering. He and some of his contemporaries criticized the nature of some rational mechanical solutions to
real, *physical* problems. They also criticized, however, the sometimes useless or randomly curious experiments of the early natural
philosophers, practitioners of *physique générale*, or personalities
of the *cabinet de physique* and the *salon*. The best early eighteenth-
century natural philosophers, like Musschenbroek and Desaguliers, rejected overspeculative hypotheses and called for physics to
be based upon experiment. At the same time, Bélidor, Frézier, and
other engineering writers took engineers to task for dismissing *la
théorie* and dealing only with *la pratique*. Each of these groups,
however, tended to overestimate the ease with which the problems
of their *pratique-théorique* duality could be overcome. They both
wrote on most or all things of interest; their investigations were
often sweeping, their nets too coarse.

The balance of physics often turns on fine-edged pivots. That
Coulomb, for example, grasped the significance of exploiting fully
the physics of torsion in thin cylinders and then moved to establish
quantitatively the idea of Newtonian central forces in electrostatics
and magnetism in place of the Cartesian-inspired vortices and effluvia, marks a major step in its evolution. Coulomb called not
only for sophistication of mathematical techniques but for reality
in experiment and in physical hypotheses. As I indicate later, perhaps natural philosophy gave the curiosity, engineering the reality,
and rational analysis the harmony that characterize physics.

However one may wish to view its evolution, the period from
about 1775 to 1825 was an exciting time for physics. Lavoisier,
Laplace, Monge, Borda: close friends, or those with whom Coulomb worked, recognized this. Lagrange recognized it as well when
he wrote d'Alembert in 1781 dispiritedly: "Physics and chemistry
now offer riches more brilliant and easier to exploit; in addition,

the taste of the century appears to be entirely aimed in this direction, and it is not impossible that the chairs for Mathematics [*Géométrie*] in the Academies will one day occupy the same insignificant position that the University chairs in Arabic occupy at present." [*Oeuvres de Lagrange*, XIII, 368.] Charles Augustin Coulomb's career moved right through the heart of this period. I hope the reader shares my pleasure in following him as engineer and as physicist in eighteenth-century France.

There exists no previous biography of Coulomb, nor any single analysis of all of his work in science and engineering. I would have been unable to complete this work without the generous help of many persons, both in the United States and France, and it is a pleasure to express my gratitude to them. I am pleased to acknowledge a research grant from Wesleyan University and the editorial assistance of Mr. Andrew Gaus. The portrait of Charles Augustin Coulomb, reproduced here, belongs to Coulomb's great-great-grandson, to whom I am grateful. I owe a great debt to my teachers at Princeton University. In his seminar on the history of electricity and magnetism, and since that time, Professor Thomas Kuhn has helped me to recognize the opportunities and to understand the difficulties of investigating the history of physics. Professor Salomon Bochner of the Departments of Mathematics of Princeton and Rice Universities has been a welcome source of ideas and inspiration in my studies. Professor Charles Gillispie has continually given me aid and advice throughout the period of preparation of this work as dissertation adviser, constant reader, and friend. Finally, and most of all, I wish to thank my wife, Rogene Godding Gillmor, for her constant support and encouragement. The typing of the original manuscript and all of the drawings in this book are the product of her talents.

CHARLES STEWART GILLMOR
Higganum, Connecticut
October 1970

Contents

Illustrations

Tables

Tables

Coulomb AND THE EVOLUTION
OF PHYSICS AND ENGINEERING
IN EIGHTEENTH-CENTURY FRANCE

One · STUDENT AND ENGINEER

Introduction

This chapter considers that period of Coulomb's life and career from his birth until his election to membership in the French Academy of Sciences in 1781. Coulomb's major contributions in the first part of his career were in the field of applied mechanics and engineering. He entered engineering at a time when its better representatives were turning toward what one might call a rational rather than a traditional empirical engineering. His studies at the *Collège royal de France* with Le Monnier and at the engineering school at Mézières with Bossut aided him in obtaining a better grasp of mathematics than that possessed by those engineers practicing a generation before.

The experience he gained in Martinique, in Cherbourg, and in many other posts in France enabled him to bring to his engineering memoirs a realistic knowledge of the behavior of structures and materials and led to his fundamental studies in the strength of materials, earth-pressure theory, and friction.

By the time of his election to the Academy, Coulomb had already gained renown as an engineer. When he then turned to physics, both his mathematical training and his engineering experience supported his physical researches in profitable ways and led directly to his discoveries in torsion and indirectly to his quantification of the fields of electricity and magnetism.

Youthful Determination

Charles Augustin Coulomb was born June 14, 1736, in Angoulême, in the Angoumois. Two days later he was baptized in the parish church of St. André.[1] Little is known of his mother, Catherine Bajet, except that she was related on her maternal side to the wealthy French family of de Sénac.[2] His father, Henry Coulomb, had begun a career in the military, then left this for a petty government-administrator post, that of *Inspecteur des Domaines du Roi*. Charles Augustin was born away from his ancestral province, for the Coulombs came from Languedoc, and the family had lived for at least several generations in Montpellier.[3] They had traditionally been lawyers and Charles Augustin's older cousin Louis was head of a branch of the family which was to remain active in politics and finance throughout the eighteenth century.

As an *Inspecteur* of the king's domains, Henry Coulomb was liable to be transferred in the course of the royal business, thus, early in Charles Augustin's childhood, the family moved to Paris, where Henry became involved in the tax-farm system. Catherine, anxious that her son become a medical doctor, saw to it that he began attending the *Collège des quartre-nations*.

The *collège*, sometimes called the *Collège Mazarin*, was founded by the will of Cardinal Mazarin upon his death in 1661.[4] Something like a private high school, it opened its doors in 1688 and for the next century taught rhetoric, mathematics, physics, logic, religion, and the classical languages to approximately thirty boys aged ten to fifteen. Although Louis XIV's *lettres patentes* stated that the *collège* would educate "gentlemen, or those children of prominent residents who live like nobles,"[5] it became more and more difficult for a potential student to be admitted without proof of four degrees of *noblesse*. Proof of such nobility was determined by the ubiquitous d'Hozier, *Juge d'armes de la noblesse de France*[a].[6] Coulomb's name does not figure on d'Hozier's lists, however, this does not completely preclude his having attended as a student. The *collège* had a good name as a school for mathematics (Nicolas Delisle, d'Alembert, Lavoisier, and Bailly studied there), and the abbé Lacaille built an observatory and taught astronomy there for many years.[7] It is probable that Charles Augustin was not a regular student but one of the many *martinets*—the numerous youths, who like little martin-swallows, flitted from place to place.[b] If Coulomb attended the *collège* at the normal age, he would have entered sometime between 1746 and 1751.

Coulomb learned of Pierre Charles Le Monnier's mathematical lectures at the *Collège royal de France*, and he began attending there. Soon, much against his mother's wishes, he announced that

[a] There was a succession of members of the d'Hozier (or D'Hozier) family as genealogists but this would be Louis Pierre d'Hozier (1685–1767).

[b] There exist no student lists for the decades during which Coulomb could have been a student, but one of his memorials[8] states that he attended there.

he was going to become a mathematician. Henry Coulomb had no strong views about the question although most likely he would have supported Charles Augustin's plans, but fate in the form of the financial market intervened and removed him from the scene. A contemporary description of Henry states that "good-natured and unsuspecting, he engaged himself in speculations which reversed his fortune. . . ."[9] Penniless, Henry returned to the family home in Montpellier and left Charles and his sisters in the charge of their mother. Charles Augustin continued to deny his mother's desire that he study medicine and was therefore temporarily disowned. Without funds, he was forced to join his father in Montpellier.

Henry Coulomb had no money but was not entirely bereft of resources; the Montpellier Coulombs held substantial positions in the community. Cousin Louis was a lawyer, subdelegate to the *parlement* from the Bas-Languedoc, and a member of the *Cour des comptes et aides de Montpellier* (the provincial financial court).[10] Louis could provide more than just the normal legal and financial contacts of a lawyer. In Montpellier, a lawyer active in politics and administration would also be close to the center of scientific activity in the city. The *Société royale des sciences de Montpellier* was fiercely proud of its 1706 charter making it the second royal scientific society in France. A majority of the founders were lawyers and professional men, and cousin Louis was in a good position to introduce Charles Augustin to the scientific circle in Montpellier.

Nothing is known of Coulomb's formal schooling in Montpellier. If, indeed, he did seek schooling he might have attended the *Collège des Jesuites*.[11] This would have provided him with more training in Latin and classical religious philosophy but little beyond Aristotle in physics. If one is to believe the *éloges* (eulogies) of members of the Montpellier *Société des sciences*,[12] the scientific instruction at the Jesuit college was such that some students came to the society itself for tutoring as student members. Coulomb was not old enough to join the organization when he first came to Montpellier, but the permanent secretary, Hyacinthe de Ratte, indicates that Coulomb was acquainted with the members for some time before his entry in 1757 as a *membre adjoint*.[13]

In spite of its title and charter, the little society must have been a rather intimate and friendly club. It was patterned after the Academy in Paris, with three regular members in each of five classes: mathematics, anatomy, chemistry, botany, and physics. In addition to the regular members, there could be fifteen student (or adjunct) members, six honorary, and four foreign members, plus an unstated number of *associés libres* and correspondents.[14] In fact, there were never more than a handful in attendance; the average attendance at each meeting in 1757 and 1758 was nine.[c,15]

The society was in financial trouble from 1752 to 1757, and in this period it met on Thursday afternoons, at the home of Augustin Danyzy, one of its mathematicians. In 1757, it moved to its new home in an observatory built on part of the medieval city wall (today, the rue des Etuves). There was room below for a medical dissecting area and a chemistry laboratory; upstairs was a meeting salon and above this were towers and walkways for astronomical observations.[17]

To become an adjunct member, one had to live in or near Montpellier and be at least twenty years old. Coulomb was twenty-one when he read his first paper to the group assembled in Danyzy's living room on February 24, 1757. His paper, entitled a "Geometrical Essay on Mean Proportional Curves,"[18] met with general approval and was said by Jean Brun, who was appointed to examine the work and report to the members, to solve a "great number of problems."[19] Coulomb's paper was actually designed as an application for membership, and it seems to have been successful, for on March 23rd, Coulomb was elected: "The society in special assembly has named to the place of Adjunct for Mathematics, Mr. Coulomb, who has given various proofs of his ability. Mr. Coulomb has been elected in the usual manner, by ballot and with the plurality of votes."[20]

The organization stated that Coulomb "has, at an early age, made considerable progress in mathematics."[21] Coulomb took an active part in the work of the society and attended twenty-seven of the fifty-two meetings held during his sixteen-month period of membership. During this time, he presented five memoirs—two in

---

c During Coulomb's membership the mathematicians were Jean Brun, Hyacinthe de Ratte, and Augustin Danyzy. The physicists were Jean-Antoine Duvidal, marquis de Montferrier; Dominique de Senés, *fils*; and Jean Baptiste Romieu. Three of this number stand out for their abilities. Danyzy was a talented architect. Among other works, his theory of arch design was important in the history of this field and will be noted in Chapter III. De Ratte was a wealthy and talented young man who became permanent secretary at an early age and remained the backbone of the society until its dissolution in 1793. Both de Ratte and Romieu were lawyers and members of the *Cour des comptes et aides*. De Ratte would become Coulomb's closest friend and adviser at Montpellier.[16]

mathematics and three in astronomy. After his first paper on mean proportional curves, he presented another on the movement of bodies on mobile planes. In astronomy, he read memoirs on calculating a meridian line and on observations of a comet and of a lunar eclipse.[22] Much of his time was spent working with de Ratte on astronomical measurements. This field work would have had great appeal for the young man. In both the eclipse and comet measurements, where he assisted de Ratte, there was a sense of contributing to the efforts of the scientific community. The comet measurements were particularly important to him; he was still interested in the project when he wrote to de Ratte from Paris a year later.[23]

Coulomb could have had a fine career as a member of the Montpellier society, but this work provided only intellectual remuneration. He needed to find a post which would provide him a living and at the same time allow him the opportunity to continue his scientific studies. There were few options which would sustain a young bourgeois or petty noble; he could become an *abbé* and obtain a sinecure from the church, or he could enter civil or military service, possibly as an engineer. An engineering career seemed the better alternative. Other military branches—marine, artillery, infantry—offered easier advancement through the ranks but did not compare in the quality of their technical standards or the intelligence of their officer corps. The choice then fell between the civil engineers in the *Ponts et chaussées* (Bridges and roads) and the military *Corps du génie* (Engineer corps). At this time, the *Ecole du génie* (School of military engineering) at Mézières was the best technical school in Europe. With his father's blessing, Coulomb decided to enter the *Corps du génie*. It would be necessary, then, to prepare for and pass the entrance exam to the school at Mézières. Several times a year, the abbé C.E.L. Camus administered the exam in Paris, and successful candidates usually had prepared for Camus through tutoring in Paris. Coulomb decided to leave Montpellier and go to Paris. In the summer of 1758, he obtained from the Montpellier society a year's leave of absence from his position as adjunct member for mathematics and headed for Paris armed with letters of introduction to members of the Academy of Sciences in Paris.[24] De Ratte was a friend of several members of the Academy, including d'Alembert and Jean Baptiste Le Roy, as well as Pierre Charles Le Monnier, whom Coulomb had heard lecture at the *Collège royal de France*. In addition, Charles Le Roy, of the

Montpellier *Société des sciences*, was the younger brother of Jean
Baptiste Le Roy.

Unfortunately for Coulomb, he arrived in Paris in September,
just when the Academy began its annual two-month vacation. Apparently he was unfamiliar with its customs for he thought it very
strange that though he knocked on many doors[25] the only two persons he met were Le Roy and Le Monnier. He sought lodging near
his fellow Languedocians on the rue du Bouloy—just across the
street from the Hôtel du Languedoc.

Coulomb's arrival in Paris marked a clear break with Montpellier and the *Société des sciences*. His friends carried him on the
attendance books well past the end of his one-year leave of absence.
Finally it became clear that Coulomb was indeed going to become
a royal military engineer; when another young candidate[d,26] came
along in 1761, the society removed Coulomb from the rolls.

Coulomb pursued his mathematical studies in Paris for nine
months; the name of his tutor, if he had one, is not known. He
then passed the abbé Camus' exam for entrance to the *Ecole du
génie* at Mézières and prepared to take up residence at the school
in February 1760.

Coulomb's reasons for leaving Montpellier to begin a career as
a military engineer may not have been entirely financial; then, as
now, it would be only natural for a brilliant young man to leave
the provinces and seek his career in Paris. In spite of the convivi-
ality and spirit of the Montpellier *Société des sciences*, it was clear
that the center of continental science was Paris. It would be many
years, however, before Coulomb could find a permanent post in
Paris, and he would come as an engineer, later to become a physicist but not a mathematician. As interesting as his early mathematical notes might have been, they were the essays of a student.
Coulomb certainly had an adequate knowledge of rational mechanics. One of the most distinguishing traits of his memoirs, compared
to other engineering memoirs of the time, is that Coulomb had the
right mathematics for each problem. He stressed the point repeatedly, however, that his mathematical treatment stopped at the edge
of reality or practicality and that he left further abstract development to the *géomètres*.[e] His work is marked by a precision and

---

[d] Coulomb was replaced as adjunct member by Pitot de Launay, son of
the famous physicist and Academician, Henri Pitot, director of the Canal
du Languedoc.

[e] Until the late eighteenth century a "mathematician" would generally be

brevity not achieved by a Bélidor. Never, though, did he go back to "pure" mathematics. Every paper he wrote after leaving Montpellier was in applied mechanics or physics. Coulomb thought like a physicist rather than a mathematician. One of the fortunate features of his life is that he realized this.

Mézières: The Making of Engineers

The history of engineering in France rightly begins somewhere in the seventeenth century when considerations of the architecture and design of buildings and fortifications began to take on aspects of formal organization. Certainly ships, bridges, and buildings had been built for centuries, but toward the end of the seventeenth century, definite rules were formed for learning and practicing these arts. Textbooks and manuals were published, and certain scholars began to earn their living as teachers of engineering. In August 1681, Louis XIV ordered the establishment of chairs of hydrography in the large maritime cities of France.[27] From this date, officers in charge of the construction of naval vessels were required to take some training in mathematics, mechanics, and in what we would call today properties or strength of materials. From the late seventeenth century through the eighteenth, the men in charge of shipbuilding were known first as *constructeurs des vaisseaux* (shipbuilders) and later as *ingénieurs-constructeurs des vaisseaux* (shipbuilding engineers).[28]

Similarly, the civil and military engineering profession grew and defined itself during the reign of Louis XIV. The *Corps des ingénieurs du génie militaire* was founded in 1675.[f] Much of this was due to the work of Sebastian Prestre Vauban.[30] Vauban was the first famous military engineer in France; his thirty-three forts were treated with veneration for decades, as were apocryphal editions of his notes.[g] Vauban was instrumental in introducing the use of statistics in governmental studies, and he realized the value of mathe-

---

known as a *géomètre*, or perhaps, if he worked primarily in rational mechanics and analysis, as a *mécanicien*.

[f] The *Corps des ingénieurs des ponts et chaussées*, however, was not established until 1720.[29]

[g] The history of what Vauban did and did not write concerning military fortification became subject for heated debate in the latter half of the eighteenth century. A good part of the supposed treatises of Vauban were altered considerably by the engineer Louis de Cormontaingne (1695–1752), who published them. For a discussion of this see Reinhard[31] and Augoyat.[32]

matical training for military engineers. He was named a *Maréchal de France* in 1703. Beginning in that same year, those wanting to enter the engineering corps had to take an examination in the mathematical sciences, introduced by Vauban. The first *examinateur des ingénieurs* was Joseph Sauveur, *Professeur royal de mathématiques* and member of the Academy of Sciences.[33] The original corps of military engineers evolved during the eighteenth century.

In 1725, about 300 engineers were formed into a *Corps du génie* headed by a *Directeur général des fortifications,* or *Commissaire.*[34] Early engineers had studied texts like Pierre Bullet's *L'architecture pratique.*[35] After the formation of the corps, more comprehensive texts were introduced—for example, the important *Traité de stéréotomie* of Amédée François Frézier[36] and Bernard Forest de Bélidor's[37] *La science des ingénieurs* and *L'architecture hydraulique.* These works exerted tremendous influence on the early growth of engineering. With the formation of the *Corps du génie,* the entrance examination required a knowledge of geometry, elements of mathematics, drafting and design, and principles of fortification.[38]

Until 1744, there was a military engineering corps, there were standard texts, and there was certainly an established tradition of engineering practice, but the *Corps du génie* still existed only in an amorphous state. A royal order of February 7th, 1744, gave the corps its first regular organization and regulations and fixed the number of military engineers at 300.[39] Impetus for the founding in 1749 of an engineering school at Mézières came from Nicolas de Chastillon, descendant of a long line of military officers[40] and later *Brigadier* and *Directeur des fortifications de la Meuse.*

The curriculum at Mézières was divided into theory and practice.[41] Three days of the week were reserved for theory with three hours in the morning for architectural design, drafting, and map work, and three hours in the evening for mathematics. Another three days were devoted to surveying, field mapping, and so forth. The "mathematics" consisted of the teaching performed by the abbé Camus, the school's examiner. In 1748, comte d'Argenson, then Minister of War, had designated Camus to prepare a course for engineers, comprising the "elements of the sciences." This course was published in three parts (in four volumes) in 1749–1752 as *Cours de mathématique*[42] and was used both at Mézières and also as preparatory material for entrance to the school. The first two volumes covered arithmetic and geometry and some knowledge of these was necessary to pass Camus' entrance exam. Volume I detailed how to count, how to manage money and systems of units, as well as decimals, fractions, and logarithms. Volume II covered basic plane geometry and a little plane trigonometry and solid geometry.

At the end of Volume II, Camus introduced a discussion of the *anse de panier* (an empirical approximation to a semi-ellipse, composed of arcs of several circles), and its use in the design of arches. This taste of mechanics led to Volumes III and IV, which were concerned with statics. There the student was instructed in composition of forces, centers of gravity, empirical solutions to arch curves, the geometrical design of gear wheels; in general, the statics of the seven simple machines. Comte d'Argenson wished the students also to be instructed in the elements of hydraulics. Camus never published a text on this subject but utilized earlier material by Mariotte[43] and Varignon.[44] Though written at a rudimentary level, Camus' volumes were quite good, especially the first two on elementary arithmetic and geometry. It must be said, however, that Camus' teaching did not involve the students in problems of higher mathematics or indeed in problems of engineering construction requiring the use of infinitesimal analysis.

As for the subjects of mapping, fortifications, and surveying, these were usually taught by one or two regular engineers assigned to Mézières as assistant commandants. The standard texts by the 1750s would have been the works by Bélidor and Frézier, cited above. Practical subjects included the art of stonecutting, study of fortifications, empirical methods of designing and constructing vaults and arches, the design of retaining walls, the operation of hydraulic, animal, and manually operated machines, and methods of bookkeeping and estimating construction costs. All of the Mézières students spent much time outdoors directing local public works.[45] They constructed bridges and arches and if these structures seemed unsafe, they were torn down; if they appeared useful, they stayed in place.[h] The students gained practice as well at being paymasters and sometimes were required to round up peasants for labor gangs. In 1756, for example, the students supervised the con-

---

[h] Between 1755 and 1758 the artillery was united with the *génie* and therefore the work at the school during this period tended more than usual toward practical projects.[46]

struction of six bridges in the Mézières area. The school was not to reach its height until after the coming of the abbé Charles Bossut (in 1752) and especially of Gaspard Monge (in 1768), and in its early years it followed a practical line and eschewed a heavy reliance upon mathematics. It is probable that until this time, extra mathematical and theoretical training was to be obtained by separate work with the mathematics master and not as a part of the regular course. Nonetheless, Mézières soon became the outstanding technical school in Europe.

To enter, the prospective student was required to provide the Minister of War with four pieces of information: (1) place of birth, (2) age, (3) family status, and (4) financial help that he could expect from his relatives. Beyond this, he had to exhibit a drafting sample made under the eyes of the Mézières drafting instructor and then pass a preliminary examination in mathematics. If he successfully met these requirements, he was given a *lettre d'examen* permitting him to present himself in Paris before Camus for the final entrance exam. He was admitted to the school upon Camus' recommendation and was given the rank of *sous-lieutenant* or *lieutenant en second*. After one year, Camus again examined the students and wrote up a class ranking. At the end of the second or final year, Camus recommended the successful for graduation and promotion to *lieutenant en premier*.[47]

Most of the Mézières students were minor nobility, although until at least 1762 it was clearly permitted for bourgeois candidates to enter the school. Camus made this clear in a letter of December 16, 1751. If two candidates were of almost equal merit and one was noble, then the noble would be admitted; however, he said, "there is no policy of excluding those who are not nobles or who have not yet served in the Corps."[48] Even after the ordinance or *acte de notoriété* of December 4, 1762, which further strengthened the class-oriented admission policy, the school continued to admit promising candidates who lacked the proper credentials of birth.[49]

Coulomb is often listed in biographical sketches as Charles Augustin *de* Coulomb, implying noble birth. In none of several hundred extant examples of his signature and those of his family does anyone ever sign himself with the particle.[50] In *all* cases, Coulomb wrote his name only as "Coulomb." On engineering documents he often added "*Cap.^{ne} au C. R. du Génie*" (*Capitaine au Corps Royal du Génie*). His father signed his name simply "Henry Coulomb." There is a 1739 copy of Charles Augustin's birth certificate in the

Archives de la guerre, but it gives no evidence of nobility.[1,51] His cousin, Louis, is listed once in Montpellier archives as "Louis Coulomb, noble"; however, on Louis' own baptismal certificate his father, Etienne, is "Etienne Coulomb, bourgeois."[52] In sum, with the exception of an unofficial listing of cousin Louis, none of the family were ever known to sign themselves as noble, to claim nobility, nor is nobility indicated on any archival records in Paris.[53]

The nobility in Europe had originated as a knightly class with military functions. After the sixteenth century, however, an increasing number of families in France gained position and status by being admitted not to the old military and landed "sword" nobility (*noblesse d'épée*) but to a new administrative "robe" nobility (*noblesse de robe*), in recognition of their service to the state. Though it never attained the social prestige of the older nobility, this much larger class grew in wealth and power, especially under Louis XIV. One could attain robe nobility by acquiring hereditary offices by purchase, by obtaining membership in one of the thirteen *parlements* (legal corporations) of France, by holding numerous types of administrative offices and by other methods. There were in reality not one or two, but many ranks within the nobility in eighteenth-century France. The highest noble, with direct access to the king, and the poor provincial squire were worlds apart.

A family, though not of the nobility itself, could gain some of the status attached to certain lower orders of the robe nobility by proving several generations of family service with officer rank in the military. It is most likely that Coulomb was admitted to Mézières by this method, on the basis of his military heritage. His father, Henry, and a paternal ancestor, Etienne, at least are known to have pursued military careers at one time. Other students entered Mézières in the 1750s and 1760s with credentials less noble than those of Coulomb.

Two types of student entered Mézières: first, young students of seventeen or eighteen years of age who had no military training and second, *ingénieurs volontaires* who had served some years in the corps.[54]

[1] It is sometimes assumed that because Coulomb quit Paris in 1794 during the Terror that he was therefore a noble. Nobility would have added little to Coulomb's dangerous situation at that time. He was a very close friend of Lavoisier; he had been purged from the committee on weights and measures; he was (or had been just previously) the king's intendant for waters and fountains, lieutenant-colonel in the engineering corps, and a member of the abolished Academy of Sciences.

A sense of the Mézières student body can be gained by looking at the class which entered in 1755.[55] Of the ten students that comprised the class, five were youths eighteen years of age with no previous military training, three were lieutenants aged twenty-one to twenty-seven with five to twelve years service,[j] and two were older officers. Nine of this number were noble and one was the son of a military officer.

The students were certainly not without class prejudice. In early 1760, for example,[56] a young bourgeois entered after making a good mark on his exam before Camus. Once at Mézières, he was asked by some of the noble students to show proof of his ancestry by exhibiting his *extrait baptistaire* or leave at once. The youth refused to show his certificate and a near-riot resulted. Chastillon severely reprimanded the students for this display and the young man remained. Things were not as dark for a bourgeois as Marcel Reinhard tells in his work on Carnot,[57] but poignant letters from the 1760 student and his father to the commandant Chastillon show that a non-noble at Mézières might have to endure much heartbreak. Noble or not, the students were subject to punishment for disobeying the rules of the school. They could be fined up to three *livres* (pounds), confined to quarters, or even sent to prison.[58]

All was not conflict at Mézières. In 1753, Chastillon had moved the school into the old palace and buildings of the deceased Governor of Mézières. These pleasant but formidable old structures faced right onto the Meuse river and the whole school was housed there. Classrooms and staff quarters were in the old mansion. The students and the engineer in charge of relief maps lived in adjoining buildings. The long axis of this three-story edifice ran parallel to the river. Several wings running at angles away from the river completed the structure. The ground floor contained a workyard for carpentry and stonecutting and space for the relief maps. The second and third floors held the library, the three classrooms for drafting and mathematics, the *cabinet de physique*, and lodging for the two commandants.[59] Each student was provided with a private room. As *sous-lieutenants*, entering students received a salary of 600 *livres* per year. The veteran *ingénieurs volontaires* received an additional post allowance of 100 *livres*.[k,60] This was not a great

---

[j] An officer could enter service at the age of twelve.

[k] Chastillon, *Commandant* and *Directeur des fortifications*, received 5,600 *livres*; Lescouet, *ingénieur ordinaire* and *Commandant en second*, received 2,000 *livres*.

sum to live upon if the student had to buy food, candles, wood, supplies, uniforms, and support his social life from it. It seems that few actually did exist upon the minimum salary because in 1772, Lazare Carnot was considered an unusual person to be able to support himself and even provide some maintenance for his brother from his 600-*livre* salary.[61] When one considers the social life at Mézières it seems that most would have used considerable sums from home. Sunday was the only official holiday at Mézières but other social evenings were arranged and the students led a not too dreary life.[1]

Coulomb entered Mézières in the winter of 1760 and studied there until his graduation in November 1761.[m,63] Circumstances at Mézières were more or less as they had been for a decade. Uniforms were "of royal blue cloth with cuffs of black velvet and red serge lining, the coat . . . trimmed to the waist with gilded copper buttons—five on each pocket and as many on the sleeves."[n,64] The students still received 600 *livres* a year and carried the rank of *lieutenant en second* until their graduation. The official student population was thirty—there were thirty-two in Coulomb's first year and thirty-four in his second.[65] Chastillon remained as commandant of the school, Camus was examiner and Bossut was now the

---

[1] Some precious indications of student life at Mézières just before Coulomb arrived are recorded in a notebook kept by Rigobert Joseph Bourgeois[62] during his first year at Mézières (1756–1757). Bourgeois was a local boy whose father was royal surveyor and Chastillon's personal architect. According to Bourgeois, the students passed their free time at music, dancing, and games. Several of the students were amateur musicians and performed in public, notably at a special concert in Charleville where thirty musicians, including Bourgeois himself, performed a score written especially for the celebration of the birth of the duc de Bourbon in 1756. The students also gave dances almost every Sunday "aux dames de Charleville." Others gambled, playing at "la mouche, ou 30 et 40, avec mises d'argent." The night of the great celebration they completed the concert, then danced until 4 A.M. in a room provided with four casks of wine—one in each corner of the room. They all then went for onion soup at a local restaurant.

The students took their meals in town, and Bourgeois relates that their favorite treats were waffles, ham, and *tourtelets* (small pieces of dough boiled and then dipped in milk or in a *sauce verte*). Then as today in small French towns, traveling carnivals and marionette shows passed through Mézières. The scope of these diversions is revealed when Bourgeois describes one carnival as having three monkeys and a lion.

[m] Coulomb passed Camus's entrance exam in Paris in the summer of 1759 and entered the school on February 11, 1760.

[n] Striking as these uniforms were they would later be changed, because it seemed that everyone mistook the gaily colored engineers for bourgeois city merchants who also wore pants and coat of red and blue.

professor of mathematics. The school continued to offer courses in carpentry, stonecutting, and drafting. Nicolas Savart[o] was employed as *aide de laboratoire* to the abbé Nollet, who began teaching a short summer course in *physique expérimentale* in 1760, during Coulomb's first year.[66]

From various secondary accounts and from archival material, it is clear that training at the school was heavy on the practical side,[p] at least until the death of Chastillon in 1765. Coulomb participated in Nollet's physics course and probably knew the material presented in his recently published six-volume work, *Leçons de physique expérimentale*.[68] This comprised general notions of matter and gravity, simple mechanics and elements of light, astronomy, electricity and magnetism, and diverse aspects of natural philosophy. Only the most rudimentary knowledge of arithmetic and geometry was necessary to study this course. For a man who was already a member for mathematics in the Montpellier *Société des sciences*, however, something more challenging than Nollet's simple textbooks would be needed. Coulomb would have had to turn to Bossut for further study. Bossut had been ordered to teach the course of mathematics as outlined in the four-volume text of abbé Camus: arithmetic, geometry and statics. He soon widened the presentation to include calculus, perspective geometry, dynamics and hydrodynamics. Coulomb would have received this in the form of lectures or notes as the texts were published after his graduation. Bossut's first text on statics and dynamics,[69] however, was presented to the Academy in Paris for its approval only six months after Coulomb left Mézières, and some of the experiments within the book were described as having been performed at Mézières. At this same time, Bossut circulated notes of his course in hydrodynamics, which appeared in print in 1771.[70]

Though a student might have learned much from Bossut (and

[o] Nicholas Savart was the father of the physicist Felix Savart (1791–1841), born at Mézières.

[p] This designation of studies at Mézières as mostly "practical" would seem at variance with Marcel Reinhard's statements[67] concerning "theoretical studies" at Mézières. First, Reinhard is concerned mainly with Mézières a decade after Coulomb attended and at a time when Bossut and Monge were both teaching there. Second, Reinhard uses "theoretical" in the sense connoted by the words "specific, empirical," such as Vauban's *theory* of retaining wall dimensions. I use the word "practical" here in the sense of learning Vauban's empirical tables of retaining wall dimensions in contrast with "theoretical" as here connoted by the words "general, analytic," such as Euler's *theory* of deformable bodies.

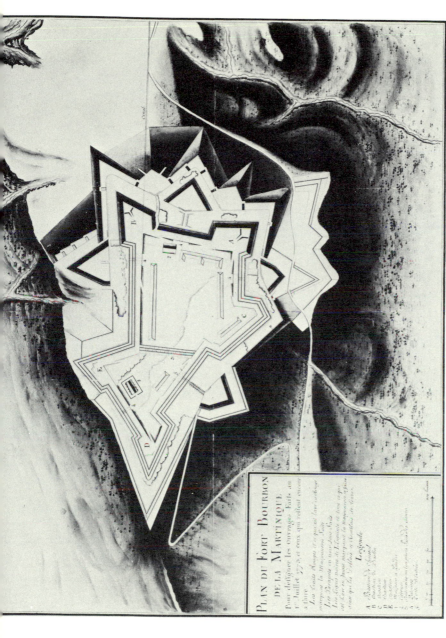

Fig. I.1. Map of Fort Bourbon, Martinique, July 10, 1773. From north to south (north is toward the upper right corner), the fort measured approximately 2000 feet; from east to west, approximately 1250 feet (Courtesy, Archives D'Outre-Mer)

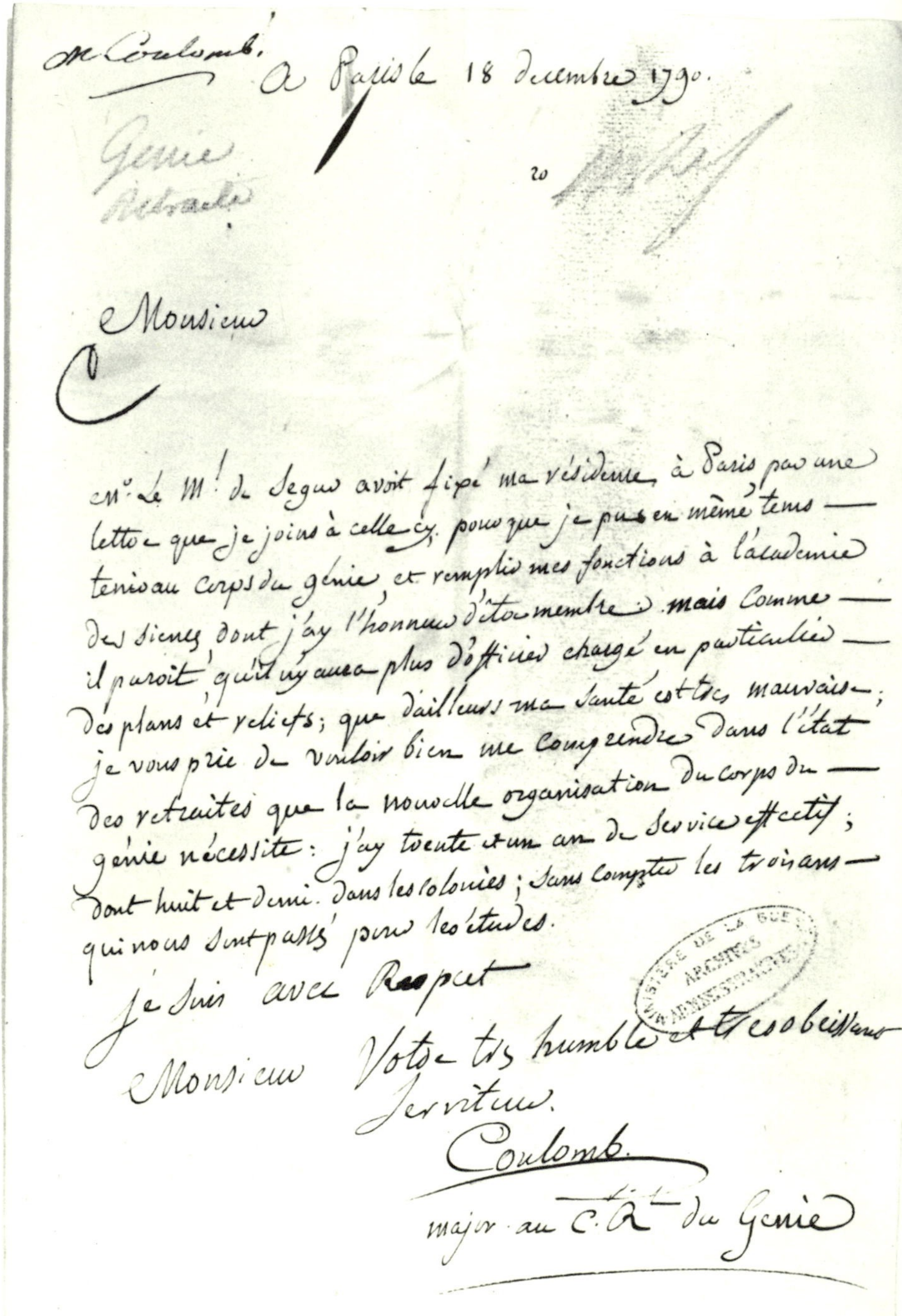

M. Coulomb.

à Paris le 18 decembre 1790.

Genie
Retraite

20

Monsieur

Mr. le Mis de Segur avoit fixé ma résidence à Paris par une lettre que je joins à celle cy, pour que je pus en même tems tenir au corps du génie, et remplir mes fonctions à l'académie des sciences dont j'ay l'honneur d'être membre. mais comme il paroit qu'il n'y aura plus d'officier chargé en particulier des plans et reliefs; que d'ailleurs ma santé est très mauvaise; je vous prie de vouloir bien me comprendre dans l'état des retraites que la nouvelle organisation du corps du génie nécessite: j'ay trente et un an de service effectif; dont huit et demi dans les colonies; sans compter les trois ans qui nous sont passés pour les études.

je suis avec respect

Monsieur Votre très humble et très obéissant serviteur.

Coulomb

major au C. Rl du Génie

MINISTERE DE LA GUERRE ARCHIVES ADMINISTRATIVES

FIG. I.2. Coulomb's letter tendering his resignation from the *Corps royal du génie* (Courtesy, Archives de la Guerre) it is clear that Coulomb did benefit in the application of analysis to numerous engineering problems), this did not guarantee the student graduating from Mézières with high marks. Since Camus avoided including much of this material in his yearly and final examinations, it was possible for a student to have done well at Mézières without coming close to Bossut or his teaching. Coulomb began a long friendship with the older man at Mézières, a friendship which ended with Bossut, an elderly misanthrope, standing in as "friend of the family" with the widow to sign legal papers after Coulomb's death. A friendship with Bossut or excellent performance in course work did not necessarily mean an excellent record at Mézières. Chastillon, not Bossut, wrote up the school's records, and Chastillon was a severe reporter. His comments on all concerned only their deportment, their drafting work, and the quality of their design techniques in a practical problem on the art of military siege. Some of the students received such comments as "his siege memoir is worthless."[71] Coulomb received this report:

> M. Coulomb is from the Academy [*i.e.* the *Société des sciences*] of Montpellier. His conduct is good, he understands and executes drafting rather well. His siege memoir is worse than average, very badly portrayed, with erasures and jottings. It is carelessly done and employs incorrect nomenclature. He supposes, as have some others with his manner of thinking, that wood for gun-carriages and wagons may simply be found in the woods; this is to have little idea of construction. He has a certain intelligence, but not that which will make him advance in the Corps. His design of the arch for a covered walkway is done with care and intelligence except for some faults of color in the slope of the profile and lack of breadth in the parapets; the scale is not made with precision. . . .[72]

This opinion was written in December 1761. Coulomb and seven other students had passed the final examination in the autumn, and Camus had recommended them for graduation. Graduation implied a promotion to *lieutenant en premier* and for the better students, a monetary gratification. Of the eight students, Coulomb and two others received bonuses. He was awarded 150 *livres* "to arouse his interest."[73] Even though Coulomb finished relatively high in his class, Chastillon's report would seem to indicate that he was a mediocre student; this is not necessarily so. Chastillon, the old soldier, wanted to improve education in the *Corps du génie*. His view of a good military engineer was one who knew well how to use the tools of drafting, one who could plan and construct field battlements in the tradition of Vauban, an obedient student—in short, a "good soldier" in the traditional sense of the term. Chastillon did not appreciate the value of higher mathematics and applied mechanics in the education of an engineer and he resented Bossut's position in the school. Consider that Bossut was appointed professor of mathematics at the age of twenty-two and that he was recommended for the post not only by Camus but probably also by d'Alembert and Clairaut. Chastillon's opinion of Bossut is indicative of his general feelings about the use of higher mathematics in engineering. In 1757, he wrote of Bossut: "The abbé Bossut, who is well educated, aspires to make a name in higher mathematics, but he is lazy and has no taste nor aptitude for the skills that are cultivated at the school, so that he is poorly fitted for the position that he occupies."[74] Chastillon requested that several students of the graduating class be kept under his direction in the Meuse area. He recommended Coulomb for transfer.

Charles Augustin graduated November 12, 1761, with the rank of *lieutenant en premier,* was given the usual leave and then was posted to Brest under the orders of Filley.[75] Filley was in charge of coast works between Brest and La Rochelle and he assigned the young man to minor coastal mapping tasks. Normally, Coulomb would have completed his two-year tour of duty at Brest and then been reassigned elsewhere. Other circumstances intervened and decidedly changed the course of his whole career. The immediate cause was that he was in Brest and available to fill the spot of an engineer who became ill. The other cause dated from 1759, when the English attacked Port Royal on the island of Martinique.

Martinique: The Proving of an Engineer

When Coulomb was ordered to Martinique he was a young engineer with less than two years of service. In Martinique he would undertake the largest construction project of his engineering career —a project that cost the state six million *livres*. It was not originally planned that Coulomb would play a large role in fortification work in Martinique, in fact, he was not even scheduled there. He was conscripted at the last moment when another young engineer fell ill. The ship, *Brillant* (a vessel of the third rank with sixty-four guns), was in the harbor at Brest, ready to sail for Martinique and

Coulomb was the first engineer available to go as replacement. Under Captain de Guichen's command, the *Brillant* left Brest in February 1764, bound for Port Royal (now, Fort-de-France), Martinique.[76]

Conditions had changed in Martinique because of the Seven Years' War. In 1759, the English had appeared in front of Port Royal with seventeen ships and 8,000 men. The English fleet and marines destroyed the town and fort and then withdrew.[77] Later they returned and controlled Martinique until 1763, when they gave it back to the French as a result of the Treaty of Paris.

After the treaty, the engineering staff in Martinique was bolstered considerably under a French "crash" technical program.[q] The French Minister of War decided that Martinique must be put into a position where it could defend itself in future engagements with the English. This called for major fortification work to be done in Martinique as well as in Guadeloupe, Sainte Lucie, and Saint Domingue. Lieutenant-Colonel de Rochemore, then chief engineer at Bordeaux, had won a competition with his plans for a new fort at Martinique. Rochemore, an old engineer with over thirty years of service, was promoted to *Directeur des fortifications des Isles du Vent* and posted to Martinique to supervise the construction of his planned fort. In April 1763, he and ten other engineers sailed for Martinique.[79]

By September, Rochemore had sent discouraging reports to the duc de Choiseul, the new Minister of War. His garrison and engineers were all ill and unable to work. Two of the engineers died within the first six months and Rochemore requested not only replacements but also more engineers to begin work on the fort.[80] Choiseul saw that there were more than problems of personnel at Martinique. The War Ministry had serious second thoughts about the cost of Rochemore's designs—fifteen million *livres*. Besides the new fort, there were added expenses for repairing the fort and buildings in the town of Port Royal. This large sum would necessitate a greater tax burden on the trading and sugar companies in the Antilles. Before any further money was spent in Martinique,

q Normally, the complement of engineers in Martinique was three: a *Directeur des fortifications* and two *ingénieurs ordinaires*. The director had the same responsibilities as in a similar position in France. He was responsible for all work in the Islands and was required to visit each site at least annually. The regular engineers worked under the director and reported to him each month.[78]

Choiseul decided there had to be a major investigation of whether such a big fort was really necessary to defend the Islands. It was thus Choiseul's order that placed Coulomb on Captain de Guichen's *Brillant*.

Charles Augustin and four other replacements arrived at Port Royal in March 1764. They brought with them orders for a council of war to decide on the proposed fort.[81] Immediately, all engineers made an investigation of the local terrain and the state of the island's defenses. On April 4, 1764, a secret meeting was held to decide whether the fort should be constructed. The group included the marquis de la Motte Fénelon (Governor of the Isle of Martinique), comte d'Estaing (Governor General of the Isles sous le Vent), Rochemore, Coulomb, and the other engineers.

Rochemore outlined his plans. He stated that the existing fortifications in Port Royal could never successfully defend the island and that a major citadel would have to be constructed behind the town on Mount Garnier. This citadel would have to protect not only Port Royal and the old fort area but also the surrounding countryside. Rochemore heard opposition from three sides. The navy felt that the funds should be spent to improve the fleet. The infantry, that only an increased number of foot soldiers could do the job. Some of the engineers believed a simple trenchwork fortification should be built in the hills and that a reconstructed Fort Royal could defend itself. On the whole, the argument was between the service branches rather than among the engineers themselves.

The council composed a long report[82] in which each engineer gave his opinion on the matter. Both governors, Fénelon and d'Estaing, were against the plan. Coulomb strongly supported it. In his defense of Rochemore he said:

> The only defense of Martinique at present is Fort Royal, which is dominated by Mount Garnier and Mount Tartanson. Experience has shown, unfortunately, how insufficient this was for the defense of this island. It is necessary therefore to argue for the occupation of these two mountains. Mount Garnier, higher than Mount Tartanson, bounded for the most part by a steep slope, delimited almost everywhere by an escarpment, and possessing but a spit of ground from which it could be attacked with ease, should have been chosen. There has never been any difficulty on this point. It is therefore only a question of knowing whether the hill must be crowned by a regular fort or whether one can

avoid this expense and be content with a simple intrenched camp.

It seems to me that since it is decided that Fort Royal is insufficient, the position on Mount Garnier must constitute all the strength of the colony. The few inducted people that the weakness of our Navy permits us to carry and maintain in time of war in our colonies causes me to think that an intrenched camp cannot suffice on this hill, since this form of defense demands a kind of equality between the attacker and the attacked. There remains only one course to follow in order to reduce expenses: to limit oneself and establish on the hill only a simple redoubt. But it seems to me that this redoubt must naturally shelter a part of the inhabitants of the countryside in case of siege and at the same time support the people from the town on the plain below Fort Royal, so that it cannot be that limited a structure. I accept therefore in entirety the projects proposed by M. de Rochemore, and I believe that it is impossible safely to avoid the expenditure that he proposes.[83]

An informal vote was taken after the individual reports were presented. Rochemore, Coulomb, and two others supported the plans for a fort on Mount Garnier; the other ten abstained.[84]

One can only guess whether the engineers who abstained did so because of real doubts about the usefulness of the fort or because of thoughts about their careers. If the fort were to be a failure it might be best to go on record with Fénelon and d'Estaing, both Lieutenant-Generals and the island's Governors.[r] Coulomb's stand

[r] This difference of opinion as to the necessity of the fort on Mount Garnier did not disappear after the council decision of April 4, 1764. Grumbling continued, questioning the need for the fort. In particular, an infantry officer, the chevalier de St. Mauris, sent a series of essays[85] in 1765 and 1766 to the comte d'Ennery and to Versailles calling for the king to "dispense with sacrificing much money for an object that I find totally useless." St. Mauris emphasized the need for a stronger marine force and said that only a simple intrenched camp was needed on Mount Garnier. Another, anonymous, report[86] complained about the high taxes and waste of government money. The local complaints were of a familiar nature: the inhabitants of the island wished France to provide them complete protection against the English, but they didn't want to pay for it themselves. There may have been some lingering doubts among the engineers as well. In his final report of 1771,[87] Le Beuf, then director of fortifications, stated that the original fort as planned for Mount Garnier had numerous faults. These faults he ascribed to the designer (evidently Rochemore). Le Beuf felt, though, that most of the defects had been corrected and that as of 1771, the fort could withstand any attack.

against authority here is characteristic of his career. He sometimes averted confrontation; he never backed down from it.

Rochemore's plan was finally adopted in modified form. Preliminary plans had called for fifteen million, and then eleven million *livres* to be spent in the mountains. The final plans allotted 6,675,-530 *livres* for fortification expenses—6,000,000 of this sum for the fort on Mount Garnier.[88]

Rochemore saw the completed fort as being able either to defeat an enemy outright or to keep him at bay until the coming of the *mauvaises saisons* (rainy seasons) forced him to choose between withdrawing or losing his army to dysentery and tropical diseases. He also believed that a strongly fortified Martinique would force the English to attack with their major forces, thus leaving their own colonies undefended. In this event, even the weak French fleet could attack the English colonies and force the English fleet to withdraw from Martinique to the defense of their own colonies.

Perhaps because of his talents, or more probably because he was one of the few to support Rochemore, Coulomb was put in charge of the work on Mount Garnier.

In March 1765, one year after the council of war, Rochemore wrote the Minister that work was progressing on the minor projects around Fort Royal and that all plans were completed for the fort on Mount Garnier and work there would begin immediately. Some months before, temporary barracks had been erected on the mountain to house the laborers and engineers working there.[89] Barracks there were, but never enough laborers. In the first year of construction, Coulomb was able to get only eighty men from the Royal Marine regiment, seventy from the Saintonge Infantry Corps, and twenty-four workers from a local mill.[90] Shortly after this, comte d'Ennery wrote Choiseul that there would soon be 600 men working on the fort. This was an exaggeration; in May 1766, Rochemore reported he could get only 240 men to work on the fort.[91]

In spite of the labor shortage, Coulomb's work showed results. Reports of the work were written by comte d'Ennery who wrote as though he were personally responsible for all construction work.[92] In truth, he rarely visited Coulomb's work site and Coulomb was never mentioned to the *Directeurs de fortification* at Versailles. Charles Augustin had the first stage of the work ready in the winter of 1767. This comprised the covered roadway, the *demi-lune* (a crescent-shaped fortification), and a large cistern; and the completion of these tasks contributed to his promotion to *capitaine* on March 4, 1767.

Illness continued to plague the corps in Martinique. Coulomb fell seriously ill several times but was forced to continue work. Deaths among the engineers made the load even heavier on the living. In requesting more engineers, Rochemore said:

> I have the honor of representing to you the necessity of sending here additional engineers to replace the dead and those whose health has required their return to France. I have remaining here only three Ordinary Engineers [out of nine]. . . . Our three gentlemen are on duty every day without having even Sundays for rest, since every week at that time they must make out the accounts for fortnightly payments—to the troops one week and to the laborers the next. . . .[93]

Things were no better in the other islands. The next winter Rochemore's chief engineer at Guadeloupe fell seriously ill and the assistant engineer went mad.[94] Illness slowed progress, but the fort on Mount Garnier was still planned for completion in 1771. Coulomb remained in full charge of the project for eight years, from the first terrain survey until near completion of the work. A six-million-*livre* investment was a tremendous responsibility for a young engineer. It is true that Coulomb was twenty-seven years old when he came to Martinique, but his field experience was very limited. His duty in Martinique was not only a success for the *Corps du génie*, it was a tremendous experience for Coulomb personally. Eight years of redesign and construction of this large fort forged the engineer. Coulomb later said of these days:

> I was responsible during eight years (and almost always alone), for the construction of Fort Bourbon and for a workgang of 1200 men,[s] where I was often in the situation of discovering how much all the theories, founded upon hypotheses or upon experiments carried out in miniature in a *cabinet de physique*, were insufficient guides in practice. I devoted myself to every form of research that could be applied to the enterprises that engineering officers undertake.[95]

[s] The fort on Mount Garnier was named "Fort Bourbon" in 1766. Coulomb mentions 1,200 laborers; apparently he was able eventually to obtain a very large work force.

Coulomb was in charge of stonecutting, earth and rock removal, masonry work, and, of course, the design of vaults, retaining walls, and other structural features. This experience resulted in several of the memoirs that Coulomb later presented to the Academy of Sciences, namely his statics memoir of 1773, "Essay on an Application of the Rules of *Maxima* and *Minima* to some Problems in Statics, Relating to Architecture,"[96] and the versions of his memoir on the efficiency of laboring men, read in 1778, 1780, and finally in 1799 ("Results of several Experiments Designed to Determine the *Quantity of Action*[t] which Men can Produce in their Daily Work, According to the Different Manners in which They Employ Their Forces").[97]

In 1770 the fort was almost completed. (For a map of Fort Bourbon drawn shortly after Coulomb's duty ended, see Fig. I.1.)[98] Once again Coulomb was seriously ill and now he asked to be allowed to return to France. His work had been exemplary, and he had been promoted to captain when only six years out of Mézières. Both Rochemore and Le Beuf,[u] the new *Directeur*, thought highly of his work. Normally, his transfer would have been approved with no trouble. Coulomb probably thought he was going home in 1771, but because of a devious trick of Le Beuf's, Coulomb had to spend yet another year in Martinique. On October 12, 1770, Le Beuf wrote to Versailles[100] that Coulomb was seriously ill and requested that he be sent home to France. He recalled Coulomb's outstanding service and several illnesses while in Martinique. He said, in fact, that Coulomb should be allowed to return home for recuperation if only in consideration of his future value to the state. This letter was certain to obtain Coulomb's transfer the following March.

Five days later, on October 17th, Le Beuf wrote a second letter which compelled Coulomb to remain for another year. This one made no mention of Coulomb's illness; it spoke instead of Le Beuf's own yearning for France. He said he himself was ill and had to

---

[t] *Quantity of action* as used by Coulomb is physically equivalent to the modern definition of *work*, although the term *work* itself (*travail*) was coined by G. G. Coriolis in the early nineteenth century.

[u] In 1768 Rochemore married and returned to France. Soulhiac, then chief engineer, took over as acting director of fortifications until the arrival of Le Beuf in 1769. Geofroy replaced Foulliac as chief engineer.[99] Coulomb remained in charge of construction at the fort throughout these command changes.

come home. The ministry could put to rest any fears about the conduct of work in his absence, he said, because everything would rest "in good hands" with Geofroy, the chief engineer, and with Coulomb, "who has been in charge of the work at Fort Bourbon since the beginning, and whom I have decided to keep here for the next year"![101]

Le Beuf did not suddenly become ill in those five days, and Coulomb certainly had not recovered in the same period. Le Beuf's double cross was not forgotten; Coulomb's widow even mentioned this unfortunate affair in a letter written in 1807.[102] The results of Le Beuf's letters were that he returned to France in June 1771, and Coulomb remained in Martinique until June 1772.[103] Coulomb's health was so affected by his illness during the eight-year tour of duty in Martinique that he was never again a well man.

Engineer and Academy Correspondent

Upon his return from Martinique, Coulomb was posted to Bouchain.[104] There were no engineering works in progress during his stay there, and he thus had the time to work on his memoir concerning civil engineering mechanics, "Essay on an Application of the Rules of *Maxima* and *Minima* to some Problems in Statics, Relating to Architecture."[v,105] He continued some experiments initiated in Martinique, but the substance of this memoir arose from his eight years of work on Fort Bourbon. He presented it to the Academy in Paris the spring after his return from Martinique. The essay covered the major problems of concern to civil engineers—strength of materials, flexure and rupture of beams, rupture of masonry piers, earth pressure theory, and design of arches.

This memoir was just the type to read at the Academy in Paris; Coulomb read it, in two sections,[106] in March and April 1773, probably upon Bossut's urging. The Academy viewed favorably Coulomb's presentation and requested Bossut and Jean Charles de Borda to examine the memoir.[107] Bossut and Borda were both friends[w] of Coulomb and were no doubt supporting his candidacy

---

[v] This memoir is the subject of Chapter III.

[w] The names of Charles Bossut (1730–1814) and Jean Charles de Borda (1733–1799) appear frequently in this study both in social and in scientific relationship to Coulomb. Bossut's part in Coulomb's life and career at Mézières and at the Academy of Sciences and the Institute is rather obvious. For additional discussion of Bossut see the article by Gillmor[108] and refer-

for membership in the Academy. A year passed before they presented their recommendations. Bossut wrote a glowing report, saying in part:

> Under this modest title, M. Coulomb encompasses, so to speak, all the statics of architecture. . . . We have noted everywhere in his researches a profound knowledge of infinitesimal analysis and much wisdom in his choice of physical hypotheses and in the applications he has made of them. We believe therefore that this work is quite worthy of being approved by the Academy and to be published in the *Recueil des savants étrangers.*[112]

The reception of his memoir brought happy consequences for Coulomb. In July 1774, Bossut and Vandermonde wrote to him to say that he had been appointed Bossut's correspondent to the Academy.[113]

The position of correspondent served more as a steppingstone to membership than as a medium for transmitting information. Six

---

ences therein. The relationship between Coulomb and Borda is less obvious; on Borda, see the article by Gillmor,[109] the biography by Mascart,[110] and comments in this note and below.

One can piece together occasional yet significant items to connect Coulomb and Borda. Each attended Mézières; their engineering paths crossed more than once (notably at Brest in the 1760s and in Brittany in 1783). Borda and Bossut reported on the first memoir Coulomb read at the Academy; again, they were both on the committee proposing the magnetism prize contest which Coulomb won. While a member of the Academy, Borda participated with Coulomb on 51 technical reports, a number exceeded only by Coulomb's reports with Bossut and with Le Roy. Borda and Coulomb served jointly on numerous committees, including weights and measures, both before and after the Revolution; in fact, each being a close friend of Lavoisier, was purged with him from the committee on weights and measures in 1793. During the Terror, Borda retired to Coulomb's property in the Loire valley. Finally, in 1799, Coulomb was one of the two Academicians chosen to visit Borda at his deathbed. Details of the private lives of each are rarely known, but Delambre, who knew each intimately, attests to their long friendship.

I cite in this book Biot and Rossel's statement[111] attributing the rebirth of exact physics in France to Borda and to Coulomb. These two names are linked, I believe, for several reasons. First, and rather trivial, the quote is taken from a memorial of Borda, thus the obvious use of his name. Second, Coulomb was one of Biot's great heroes, and Borda was the same for Rossel, a naval officer. Much more important is the similarity in their careers. Each was an engineer whose fame has come down to us as well in physics and mechanics. Each was concerned with the science of quantitative, precise measurement, and the invention and development of new measuring devices. Each worked toward the extension of the analytical methods of rational analysis coupled with experience gained in engineering situations to develop new fields in physics, such as magnetism and fluid mechanics.

times in seven years, Coulomb entered the arena of the Academy to read a memoir as Bossut's correspondent, but he read these personally and refrained from sending in bits of information for Bossut to relay to the Academy members. His visits to the Academy occurred during leaves of absence from his various military posts.

Coulomb learned of his appointment in Cherbourg, for he had been posted there from Bouchain. This new post was interesting for him. First of all, it was on the coast, and he wrote that the coastal cities were the only ones of real engineering interest for a military engineer. Also, the city of Cherbourg had a fledgling amateur scientific society which, though Coulomb found it rather unproductive, must have at least been entertaining.[114]

There were no major engineering projects at Cherbourg during Coulomb's stay from 1774–1776, but there were changes in the wind. Several of his exploratory memoirs helped establish recognition of the need for renovation of the fort and port of Cherbourg and its environs.[115] The story of engineering at Cherbourg really centers around Coulomb's chief, Pierre Jean de Caux, an old and clever engineer. After Coulomb left Cherbourg, de Caux supervised a long series of constructions and experienced numerous difficulties with the Department of the Marine and with the *Ponts et Chaussées*. Fortunately, de Caux had three good engineers in succession at Cherbourg: Coulomb, Lazare Carnot, and Jean Baptiste Meusnier!

Coulomb continued his scientific work in Cherbourg in his free time and during the slack winter periods. He spent most of his time at La Hougue, near Cherbourg, and it was here that he completed perhaps the most important essay he ever wrote—the "Investigations of the Best Method of Making Magnetic Needles."[x,116]

It is not certain why Coulomb left the field of engineering investigation for physics. Perhaps it was due in part to his friend Borda who had worked for some time on the improvement of magnetic compasses. Perhaps it was to relieve the periods of boredom that accompanied his stay in provincial duty posts. Most probably, Coulomb was spurred on by the Academy prize contest for 1777. In 1773, the Academy announced a contest on the best means of constructing magnetic compasses and set the date for 1775. No winner was chosen in 1775, and the Academy doubled the prize and reset the contest for 1777. Coulomb's memoir, which he com-

---

x This memoir is discussed in Chapters V and VI.

pleted in 1776, was to share the double prize with J. H. Van Swinden's work. The importance of this memoir for Coulomb's subsequent career in physics is that it contained elements of all of his major physical studies: the quantitative study of magnetic phenomena, torsion and the torsion balance, friction and fluid resistance, and the germ of his theory of electricity and magnetism. It was important to Coulomb personally in that it provided the major impulse for his election to the Academy in December 1781.[y]

One other event during Coulomb's stay at Cherbourg was to raise his reputation in the eyes of the *Corps du génie*. This was his submission of a memoir on the proposed reorganization of the *génie*. The comte de St. Germain became Minister of War in October 1775, during the Turgot administration. Coincident with Turgot's reforming aims, St. Germain announced a planned reorganization of the *Corps du génie* and called for memoirs on the question. Coulomb contributed one of the memoirs[z,118] that St. Germain would utilize in designing the new corps.

Marcel Reinhard[119] has attributed the tensions within the *Corps du génie* to the frustration of the individual and the limited upward mobility of engineers of non-noble birth. Coulomb did not see the problem of the *génie* in terms of individual frustration but in terms of efficiency and utility. His "Memoir on the Service of Officers of the *Corps du génie*"[120] was organized around two entities: the individual and the state. He sought to define the maximum utility to be obtained for each and to show that the best use of the *génie* brings the most to each individual. To obtain the best from the *génie*, the state must consider the total goals to be obtained from the art of fortification. The military defenses of the country must be viewed as a whole, and then the defense of France must be designed to fit into the overall plan of progress of the country.

---

[y] Coulomb was clearly a front-runner for candidacy by 1779. Bézout's promotion to *pensionnaire mécanicien surnumeraire* in December 1779, left a vacancy in the section of mechanics at the Academy. L'abbé Rochon was elected to fill this chair but Coulomb received the second place in the voting.[117] From this date, he was in a strong position to be elected at the next vacancy. Van Swinden gained as well. He was immediately elected correspondent to J. B. Le Roy at the Academy. He continued a steady relationship with the Academy and after the Revolution participated as a foreign delegate in the weights and measures work of the Institute.

[z] For the text of Coulomb's memoir, see Appendix C. Other authors consulted were Du Vignau, Le Bègue du Portail, d'Arcon, and the comte de Robien.

From a military standpoint, the alignment of engineering forces in 1776 was incoherent. Coulomb recalled that since a good military strategy requires a total plan, engineering works also necessitated such a program. He illustrated this by showing that the *Ponts et chaussées* were charged with the construction of port facilities, while the fortification works dealing with construction foundations were planned by the *sapeurs* (sappers) and *mineurs* (then under the control of the artillery). Greater advantage would be obtained from all, Coulomb claimed, by uniting the *sapeurs* and *mineurs* with the *génie* and by charging the latter with the construction of port facilities as well. Thus, for example, the immovable defenses of a port would be planned and built by a single authority. This would in turn provide the *génie* with more opportunity to engage in interesting and instructive projects. Not only would it fully justify its existence, each member would benefit from the challenge of work. Of the engineers, Coulomb said: "The more they are occupied during peacetime, the more they will acquire the means to be useful during wartime. . . . It is the same with the Spirit as with the Body; both have need of exercise for their preservation."[121]

This same philosophy obtained for the foot soldier. Why, asked Coulomb, leave 150,000 soldiers to languish in their garrisons and to become financial burdens both to their families and to the state? In time of peace, the *génie* could direct troops in the construction of "great highways, and navigable canals . . . and if we still have extra hands, then drain the marshes, and open up uncultivated lands. . . ."[122] As with the officers, so with the men: "The best means of increasing our wealth is to draw the greatest profit from every man."[123] Coulomb presented the Romans as the best example of all that an army could do: ". . . This warlike people proceeded to the conquest of the world only after having employed its legions in public works."[124] Talent and utility were the keynotes to this program. The state receives the most good from a system where men and programs are rigorously judged on their usefulness.

Coulomb stated that this judgment of utility could be obtained only by engineering decisions arrived upon within the *génie* itself. To this end, he proposed evaluation committees both at the local and national level. Local committees would review the works in their districts and a national one would review annually the projects undertaken or proposed by each district. This committee, composed of engineers, would provide the Minister of War with a fair appraisal of services rendered by the *génie*. Each engineer, even a lieutenant, would receive recognition based on the merits of his own work. The number of chief engineers would not be rigidly fixed but would vary with the amount of important projects to be done. With this new system, Coulomb contended, the existing number of engineers in the *Corps royal du génie* would be more than sufficient.

This was indeed a hardy proposal. The engineering corps would be reduced in number, and advancement within it would be on the basis of talent. Realizing that France was not always at war, Coulomb proposed to employ the army to undertake vast public works projects. Talent requires inspiration to be useful; usefulness necessitates continuous service to avoid boredom and waste. The *génie* would serve in peace as well as in war and render to France the maximum benefit from the science of engineering. The *génie* would and should be the pride of France and no more should a young engineer have to support the boredom and monotony of his service by devoting himself "to some branch of science or literature absolutely foreign to his work."[125]

Coulomb's memoir was among the few that figured in the reorganization of the *génie* in 1776. His suggestions for a national review committee bore some resemblance to the subsequently established board of thirteen *Directeurs des fortifications*. His plan for the use of troops for public works during peacetime was hardly realized. Troops had always been used for occasional public works projects (they would be used, for example, in the Brittany canal work in the 1780s), but no major program for the use of troops would emerge. Coulomb's call for advancement on the basis of ability and his characterization of the *génie* as a *Corps à talent*[126] would appear again in the works of Lazare Carnot and others. This ideal situation would never come about; inter-service waste and rivalry with the *Ponts et chaussées* would continue under the old regime.

Coulomb expressed a clear dissatisfaction with the condition of the *Corps du génie*, but his call for reform never bore that sense of frustration of the individual or perception of the state as an archaic monolith designed to crush the free man. He never framed his conceptions in the tones or phrases of Prieur or Carnot, of that later group of *ingénieurs-revolutionnaires*. Coulomb stressed not the evils of the state but the potential of the state and individual in balance. Talent, experience, inspiration—as parameters in a variational calculus of the human condition—could find a maximum of utility in engineering fused into a social technocracy.

In 1777, Coulomb was posted from Cherbourg to Besançon.[127] His duties there concerned only some small reparations to the fort and town of Salins. This limited duty and his good relations with Damoiseau, the *Directeur des fortifications à Bensançon*, permitted Coulomb to spend a large part of his time working on various engineering memoirs. One of these, "Memoir Containing the Description of a Pontoon Bridge, with Freely Submersible Sluices, for Clearing a Channel, or Closing a Dry-dock, with an Addition to This Memoir on a Means of Eliminating Friction in Arched Doors and Giving Them the Same Mobility as a Floating Body,"[128] was written in 1777 as a "classified" defense report and filed in the Ministry of War.[aa] A second memoir gained immediate popularity. The Academy of Rouen had given as the subject for a 1779 prize contest: "It Is Proposed to Remove a Boulder Which is Submerged under Water at All Times and Which Interferes with Navigation on the Seine near Quillebeuf. . . ." Coulomb wrote on this subject, intending to enter the memoir in the contest at Rouen. His *Investigations of the Means of Executing under Water All Types of Hydraulic Works without Employing Any Drainage Systems*[129] describes a floating chamber that could be lowered over an obstacle in a river. Once lowered into place, workers could enter a sealed chamber and proceed to remove the obstacle by ordinary means. The chamber was evacuated by pumps and while the men were working inside, other workers operated air pumps to keep a steady supply of fresh air entering the chamber. The men could remove the material dredged from the bottom through a series of air locks. Coulomb calculated the size of the working chamber and air pumps so that several men could work in the chamber at one time.

According to Coulomb, his fellow engineers thought it such a useful essay that they urged immediate publication. Thus, instead of presenting this caisson design to the Academy at Rouen, Coulomb read it in session at the Academy of Sciences in Paris (May 1779).[130] Le Monnier, Bossut, Bory, and Lavoisier quickly reported back to the Academy that the design was valuable and merited being published under the auspices of the Academy. As was

[aa] The present location of this manuscript is unknown.

his manner,[bb] Lavoisier suggested[132] some slight corrections, in this case concerning the amount of air a man would consume in breathing. The Academy sponsored the first edition of this memoir in 1779. It became an engineering best seller and was issued in later editions of 1797, 1819, and 1846. It is true this memoir was quite popular, and Coulomb's fellows no doubt did urge him to publish it. His reasons for withdrawing it from the Rouen contest were, however, more likely because it seemed a good memoir to read at the Academy in Paris. It is clear from Coulomb's letters and from his numerous leaves to Paris that he hoped for membership in this body. Memoirs read in provincial academies did not gain one entrance to the Academy in Paris. It is more likely that having been convinced of the novelty and usefulness of this engineering device, Coulomb sought to increase his chances for membership at Paris by reading it there.

Coulomb visited Paris and the Academy more than once during his duty in the brigade at Bensançon. D'Aumale, the younger, his chief, spoke very highly of Coulomb in the annual reports and supported his requests for leave.[133] In February 1778, Coulomb went to Paris to supervise publication of his magnetism essay which had shared the Academy prize of 1777. While there, he took the opportunity to read two other memoirs that he had written: one, "On the Most Advantageous Manner of Applying Force to the Movement of Machines," and the other, "On the Limits of a Man's Force and on the Impossibility of Imitating the Flight of Birds."[cc,134] Part of this work originated in Coulomb's experiences in Martinique and was written up in 1774, while he was at Bouchain. After reading the manuscripts at the Academy, he withdrew them to develop them further.

Following his service with the younger d'Aumale at Besançon, Coulomb was to be posted to Marseilles for 1779.[136] It is not known if he ever went to Marseilles, for two events were to change his route. The first was the death of his mother and the second the figurative rebirth of the marquis de Montalembert.

Coulomb's father, Henry, died sometime in the years when Coulomb was fort-building in Martinique. His mother died early

[bb] Note how Lavoisier corrected some passages relating to chemistry of the air in the memoir on the Hôtel-Dieu, written by the Hôtel-Dieu hospital committee and read at the Academy September 22, 1786.[131]

[cc] The manuscripts for these memoirs are lost. They probably appear in part in Coulomb's 1798 memoir on the efficiency of laboring men,[135] discussed in Chapter II.

in 1779. Ordinarily there would have been no need for an extended leave, but it seems that a businessman of dubious honor was mishandling Catherine Bajet Coulomb's estate, and Coulomb felt he had to get to Paris to save her considerable funds from dissolution.[137] The stubborn mother had temporarily disowned the stubborn son when he had rejected the career of a medical doctor, but she relented in the end, and Charles Augustin was to share in the inheritance with his sisters. And, while he was in Paris, there would be another good opportunity to read a paper at the Academy. It was, in fact, this time that he chose to present his description of the underwater dredging caisson.

Coulomb visited the Academy three times in the first week of May 1779,[138] to read and to discuss the paper on the dredging machine. His scientific conversations were cut short, however, by the arrival of orders directing him to proceed immediately to Rochefort.[139] His mother's affairs still unsettled, he left for the west coast of France knowing only that he would be involved in the construction of a fort near Rochefort; he would be under special orders to construct a new, experimental wooden structure and would serve under the engineer, de Carpilhet.[140] Though officially registered as serving in the Brigade of Toulon at Marseilles, Coulomb, with de Carpilhet, would be working on the tiny Ile d'Aix, some eight miles northwest of Rochefort at the mouth of the Charente river. What Coulomb did *not* know was that he would be serving under the overall command of the marquis de Montalembert—the *bête noire* of the army. Montalembert, an artillery officer and Lt. General, had a hatred for General Fourcroy de Ramecourt, the chief military engineer, and little regard for most of the members of the *Corps royal du génie*. Coulomb became embroiled at Aix in a personal battle between Fourcroy and Montalembert; a battle that began in 1761 and that continued until Fourcroy's death in 1791.

Numerous studies have discussed the merits of the controversial ideas of the marquis de Montalembert.[141] He fought against the traditional system of bastions and ramparts and relied on sheer firepower for the strength of his system. In place of the older bastioned systems, he suggested a system of *fortification perpendiculaire*, polygonal forts having several times the number of cannon usually employed in land fortifications. The spirit of Montalembert's system was reminiscent in fact of a landlocked man-o'-war. He became, and remained, a *cause célèbre* in French military engineering for many years, and the center of the controversy was the fortification of the Ile d'Aix—a tiny spit of land no more than a mile across. War with England was again at hand,[dd] and the Ministry saw no chance of building any kind of large fortifications at Aix in time. Montalembert jumped at the chance to prove the efficiency of his system. He claimed that he could build a usable fort of wood in just one month's time. He argued that the tremendous firepower would compensate for the lack of stone in its construction and that the cost would be only about three per cent of that of a conventional fort.

Major work on the wooden structure lasted from May until December 1779.[142] In the first months the carpenters worked in the shipyards in Rochefort preparing the wood. Pieces were designed and cut there and then transferred the eight miles to Aix. By the time the wood reached Aix it had warped, and Coulomb said it took an eternity to recut and fit each piece. According to him, Montalembert changed his mind almost every day about the design of the fort.[143] This is very probably true. As one advances through the archival reports, the estimate of cost, the number of cannon batteries, and other items concerning the design change from one report to the next. In January 1779, Montalembert said the fort on the Ile d'Aix would cost 600,000 *livres*.[144] In February 1779, he said 700,000.[145] By 1783, he had listed 1,170,000 *livres* spent for the fort and the town of Aix.[146] (Apparently, 720,000 of this was for the fort.) A year later, in 1784, he said that the fort had cost 490,000 *livres*.[147] It is very difficult to get an idea of just how much was finally spent on it. Carpilhet's estimate was 1,100,-000 *livres*;[148] Fourcroy's was 1,800,000 *livres*.[149]

Coulomb's criticisms[150] mirror these confusions; Montalembert changed the design plans constantly and kept little in the way of financial records. Coulomb was forced to go from the shipyard at Rochefort to the construction site at Aix three times a week. Each time, he said, he became sick on the way[ee] and each time he spent the day at Aix doing nothing. Montalembert had claimed that he could put together a partially built but usable fort within a month, but in October 1779, after six months' work, Coulomb said that the cannon were not yet installed. The odious climate added to Montalembert's personnel problems. The damp air arising from

[dd] England declared war on December 21, 1780.
[ee] It is not clear whether Coulomb became sick from the coach ride or from the boat ride from the mainland to Aix or both.

the terrible Rochefort marshes made most of his carpenters fall sick, and he was then forced to requisition workers from Bordeaux, Tours, and Nantes.

Fourcroy de Ramecourt was kept aware of the situation at Aix through letters from Filley and others and from maps and reports that Coulomb had sent to Versailles. In addition, the comte de Broglie had visited Aix and reported in writing on the bad condition of the fort.[151] Fourcroy visited Aix in October 1779. It had been a very rainy summer and the miserable fort was in an even worse state than his prejudices had led him to believe. Upon his return, he issued a scathing report[152] to the prince de Montbarey, the Minister of War.

Fourcroy said the wooden fort would soon rot in the damp climate. The interior humidity due to rain leakage would be terrible for the health of the troops and would ruin the powder stored in the magazines. The fort was almost unprotected at the back; thus, the enemy could land on the other side of the island and easily take the fort from that side. With only two feet between the batteries on the ground floor and the batteries above, enemy fire would soon knock out the flooring and the second story would collapse. During an attack there would be great danger of fire destroying the wooden structure. Many interior walls were placed nearly parallel to the line of fire, and Fourcroy said that cannon balls entering the fort would ricochet off the walls and kill most of the defenders. Montalembert had compared his fort to a man-o'-war, but Fourcroy noted that even in a moving ship, the smoke from the cannon between decks made breathing difficult. In a fixed, enclosed fort with cannon every nine feet, the smoke would seriously hamper the operations of the cannoneers. Finally, the shock and vibration of the enemy cannon fire would eventually make the wooden structure unstable—even if it withstood everything else. In sum, Fourcroy said that the fort could serve only as a temporary hideout (*cachot*) and that the same defensive capability could be achieved for a sum of 40,000 *livres* by using the battery external[ff] to the fort and by supplementing it with another eight or ten mortars and twenty-five cannon.

Montalembert immediately riposted through a memoir sent to the prince de Montbarey and the fight was on.[153] Coulomb had requested Montalembert to give him leave to Paris so that he could

[ff] The external battery already contained eight 12-inch mortars and fifty-five 36-pound cannon.

go back to settle his mother's estate.[154] He received this leave
and also his next orders; he was to be transferred to Lille for 1780
and 1781.[155] One would assume that he was now out of the fight,
but this was not entirely so. Fourcroy and Montalembert continued
their battle—sometimes under the auspices of the Academy of
Sciences. One of the major reasons outlined in Coulomb's subsequent request for transfer from Lille to Paris in 1781 was so that
he could then become a member of the Academy. Coulomb
strongly suggested that the *Corps royal du génie* would benefit
from having an officer take the position of regular member of the
Academy. This would permit the member, he said, to advise and
examine all proposals dealing with engineering and fortification
problems. So Coulomb remained in the Montalembert-Fourcroy
affair, not as an Academy referee in the scrap, but as a supporter
of Fourcroy. When Montalembert read extracts of his continuing
volumes on *fortification perpendiculaire*, Coulomb would avoid being named a member of the examining committee.[156] When Fourcroy presented his replies to Montalembert, Coulomb would be
one of those who examined his work.[157]

Coulomb was not wholly preoccupied with Montalembert during
his stay at Rochefort. In 1777, the Academy of Sciences in Paris
had proposed as the prize for 1779 the solution of problems of
friction of sliding and rolling surfaces, the resistance to bending in
cords, and the application of these solutions to simple machines
used in the navy. No winner was judged in 1779, and the Academy
then doubled the prize and rescheduled the contest for 1781. Coulomb decided to enter. He was in a good place to undertake the
experiments (Rochefort was one of the newest French shipyards,
though not the largest), and his friendship with the port commander, Latouche-Tréville, permitted him to obtain the services of two
men and the use of a shipyard to conduct the experimental tests.
Coulomb had noted with annoyance that several times his various
experiments had been interrupted when he had been moved from
post to post, thus he may have begun the friction studies before
coming to Rochefort. In any case, the work at Rochefort began
in the late fall of 1779 and continued for several months. Coulomb
considered Amontons' original theory of friction (1699) and those
of Desaguliers and others. From these works and from his own numerous experiments, he developed a generalized theory of friction
and a series of empirical formulas that soon became the standard
work in the field and remained so for a century. He completed

work on this long essay and submitted it to the Academy during 1780, as an entry for the contest to be judged in 1781.[gg] In the spring of 1781, he was named winner.[159] This second, consecutive victory in the Academy's naval prize contests (recall he won the 1777 contest with his essay on magnetic compasses) ensured his election to the Academy in December 1781. Following his service at Rochefort and Aix, Coulomb took his leave in Paris and worked out the legal arrangements for the settlement of his mother's estate. As usual, he took the opportunity to enter and read at the Academy. On April 19, 1780, he read a revised version of an earlier memoir in the form: "On the Limits of Man's Force and on the Greatest Action that One Can Exert for some Seconds, from Which is Concluded the Impossibility of Flying in the Air like Birds."[160]

A week later he read "The Description of a New Magnetic Compass for Observing the Diurnal Differences in the Variation of the Compass."[161] This second memoir was an addition to his prize memoir on magnetic compasses, and, therefore, it was referred to the Academy's prize committee—Le Monnier, Borda, Bory, Le Roy, and Bossut.

He went on to Lille in the late spring of 1780. There he immediately began a study of windmill design. This work, too, would result in a paper submitted and read at the Academy of Sciences.[162]

From Engineer to Physicist and Public Servant

Coulomb constantly kept busy. Like Gaspard Monge, his contemporary in mathematics, he seemed to apply his engineering talent to whatever was at hand. He took advantage of the peculiarities of each military post where he was assigned to study and write about work with which he came in contact. During the building of the large fort in Martinique, he began his studies of earth pressure, column rupture, beam flexure, arch design, and the efficiency of laboring men. Harbor planning at La Hougue and Cherbourg led to his "classified" memoir on coastal defense and harbor improvements and to the beginning of his study of magnetism and the torsion balance. At Salins and Besançon he composed his essay on the underwater dredging caisson. The shipyard at Rochefort permitted him to work on his theory of friction in simple machines. In Lille, where there were windmills within a half mile of the fort

[gg] Coulomb's memoir, "Théorie des machines simples,"[158] is the subject of Chapter IV.

walls, Coulomb wrote on the theory and design of windmills. Every post presented different engineering problems, and Coulomb wrote on each one.

The unity in Coulomb's engineering studies lay in his desire to complete a series touching all aspects of the work of the *Corps royal du génie*; in short, he wanted to write a text on engineering mechanics and his various engineering memoirs were designed for that purpose. He wanted to do this because, as he said, the standard works were out of date not only in detail but in approach. Coulomb mentioned Bélidor's famous *L'architecture hydraulique*. This important study ran to four parts, and with its companion work, *La Science des ingénieurs*, the author had presented a complete course in engineering studies. Bernard Forest de Bélidor was not an engineering officer himself but a teacher of engineering mechanics at La Fère. His texts in the field were the most famous of the eighteenth century, and he wrote on every subject that touched engineering. In reality it was Bélidor, not Cormontaingne, who was the most famous disciple of Vauban. Bélidor cited every important study relating to friction, machines, fortification, and artillery. He made valid and original contributions to many of these subjects.[hh,163]

At the same time, Bélidor wrote on such a broad range of topics that sometimes he blindly accepted another's ideas. At times his own theories were based on guesswork or on faulty experiments made on the scale of a *cabinet de physique*. Coulomb admired Bélidor's work but felt it was erroneous in much of its theory and out of date in its practical information. Coulomb wanted then to issue "a revised edition of M. Bélidor's *L'architecture hydraulique*; this work, though its outline is useful, is founded almost entirely on false theories; moreover, techniques have been perfected a great deal in the past thirty years, and this book must be rewritten."[165]

Thus, Coulomb's plan was to present no less than a complete, new course of engineering—not a course of mathematics or engineering drawing for the student, but a manual and method of approach for the practicing engineer. Then, as now, the engineer acquires his basic abilities at the technical institute; but he only becomes a real professional in the field.

To complete his project, Coulomb wanted to secure a permanent

---

[hh] For example, Bélidor's original proposals for the use of explosives in artillery mortars resulted in his expulsion by the artillery corps. Later, after 1766, the corps incorporated many of Bélidor's suggestions.[164]

post at Paris where he could obtain "the help of books and technicians which are necessary to me to perfect the theory and, especially, the experiments which serve as the base for theory. . . ."[166] He not only wished to pursue his engineering hopes, he had also become intrigued with his work on magnetism and torsion. Now, to get to Paris, Coulomb had to find good reasons for the *corps* to change his post. He soon found them. In July 1781, with the aid of Pontleroy, his chief at Lille, Coulomb presented a memoir and application[167] for permanent transfer to Paris.

In the memoir he listed his reasons for transfer. First, it was necessary for him to be in Paris to oversee the correct edition and publication of his various memoirs. According to him, those memoirs that he had not been able to proofread himself "are so incorrect that it is not possible to read them."[168] In addition, several times he had been forced to abandon a set of experiments when he was moved to another post. Always he had paid from his own funds for the cost of these works. A permanent post would allow him the chance to continue his work uninterrupted. He next mentioned his plan to publish a revised edition of Bélidor's work.

His strong showing at the Academy election of the previous December had put Coulomb in a good position to be elected on the next ballot. Since that time he had gained his second Academy prize and had read two more memoirs to the membership. Coulomb must have been tipped off that he would be in line for election if he could manage to live in Paris for at least five months of each year. He wrote: "A residence in Paris would put me in the position to occupy a place at the Academy of Sciences, where the two prize contests I have won give me considerable promise [of election]."[169]

He stressed also the importance to the *Corps royal du génie* of having one of its officers as a regular[ii] member of the Academy, "whose various discoveries are often related to our works; that way

---

[ii] Of course, there were numerous noble military officers who were accorded honorary membership in the Academy, including, as of 1781:[170] Jean Paul François Noailles, duc d'Ayen; Marc Antoine René de Voyer, marquis de Paulmy d'Argenson; César Gabriel Praslin, duc de Choiseul; Yves Marie Desmarests, marquis de Maillebois; Louis François Armand Duplessis, duc de Richelieu; Louis Elisabeth de la Vergne, comte de Tressan; Joseph Bernard, marquis de Chabert; Marc René, marquis de Montalembert; Gabriel, chevalier de Bory; and le chevalier Etienne François Turgot, marquis de Sousmont. These men, however, were all *membres honoraires* or *associés libres* and none of this group were officers in the *Corps royal du génie.*

one would establish a closer communication between the two bodies, and theory and practice would enlighten each other."[171]

Coulomb suggested that he could be assigned to work under Colonel Larcher d'Aubancourt at the Bastille. This move, he foresaw, would benefit his own career, the *Corps royal du génie*, and the relations between the corps and the Academy.

Coulomb applied almost simultaneously for the *Croix de Saint Louis*, a military decoration awarded to officers with many years of service. After the law of June 1770, an officer had to satisfy certain requirements of length of service and rank before he could apply for the *croix*.[172] As a captain, Charles Augustin was required to have served the equivalent of at least twenty-five years. Campaign services (that is, service during wartime or in the colonies), counted as double time, and time spent traveling to and from campaigns counted as time and a half. Coulomb submitted his request for the award on July 12, 1781.[173] He listed his service as twenty-one years, six months (from his entrance to Mézières in February 1760 through July 1781). In addition, he listed eight years, five months of duty in Martinique making a total, he said, of thirty years of service in the *Corps royal du génie*. He was seconded in his request for the award by his chief at Lille, Pontleroy, and by Foulliac,[174] an old Martinique comrade who attested to his colonial service. He didn't have long to wait either for his post in Paris or for his *Croix de Saint Louis*. Ségur, the Minister of War, wrote Coulomb and Pontleroy in the first part of September to announce that Coulomb was to be posted immediately to the Bastille under the orders of Lt. Colonel Larcher d'Aubancourt, who was "responsible for works at the Bastille" and curator of relief maps.[175] By then it was a sure thing that Coulomb would receive the *croix* as, in writing to acknowledge his transfer, he said: "I still have some papers to get in order, and I don't plan to leave here until around the 25th of September. If it were possible for the Cross [of St. Louis] to reach me before this date, M. de Pontleroy could receive it for me."[176]

Coulomb moved to Paris at the end of September. He was awarded the *Croix de Saint Louis* on September 30th[177] and elected to the Academy of Sciences in Paris as *adjoint mécanicien* (adjunct member in mechanics) on December 12, 1781.[178]

The year 1781 marked a decisive turn in his life and career. It found him a *Capitaine en Premier de la Première Classe*—the highest rank of captain—in the *Corps royal du génie*, holder of the *Croix de Saint Louis*, and a member of the Academy of Sciences.

From this date, his life and his work changed. Permanently stationed in Paris, he could find a wife and raise a family. No longer would he be considered a regular engineer; henceforth his duties would be as a specialist or consultant on machines, canals, and navigation. His numerous memoirs had brought him to the Academy and freed him from the boring provincial posts that had filled his life for twenty years.

His scientific work changed too. He had access to the books, the equipment, and especially the company of his fellows at the Academy. His last engineering memoir (on windmill design), was composed at Lille and read at the Academy in his first month as a regular member. He continued work on his memoir concerned with the efficiency and "quantity of action" of laboring men; save for this, the rest of his scientific work would be in physics and instrumentation. He never completed his plans to write a text or rework Bélidor's *L'architecture hydraulique*. Others, namely Bossut, Prony, and later, Poncelet and the early nineteenth-century French engineering mechanists would weave Coulomb's contributions to rational and applied mechanics into the curricula of engineering education.

One can say that 1781 brought to an end a brilliant career as a theoretical engineer, as the term would be understood in the eighteenth century. Now Coulomb's role as scientist would begin. Of course, Coulomb had worked in science well before 1781 and his engineering consulting work would continue. This year marks a break, however, since the enormous change in his environment and his opportunities after this time allowed his work to turn to physics. This change *permitted*, though it did not *cause* Coulomb to emerge as a physicist. His talent was such that he would have investigated natural problems no matter where he was stationed. It would be only after he lived permanently in Paris that he could possibly undertake the continuous and delicate series of experiments that form the corpus of his work in physics.

TWO · PHYSICIST AND PUBLIC SERVANT

Introduction

In the year 1781, the turning point of Coulomb's career, times were changing not only for him but for science as a social force and for physics as a stepchild of mechanics or natural philosophy. Physics as it is today was emerging from the *cabinet de physique* and the *salon* to become an independently recognized discipline.

Until the eighteenth century, the exact physical sciences comprised, at most, theoretical mechanics, astronomy, and geometrical optics. The fields of heat, light, electricity, and magnetism were descriptive and empirical rather than analytical. During the course of that century, the empirical physical disciplines began to develop into exact and quantitative sciences. Some of these fields fully emerged during Coulomb's manhood.

In this chapter, Coulomb's later life and career will be considered, including his work in the Academy of Sciences, his studies in physics,[a] and his contributions as a French public servant.

Academician and Physicist

WORK IN THE ACADEMY.[1] To qualify for resident membership in the Academy of Sciences, a candidate had to live in Paris for at least five months of the year. In the early years, this regulation was honored in the breach, and some members rarely put in an appearance at Academy sessions. After the first half of the eighteenth century, however, regular participation was required and several academicians were dropped from the rolls for lack of attendance.

Meetings were usually held twice a week—on Wednesday and Saturday afternoons.[b] Before each, all members present were required to sign the register book. At the appointed time, the secre-

[a] See also Chapters v and vi.
[b] After the Revolution, the Institute met twice each *décade* (the ten-day week used in the period from September 22, 1792 until January 1, 1806).

tary drew a line under the signatures; those who were absent or tardy did not share in the small payments given for attendance. Members from all classes were entitled to deliver reports on their research work either informally, orally, or as formal, written research papers. In some cases, the member presenting a report would enlighten the Academy by performing demonstrations of experiments or showing pieces of experimental apparatus.

In addition to receiving or judging work emanating from within the Academy, the members examined numerous reports, plans, and inventions submitted by other individuals or organizations. For instance, the royal household and the various war ministries asked advice concerning plans for buildings, canals, insurance schemes, etc. The usual method of handling these requests was to name a committee of members to examine a particular memoir or invention in detail and to give a written report to the Academy at large.

Administrative affairs were conducted through several standing committees: the prize committee, the library committee, the committee on election of new members, and others.

In sum, each resident member might have responsibilities in three areas: (1) presenting his own research before the membership,[c] (2) serving on a committee for the examination of outside proposals and inventions,[d] and (3) engaging in the administration of the Academy itself.

Coulomb participated in each of these three areas. He read thirty-two scientific memoirs to the Academy and to its successor, the *Institut de France*, from 1773 to 1806—seven of these before his admission as member in December 1781; sixteen from this date until the abolition of the Academy in 1793; and nine as a member of the Institute from 1795 until 1806. Of these thirty-two memoirs, twenty-two were in physics, eight in mechanics, and one in plant physiology. Two won Academy prizes, one in physics, one in mechanics. Although he occasionally consulted others regarding his scientific memoirs, there is no evidence that he ever wrote one with a colleague.

None of Coulomb's scientific manuscripts remain in the archival files of the Academy of Sciences. Two of his laboratory notebooks are deposited in the library of the Institute.[2] He apparently with-

---

[c] A list of memoirs that Coulomb read to the Academy will be found in Appendix A.

[d] A list of notations regarding Coulomb and his reports to the Academy will be found in Appendix B.

drew his manuscripts from the Academy files, as was the custom, either to work on them further or to supervise personally their printing in the memoirs of the Academy.

In studying Coulomb's work in the area of Academy reports on plans and inventions, he is seen to have associated with a large number of academicians on a variety of subjects. Many of these reports are filed in the dossiers of the meetings in the Academy archives. Ideally, for each session there should have been a list in the minutes of those members in attendance, a brief mention of the memoirs or reports read at the meeting, and a summary of the business acted upon. Sometimes a check of the original notebook of the permanent secretary provides additional information about a given meeting.

For an appreciation of what an eighteenth-century Academy scientist did, one must go farther than a study of his published writings. For instance, a study of Lavoisier's writings on chemistry alone would not reveal Lavoisier the organizer and administrator who spent much of his time going back and forth between the Academy and the Arsenal, guiding and prodding the project to increase France's supply of gunpowder. In Coulomb's case, there exist few letters or memorabilia to indicate who might have been his scientific friends and co-workers. Often the only knowledge of his day-to-day whereabouts is provided by the Academy's attendance records.

Individual academicians usually were asked to report on subjects related to their special fields of interest, though a considerable portion of their time might have been devoted to examining seemingly irrelevant matters. Between 1781 and 1806, Coulomb participated in 310 committee reports. Not all those assigned to a committee were acted upon. Certainly, errors in the manuscript minutes make precise calculations impossible. Of the total of 310 reports, 163 were for the period 1781 to 1793 and 147 for 1795 to 1806. The subjects may be divided by frequency of occurrence into seven categories (see Table II.1).

Table II.1 shows that most of the reports concerned machines, with physics in second place. Public safety, health, or education, and canals and navigation occurred frequently, while a number of miscellaneous subjects accounted for about 15% of the total.

There is a significant shift in the number of reports by category if selected before or after the Revolution. Coulomb was involved in many on engineering or mechanics before 1793; after 1795 there

TABLE II.1

COULOMB'S REPORTS TO ACADEMY OF SCIENCES,
1781–1806

Category of Report*	Number of Reports Assigned or Given			
	1781–1793	*1795–1806*	*Total Number*	*Total Percentage*
Machines	70	39	109	35.1 %
Physics (including instrumentation)	18	34	52	16.7
Miscellaneous	20	25	45	14.5
Public safety, health, education	16	24	40	12.9
Canals and navigation	20	11	31	10.0
Structural engineering	9	9	18	5.8
Military	10	5	15	4.8 %
Totals	163	147	310	100.± %
Ratio of reports per month	1.16	1.14	1.15	

* The categories are my own.

is a shift towards physics and public service. This distribution lends weight to Coulomb's statement[3] that one purpose for a member of the *Corps royal du génie* obtaining a place in the Academy would be to ensure that those memoirs of interest to the *génie* could be examined before the Academy by an officer of the *corps*, and Coulomb remained an officer until 1791. No doubt the veteran members of the Academy had considerably more leeway in accepting a particular commission. Thus, as Coulomb became a senior member, he could choose subjects that seemed to be in closer accord with his increasing preoccupation with physics.

Coulomb worked on reports with 93 different people at the Academy (see Tables II.2 and II.3). Obviously he could not have cooperated much with those who died soon after he was elected to the Academy, or conversely, with those who were elected just before his own death. For example, he worked with d'Alembert on only two reports; d'Alembert died in October 1783, less than two years after Coulomb's election to the Academy.

If one examines, say, the ten men with whom Coulomb worked most closely in this area, nine of the ten were either *géomètres,*

TABLE II.2
ACADEMICIANS PARTICIPATING WITH COULOMB
IN ACADEMY REPORTS, 1781–1806

Name	Number of Reports	Name	Number of Reports
Bossut	76	Tessier	3
Le Roy	53	d'Alembert	2
Borda	51	*Aeneas	2
Prony	48	Bonaparte	2
Laplace	36	Cadet	2
Desmarest	25	Cels	2
Périer	25	*Ciscar	2
Monge	24	Cuvier	2
Bory	22	Desfontaines	2
Vandermonde	21	De Fouchy	2
------------		Duhamel (J.P.F.G.)	2
Charles	18	Fourcroy (de R.)	2
Condorcet	18	Huzard	2
Cousin	15	Lassone	2
Legendre	15	Lassus	2
Lavoisier	14	Legentil	2
Tillet	14	Lelièvre	2
Brisson	13	Mascagni	2
Berthollet	11	Parmentier	2
Darcet	11	*Pédrayèz	2
Delambre	10	Sage	2
Fourcroy (A. F.)	10	*Trallès	2
Lagrange	10	Vassali	2
Hallé	9	Van Swinden	2
Lefèvre-Gineau	8	Vauquelin	2
Méchain	8	Baumé	1
Meusnier	8	Cassini (IV)	1
Haüy	7	De Gua	1
Levèque	7	Des Essartz	1
Perronet	7	Dionis du Sejour	1
Rochon	7	Dolomieu	1
Bailly	6	Forfait	1
Berthoud	6	Fougeroux	1
Guyton	6	Franklin	1
Biot	5	Labillardière	1
Carnot	5	Lamarck	1
Chaptal	5	La Croix	1
Tenon	5	La Curée	1
Vicq d'Azyr	5	La Rochefoucauld	1
Bougainville	4	Le Blonde	1
Lalande	4	L'Heritier	1
Sabatier	4	Maillebois	1
Bochart de Saron	3	Marescot	1
Daubenton	3	Messier	1
Lacepède	3	Mongez	1
Le Monnier	3	Sané	1
Pelletan	3		

* Aeneas, Ciscar, Pédrayèz, and Trallès were neither members of nor correspondents to the Academy (or Institute) but participated with Coulomb in reports only as foreign members of the commission for weights and measures in 1798.

TABLE II.3

ACADEMY REPORTS AND ACADEMICIANS,
1781–1806

Total number of men reporting with Coulomb		93
Total number of reports		310
Total number of men on all reports (Coulomb)	310	
(Others)	746	
Total		1056
Number of Academicians assigned to each report (average) $\dfrac{1056}{310} =$		3.41

mécaniciens, or *astronomes*.[e] These colleagues were either mathematicians who were strongly interested in physics (Laplace, Monge, Bossut, Borda) or men interested in the application of mathematics and physics to the principles of engineering (Prony, Périer, Le Roy). Bossut figures largely in those cooperating with Coulomb in the Academy reports because Coulomb was Bossut's correspondent to the Academy from 1774 to 1781 and then his very close friend for life. Similarly, Borda and Le Roy had been friends of Coulomb since his days at Mézières.

Writing out the reports was often a dull task. For the first few years of his membership, Coulomb usually wrote those assigned to him on a given committee and the other members signed. This is understandable; the freshman member would be required to undertake most of the work. The reports varied in length and quality. Some had obviously involved much work—checking calculations, reading long manuscripts, in some cases even verifying experiments. On major undertakings like the project for hospital reform, for instance, they might run to over a hundred pages; some of Coulomb's reports on scientific manuscripts or inventions were as much as twenty-five quarto pages. Other plans (perpetual motion machines or obviously worthless inventions) were dismissed in two hundred words or were deemed unworthy of being written up at all. Reports were rarely given to one man alone; the usual committee size was three or four members (see Table II.3).

The *ancienne Académie* has been characterized as haughty in its rejection or dismissal of material submitted to it by outsiders. Two comments seem in order here. First, if one examines the many

[e] The single exception, Desmarest, though in the class of *mécanique* until 1785, was in reality a geologist and mineralogist.

absolutely worthless inventions or plans submitted to the Academy for inspection there is a good case to be made for their rejection. Sometimes these plans consisted of a single sheet of paper bearing a poorly drawn figure. Some indicated a complete lack of both drafting ability and scientific knowledge. Second, at least in the case of Coulomb, the Academy looked at almost the same number of plans and inventions per year before as after the Revolution. Coulomb's own rate of committee work, both before and after the Revolution, was about fourteen reports a year.

He participated in important work in the committees on hospital reform and on amendment of the system of weights and measures.[f] And in reviewing the design and first operation of the Périer brothers' water pump at the Palais de Chaillot, Coulomb was the first in France[4] to describe publicly the principles of Watt and Boulton's improved steam engine. These are exceptions, however. In examining the actual reports that Coulomb wrote, one must say that few contain much of scientific interest. Most, after all, are engineering opinions on the desirability of developing a particular canal or hydraulic machine or they are "book reviews" of a manuscript submitted for the approbation of the Academy.

In addition to reporting on submitted plans and inventions, Coulomb worked in several areas of the internal administration of the Academy. As mentioned above, he served on the committees for hospital reform and for weights and measures. He worked for a number of years on the Academy's library committee, in the secretariat, and, after the Revolution, on the commission *des arts et manuscrits*. Both before and after the Revolution he was involved in nominating candidates for membership and in judging entries for the Academy's prize contests. Some of these were time-consuming tasks; for example, the contest for design of a new water pump at the Pont Notre-Dame produced 45 entries.[5] Finally, he was elected to the (largely honorary) position of *Président* of the *Première classe* of the *Institut de France* for a six-month period in 1801.[6]

THE PHYSICS MEMOIRS.[g] Before his election to the Academy in 1781, all but one of Coulomb's memoirs had been concerned with engineering mechanics. The exception was the memoir which won the Academy's prize contest for 1777, "Investigations of the Best

[f] This work will be discussed below.

[g] Coulomb's work in torsion and fluid resistance will be examined in Chapter v. Chapter vi considers his studies in electricity and magnetism.

Method of Making Magnetic Needles."[7] This essay was very important for his later career, since it contained the outlines of several of his further researches—torsion, fluid resistance, and magnetism.

After Coulomb moved to Paris and was established with the Academy, he could again turn to physics studies. Several things had prevented this while he was on engineering duty in the provinces. First, he was often occupied with his normal engineering duties. Second, he was transferred from post to post frequently and was unable to establish a permanent laboratory. Finally, while in the provinces, he was denied access, as he said, to "the help of books and technicians which are necessary to me."[8]

Not only did Coulomb's 1777 magnetism memoir presage his further physics researches, but events connected with the reception of it led him back into studies of physics. A torsion suspension magnetic compass developed by Coulomb and described in his 1777 magnetism memoir was adopted by Jean Dominique Cassini for use at the Paris Observatory. Cassini encountered technical problems in utilizing the compass for measurement of the diurnal variations in declination of the terrestrial magnetic field. He asked Coulomb for help in modifying the compass. The study subsequently undertaken by Coulomb guided him back to research in torsion and from this emerged his major torsion memoir, "Theoretical and Experimental Investigations of the Force of Torsion and of Elasticity in Metal Wires."[9] In this work, he sought not only to extend his previous experimental work to torsion in different materials but also to grapple with it as a problem within the theory of elasticity. He determined the correct laws for torsion in cylinders and thereby developed his torsion balance. The balance was later applied to his famous studies of electrostatics and magnetism and to other work in fluid resistance studies and in determination of moments of inertia. Coulomb investigated the mechanism of torsion itself "in order to determine the laws of coherence and elasticity in metals and all solid bodies."[10] Working with brass, silver, and iron wires, he found the elastic limits (beyond which permanent set occurs) and studied the effects of work hardening and annealing in changing the elastic limits of metals. He developed a molecular theory of elastic behavior in supposing that strains *within* molecules are elastically restored up to a certain limit. Beyond this limit, he supposed, the stresses become enough to break the cohesive bonds *between* molecules; then the material fractures or flows along molecular planes. In the region above the elastic limit but below the rupture point, the material is rearranged, but the (elastic) response within the molecule remains the same. This explained why hammering or "working" metals changes their elastic limits but leaves their elasticity unchanged.

This work was undertaken in the early 1780s, and Coulomb read his major torsion memoir in September 1784. He utilized the torsion balance itself in most of his later physics studies.

He presented memoirs of his work in electricity and magnetism throughout his period of membership in the Academy, but his major studies came in the famous series of seven memoirs that he read from 1785 to 1791.[h] In his electrical studies, Coulomb determined the quantitative force law for electrostatics, gave the notion of electrical mass, and studied charge leakage and the surface distribution of charge on conducting bodies. In magnetism, he also determined the quantitative force law, studied magnetic momenta, introduced the idea of the demagnetizing field, and created a theory of magnetism due to molecular polarization. His concern was in establishing electricity and magnetism on the basis of attractive and repulsive forces and determining quantitative relations answering to the phenomena. In doing so, he believed it necessary to replace the old theories of electric atmospheres and magnetic vortices because the important assumption now was that all particles acted upon each other at a distance.

In his First (1785) and Second (1787) Memoirs, Coulomb presented the details of his electric torsion balance and firmly established the force laws. In his Third (1787) Memoir, Coulomb examined the losses due to leakage of electric charge. In the Fourth (1787), Fifth (1788), and Sixth (1790) Memoirs he conducted an extensive investigation of charge distribution on conducting bodies of varying sizes and shapes.

Coulomb saw all matter as being either a perfect conductor for electricity or a dielectric (complete nonconductor). He explained conduction across dielectrics as being due to surface contamination, but between the contaminating conductive particles, he postulated a dielectric interval having a physical resistance. Electricity could pass across this only if the electric intensity was sufficient to over-

[h] Coulomb himself called these his "seven" memoirs in electricity and magnetism. The dates given here and below are not publication dates but rather those dates when Coulomb first read the memoirs before the Academy.

come the "coercive force" offered by this dielectric interval. Though he only hinted at conduction across uncontaminated dielectrics, he supposed that *any* dielectric substance would break down under sufficient electric intensity.

Coulomb turned again to magnetism in his Seventh (1791) Memoir. After attempting unsuccessfully to work within the existing one- and two-fluid macroscopic theories of magnetism, he presented a theory of molecular magnetic polarization. The "magnetic fluids" were allowed to move only *within* each molecule, he posited; thus each molecule within a magnet could become polarized.

His further studies in magnetism centered on the effects of heat and elastic stress on magnets, on their magnetic properties, and on the extent of magnetism in all matter. The concept of a "coercive force" ties Coulomb's theories—both of electricity and of magnetism—to his earlier work in torsion, friction, and strength of materials. For example, in magnetism he saw this coercive force as responsible for the limiting value of magnetization that could be obtained in a given material. Somehow, soft iron could easily be magnetized and it also lost its magnetism easily. Steel was difficult to magnetize but it held its magnetism afterwards. Perhaps, he thought, these properties were due to a coercive force that, like friction in machines, provided an upper limit to the stresses that a given material could withstand. In his last magnetic researches, after the Revolution, Coulomb was really investigating the nature and properties of this coercive force in matter.

Coulomb's physics researches were more than a juncture of experiment and rational analysis. They benefited from his experience in three areas: rational analysis, the tradition of *physique expérimentale*, and another type of experimentation and method of investigation which developed largely from elements within the French engineering profession.

Coulomb's researches in electricity and magnetism form a major contribution to the history of physics. These were only a part of his later career, however, for the members of the French Academy of Sciences were responsible for duties beyond their own research.

Public Servant

CANALS IN BRITTANY. The story of Coulomb's involvement in 1779 with the marquis de Montalembert at the Ile d'Aix illustrates the inter-service rivalries that existed between the military engineering corps and other branches of the army. These same tensions were mentioned by Coulomb in his 1776 memoir concerning the reorganization of the *génie*. Another episode in his career points up the problems between the engineers and other government organizations—only this time it was a local civil body in Brittany that clashed with the *génie*.

Because of his reputation as an engineer, Coulomb was called to consult on two projects proposed by a provincial canal commission in Brittany in 1783—one a canal system linking Angers, Nantes, and St. Malo, and the other a harbor development at St. Malo. What the Breton canal commission really wanted was to approach the king for funds for the canal and harbor projects and to support this request with the politically important recommendations of a famous engineer. Coulomb, and the other members of the consulting team, insisted on assessing the harbor scheme as it really was— a project that would be both economically and technically unfeasible. Before the consulting job was finished, Charles Augustin was arrested on the military charge of quitting his post without permission and subsequently served a token sentence of one week in prison. Technically the charge was correct, but Coulomb was made the scapegoat of the affair by Ségur, the Minister of War. The charge was brought against Coulomb by the Breton canal commission which was offended by his insistence on giving only an engineering, and not a political, judgment on the projects.

Canal development throughout France was an important question in the eighteenth century for various reasons, but it was British marine supremacy that created the need for canals in Brittany.[11] Timber, rope, tallow, and other military supplies as well as foodstuffs could not reach their destinations in Brittany along the western coast of France because of the British coastal raiders. Supplies coming out of Bordeaux or out of the Charente at Rochefort were stopped by the British before they could reach Brest or L'Orient. Similarly, materials from Flanders or the Low Countries were stopped in the English channel before they got to Cherbourg, St. Malo, or other ports in Normandy or northern Brittany.

About the same time as port works began at Cherbourg in the 1770s, projects were suggested to provide an *interior* route for supplies coming to Britanny.[12] Generally, it was hoped to connect Angers, Nantes, Redon, Rennes, Laval, and St. Malo through the rivers Loire, Mayenne, Villaine, Rance, and others. This work would require the construction of several systems of locks and

canals, and the port of St. Malo might have to be fortified to protect the Rance river from the British.

In January 1783, the Estates of Brittany formed a canal commission headed by Rosnyvinen, comte de Piré. This commission
soon reported its plans to seek outside advice in forming specific
plans for the canal system.[13] The comte de Piré went to Paris to
arrange for Ségur, then Minister of War, to assign an eminent engineer from the *Corps du génie* as consultant. Ségur named Coulomb
as that engineer in April 1783. At the same time, the abbé Rochon,
a native Breton, member of the Academy of Sciences, and Director
of the Marine Observatory at Brest, declared he wanted "to be of
use to his country."[14] Rochon volunteered to join the canal efforts
as consultant.

Meanwhile, Piré had heard the criticism that there were no engineers from the *Ponts et chaussées* among the consultants on his
commission. To allay this, he succeeded in getting the Controller
General to assign two *Ponts et chaussées* men to his force. He did
rather well, obtaining the services of the engineer Liard, and also
of no less a person than Chézy, *Inspecteur-Général des ponts et
chaussées* and assistant to J. R. Perronet, the Director.[15]

Rochon and Coulomb left Paris about May 18, 1783 for Rennes,
the seat of the Estates of Brittany. On the twenty-second, the comte
de Piré presented them to the assembled Estates. Chézy and Liard
arrived a few days later, and on May 30, a large group of commissioners and consultants went downriver from Rennes to Redon,
then upriver from Rennes to Cesson on a preliminary inspection.[16]
After the first trip, Chézy and Liard began their sorties into the
country while Coulomb and Rochon went in other directions. During June and July, Coulomb and Rochon made a series of excur-
sions to investigate the proposed canal sites—in particular the links
between Rennes and St. Malo.[i]

Chézy returned to Paris on July 19; just before leaving, he gave
his report to the Breton canal commission. He stated that there
must be a minimum of four feet of water in the canals for navigation. He recommended that the length of the canal locks be increased
from 66 to 106 feet so that all river barges could use the canals.
His cost estimate was 615,000 *livres*.[j] Coulomb generally agreed
with Chézy's analysis but recommended some changes in the place-

---

[i] This path would join the Villaine river to the Rance via either the small
rivers l'Isle and Linon or the rivers Meu and Garun.[17]

[j] Chézy later revised this estimate upwards to 861,000 *livres*.[18]

ment of the canal locks. He said the dredging of the rivers would account for the major expense and he felt that the canals should be no less than six feet deep, rather than four.[k,19] The new locks and canals would leave the interior lands open to invasion, for, as at Redon, the tides caused the river to rise nine feet. To assess this danger fully, Coulomb strongly recommended a complete survey of the river Villaine up as far as Rennes, with depth soundings every 120 feet.[l,20]

In the meantime, the comte de Piré had been a busy man. He had not only sought support for canals in Brittany, he had also persuaded the Minister of the Marine, Maréchal de Castries, that the port of St. Malo merited major harbor and fortification works. Piré saw St. Malo as a potentially great port and as a protection for the northern end of his proposed canal system. Castries wrote Coulomb and Rochon in care of Piré and told them to present themselves in St. Malo on September 10 to consult on the desirability of the project. M. Bavre, an engineer, and Coulomb's old friend, Jean Charles de Borda, would join them as members of the team.[21]

Coulomb answered Castries on August 21, saying that pending further instructions, he would be there on the proper date.[22] Two days later he wrote Ségur[23] from Rennes and asked that his duty at Rennes be terminated. He said that as the engineers from the *Ponts et chaussées* had terminated their work, there was nothing more to be done until the Estates of Brittany received an answer to their request for funds for the canal projects. In any case, he said, there could be no further work until spring and he had duties at the Academy of Sciences. Curiously, he made no mention of the upcoming assignment for Castries.

Before going to St. Malo, Coulomb still had to examine the upper reaches of the Villaine river near the source of the Mayenne.[24] He and Robinet, one of the commissioners from Rennes, left August 25 by coach for Vitré and then spent a week on horseback examining many watermills and streams between Vitré, Bourgon, and the river Ernée. The mill visits were a clever way for Coulomb to obtain a detailed knowledge of river conditions, because each

---

k In Coulomb's opinion, the dredging would be the major expense because the canals had to be dug out to forty-eight feet wide by six feet deep at a dredging cost of ten *livres* per cubic *toise*. (A cubic *toise* equals about eight cubic yards.)

l This survey was begun and completed the next summer (1784).

mill owner was a local expert. He found that water levels were generally very low everywhere and that the difficult, hilly terrain necessitated a further, intensive survey before a path could be chosen to link the Villaine and the Mayenne. On September 1, Coulomb and Robinet went back downriver to Rennes. In the next week, Coulomb prepared his reports to the commission.

On September 9, the evening before their departure, Coulomb and Rochon dined with the canal commission. Coulomb[25] said that everyone expressed satisfaction at the job done by him and Rochon. Only one member of the commission, he said, mentioned in passing that it was too bad that Coulomb couldn't spend the winter in Rennes. The commission later recalled the incident quite differently.[26] They said that upon learning of Coulomb's decision to spend the winter in Paris, they all expressed their *vifs regrets* and exhorted him to stay in Rennes.

The next day, Coulomb and Rochon went on to St. Malo and awaited Borda and Bavre, who arrived a few days later.[27] Unknown to Coulomb, Ségur had meanwhile deferred judgment on his request for a leave to Paris. Ségur sent the request to the Maréchal d'Aubeterre, Commandant of the Province of Brittany.[28] In turn, d'Aubeterre sent it on to Piré and the canal commission.[29]

At St. Malo, Coulomb and the others were presented with the comte de Piré's second plan[30]—two grand ports for St. Malo. One would be military and one commercial. The port area would be over 800,000 square meters (twenty-seven times as large as Vauban's port at Dunkerque). Woodshops and shipyards were planned in addition to the ports.[31] The consulting team didn't release their report until December 19, but Piré's plans were so exaggerated that no engineer could have approved them. The project would cost over 30 million *livres*, including 13.5 million for the dredging alone.[32]

In 1692, on one occasion, twenty-one French ships had escaped the British by running up the estuary at St. Malo. This episode was held up by local people as evidence of the port's possibilities. This hope was hauled down after Coulomb's team used rowboats to take soundings all over the harbor and out to the nearby islands of Rimains and Landes. They found that with the deeper-draft vessels in use in 1793, it would be impossible to move more than six large ships in or out of St. Malo on a single tide and they recommended that only some small fortifications be constructed. They concluded:

This fact proves in a manner which can leave no doubt that St. Malo can serve as refuge to a small number of vessels attacked by bad weather or by superior forces. . . . But if one considers this port relative to the importance it would have in time of war for military operations in the Channel, one will see that its advantages do not in any way correspond to the grandeur of the establishment that is proposed for it.[33]

If any place on the surrounding coast should be developed, they said, it should not be St. Malo but Brehat Island and the Pontrieux river, near Cherbourg.

Piré's plans were not rejected entirely. The group of consultants expressed strong support for the Nantes-St. Malo canal plan "because then this latter city could obtain through Nantes not only the wood, iron, anchors, artillery, etc. which would go down the Loire, but also all supplies coming from Bordeaux and from Rochefort; in addition to that, the wood from Havre would arrive there more promptly and safely than at Brest."[34]

Coulomb had as yet received no answer to his request for leave. He had no reason, however, to suspect that it would be denied, since there was nothing for him to do at Rennes. It was never a question of duties other than the canal project in Brittany because the *Corps du génie* already had enough regular engineers serving there. The St. Malo team of Borda, Bavre, and Rochon announced their intention to return to Paris and there to prepare their report for Castries. They intended to file their report in person upon Castries' return from Fontainebleau. They suggested that Coulomb accompany them because, as a member of the St. Malo commission, Coulomb also was responsible for the presentation.[35] There could have been very little coaxing, for this was exactly the type of excuse Coulomb needed to justify his return to Paris.

After receiving the Breton canal commission's letter of September 21, expressing their regrets at his absence, Coulomb answered them from Paimpol[36] saying that the St. Malo consultants were returning to Paris. He assured them that he would be available if he were really needed.[m] On October 17, le Sancquer (*Commissaire et chef du bureau des fortifications et de l'artillerie à Versailles*)[n]

[m] The Breton canal commission had also written Chézy and Liard and requested their return. They were unsuccessful in this attempt as well.

[n] Le Sancquer was not a military engineer, but as chief bureaucrat in the headquarters of the *Corps du génie*, he was a person of great power. His role has not been recognized in histories of French engineering. He was, in

wrote Coulomb at Rennes[38] and announced that his leave had been refused on the orders of Maréchal d'Aubeterre. Coulomb never received this letter[39] because he was then at St. Malo. Upon his return to Paris in late October, Coulomb wrote le Sancquer to let him know of his arrival.[40] Le Sancquer answered curtly:

> However interesting may have been the motive for your journey, I doubt whether the Minister [*i.e.*, Ségur] may not have cause to be surprised that you have proceeded to Paris without obtaining the leave that you requested. . . . You will receive directly, no doubt, the letter of advice which was addressed to you at Rennes, and which absolutely contradicts the action that you have taken in coming to Paris on your own authority.[41]

Coulomb received a similar letter from d'Aubeterre. On November 3, 1783, he replied to d'Aubeterre:

> The letter, sir, which you have honored me by writing is very harsh; I would not have believed that this should be the result of all the attention that I have given to your province. If you would look through your records, you would see that I have never before received treatment like this: I am writing to Monsieur the Maréchal de Ségur to submit my resignation. I will relate to him in detail my actions, which are beyond reproach.[42]

The same day, Coulomb wrote a long letter to Ségur giving his account of the event at Rennes and St. Malo and tendering his resignation from the *Corps royal du génie*.[43] He stated that the general decline of his health, especially the return of [chest ?] congestion and of hemorrhoids, forced him to resign. This was not his motive, but the week of horseback riding on the Mayenne, for instance, could certainly have led to the return of his intestinal problems. He *was* resigning, of course, because of his humiliation over the Breton canals affair. He described his actions to Ségur and listed the drawbacks of the job: there was no one in power to give a final decision on actions to be taken with regard to the

---

fact, the link between all correspondence concerning engineers in the field and the higher command in Versailles. Le Sancquer read everything destined for Ségur or Fourcroy. In Fourcroy's absence, he actually ran the *Corps du génie*. At any time, he might intervene and carry on correspondence independent of the *Directeurs des fortifications*. Le Sancquer had seen fit to disregard Coulomb's letter from the Isle of Aix in 1779.[38] This time he entered into personal correspondence with him.

canals; the *Ponts et chaussées* were not working in accord with the *génie*; the Breton commission wanted not an engineering decision but only positive support for their project.

To coordinate this operation, Coulomb said, "It would be necessary for the officer in charge of operations to be of considerable rank, have the required ability, be able to speak with ease, and, especially, have the talent of leading men, always keep on good terms with everyone, and attempt continually to reconcile those persons who are unable to get along with one another: as for myself, I recognize my inadequacy."[44] In addition, Coulomb said that even if he hadn't resigned he would have requested that another officer finish the Brittany job.

This was something that Ségur hadn't expected. He sent Coulomb's letter of November 3 to le Sancquer and wrote across the top of it, "Report to me on this promptly and in detail."[45] A meeting was held on the sixth. The engineering committee which judged the affair took Coulomb's side in the case and recommended that his leave be granted, stating that he was justified in his actions. As to Coulomb's resignation, they advised Ségur to refuse it, for "It would be a real mistake to grant it to him, since it would be a great loss for the King's Service."[46]

Ségur was caught between the *génie* and the Estates of Brittany. To save face, he made Coulomb the scapegoat, sentencing him to one week in prison[47] at the Abbaye de St. Germain. Coulomb served his sentence sometime between November 7 and 20, 1783. The functionary who led him to prison remarked that before an officer in Paris without leave was arrested, he was nearly always warned.[48] Coulomb certainly felt that he was the object of a case involving more than himself. The Breton canal commission had no need of him, and he said their action was like "a patient who wants his physician near him, not so that the physician can seek remedies to cure him, but so that if his sickness grows worse, he and the public can blame the physician."[49] And as for Ségur, Coulomb said, "the reason that was given in the order for my imprisonment can only be the pretext that a poor devil, hard pressed by his mistakes and his conscience, employs to escape the pressure."[50]

Although Coulomb withdrew his resignation, he asked Fourcroy to relieve him of the Breton canal job. The bad situation at Rennes would only become worse, he felt, when the canal commission and the Estates of Brittany learned of his prison sentence. To avoid embarrassment both to himself and to "the uniform I wear,"[51] Coulomb preferred that another officer take over the position. The canal commission wrote to him in December 1783, and asked him to return. He answered saying that the state of his health would not permit it. They petitioned him again in January 1784, and again Coulomb refused, although he agreed to spend three months there in the summer if they would request the services of another engineer as assistant. He suggested the chevalier du Dezerseul, engineering Captain at Rennes, to serve in his absence.[52] The Breton canal commission followed Coulomb's lead, and on February 9, 1784, Ségur named Dezerseul as assistant and ordered Coulomb to go to Rennes in May.[53]

Coulomb left Paris in early May 1784, and spent two months in Brittany.[54] The marquis de la Rosière was named to command the troops and laborers assigned to do the work. This force included 880 soldiers from two Breton regiments and up to 360 peasants. Work began June 15 and continued until October.[55] Coulomb returned to Paris and the Academy in early July. His troubles with the Bretons were over.

Work on the Breton canals died out and the projects remained dreams for years. In 1786, Bossut, Rochon, Condorcet, and Fourcroy (de Ramecourt) examined the Breton canal problem for the Academy all over again.[56] Their generally favorable report was similar to the observations of Coulomb and Rochon in 1783. Charles Augustin steered clear of this committee; it is interesting, however, to note that some of the 1786 report's phrases were very similar to those used by him in his November 1783 letter to Ségur.°

There was a happy ending to Coulomb's experiences in Brittany. In May 1785, the Estates of Brittany asked the *Corps du génie* for permission to give both him and Dezerseul a bonus for their efforts. Dezerseul was given 4,000 *livres*. The commission wanted to give Coulomb a *boîte d'or* (golden box) in lieu of a monetary gift because he had acted with such disinterestedness that "he did not

---

° The 1786 report concluded: "Finally, we believe that it is appropriate for us to add that, in order to assure the success of these different projects . . . it would be useful to entrust general direction to a single man, one to whom the province would accord its entire confidence concerning all that relates to the discipline of engineering, and one who would be attached solely to the engineering service. This is the only means of organizing and unifying the different works, of avoiding a multitude of incidental and useless expenses."[57]

wish to accept any fee nor even to receive reimbursement for his travel expenses."[p,58]

The canal and harbor projects in Brittany were Coulomb's last major consulting duties as an officer of the military engineering corps. Throughout his career, however, he was presented with many similar tasks in his position as a member of the Academy of Sciences. His excellent reports on various problems of canals and water supply systems and pumps brought him to the attention of the comte d'Angiviller, who was charged with directing all royal buildings, gardens, and water systems. Just after completing his work on the canals, Coulomb was named by d'Angiviller to take over the management of the royal water supply systems. This was a formidable task which occupied much of his time until the position was abolished in the Revolution.

THE KING'S INTENDANT FOR WATERS AND FOUNTAINS. In July 1784, Coulomb was named *Intendant des eaux et fontaines du roi*.[62] Thus, he became the administrator of a system dating back to the construction of the first Paris aqueduct, in the reign of the emperor Julian.[63] This first system, at Arcueil, was destroyed by the Normans in the ninth century. It was reconstructed under Philippe Auguste about A.D. 1200, and public fountains were installed at the city markets during this period. The first private concession for sale of water was awarded to the Couvent des Filles-Dieu in 1265.

The sixteenth century saw the first rapid growth period, both in the construction of public fountains and in the awarding of private water rights. This practice of granting private rights eventually reduced the public portions to such an extent that Henry IV revoked many private concessions in 1594. The Latin Quarter of Paris had traditionally been poorly supplied with water; there were sixteen public fountains in Paris by 1600 but none on the left bank. Henry IV and then Louis XIII hoped to improve the situation by repairing the Aqueduc d'Arcueil. Louis XIII laid the first stone for the improvements at Arcueil in 1613, and by 1617, the aqueduct was

---

[p] Biot[59] and Delambre[60] said the gift was a fine clock with second hand that Coulomb often used in his experiments. Investigation of the probate of Coulomb's estate in the *Minutiers centrals*[61] reveals that he possessed a watch with a jeweled gold case. This is probably the gift of the Breton canal commission.

providing thirty *pouces*[q] of water—eighteen for the royal household and twelve for the city.

Claude Regnault proposed building a large water wheel on the Seine to supply the Faubourg Saint-Germain, but in 1666, Louis XIV rejected the plan as being dangerous to river navigation. At the time of Regnault's proposal, there were thirty-four public fountains giving a total of 13 *pouces* 27 *lignes*[r] and 152 private concessions giving 10 *pouces* 6 *lignes*. Because of the increasing complexity of the water system, it became traditional about this time for city officials to conduct an annual inspection tour of water facilities. This tradition continued through Coulomb's term as *intendant*.[64]

In 1669, a committee composed of Thomas Francini, Petit, Blondel, and Roberval[s] approved a plan for pneumatic pumps. These were put into operation but soon began breaking down, so that in 1680, the city appointed a permanent inspector of pumps. Many designs for pumps were proposed in the last two decades of the seventeenth century. The first example of a real engineering study of these pumps came when Bernard Forest de Bélidor was chosen to examine and report on the machine at the Pont Notre-Dame in 1737. Bélidor's report[65] contained improvements which increased the flow from 100 to 150 *pouces*.

During the middle of the eighteenth century, the Academies first began to study seriously the chemical purity of the water supply. An early plan had suggested using sponges to filter the water. In 1749, Mathieu Tillet had Reaumur and Grandjean de Fouchy give an account to the Academy of Sciences on means of filtering the water. Then in 1766, the *Faculté de médicine* appointed a committee composed of Jean Hellot and Macquer (of the Academy), and Majault, Poissonier, la Rivière (le jeune), Roux, and Darcet (for the *Faculté*), to examine the purity of the waters in the Paris region. The committee called the public's attention to the dangers

[q] The *pouce* as a flow-rate measurement (as here), was equal to 14 pints per minute. The linear *pouce* was about an inch.

[r] The linear *ligne* was equal to one-twelfth of a *pouce*. Thus, the *ligne* as a flow-rate would be 1/144th that of a *pouce*, or about a tenth of a pint per minute.

[s] Francini (or Franchini) was the *Surintendant des eaux du roi*. Though the title changed, this was the same position Coulomb was to hold. Petit and (Nicolas-François) Blondel were engineers and Gilles Personne de Roberval was the celebrated mathematician.

existing in the consumption of the highly polluted waters, but most of the eighteenth century passed with water purification methods remaining within the scope of physical filtration.

With the development of pumps during the eighteenth century, two types of water supply systems were provided: pumps, and the more traditional systems of canals or aqueducts. In 1771, Lavoisier gave the opinion that pumps would be most economical if water was to be raised less than sixty feet. To obtain water in very large quantities, Lavoisier recommended canals as preferable. About the same time, Perronet and Chézy considered the problem and also opted for a canal to supply the city of Paris.

Private water companies at this time serviced a good part of the city with pumps carried on boats, and hundreds of porters carried water from the Seine to the neighborhoods on either side. In 1777, the Périer brothers were given a fifteen-year monopoly to provide 150 *pouces* of water to Paris. They received a healthy 45,000 *livres* plus ten percent of the profits for this service. Their first operating site was at the Palais de Chaillot, where they installed two steam engines to raise the water 110 feet and distribute it in a one-foot diameter iron pipe. The Chaillot installation went into operation in July 1782, using designs and some parts obtained from Watt and Boulton. Thus, the Périers were the first in France to operate the improved steam engine successfully.[66] Though their company's stock lost value in the late 1780s, the brothers were as ingenious in business as in engineering.

In February of 1783, Le Roy, Bossut, Cousin, and Coulomb were named to examine the Périers' steam engines and give an account to the Academy. After several observations and tests with the engines, the committee gave its report on March 19, 1783.[67] It was written and delivered by Coulomb. He clearly outlined the principles behind Watt's designs and indicated the Périers' contributions. It was thus Coulomb who first *publicly* introduced the principles of the improved condenser steam engine in France. Coulomb reported on some fourteen schemes for pumps and canals between the time of his election to the Academy in December 1781 and his appointment as *Intendant des eaux et fontaines* in July 1784.[t]

---

[t] The histories of hydraulics and the water system of Paris[68] fail to mention Coulomb's work as *intendant*. There are two reasons for this. First, after 1783, the duties of the *Intendant des eaux et fontaines* seldom appear in the *Registres de la Ville de Paris*. Second, supervision of the water supply for

In particular, he joined Bossut, Borda, Périer, and Monge in a commission to study the comte d'Angiviller's plan for a contest to design a new hydraulic machine at Marly.[69] Since 1774, the comte d'Angiviller had been *Directeur général des bâtiments, arts et manufactures du roi.*[70] This post included the administration of the "Academies of painting and sculpture, the Sèvres porcelain and the Gobelins [tapestry] manufactories, cloth and soap works, the Observatory, the royal gardens, promenades, palaces and châteaus, and the French Academy in Rome."[u,71]

At the time of Coulomb's appointment in 1784, Paris was supplied with six types of water delivery systems:[72]

1. The new pumps
   a. Quai de l'Hôpital
   b. Quai de la Grève
   c. Port au Plâtre
   d. Port du Recueillage
   e. Palais de Chaillot
2. The old pumps
   a. la Samaritaine
   b. Pont Notre-Dame
   c. Pont Neuf
3. Filtered water taken directly from the Seine on the Ile Saint-Louis
4. The *bateaux covertes* (pumps mounted on boats)
5. The aqueducts
   a. Arcueil
   b. Rungis
   c. Belleville
   d. Pré Saint-Gervais
6. The system of lead piping.

As mentioned above, Coulomb's duties as *intendant* covered the

---

Paris and for the king's properties had been divided, with an *intendant* to administer the royal properties and a committee from the city of Paris to administer the public water supply. Thus, most secondary sources concern the history of the public water supply system rather than that of the royal properties. In spite of regulations defining the authority and duties of each, the king's *intendant* was in fact often involved in outside problems concerning both public and private water supplies.

u One of d'Angiviller's assistants was the mathematician Jean-Etienne Montucla, who was charged with the administration of the Gobelins, Sèvres, the Observatory, the soap works, and laboratories at Autueil.

administration of the waters of the royal properties but not those of the public.[73] The city of Paris administered its portion of the waters through a committee which included the *Prévôt des marchands*, the *Procureur du roi*, and the *Lieutenant de police*.[74]

As *intendant* for the royal waters, Coulomb was solely charged with the "Pump at la Samaritaine, and also with a portion of those pumps at Rungis (called 'The King's waters,' because the expense of these establishments had been drawn from funds of the Royal treasury)."[75] Coulomb also directed "the distribution and use of that portion of the public waters which have just been mentioned,"[76] the "Château of waters located at the Observatory"[77] (the *Château d'eau* was a water reservoir, with accompanying buildings, where water could be supplied under pressure to pipelines or aqueducts leading to various sections of the city), and the supplies for Versailles, Fontainebleau, Saint-Germain-en-laye and the other royal residences.[78] This amounted to seventeen kilometers of ducting for the Rungis and Arcueil aqueducts alone.

Within the city, he was responsible for the royal buildings as well as the fountains at the Louvre, the Tuileries, and several neighboring quarters. The edifice at the Samaritaine, for instance, was a Baroque castle with a hydraulic clock "which played tunes every hour," in particular the air, "Where better to be than in the bosom of one's family. . . ."[v,79]

Louis XIII gave the title of *Surintendant des eaux* to Thomas de Francini, comte de Villepreux, in 1623,[81] and the position remained within the Francini family until the death of the last comte de Villepreux in 1783. On d'Angiviller's recommendation, Coulomb was then awarded the *intendancy* as a hereditary post. His salary for this position is not known, though earlier in the century the salary was 3,000 *livres* a year.[82]

Immediately upon taking the position in July 1784, he received notice from the city of Paris that the annual inspection of water facilities would be set for July 22. Coulomb asked d'Angiviller to send him all papers and studies relative to the properties for which

---

[v] A further description of this amazing hydraulic structure is as follows: "At the base of the clock-face is a great gilded receptacle which receives water from a reservoir in order to transmit the water in its turn into the pipes which carry it to its destination. The water, in falling onto a shell, and from there into a basin, forms a very attractive waterfall. The basin is adorned with two figures of bronzed and gilded lead, one representing the seated Jesus Christ, and the other the Good Samaritan, drawing water from Jacob's well and stopping to listen to Christ."[80]

he was responsible. He expressed his anxiety at not being ready for the inspection.[w,83] He received the use of a château at Arcueil but his health was such that he never took possession of this property;[85] he preferred to live in Paris nearer to the Academy. Coulomb's position was not in the least a sinecure, however. D'Angiviller published two reports of the work performed under his direction from 1774 to 1789.[86] The exact funding of Coulomb's work is not disclosed; however, the total funds for d'Angiviller's department of the *Bâtiments du Roi* were fixed at four million *livres* per year in 1783. In his reports, d'Angiviller listed large items of work on aqueducts and water systems included between 1783 and 1789:

Versailles—reconstruction of the major part of the reservoirs— immense aqueducts in the city.
Paris—at the Arcueil aqueduct.
Compiègne—the installation of a hydraulic machine (pump or water wheel) for the security of the château and the whole city.[87]

Coulomb not only had to supervise the water supply for the king but also for various villages between Rungis, Arcueil, and Paris that took theirs from the king's aqueducts.[88] He was faced with tax questions and litigations regarding private concessions.[89] Once, the old lead piping under the rue des Francsbourgeois ruptured.[x] Coulomb was confronted by citizens complaining that their basements were flooded. He had to supervise the reparation and inspect each basement to insure that the leakage was stopped. Similar day-to-day problems appeared: gravel in the water lines, leakage all along the line between the Observatoire and the Luxembourg gardens, discussions over taxes on the château at Arcueil.[90] There was a movement to increase the water supply to the Latin Quarter by adding a new aqueduct. Coulomb felt that this was a desirable project but he reported to d'Angiviller that it was too expensive for the state budget at the time.[91]

Silvestre de Sacy's recent biography of d'Angiviller[92] shows him to have been a devoted, able, public servant. He was one of those who shared in the reforming ideals of Turgot. He took over the position of *Directeur générale des bâtiments du roi* from l'abbé Terray in 1774, the same day, said d'Angiviller, that the king

---

[w] The inspection showed that Arcueil provided 58 *pouces* flow of water as compared to 28 for the preceding year.[84]

[x] The old rue des Francsbourgeois was then located in what is now the 5e *arrondissement*.

placed "at the head of his finances M. Turgot, with whom I was united since 1751 by a friendship which died in his heart only on the day of his death and which still lives completely in mine."[93] D'Angiviller's staff at the *Bâtiments du Roi* included others as talented as Montucla. D'Angiviller chose Coulomb because of "his profound knowledge, in the use of which he has distinguished himself in all the details which have been confided to him. . . ."[94] One can judge that as a man devoted to the idea of a *corps à talent*, Coulomb shared some of the same ideals as d'Angiviller and that his years as *intendant* were as fruitful as his other services as an engineer.

One is not sure exactly when he terminated his services as *Intendant des eaux et fontaines*.[y] According to Girard,[96] the *intendancy* ceased to function in 1792. Beltrand,[97] however, believes 1790 to be a more likely date, for many municipal functions were suppressed in that year. Coulomb's position was not for the city but for the royal household, thus, Girard's estimate is more probably correct. In addition, Girard knew Coulomb personally before 1792.

HOSPITAL REFORM. Coulomb's role as an academician in hospital reform work has been mentioned briefly above. In addition to his role as consultant on reports and inventions concerned with machines and canals, Coulomb participated in the Academy's activities in public health planning. This social engineering, as indeed it should be defined, occupied the Academy during the 1770s and afterwards. Prizes were offered for solutions to problems of street lighting, water supply systems, and insurance programs.[98] Not only was quantity a factor in the question of the Paris water supply system, but Macquer, Darcet, and others introduced chemical analysis into the investigation of the purity or quality of the water.[99] Problems that formerly were considered as *mécanique appliqué* now concerned the chemist and biologist as well.

Coulomb's interests in hospital reform were not first kindled at the Academy. In an essay written in 1775, he called attention to the deplorable conditions in the hospital at Cherbourg:

> This hospital cares for 200 indigents. It takes in children, the sick, the feeble, and the wounded. When there are troops quar-

[y] The last known letter from Coulomb as *intendant* to d'Angiviller is dated May 1790.[95]

tered in Cherbourg, ailing soldiers find beds there. The income of this hospital does not exceed 3000 *livres*, and its annual expenses are more than 10,000 *livres*. Work by the poor and public charities does not always suffice to cover the excess expenses, and the patients there often lack bread. One would hope that enough [aid? word illegible] could be supplied to this establishment to put it in a state to be able to receive the crowds of beggars who wander continuously through the city.[100]

The hospitals of Paris were in a poor state compared to similar institutions abroad and even to those in other cities in France. Accordingly, the death rate at the Hôtel-Dieu in Paris was several times that of hospitals in Edinburgh and Rome and three times as high as those at Lyon and St. Denis. Jean Baptiste Le Roy had submitted to the Academy in 1777 a plan calling for reform of the Paris institutions. In 1785, the Academy appointed a committee composed of Lassone, Daubenton, Le Roy, Tenon, Bailly, Lavoisier, Darcet, and Laplace to examine a M. Poyet's memoir concerning reform of the Hôtel-Dieu. The committee initiated a full investigation of general reform of the hospitals in Paris. Since Le Roy's plan of 1777 was included for discussion, Coulomb was appointed to replace Le Roy on the committee. This group worked for ten months before issuing a 158-page report.[z,101] It detailed the shocking conditions at the Hôtel-Dieu and criticism crossed several disciplines: architecture, public health, control of communicable diseases, and design and maintenance of utilities supply systems (heating, water, waste).

The committee recommended immediate construction of four hospitals of 1,200 beds each. They acknowledged the need for about 5,000 beds but outlined why four medium-sized buildings were preferable to a single large one: hospitals of 1,200 beds would be easier to administer and to provide with food and supplies; they would be more accessible to the patients, since each would be in a different quarter of Paris; most importantly, the spread of infection and communicable disease would be too difficult to control in a large hospital. In sum, rather than renovate the old Hôtel-Dieu, the committee recommended the conversion of two existing institutions (St. Louis and Ste. Anne) and the con-

---

[z] Signed by all but Laplace. Maury[102] indicates that it was Bailly who wrote this report.

struction of two new buildings, the first to be located near the Celestin and the second near the Ecole Militaire.

The Academy continued the general investigation. Subsequently, in 1787, Coulomb and Jacques René Tenon were named to travel to England to survey the newest hospital design and operative methods in use there.[103] Coulomb and Tenon spent eight weeks in England, visiting, among others, Sir Joseph Banks and James Watt, and seeing the cities of London, Birmingham, and Plymouth.[aa]

Tenon played the major role in the hospital reform committee, and it was his written reports that the Academy considered in later meetings. Coulomb contributed an active though not a leading part in this work. Perhaps the importance of this episode lies not so much in any substantive action Coulomb took with regard to hospital reform, rather it indicates that a number of academicians were deeply interested in various problems of "social engineering" long before the Revolution called for these reforms under the rubric of democracy. The haughtiness of the Academy toward solutions offered by outsiders stemmed not so much from the aristocratic nature of mathematics or the Academy itself, but from hardheaded refusal to accept vague, romantic solutions to problems—be they human or natural.

RELIEF MAPS. Beginning with Colbert's administration and continuing through the nineteenth century, the French military constructed elaborate scale model relief maps (*plans en relief*) of fortified ports and cities. These models were sometimes up to thirty feet on a side and represented in detail all parts of the city and its surrounding terrain. Unlike flat maps, which could be conveniently stored, the relief maps required a great deal of space. They were stored in the Louvre during most of the eighteenth century under the care of five to seven employees. When the comte d'Angiviller created the Louvre museum in 1776, they were moved to the Invalides. At this date, there were 127 maps.[105] The collection was considered highly secret, and *all* officials were required to obtain explicit permission from the Secretary of State to visit the gallery. The public was never allowed to visit the collection.

[aa] Coulomb and Tenon were abroad from about the middle of June until the second week of August 1787. Their letters to the Academy are lost but there are several letters from or about them preserved in the Joseph Banks Collection.[104]

Larcher d'Aubancourt, an officer in the *Corps royal du génie*, was in charge of the maps from 1758 until his resignation in 1791.[106] By the law of July 10, 1791, the relief maps were combined with engineering maps in general, in a new *Dépot d'archives des fortifications* under the command of Lt. Col. d'Assigny.[107]

Coulomb may have participated in the direction of this collection. It is impossible to be sure, however, for there are numerous conflicting sources. Three sources state that he was given the "survivance" to the position of *Conservateur des plans en relief* in 1786: Delambre mentions this in his memorial;[108] Biot states this and also adds that Coulomb received the survivance "without having requested it";[109] finally, Coulomb's service record at Vincennes states simply "Conservateur des plans & reliefs . . . 1786."[110]

In addition to these sources, Coulomb mentions the post in his letter of resignation from the *génie*, December 18, 1790. He gives as one of his reasons for resigning: "as it appears that there will no longer be an officer charged in particular with maps and relief maps. . . ."[111] This latter statement, however, implies only that Coulomb was not to have the job.

Coulomb is never mentioned in the archives at the present *Musée des plans-reliefs*. The employees are listed, and there is a record of Larcher d'Aubancourt's transfer of the post to d'Assigny, Coulomb's name is never cited in the few studies concerning the collection of *plans en relief*. Some of these contradictions may be resolved. Charles Augustin was under Larcher's orders for ten years—from 1781 to 1791. It is possible that he was given the promise of the post after Larcher's retirement. He could not have been given this officially, however, because Larcher did not have the authority to appoint his successor.

Delambre knew Coulomb from before the Revolution, and therefore his memorial must be accorded considerable weight as evidence. Biot knew Coulomb only some years after these events, and his 1813 article on him may have been taken from Delambre. In any case, he makes the same statements. And as for the service record at Vincennes, a note at the bottom indicates that Delambre's memorial was used in compiling the record.

Given Coulomb's statement in his letter of resignation, it is clear that he must have thought, at least, that he would obtain the post of *conservateur*. I have found, however, no records to indicate that Coulomb was given either the post or its survivance. In any case, the job was a kind of sinecure and required little or no work. Coulomb played no role there and this episode must remain an unexplained but trivial event in his career.

WEIGHTS AND MEASURES. The diverse and chaotic character of weights and measures used in eighteenth-century Europe called forth numerous plans for reform. The first real step in this direction in France, however, occurred in 1788 when the Academy appointed a preliminary commission to study the question of a new system of weights and measures. The commission, composed of Borda, Lagrange, Laplace, Monge, and Condorcet, reviewed the matter and submitted a proposal to the Academy and to the National Assembly in March 1791.[112] Their plan called for the establishment of five commissions to develop a new system. The commissions and their members as appointed April 13, 1791 were:

I. Triangulation and latitude determination:
   Cassini (IV), Méchain & Legendre
II. Measurement of standards (of length):
   Monge & Meusnier
III. Length of the seconds pendulum: Borda & Coulomb
IV. Weight of a standard volume of water:
   Lavoisier & Haüy
V. Comparison of provincial standards with those of Paris:
   Tillet, Brisson & Vandermonde[113]

In practice, these commissions were not fixed, for Delambre replaced Cassini and Legendre on the first; Monge and Meusnier were usually replaced by Méchain and Delambre on the second;[114] and Cassini claims he himself replaced Coulomb for the work on the third.[115] It is not our intention here to give a history or sketch of the evolution of the system of weights and measures, for this story has been ably told elsewhere.[116] An attempt will be made, though, to trace Coulomb's part in this work.

If one goes strictly by secondary histories it might appear that Cassini did Coulomb's work and that Coulomb played no role at all. This is probably inaccurate for several reasons. First, Cassini was never noted for his modesty. If one relied on his story in the instance of the magnetic observations (mentioned in Chapter I), one could easily get the false impression that the development of the measurement of the diurnal variations of the earth's magnetic field was all Cassini's work. Second, Coulomb participated in the commission's tasks in matters other than determination of the pendulum standard. Finally, he was again involved in weights and measures after the Revolution. Though his role may have been a small one, it is worth considering.

The pendulum commission conducted its measurements from June until August 1792. Cassini stated that he used a pendulum "constructed by Le Noir, after the design of Borda and under his direction, with which I made all the observations that served as the basis for the Memoir in which this academician [Borda] standardized the length of the pendulum. . . ."[117] That Coulomb played some role in this, however, is evidenced by archival materials at the Observatory of Paris which contradict parts of Cassini's story; Lavoisier's later mention of Coulomb in connection with the third commission;[118] and Borda's report to the National Convention, November 25, 1792, which read, in part, "The operation relative to the length of the pendulum, the objective of the Third Commission, is already well underway; numerous experiments have already been done at the Observatory, by citizens Borda, Coulomb and Cassini, in order to determine first, the length of the seconds pendulum at Paris."[119]

The commissions on weights and measures were suppressed simultaneously with the suppression of the Academy on August 8, 1793. The importance of the commission's occupation did not escape the convention, however, and they adopted Fourcroy's proposal that it be continued. On September 11, 1793, the convention named a *Commission temporaire* and stated that they would maintain "the respective operations which have been confided to them."[120] By this time Tillet was dead, Meusnier had fallen at Mayence, and Condorcet was in prison. The *Commission temporaire* was then composed of Borda, Brisson, Cassini, Coulomb, Delambre, Haüy, Lagrange, Laplace, Lavoisier, Méchain, Monge, and Vandermonde.[121] In early December 1793, Coulomb replaced Lavoisier as treasurer. Two weeks later, on December 23, 1793, Coulomb was purged from the committee. The purge issued from the pen of Prieur de la Côte d'Or and the *Comité de salut public*.[122] As with so many other things during the Reign of Terror, this change came not from long-standing administrative errors or injustice toward the "people" but simply from personal animosity. Prieur had submitted a proposal for a new system of weights and measures in 1790 (when he was still Prieur Du Vernois and a mere "officer in the *Corps royal du génie*"),[123] and this had been rejected by the commission.

In his biography of Borda, Jean Mascart (citing Delambre) has shown that Prieur was usually at odds over political subjects with Lavoisier and with Lavoisier's supporters—Borda and Coulomb.[124] Thus it is not surprising that Coulomb was included among those purged from the commission.[bb] After their removal, Coulomb and Borda retired to some property Coulomb owned near Blois.[126] Charles Augustin would not return again to work in Paris until sixteen months later, when he was called to continue the study on weights and measures.

The purging of December 1793 was much more than symbolic. The remnants of the temporary commission did little in the next year. Weights and measures work began again with the naming of a new commission by a decree of April 17, 1795. The twelve Academicians forming the new group met in the "offices of the *Comité d'instruction publique.*"[cc,127] Specific duties were outlined for all in the group save Coulomb and Lagrange.[128]

In the beginning of the Revolutionary year 7 (September 1798), the *Directorate* invited eleven foreign delegates to participate in the study on weights and measures.[dd] This combined group of French and foreign academicians[ee] was divided into three subcommissions, and Coulomb was named to two of these: the group charged with comparing the standards of length used in the measure of base lines with the standard *toise* and the commission for the determination of the unit of weight.[130]

He continued as a member of the weights and measures commission through 1799. He participated in a large number of studies connected with the establishment of a system of weights and

---

[bb] Others purged were Borda, Lavoisier, Laplace, Brisson and Delambre. Those added were Buache, Berthollet, Hassenfratz, and Prony.[125]

[cc] The group comprised Berthollet, Borda, Brisson, Coulomb, Delambre, Haüy, Lagrange, Laplace, Méchain, Monge, Prony and Vandermonde.

[dd] The delegates were:[129] Batavian Republic, Aeneas and Van Swinden; Cisalpine Republic, Mascheroni; Denmark, Bugge; Spain, Ciscar and Pédrayèz; Helvetian Republic, Trallès; Ligierian Republic, Multedo; Kingdom of Sardinia (replaced by the Provisional Government of Piedmont), Balbo (replaced by Vassali Eandi); Roman Republic, Francini; Tuscany, Fabroni.

[ee] By this time the French commission comprised: Borda, Brisson, Coulomb, Darcet, Haüy, Lagrange, Laplace, Lefèvre-Gineau, Méchain, and Prony. Darcet and Lefèvre-Gineau replaced Berthollet and Monge, who were in Egypt.

measures, but it seems that he did so in a minor way, probably as a consultant. His skill with measuring instruments and his previous Academy experience (for instance his reports on proposals for the minting of coins)[131] would have made him a natural person to consult.

THE REVOLUTION AND THE FIRST YEARS OF THE INSTITUTE. The Revolution of 1789 caused little outward change in Coulomb's activities. He was in the midst of his great series of memoirs on electricity and magnetism; in fact he finished and read the Seventh Memoir only in July 1791. Committee reports for the Academy continued as usual. Coulomb reported on the establishment of new trades and manufactures, the minting of coins, plans for a new monetary system, and various schemes for improvement in canals, navigation, and machines.

In the first two years of the Revolution, the National Assembly overturned or reorganized in detail many of the institutions of the *ancien régime*. The *Corps royal du génie* was similarly affected by decrees issued from October 1790 through the spring of 1791. The laws of October 24-31, 1790 reduced the effective number of engineers by about twenty percent, from 380 to 310. Most of the cuts came from the lower ranks—the number of Mézières students was cut from twenty to ten; the number of lieutenants from one hundred to sixty. Coulomb had been promoted from captain to major on March 23, 1786.[132] Henceforth, this rank would be abolished and all majors would become lieutenant-colonels, and in addition, the years of study in preparation for entrance to Mézières would now be counted towards retirement benefits or seniority.[133] Another decree, issued December 15, 1790, favored the advancement of captains and held the door open to retirement for many older members of the *génie*.

On December 18, 1790, for the second time in his career, Coulomb tendered his resignation.[134] This time it was accepted. He gave two reasons: first, he had heard that the department of *Plans en relief* would be combined with another, thus eliminating the position of officer in charge of relief plans; second, his health was such that he could no longer perform the duties of an engineering officer. As Reinhard indicates,[135] the decree of December 15, 1790 provided older officers the opportunity to leave for personal reasons. It was this reorganization that caused the first large-scale resignation from the corps. Nearly all of the *génie militaire* had remained loyal to the Revolution, at least through 1790, and only a few had resigned or fled the country before 1791. In fact, only one captain quit in 1789 and another decamped in 1790.[136]

Coulomb's resignation was accepted April 1, 1791. He obtained a pension of 2,240 *livres* in January 1792, based on his rank of major and his thirty-one years of service in the corps.[ff,137] This pension was cut to 1,287 francs per year in 1799[138] and further reduced to 746 francs sometime after 1803.[139] His resignation from the corps did not affect his responsibilities at the Academy. Since moving to Paris, his work for the *génie* had been limited largely to reading reports submitted to the Academy (except for the two seasons of wrangling with the Breton canal commission). Neither did the termination of his position as *Intendant des eaux et fontaines* affect his duties at the Academy. There were a few plans submitted by the National Assembly, and in November 1791, Coulomb and fourteen other academicians[gg,140] were named to the Academy section of the *Bureau des consultation des arts et métiers*, an organization decreed by the Constituent Assembly.[hh]

General war was declared in February 1793 and the Academy turned in its last months to almost full-time consideration of military inventions. As a specialist in applied mechanics, Coulomb was in demand. He reported on only five inventions or plans in 1793—all concerned the military.

His final appearance at the Academy was at the last meeting in July 1793.[141] Immediately after this he went to his house in the country north of Paris, near the château Chaumontel at Luzarches.[ii] It was a very dangerous time to be in Paris. The war was going badly; the Paris Commune had invaded the Convention and ar-

---

[ff] Coulomb's *total* effective service was:

service	31 years
campaigns	9
Mézières and study	3
Total	43 years.

[gg] The members elected were: Le Roy, Bossut, Lavoisier, Desmarest, Borda, Vandermonde, Coulomb, Berthollet, Meusnier, Brisson, Périer, Rochon, Duhamel, Lagrange, and Laplace. In addition to these fifteen, Legentil acted as secretary. Lavoisier had a double post as member and treasurer.

[hh] Coulomb seemed to play no important role in this body for his name does not appear in its subsequent records at the Academy.

[ii] It is not known when Coulomb obtained the Luzarches property. He sold it some years before his death in 1806 but neither the exact year of sale nor the extent of the property is known.[142]

rested many Girondist leaders; Condorcet was in hiding. On August 6, 1793, two days before the Academy was abolished, Coulomb wrote Lavoisier from Luzarches asking him for a small favor. The galley proofs of his memoir on pivot friction needed correction. Coulomb asked Lavoisier to get these from the printer and to send them to him. At this date then, he assumed that things at the Academy would continue as usual. He was certainly aware of the danger in Paris, however, for he begged of Lavoisier: "Have also the kindness to write your steward and ask him whether you still have any traces of coats of arms or feudal artifacts proscribed by the law and to destroy any found."[143]

The Reign of Terror for science began two days later when the Academy was abolished and seals were placed upon the buildings and all papers therein. Coulomb remained close to Paris, for there was still work to do for the commission on weights and measures. He continued for two months until Prieur and the *Comité de salut public* purged the *Commission temporaire* in December 1793.

After this occurred, Coulomb and his friend Borda retired to property Coulomb possessed near Blois,[jj] to get farther from the Revolution. It was here that Coulomb brought his family during the Reign of Terror. Charles Augustin had taken as his wife a Doué girl in her twenties, Louise Françoise Le Proust Desor-

[jj] The state of Coulomb's property holdings at any one time is difficult to determine. Grimaux[144] notes that in 1793 Lavoisier sold to Coulomb the *habitation* of Thoisy, for the sum of 44,000 *livres*. Thoisy is about a mile and a half south of Lavoisier's château at Fréchines, and eight miles north of Blois. It is probable that this property is where Coulomb and Borda spent the period of the Reign of Terror and where Coulomb made his observations in plant physiology. Later, however, in 1803, Coulomb purchased property some ten miles south of Thoisy and three miles west of Blois, for the sum of 23,700 francs. This was (and is) a farm of about fifty acres called "la Justinière," near Groix (Grouets) in the communes of Blois and Chousy. The property contains four tenant houses, or *closerie* (one at each corner of the property), with the main house in the center. This modest structure consists of a two-story stone and slate house built about 1700 with an attached toolshed and barn.

The difficulties here are that Coulomb's probate mentions his former ownership of the house near Luzarches, and of his purchase of "la Justinière" but makes no mention of any property at Thoisy or any purchase of property from Lavoisier. Coulomb's probate, however, indicates that various items indicated only by number "n'ont été plus amplement décrites."[145] Grimaux obtained his information from an official at Blois, and given Coulomb's friendship with Lavoisier, the reported sale of the Thoisy property to Coulomb is not unreasonable. His widow mentions that much was lost during the Terror, thus there may actually be no record of eventual sale by Coulomb.

meaux.[kk] His first son, Charles Augustin II, had been born in Paris on February 26, 1790.[147]

Coulomb passed the time at Blois with his family and initiated several experiments in botany. Just as in his old engineering days, he was inquisitive and investigated what was at hand; friction in Rochefort, coastal defenses in Cherbourg, windmills in Lille, and at Blois, Coulomb studied plant physiology.

In the manuscript notes of his memorial of Coulomb, Delambre writes that Coulomb did a considerable amount of botanical physiology and that he had looked through a number of his notes and memoirs concerning this.[148] Unfortunately, except for two of his laboratory notebooks for the period circa 1802, none of his original scientific manuscripts are known to exist today. We have only his printed works. The only evidence of his botanical investigations concerns some work he performed in 1796 and published in the *Mémoires de l'Institut* as "Experiments Concerning the Circulation of Sap in Trees."[149]

Coulomb had some Italian poplars cut down in the spring of 1796. He noticed that when one cut into the core of a tree, the trunk emitted a sound similar to that of air bubbling to the surface of a liquid. He ordered some more poplars cut and discovered that the noise occurred only when the trunk was cut very near the core. Other trees were then cut all the way around so as to leave a central core of three or four centimeters untouched. When these trees were pulled down the center core often bent without breaking. A considerable amount of bubbles issued forth, much more so than in sap which flows from a cut in a tree. The bubbles came forth with a clear water that had no taste. To investigate this further, Coulomb drilled holes horizontally into the center of some poplars at the height of one meter above the ground. Within two or three centimeters of the core, the clear fluid began to flow copiously and was always accompanied by the air bubbles and the bubbling noise. He noticed that this noise diminished as the summer progressed but that it continued through the seasons, stopping only during the night and on cold and humid days. The phenomenon increased as "the heat of the sun increased the leaf transpiration."[150]

Coulomb suggested that this indicated that the circulation of sap in trees occurs through their central medullary canals. He gave no

kk Coulomb legitimized his marriage on 17 *brumaire, an* 11 (November 8, 1802).[146]

further suppositions on this experiment but promised to repeat it. He later did so with members of the botanical section of the Institute in attendance.[151]

Coulomb loved the country, and he spent much time tutoring his small son Charles. This must have been a pleasant place for him, because as Delambre notes, Lavoisier and others had often visited him there before the Revolution.

He left the property near Blois only once during the Reign of Terror; in May 1794, he risked his life to enter Paris for Lavoisier's funeral. He next visited Paris in April of 1795 when he was appointed a member of the reconstituted commission on weights and measures. As mentioned previously, he played only a minor role in the weights and measures work after the Revolution. Until the founding of the Institute in December 1795, he preferred to spend most of his time with his family in the Loire.[152]

Coulomb was elected *membre résident de la section de physique expérimentale* in the new *Institut de France* on December 9, 1795.[153] This change from his former position as a member of the class of *mécanique* indicates not only that the thrust of his work was now in physics rather than in mechanics but more importantly, that the rapidly evolving physical fields of light, heat, electricity and magnetism (the Baconian fields, as Thomas Kuhn calls them) were now recognized as worthy of a separate position in the Academy.

Coulomb had purchased a house in Paris on the rue du Chantre in May 1791, just after his retirement from the *Corps du génie*. The *Almanach royal* lists his residences for 1795 and 1796 as "rue Favart, no. 4" and "rue Coquéron, no. 56." He had definitely moved into the house (known as the Hôtel d'Armagniac) on rue du Chantre by 1797, because his second son, Henry Louis, was born there on July 30, 1797.[154] The home was just next to Notre-Dame on the Ile de la Cité, and Coulomb went regularly from there to the meetings of the Institute. His role in that organization continued as before the Revolution. He still had to report on devices for wagons, artificial legs, machines of various kinds, and even literary novels. His own memoirs given in the first years of the Institute (1795–1799) were based largely on previous work. He read the memoir on root pressure that he had written at Blois and, finally, he submitted one on the efficiency of laboring men. He had begun this latter study in Martinique, had delivered preliminary versions of it to the Academy in 1778 and 1780, and then had taken it up again at Blois during the Reign of Terror. At last, in 1798, he read it in final form.

Coulomb had studied the work habits of men at various times during his engineering career. He solved important problems of maximizing output in his memoir "Results of Several Experiments Designed to Determine the Quantity of Action that Men Can Supply in Daily Work According to the Different Manners in which They Employ Their Forces."[155] The basic unit employed by Coulomb in this study was dimensionally equivalent to work (or, a force acting through a distance), and he defined work as "quantity of action"[156] or "effect of work."[157] In output, he distinguished between two things in men and animals: "the effect that can be produced in the use of their forces as applied to machines, and the fatigue that they experience in producing this effect."[158] The aim of this memoir, then, was to determine means to "increase the effect without increasing the fatigue."[159]

Coulomb departed from earlier studies of this subject in showing that fatigue in humans and animals is not proportional to the maximum work obtained but is a function of weight, distance, and time. Utilizing the calculus of maxima and minima, he examined numerous types of physical labor and determined the maximum useful work deliverable under these conditions for varying periods. Among his findings was that frequent rest periods in certain tasks produce higher overall output. He believed to have proved that maximum output occurs with seven to eight hours labor per day for heavy tasks and ten hours per day for shopkeeping and lighter tasks.[160] Above this, greatly increased fatigue results in lower overall output. This study produced findings important for the theory of labor planning and distribution, and though little noticed, it was one of the most significant early studies in the science of work, or what we today call ergonomics, until the studies of F. W. Taylor[161] almost a century later.

Another memoir, read by Coulomb in 1800, concerned an application of his torsion balance.[11,162] Since the time of Newton, investigators had attempted to discover the laws of fluid resistance. D'Alembert, Bossut, and others had conducted experiments on a large scale, using rowboats pulled across a small pool. In spite of all experiments, there was doubt that the correct law of fluid re-

---

[11] This memoir is discussed further in Chapter v.

sistance could be known unless fluid motion could be studied at very slow, precisely controlled velocities.

Coulomb saw a solution to this difficulty through the use of his torsion balance. Because of its cylindrical symmetry, the balance could oscillate in place, thus moving through the fluid only in the sense of rotation and not of translation (at least to lower-order approximations). At the same time, the cylindrical object at the end of the torsion balance varied negligibly in vertical displacement. The cylindrical test object could be chosen at will to have periods from a fraction of a second to many seconds, and Coulomb could produce fluid motion at almost any desired velocity without involving translation of the object through the fluid.

These memoirs presented between 1795 and 1799—plant physiology, efficiency of laboring men, fluid resistance—though interesting in themselves, were not at the core of Coulomb's scientific concerns at the end of his life. His last major studies were aimed at discovering the limits of electricity and magnetism and their relations to heat and the constitution of matter.

These first two chapters have presented Coulomb's life as student, engineer, physicist, and public servant. His engineering and physics memoirs have been mentioned at appropriate points in the biography, but I have not attempted to analyze them in detail. However interesting Coulomb's life and career may have been, it is his engineering and physics works that gained for him the place he has in the history of science. These studies are examined in succeeding chapters.

Three · COULOMB AND EIGHTEENTH-CENTURY CIVIL ENGINEERING

Introduction

On March 10, 1773, Grandjean de Fouchy, permanent secretary of the Academy of Sciences, noted in the minutes, "M. Coulomb entered, and began the reading of a memoir entitled: 'Essay on the Application of the Rules of *Maxima* and *Minima* to Some Problems in Architecture.' "[1] This was the beginning of a career as correspondent and member of the Academy that would extend over three decades and more than thirty memoirs.

Coulomb is generally remembered for his outstanding work in electricity, magnetism, and torsion, yet he was trained at Mézières and had worked as a military engineer for twelve years prior to reading this first memoir at the Academy. He was an engineering officer from 1761 until 1791 and was fully concerned with the subject for the greater part of his adult life. In the impact of his studies, Coulomb can be considered one of the great theoretical engineers in France and indeed in Europe in the eighteenth century. In this chapter and the next we shall consider some specific developments of his engineering research. The subject is important not only because of the intrinsic interest of the work itself, but because it illustrates how Coulomb came from this field to his later work in physics, and even how his method in engineering would fuse with rational mechanics and with *physique expérimentale* in the new formulation and maturation of the "empirical" physical disciplines.[a] Here we will focus on Coulomb's 1773 memoir, "Essay on an Application of the Rules of *Maxima* and *Minima* to Some Problems in Statics,

[a] By the "empirical" physical disciplines I mean heat, light, electricity, and magnetism; that is, those parts of physics exclusive of the earlier matured sciences of rational mechanics, geometrical optics, and astronomy.

Relating to Architecture."[b,2] This short essay on mechanics was perhaps the finest *engineering* memoir delivered at the Academy during Coulomb's lifetime. It contained important and even fundamental ideas in the fields of strength of materials, soil mechanics, and the design of structures.

Coulomb was thirty-six years old when he delivered his 1773 statics memoir at the Academy. Except for the short notes he had read to the *Société royale des sciences* in Montpellier in 1757, it was the first scientific or technical memoir he had presented publicly.

Of course, as a cadet at Mézières he had produced a number of student papers. If one can judge by the comments of the school's commander, Brigadier Chastillon, those Coulomb wrote were mediocre.[3] If, as Coulomb states below, he considered the work required of an engineer often boring and monotonous, it is not surprising that he was no star pupil in the drafting of these school exercises. Often they were merely fragmented exercises, such as "design a walkway" or "plan a cistern", which, though quite appropriate for an engineering curriculum, may have seemed uninspiring to the young student. After his graduation, routine work continued for Coulomb. In his first duty at Brest he was kept busy with minor mapping tasks along the coast of Brittany.

It was during the strenuous eight years in Martinique, from 1764 to 1772, that he found the opportunity for his first creative work. Few men posted to such arduous locations could do more than live from day to day and try to obtain a release from colonial duty. Not much came out of the work of the score of engineers who filled the positions at Martinique, Guadeloupe, and Santa Lucia in the 1760s. All had to fight malaria and avoid sunstroke. Many died and those who remained were overworked until replacements could be sent from France.[4] It was during this difficult period that Coulomb formed his plan of attack against mental stagnation. He later wrote, "A young studious subject who graduates from the School [of engineering] has no other choice in order to bear up under the boredom and monotony of his occupation than to devote himself to some branch of science or literature absolutely foreign to his work."[5]

In the mid-eighteenth century, civil engineering as practiced in France among the *Corps royal du génie* and the *Corps des ponts*

[b] Hereafter, this memoir will be referred to as Coulomb's 1773 statics memoir.

et chaussées had advanced beyond that practiced in the rest of Europe. Vauban's tables of retaining-wall dimensions and his fortification designs had circulated among the *génie* for sixty years. Complete engineering manuals like Bélidor's *La science des ingénieurs*[6] were in common use. Empirical as these treatises were, bridges stood, and sometimes walls successfully repulsed cannon shot. Engineering had so far done with little interaction from science.

Coulomb's work in Martinique went beyond the requirements of the task. For all its use in everyday practice, he was not satisfied with the existing engineering literature. He wrote in his 1773 statics memoir, "This Memoir, composed several years ago, was meant at first only for my own use, in the different tasks for which I am responsible in my occupation."[7]

Until this time there were two types of mechanical investigators. On the one hand, there was the worker in *physique expérimentale*, best exemplified by Musschenbroek (and described by Pierre Brunet).[8] On the other hand, there was the geometer, like Euler, who worked in applied mechanics only as it could serve to show the comprehensive power of analysis. I do not mean to slight either the experimentalist and empiricist or the pure analyst. However, one of the broader theses of this book is that the great development of the fields of "empirical" physics in the late eighteenth century came not only from improved and sophisticated experimental techniques and the wide use of mathematical analysis but from a fusion of these methods of investigation as seen in the work of a man like Coulomb.

Experimentation had to be focused and brought to bear on real problems. The experimenter had to go out of his *cabinet de physique* if necessary to obtain a meaningful and general solution. This feeling was to grow among the new type of engineer-physicist until by the end of the century Coulomb, Lazare Carnot, Prony, and Bossut, for example, had all called for the rewriting of Bélidor's standard engineering works.[9] Not only had experiment to be related to the physics at hand; mathematical analysis had to be used as a tool for development of physics. The theological reason-for-being of rational analysis, as expounded by Euler and others, was not to call the tune for the new physics. Physics would not be regarded as a tennis game at which analysts could test their skill.

After pronouncing the Euler works "the most beautiful and ample body of analytical science that the human mind ever produced,"[10]

Bossut said of the same works as applied to physics, "they can be considered only as geometrical truths of great intrinsic value, but not adapted to guide the practitioner to a knowledge of the actual and physical."[11] It was a fusion of these two types of investigation, the physical and the rational, that Coulomb proposed. This was not a simple process of superposition. It was not merely a mathematization of *physique expérimentale*, for experiment itself acquires new definitions and is performed differently and for different reasons. The mathematics must give real solutions relevant to physics and not metaphysics, and the experiment must be pertinent.

The 1773 Statics Memoir

As in all of his memoirs, Coulomb here gave a lucid introduction outlining the various points that he would consider. He said in part: "This Memoir is designed to determine, as much as a combination of mathematics and physics[c] can permit, the influence of friction and of cohesion in a few problems in statics."[12]

Friction and cohesion had to be considered because of the role they play in real physical interactions. As long as physics was reflected in the ideal world of analysis or in the traditional tables of empirical engineering, friction and cohesion could either be thought away or else lumped into an observed result. These properties of material interaction, however, troubled the eighteenth-century investigator. From either end of the spectrum—traditional empiricism or pure analysis—attempts to grapple with materials in their interactions were unsuccessful if there were no search for a theory or if the theory were an oversimplified attempt to reflect the harmonies of nature.

In his statics memoir Coulomb was doing two things: first, introducing the use of variational calculus[d] in engineering theory; second, bringing the major civil engineering problems to consider the complexities of nature. Coulomb's statics problems might seem disconnected, but they were at the heart of eighteenth-century engineering. If one examines Bélidor's classic *La science des ingénieurs*,[13] or Amédée Frézier's *Traité de stéréotomie*,[14] one finds the main engineering topics to be the strength of masonry materials,

---

[c] Coulomb's phrase was "*mélange du calcul et de la physique*."

[d] I make no claim whatsoever as to the originality of Coulomb's *mathematical* technique. Taken by itself the maximum-minumum solution here is rather elementary.

the design of retaining walls, and the design of arches. These are precisely the problems that Coulomb attacked in his 1773 statics memoir.

At the beginning of the body of the essay,[15] Coulomb introduced three propositions of mechanics. Briefly, they are as follows:

> PROPOSITION I. Let the plane figure *abcde*[e] (see Fig. III.1)[16] resting on the plane *AB* be acted upon by any planar forces whatsoever. In equilibrium, the resultant of these forces will be perpendicular to line *AB* and will fall between the base points *a* and *e*.

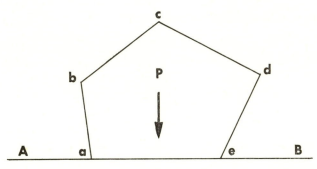

FIG. III.1. Coulomb's figure illustrating three basic propositions of mechanics

> PROPOSITION II. If all of these forces are resolved parallel and perpendicular to *AB*, the sum of forces parallel to *AB* will be equal to zero and the sum of forces perpendicular to *AB* will equal the weight of the plane section, *P*.
>
> PROPOSITION III. If one includes the reaction force to *P*, the sums of the forces resolved along *any* two perpendicular directions will be equal to zero.

These three propositions were important to Coulomb, and he recalled them constantly in the succeeding sections of the memoir. They are not original, but it is unusual to see them specifically relied on in engineering literature at this period. They indicate that Coulomb sought general solutions based on fundamental principles of static mechanics. Once he had established these propositions he proceeded into the memoir. The calculus served as a device for

---

e To facilitate reference to Coulomb's memoirs, his original notation is employed throughout whenever possible.

describing and solving the engineering problems that Coulomb treated. The content of the problems themselves, however, fell into two categories: elasticity and the strength of materials, and structural mechanics. The consideration of friction and cohesion was central to this investigation, and it involved him in giving virtually a theory of the flexure of beams and rupture and shear of brittle materials. The second half of the memoir was then devoted to structural mechanics problems of earth pressure in retaining walls and the stability of arches.

Coulomb's method was the same for all of the problems he studied. Complex statical phenomena in physical problems could give the physicist only an approximate idea of their effect. The individual physical factors like shear, arch friction, or the shape of the wedge of earth pressure could not be calculated accurately.[17] Coulomb sought to determine the *limits* of their action. Throughout the memoir he let the unknown factors vary and solved for the limit value of the pressure at the point between equilibrium and rupture. He dealt similarly with earth pressure, compressive rupture in columns, and the stability of arches. It is rather incidentally that he treated the flexure of beams, but all of these solutions required values for the physical effects: friction and cohesion.

Friction and Cohesion

For the applied mechanician, friction and cohesion are the links between geometry and physical reality. In the next chapter we will see that Coulomb obtained a successful theory of friction, successful at least in that it seemed to account for the phenomena and in that it established itself as the classic theory. He continued to study friction throughout his career. Cohesion, on the other hand, was seen as quite different. In the 1773 statics memoir, in the 1781 essay on friction in simple machines, and in other memoirs, the role of cohesion was studied, though its effects in friction phenomena were very difficult to measure.

Coulomb often associated friction with the mechanism of shear, though he never explicitly defined it thus, nor used the term. When one body was moved over the surface of another, Coulomb imagined it either sheared off small irregularities or else it bent them. Cohesion he usually saw in terms of tensile or compressive strength or of shear. The terms *cohérence, adhérence,* and *cohésion* were used by Coulomb and most eighteenth-century writers to describe the same general phenomena. A beam, for example, loaded under tension would resist rupture until a certain limit at which the cohesive forces holding the molecules together would be exceeded and the beam would rupture. When Coulomb dealt with compressive rupture of columns or tensile rupture of stone, described below, he used the term *cohésion* in this sense. When he discussed torsional shear on a molecular level in metals, cohesion also was seen as the force holding molecules together until rupture due to shear. In both cases—friction and cohesion—whatever Coulomb may have inferred from his experiments, he got results that were quantitative on a *macroscopic* scale. That is, he obtained quantitative coefficients and laws for friction which hold for macroscopic situations. Though he may have speculated about molecular structure, he got no quantitative results applicable on the level of individual molecular interaction.

For some eighteenth-century figures, friction and cohesion were seen as opposed concepts. (See Fig. III.2.) Friction could be imag-

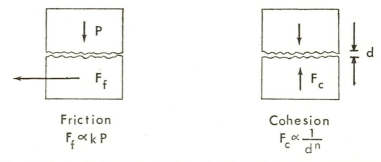

Friction
$$F_f \propto k P$$

Cohesion
$$F_c \propto \frac{1}{d^n}$$

FIG. III.2. Author's representation of eighteenth-century conceptions of mechanisms of friction and cohesion, where friction force F_f is proportional to normal force P; and cohesion force F_c is inversely proportional to some function of the distance of separation, d, for d very small and with the exponent n being greater than 2

ined as contact action wherein one body collided on a molecular level in some way with another even though the interaction appeared tangential on the large scale. Cohesion, however, did not necessarily imply contact action but only the close approach of one body to another. Spurred on by their interpretation of Query XXXI of Newton's *Opticks*,[18] Desaguliers, especially, and others would attempt to see in nature proofs of cohesive forces of attraction acting over very small distances and possibly following a law of attraction other than the inverse square law of gravitation with regard to the distance of separation of the bodies.[f] In other words, there might be some close-acting force law varying as the inverse cube or some other power of the distance. Never does Coulomb propose to identify any such law. To the extent friction depended upon the normal force acting between two bodies rather than upon their common surface area of interaction, it implied the surface roughness theory. To the extent friction depended upon the surface area in contact it could imply cohesive forces as Desaguliers thought, or the surface film effects which Coulomb supposed as an alternative.

In any case, Coulomb's experiments in friction showed that the surface area effect was always less than a few percent of the total friction for any situation where the normal forces amounted to several pounds or more.

In Articles IV and V of the 1773 statics memoir Coulomb noted that friction and cohesion are measured by the *limits* of their resistance. That is, they are never active forces like gravity but rather "coercive" forces. Here, he accepted Amontons' theory of friction,[19] that between bodies it is mainly proportional to the force acting normal to the surface of contact of the bodies and not to their surface areas. He noted, however, that this law of friction is not strictly observed and that with nonfibrous materials, such as stone, it is necessary to test the friction coefficient of each type of stone that one would use because "tests made for one quarry can never serve for another."[20] For the sample of stone he tested, Coulomb found the coefficient of friction to be equal to ¾.

Cohesion, according to Coulomb, is measured by the resistance that solid bodies oppose to direct "disunion" of their parts. In a homogeneous body each part resists rupture with the same degree of resistance. Therefore, total cohesion is proportional to the number of parts to be separated and thus to the surface area of rupture.

To determine the amount of cohesion in brittle material, Coulomb employed a block of white Bordeaux stone cut and suspended as shown in Fig. III.3,[21] so that the area to be ruptured was equal to two square inches. He loaded this stone until rupture occurred, at a value of 430 pounds. Next he fixed a stone slab of similar cross section and subjected it to a purely shear force which resulted

[f] See Chapter IV.

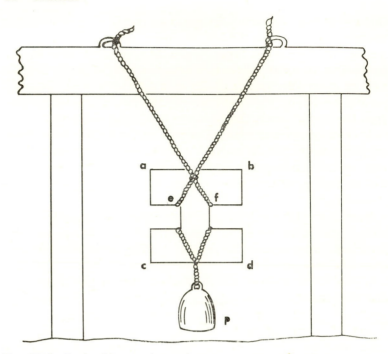

Fig. III.3. Coulomb's experimental apparatus for tests of tensile rupture in stone

in rupture at 440 pounds. After several trials he concluded that the force necessary to produce shear rupture was always a very small amount greater than that which produced tensile rupture. On the basis of these experimental results, he assumed that cohesion for brittle materials was about the same following any plane of rupture. Recalling his experiments in Martinique, he cautioned that climatic conditions greatly affected the rupture strengths of mortar and that as with friction, one must test a sample of each type of building stone before beginning design calculations. Thus having obtained coefficients for friction and "cohesion" in stone, he proceeded to an investigation of the flexure of beams.

Flexure of Beams

In this work Coulomb solved an outstanding problem in mechanics. The problem began with Galileo, and various facets of it became of central concern in the history of mechanics. The "first" science that Galileo founded in his *Two New Sciences*[22] in 1638 was that of the strength of materials. In the second dialogue of this work, Galileo gave 17 propositions regarding fracture of rods, beams, and hollow cylinders. He described the parabolic shape of the solid of equal resistance—that beam shape that is the minimum thickness for a given length. He then stated that the beam resistance is proportional to the second power of its vertical dimension.

Galileo's great work was the impulse for all future work on the rupture and strength of beams. As with all theories, uncritical acceptance can lead to continued error. This occurred with regard to Galileo's ideas of flexure and rupture in beams.

Galileo had no concept of elasticity. His beams suffered neither extensive nor compressive strain; they just ruptured. Given a cantilever beam set in a wall (see a representation of Galileo's famous sketch in Fig. III.4),[23] he assumed the tensile stresses in the beam to be uniformly spread over the cross section. He then equilibrated this resultant with the statical moments of the external load. From this he obtained the correct solution: in a beam of rectangular cross section the bending strength is proportional to the width and the square of the height. Galileo did not obtain a correct solution for the ratio of the bending strength to the tensile strength because of his ignorance of elastic conditions.

Robert Hooke would provide the next clue to the solution of the problem of the flexed beam. His cryptic phrase *Ut tensio, sic vis* (published in 1678),[24] provided the principle of proportionality of stretching force to change of length that was to be a basis for the future development of theories of elasticity. Searching for the proper dimensions for water pipes, Edme Mariotte conducted some flexure experiments and presented what was, in effect, Hooke's Law in his *Traité du mouvement des eaux* (1686).[25]

At first Mariotte, as Galileo, assumed that the bending moments are taken about a point on the lower edge of the beam. He later assumed that in a bent beam, the upper half of the beam fibers would be extended and the lower half compressed. In this work, Mariotte became the first to speak of the *neutral line*—the curve in the beam where the fibers are neither extended nor compressed.

Leibniz commented on this in a short note in *Acta Eruditorum* (1695).[26] Those who were to study elasticity in the eighteenth century took the Mariotte-Leibniz hypothesis on proportionality of stress and strain and ignored the original work of Hooke. Except for an almost unknown reference to Hooke in a mediocre

FIG. III.4. Galileo's famous sketch to illustrate rupture in beams

paper by James Jurin in 1744,[27] Hooke's work in elasticity was completely forgotten until Thomas Young mentioned "Hooke's Law" in 1807.[28]

From the time of the explosion of work in the founding of the calculus, through most of the eighteenth century, physics was the maidservant to the development of the calculus. The brilliant figures in the history of rational mechanics turned to structural problems to illustrate the power of analysis. One of the favorite problems was that of the elastic curve. This was beautifully investigated by Leonhard Euler in his *De curvis elasticis* (1744).[29] In developing the elastic curve theory, mathematicians assumed the curvature to be proportional to the bending moment. There was little attempt to study how the stress is distributed in the beam. Two men, Parent and Coulomb, diverged from this approach.

In a memoir published in 1713,[30] Antoine Parent showed that a single point could not support bending forces in a beam and that therefore a sizable portion of the beam cross section must act in support of compression. As Coulomb was later to do, Parent then showed that the sum of the resistance of the compressed fibers equals the sum of the resistance of the extended fibers.[31] Most probably Coulomb was unaware of this portion of the other man's work. Parent had an unhappy career in the French Academy and never advanced beyond the rank of adjunct member. Many of his memoirs were little known even in his own day.

Coulomb began his study of flexure in beams[32] by employing a rectangular cantilever beam (see Fig. III.5).[33] He imagined it cut

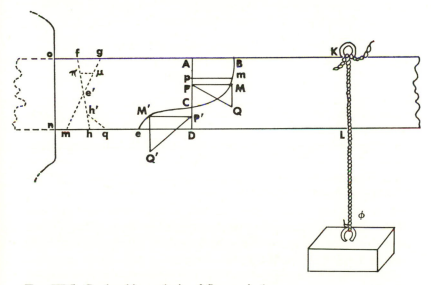

Fig. III.5. Coulomb's analysis of flexure in beams

by a vertical plane *AD*. He stated that there must be some upper portion of the beam that resists extension and another, lower portion that resists compression. His first move was to resolve all forces into horizontal (F_h) and vertical (F_v) components. The end of the beam (*ADLK*) must then be acted upon by horizontal as well as vertical forces, including the weight ϕ hanging at the end.

Under equilibrium conditions and following his preliminary Proposition III, the following condition must hold:

$$\Sigma F_h = 0.$$

From this he drew the fundamental conclusion that the area under compression (*Ced*) must equal the area under tension (*ABC*). Further, by the same proposition, the sum of the vertical forces (*QM*) must equal the weight (ϕ): $\Sigma F_v = \phi$. He next observed that the moment of this load (ϕ) about point *C* must equal the sum of the internal moments of the beam.[g] This gave him the equation[h] (see Fig. III.5).

$$\int [Pp] \, [MP] \, [CP] = \phi[LD]$$

Coulomb noted that this equation is independent of any relations between the cohesion and the elongation of the fibers of the beam.

Using these three formulated statements:

(1) $\Sigma F_h = 0$; therefore, Δ compression $= \Delta$ tension;

(2) $\Sigma F_v = \phi$;

(3) $\int [Pp] \, [MP] \, [CP] = \phi[LD]$.

Coulomb presented the first correct analysis of the equilibrium state of a beam. Equation (1) shows that the tensile forces in a beam must equal the compressive forces. Equation (2) is the first recognition of the significance of shearing force in a beam, and (3) shows that the moment of resistance of the beam must equal the bending moment of the load.[34]

Coulomb next took a small element (*ofnh*) near the fixed end of the beam and examined this under bending forces. Under such conditions the plane section represented by *fh* will orient itself around a point *e′* to take some position *gm*. Coulomb assumed the resulting small triangles *fge′* and *e′mh* to represent the compressive and extensive forces. Designating δ (represented by the vector *fg*)

---

[g] Notice that although Coulomb took a perfectly elastic beam as an example in calculations, he realized the line *BMCe* could be *any* sort of curve, and he actually drew it as some sort of curve in Figure III.5. He will make similar observations in the articles concerned with earth-pressure theory.

[h] Coulomb uses *Pp* as the derivative of *CP* (*i.e.*, $Pp = d \, [CP]$). The integral is therefore along the vertical from *D* to *A*, or of the form:

$$\int_D^A [MP] \, [CP] \, d[CP] = \phi \, [LD]$$

to equal the tensile forces at point f, fe' equals $\frac{fh^1}{2}$. Since these are isosceles triangles, Coulomb found that the moments of the small triangles fge' and $qe'm$ equaled $\frac{\delta[e'f]^2}{3}$ and $\frac{\delta[e'h]^2}{3}$. Then the sum of these momenta $(\frac{\delta[fh]^2}{6})$, is equal to the momentum of the load $(\phi[nL])$; or

$$\frac{\delta[fh]^2}{6} = \phi[nL].$$

Coulomb considered a *long* rectangular beam here; therefore he made the important statement that the "thrusts such as at $[MQ]$ have only very little effect on the resistance of bodies."[35] In other words it is reasonable to neglect shearing forces here.

The above case was for the bending of an elastic beam. Coulomb next considered the perfectly inelastic case, where the fibers are "rigid, or are not susceptible either to compression or to extension."[36] In this supposedly inelastic situation he placed the neutral line at the bottom edge (h) of the beam. Here, uniform stress would exist in each element along fh and the equation for ultimate load would be equal to

$$\frac{\delta[fh]^2}{2} = \delta[nL].$$

Coulomb recalled Bossut's memoir on construction of dikes,[37] where it was stated that one should treat wood as elastic and stone as inelastic. Coulomb did not take this as fact but *tested* this hypothesis by examining his work on the rupture of stone. In these experiments[38] he had obtained a tensile breaking strength for stone of 215 pounds per inch². If stone were perfectly inelastic his experiment in Article v, performed with a lever arm of 9 inches, would give a quotient of 215/9 pounds per inch³ or almost 24 pounds per inch³ for equivalent shear. His experiments in Article v, however, gave this quotient as 20 pounds per inch³. This discrepancy led Coulomb to conclude that stone must *not* be perfectly inelastic.[j] As he observed, for this to have been so, point h would

[i] This is for the case of a perfectly elastic beam where triangle fge' would equal triangle $qe'm$ (that is, tensile stresses equal compressive stresses).

[j] There are two factors not considered by Coulomb that would have further increased the discrepancy between his experimental results and the

have to support all the pressures. Since the "cohesion" at point h is not infinite the neutral line must be placed higher in the beam.[k] He then solved for the probable neutral line (through point h' in Fig. III.5).

Rupture of Masonry Piers

Before passing to the parts of Coulomb's memoir concerned with structural design in retaining walls and arches, his theory of the rupture of masonry piers (short massive columns) will be presented.[41] This section serves to join the first and second halves of the memoir. It deals with the rupture strength of masonry, but it uses the same mathematical method and the same theory of matter as in the work of the later articles. This is an interesting section because Coulomb contested earlier theory concerning compressive rupture of columns and because his own theory, while ingenious, is not strictly true. Coulomb's physical conceptions here would appear again in his work on torsion. Right or wrong, Coulomb's theory of pier failure was employed by some engineers until the middle of the nineteenth century.[42]

In his investigation of masonry rupture Coulomb supposed a homogeneous pier $ABMD$ loaded with a weight P (see Fig. III.6).[43] He proposed to find the limiting load and the angle at which the pier would rupture along any given plane CM perpendicular to a side of the block. From the results of his experiments on shear and tensile strength in stone he assumed the ultimate shear strength equal to ultimate strength in tension.

In order to limit his solution to one rupture plane he assumed that the adherence of the block is infinite everywhere except along the unknown rupture plane. Thus, in effect, he was looking at a series of two blocks: the upper block ($ABMC$ in Fig. III.6) and the lower block (CMD). He then sought the plane angle x (angle $r\phi q$ in Fig. III.6) which would be a minimum for the component of the load (P) to become larger than the cohesion (shear resist-

---

assumption of perfect inelasticity in a beam. Both nonlinearity of extension and also inequality of fiber resistance to extension and compression make the rupture resistance of beams to bending higher than accounted for in Coulomb's theory.[39]

[k] This is the same argument used by Parent and Bulfinger[40] although Coulomb may have been ignorant of Parent's work and most probably was ignorant of Bulfinger's work.

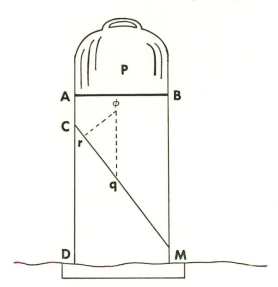

Fɪɢ. III.6.
Coulomb's figure for
analysis of rupture in
masonry piers

ance) along the plane of rupture (*CM*). Summing up the forces,
he obtained (see Fig. ɪɪɪ.6):

(1) $$P \sin x = rq$$

(2) $$\delta\, CM = \frac{\delta\, a}{\cos x}$$

where $P \sin x$ = force component along the rupture plane.

   $x = \angle\, r\phi q = \angle\, CMD$, the angle between the rupture
   plane and the horizontal.

   δ = "cohesion" (that is, the shear resistance which he
   took here as equal to the resistance to tension).

   CM = side of rupture plane.

   a = side of base.

Therefore, for equilibrium, $P \sin x = \dfrac{\delta\, a^2}{\cos x}$

or

(3) $$P = \frac{\delta\, a^2}{\sin x \cos x}\,.$$

Now $\sin x \cos x$ must be a maximum in order to find the minimum
load (*P*), needed for rupture. Thus, differentiating *P* with respect
to *x* :

$$(4) \qquad dP = \frac{\delta\, a^2\, [-\, dx(\cos x)^2 + dx(\sin x)^2]}{(\sin x \cos x)^2} = 0,$$

and $\therefore$ $\sin x = \cos x = 45°$.

Substituting $x = 45°$ into Equation (3) gives

$$(5) \qquad P = \frac{\delta\, a^2}{\sin x \cos x} = \frac{\delta\, a^2}{0.5} = 2\,\delta\, a^2.$$

Therefore, by statical means Coulomb has shown that the homogeneous masonry pier would tend to rupture at an angle of 45° under a compressive force twice that of the ultimate tensile strength. Using projective geometry, he then sought to generalize this result by letting plane CM be situated at any angle to the base.

In Article IX,[44] he added the retarding force $\dfrac{P \cos x}{n}$, which is due to friction. Thus,

$$(6) \qquad P \sin x = \frac{\delta\, a^2}{\cos x} + \frac{P \cos x}{n},$$

where $1/n$ = coefficient of friction, or,

$$(7) \qquad P = \frac{\delta\, a^2}{\cos x\, (\sin x - \dfrac{\cos x}{n})}.$$

To make P a minimum for the case with friction he again differentiated with respect to x and set the result equal to zero:

$$(8)\quad dP = dx\, [\sin x\, (\sin x - \frac{\cos x}{n})] - dx \cos x\, (\cos x + \frac{\sin x}{n}) = 0,$$

$$(9) \qquad \sin^2 x = \cos^2 x + \frac{2 \sin x \cos x}{n},$$

and

$$\tan x = \frac{1}{\sqrt{1 + \dfrac{1}{n^2} - \dfrac{1}{n}}}.$$

In order to define x in numbers he must have a value for the coefficient of friction. In the first part of the memoir he stated that this coefficient is about ¾ in the case of brick. Since he was going to compare this value with Musschenbroek's experiment with a brick column, he let $\dfrac{1}{u}$ equal ¾ here; therefore:

$$\tan x = \frac{1}{\sqrt{\frac{25}{16} - \frac{3}{4}}} = 2; \quad \cos x = \sqrt{\frac{1}{5}}; \quad \sin x = 2 \cos x; \text{ and}$$

(10) $$P = \frac{\delta \, a^2}{\cos x \, (\sin x - \frac{\cos x}{n})}$$

or

(11) $$P = \frac{\delta \, a^2}{\sqrt{\frac{1}{5}} \left(2\sqrt{\frac{1}{5}} - \frac{3}{4}\sqrt{\frac{1}{5}} \right)} = 4 \, \delta \, a^2.$$

The angle for the rupture plane is then $x = 63° \, 26'$ and the compressive rupture limit is four times that of the limit for tension.

Coulomb assumed a rectangular masonry pier and asked what load would break the pier and under what angle the plane of rupture would occur. Others had considered problems similar to this. Specifically, Musschenbroek[45] (experimentally) and Euler[46] (analytically) obtained formulas for the rupture of columns. They did so under the assumption that the column would first *bend* and then rupture under the resultant transverse stresses. It is clear that this method of envisaging column failure employs elastic considerations, however implicitly. Coulomb never saw the problem in this light. For him it was simply a case of compressive rupture due to sliding along a plane surface. We shall see that in his work on torsion, this same assumption led him to the brilliant, and correct, guess that molecular failure occurs by slipping along the crystal plane after forces have produced preliminary distortional strain. This will be the base of Coulomb's physical theory of torsion. The (Hooke) law of the proportionality of stress and strain will be explained as linear distortion set up between the molecules in a body. Nonlinearity and extension beyond the linear (Hooke) limit will be seen as due to actual slippage of the materials along molecular planes so that the material does not return to its original state.

Coulomb's fixation upon rupture due to sliding along a plane becomes understandable when one considers both the problems he observed as an engineer and the eighteenth-century classification of materials as fibrous and nonfibrous.

In engineering practice fibers were seen to play a role in elastic bending and rupture of *wooden* beams and columns. Other materials used in construction (stone or masonry and earth), were observed to fail due to rupture and slip. Coulomb considered here the failure of what we would call a masonry pier, that is, of a structure whose length and width are sufficiently comparable to its height so as to preclude observations of flexure. The similarity between failure in masonry piers and failure in retaining walls will be evident if one examines Fig. III.7A and B.[47] The former is Coulomb's figure for earth-pressure failure in retaining walls. The latter is his diagram for analysis of compressive rupture in masonry piers; the diagram is simply rotated through 90° so that it is presented, so to speak, on its side.

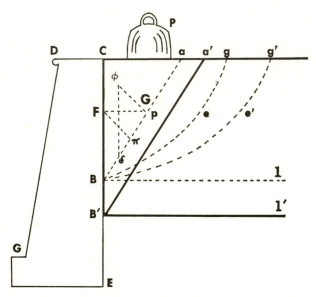

FIG. III.7 A. Coulomb's figure illustrating his earth pressure theory

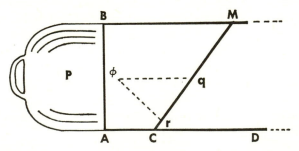

FIG. III.7 B. Coulomb's figure for rupture of masonry piers, rotated through 90°

In comparing these figures, note the conceptual similarity. In this view it is clear why Coulomb said the problems were of the same genre and were to be treated by the same mathematical method. In both cases it is a wedge of material that is sliding along a planar, or near-planar, section. The problem is reduced to finding that angle which will produce a maximum or minimum of pressure.

Coulomb realized that stone is not perfectly inelastic. Indeed, in this same memoir he showed that in rupture of stone blocks the rigidity cannot be perfect. In Article VII, however, he noted that the beam there under analysis was much longer than its cross section (9:1). In the masonry pier examined here the ratio of height to side is only about 4:3, so he assumed the stone to act as if almost rigid. He took issue with Musschenbroek over the case of a rectangular brick column 5/12 of an inch on a side and 11 inches high.[1] Musschenbroek found this column to rupture under a load of 195 pounds. Based on calculations from his own theory Coulomb predicted rupture of Musschenbroek's column at a load of 208 pounds, a quantity "differing little," he said, from Musschenbroek's experimental results.

Musschenbroek stated that columns would bear loads in inverse square ratio to their lengths and directly as the cube of their sides:[48]

$$P = \frac{k\, a^3}{l^2}.$$

According to Coulomb's theory, "the [bearing] forces in homogeneous columns are proportional to their horizontal sections."[49] There is a direct disagreement between Coulomb and Musschenbroek. Further experiments with slender columns should have indicated the areas of disagreement, but Coulomb merely dismissed Musschenbroek offhand with the remark, "Moreover, I am obliged to note that the manner in which Mr. Musschenbroek determines the forces in a masonry column has no relation to the method that I have just employed."[m,50]

There are two difficulties here. First, neither man was speaking to the same problem. Musschenbroek considered rupture due to flexure in long columns. Coulomb examined compressive rupture in masonry piers. Second, not only is Coulomb's theory of rupture

[1] This was clearly only a scale-model experiment. It would be a rare case where brick columns of such dimensions were employed in practice!

[m] This is one of the very few times that Coulomb dismisses another man's work without completely testing the results himself.

oversimplified, but it is based on a meager set of experiments. He had, of course, seen dozens of ruptured piers in his career; the fault is that his observations were probably limited to piers of the same materials and ratios of length to cross section. The ratio of shear to tensile strength in stone is closer to 0.8 than Coulomb's value of 1.0,[n] which would give him a value of 1.6 instead of 2.0 for the ratio of compressive to tensile rupture in the masonry pier described in Article VIII of his memoir.

Coulomb had excessive confidence in his theory that the ability of columns to bear weight is in direct proportion to the square of their sides. He went on to say that a column could be raised to 600 or even 1,200 feet without encountering rupture. He seemed to forget his sense of engineering reality and held steadfast to his theory. His statements here resemble the fantasy of Archimedes' and Stevin's "infinitely" powerful winches. In spite of this exaggeration, Coulomb's theory gave reasonable results for massive piers, and numerous nineteenth-century engineers employed his theory in this type of design.

Earth-Pressure Theory

Study of the problem of pressure against retaining walls, like the problem of friction in machines (discussed in the next chapter), began at about the turn of the eighteenth century. That is, attempts to solve this problem using the principles of mechanics and some theory of material interaction started around 1700; of course, empirical solutions to most civil engineering problems have existed for centuries. It was the eighteenth-century French engineer who first attempted general solutions for these types of engineering problems.[o,52]

Most physicists and historians of science will be acquainted somewhat with researches in elasticity, structures, and so forth, as they pertain to rational mechanics. The science of *soil mechanics*, however, may be sufficiently unfamiliar to some that a clarification of the limits of this discipline be briefly given here. Karl Terzaghi's

[n] He found it to be 0.977, precisely. Later experiments on cast iron have given figures for this compressive/tensile ratio as high as 4:1 to 9:1.[51]

[o] A large bibliography exists for eighteenth-century earth-pressure treatises. This essay will discuss only those investigators who affected the *theory* of earth pressure. For information on the many works extant see the bibliography listed under Reference 52.

definition of soil mechanics is "the application of the laws of mechanics and hydraulics to engineering problems dealing with sediments and other unconsolidated accumulations of solid particles."[53]

The classical problem in the field of soil mechanics is the earth-pressure problem. The most important work on this was given in Coulomb's statics memoir of 1773. Most theories pertaining to soils were developed by 1900, but the knowledge of the real, physical properties of soil has come about only in recent decades. The necessity of a simple, general solution to these problems should be emphasized even today. To quote Terzaghi again, "In many advanced papers on soil mechanics the mathematical refinement is out of proportion to the importance of the errors due to simplifying assumptions."[54] This is an important point to bear in mind when considering Coulomb's work. Often, the characteristics of particular soils cannot be determined by test borings. The applied mechanics employed then rests on the assumptions made concerning the soil. The history of this discipline has been that theories were established and overturned on the basis of insufficient knowledge of the physical interactions involved. At one time in the nineteenth century Coulomb's theory was rejected because it produced discrepancies in an area beyond that for which he intended it. Nevertheless, it remains today as the one most generally used in basic engineering practice, and "Coulomb's Equation" can be found on page one of modern texts on soil mechanics.

Its value rests in its generality. Coulomb assumed homogeneous soil; this is often still done today. In practical cases he supposed the soil bank to fail along a plane. In most situations, this treatment is still adequate.

Until the eighteenth century, earth-pressure problems were not particularly recognized as of major importance in engineering construction. Empirical rules-of-thumb must have existed; fort sites were usually chosen on rock or firm ground, and cannon balls often proved to be the test of the construction. During the eighteenth century the great increase in the construction of roads, and especially of canals, indicated the need for an earth-pressure theory. For the first time, cut banks and retaining walls figured largely in construction work. The problem then began to be treated in a more systematic fashion. The famous engineer Vauban compiled tables for the design of retaining walls from 6 to 80 feet in height. These tables were published by Bélidor[55] and were used extensively. They were employed as empirical data useful for the construction of walls. However, they hardly constituted a theory of earth pressure, since Vauban did not account for the properties of the soil.

Although a large part of the French engineering profession accorded Vauban's work the status of an engineering bible, some theoretical studies emerged as early as 1691. Before Coulomb there were three prominent contributions to the study of earth pressure—the studies of Bullet, Couplet, and Bélidor. These merit some discussion here.

Pierre Bullet[56] first attempted to construct a theory of earth pressure by assuming the soil to be composed of ideal spheres. In vertical cross section, he assumed these spheres would form an equilateral triangle[p] with a 60° angle of repose. Bullet then assumed the individual soil particles would tend to slide along the side of this triangle at an angle of 60° to the horizontal.

Bullet's theory was completely arbitrary. Quantitatively, it provided no support for future work. His conception of soil as tiny spheres was important, though, in setting the tone for much later work. Soil was conceived to be of this composition in many earth-pressure papers until as late as 1890.[57]

Pierre Couplet criticized Bullet's work in memoirs presented to the Paris Academy in the late 1720s.[58] Couplet noted that Bullet's theory was based on a false principle because Bullet assumed the wall to provide only a lateral thrust. For the theory to be correct therefore, the wall must provide also an upward thrust component in the direction of the inclined plane. Couplet stated that the ball of earth would not tend to slide along the 60° plane (*CB* in Fig. III.8),[59] but rather along the tangent line (*LK*). This would give an angle of repose of 30° with the center of the wall pressure placed at two-thirds the height of the wall. In this theory, Couplet continued to use Bullet's conception of soil as small frictionless spheres.

The first to consider actual soil properties was Bélidor,[60] who made the practical observation that soils rarely stood at slopes greater than 45°. He then assumed the angle of repose to be 45° and constructed an isosceles right triangle (see Fig. III.9).[61] He sought the horizontal force which would keep an earth ball (*M*, with weight *P*) in equilibrium on this plane, and he assumed friction to reduce the necessary wall thrust by one half. This, then,

---

[p] Note that this configuration would not represent maximum packing density for the case of spheres packed in three-dimensional space.

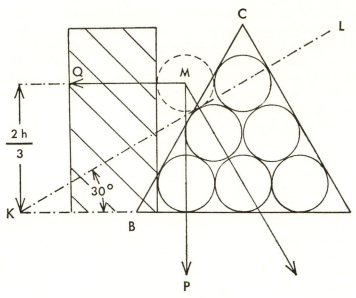

FIG. III.8. Couplet's theory of earth pressure

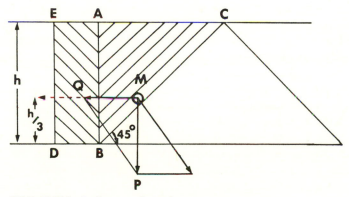

FIG. III.9. Bélidor's theory of earth pressure

gave the center of thrust of the wall (*ABDE*) at one-third of the wall height and the horizontal wall pressure equal to

$$Q = \frac{gh^2}{4}$$

where h = wall height, and
        g = earth density.

Bélidor's formulas became the accepted standard for most of the eighteenth century and gave results in satisfactory accord with contemporary practice, but in reality his theory was based mostly on purely geometric considerations. Small-scale experiments carried out by Gadroy, Papacini D'Antony, and Rondelet[62] were inconclusive enough as to offer no challenge to Bélidor's theory. Thus, until the late eighteenth century, earth-pressure problems were treated with an empirical approach based on idealized geometry. Except for Bélidor's observational assumption of a 45° angle of repose, there was little concern for the real properties of soil.

In studying the pressure of earth against vertical retaining walls, Coulomb sought to include another engineering problem within the limits of the variational calculus. Comparing earth pressure to the structural problems he said in the memoir, "the Method is absolutely the same."[63] As observed earlier, both the mathematical method and the physical conception were the same; Coulomb saw in both cases the sliding of an approximately triangular form along a rupture plane. All others, including Bélidor, had assumed the earth bank to rupture and slide along a plane on the angle of repose of the soil. Coulomb, however, noted that rupture occurs in *two* stages. The angle of repose of a free-standing bank of earth is not the same as the angle of formation of the rupture plane. Whatever the angle of repose after the wall collapses or separates from the bank, this angle can obtain only after the sliding wedge has moved the wall. Therefore, assumptions of 45° or 60° for the rupture plane were completely arbitrary. Supposing homogeneous earth and retarding forces due to cohesion and friction, Coulomb sought the angle (*CBa* in Fig. III.10)[64] under which the soil would crack. Since the system is investigated in an equilibrium state, Coulomb's force diagram is closed. It consists of the three forces: *A*, the horizontal reaction of the wall (applied at *F* in Fig. III.10); ϕ, the weight of the sliding wedge of earth; and *R*, the reaction due to friction and cohesion. Now, if this were the hydrostatic case where friction and cohesion are assumed zero, then there could be only one equilibrium value for the force *A*. That is, if the force were increased, the level of the ideal fluid would rise; if decreased, it would fall. For the case of solids or semisolids the existence of friction and cohesive forces widens the curve *Ba* (see Fig. III.10) into a family of curves lying between the limits *Ba* and *Bg'*. Coulomb observed that in this real case one can apply a variety of forces between the limits *A* and *A'* without causing the wedge of

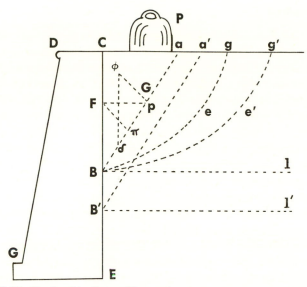

FIG. III.10. Coulomb's figure illustrating his earth-pressure theory

earth to move. The frictional forces must be overcome for both upward and downward movement. To solve for these limits Coulomb
equated the forces and found the limit conditions where A is a
minimum and A' a maximum.

He was only concerned here with the minimum force necessary
to keep the wedge from sliding downward, thus he solved only for
the force A.[q] He observed that the rupture curve need not be a

[q] Let $CB = a$, $Ca = x$, δ = cohesion, $1/n$ = friction coefficient,
$\delta(a^2 + x^2)^{1/2}$ = "adherence" of line Ba, ϕ = weight of $\triangle\ CBa = \dfrac{gax}{2}$,
where g = density of soil triangle.

For equilibrium

$$A = \frac{\phi(a - x/n) - \delta(a^2 + x^2)}{x + a/n}$$

and

$$A = \frac{(gax/2)\ (a - x/n) - \delta(a^2 + x^2)}{x + a/n}$$

$$\frac{dA}{dX} = \frac{(g\ a/2n + \delta)\ (a^2 - 2ax/n - x^2)}{(x + a/n)^2} = 0$$

from this, $x = -a/n + a\ \sqrt{1 + 1/n^2}$; this value for x is then substituted
in the expression for A above.

Note that Coulomb used the coefficient of friction $(1/n)$ as equal to the
tangent of what is today called the angle of internal friction. Thus, in the
modern form of "Coulomb's Equation" concerning shear resistance, $\tan \psi$
is substituted for $1/n$.[65] The modern "Coulomb's Equation" is

straight line but could be any curve whatsoever, but as with the case for rupture of masonry piers, he cited experience to show that rupture always occurs in a curve closely approximating a straight line. He found that cohesion had little effect on the curve of rupture compared to the effect of friction. In soil with little friction (such as dry sand), the curve of rupture will assume an angle of 45°.

To determine the actual dimensions of the retaining wall, it is necessary to find the momentum of force A (applied at F in Fig. III.10) around point E, the base of the wall. Integrating, Coulomb found the momentum around point E^r must equal or surpass the momentum of force A for equilibrium to exist. Coulomb then proceeded to calculate some examples of his method. He obtained a ratio of wall height to base of $7:1$. He noted that Vauban recommended a ratio of $5:1$ for nearly all the forts that he constructed and that he added buttresses to the walls for additional strength. Coulomb courteously defended Vauban's conservative designs with the statement, "This increase in strength must not be regarded as superfluous in fortification works, where the exterior walls must never be overturned by the first cannon shot."[66]

As with the other subjects in his statics memoir, Coulomb's work in soil mechanics remained virtually unknown until it was used by Prony. Prony wrote not only for the engineering profession[67] but also specifically for the students at the *Ecole polytechnique*[68] and the *Ecole des ponts et chaussées*.[69] It was in this form that most of Coulomb's mechanics memoirs entered the curricula of engineering studies in France. In two papers[70] published for these engineering schools, Prony simplified Coulomb's analysis of earth pressure. He noted that the plane of maximum earth pressure (*Ba* in Fig. III.10) actually bisects the angle between the back of the wall and the line of natural slope of the soil. He then presented

---

$$S = C + \sigma \tan \psi$$

where S = Shearing resistance
C = Cohesion
σ = Effective normal stress of the surface of sliding
ψ = Angle of internal friction.

[r] A [FE] $= \dfrac{m - b^3}{3} - \dfrac{\delta l \, b^2}{2}$, where b = total height of wall CE,

δ = cohesion; l, m = constant coefficients of friction.

a simple graphical method of designing retaining walls. He noted, however, that he was employing Coulomb's theory in this work.[8]

Graphical methods of solution for the problem of earth pressure were later developed by Poncelet[73] and others.[74] In 1857 Rankine[75] published his conjugate stress theory of soil pressure. For a time this supplanted Coulomb's method, but modern authorities[76] agree that Coulomb's wedge theory not only is simpler than Rankine's, but also accounts more accurately for observed data.

Theory of Arch Stability

"Concerning the equilibrium of arches, before Coulomb one possessed only mathematical considerations or very imperfect empirical rules based on limited hypotheses, the majority lacking that character of precision and certainty which alone can recommend them to the confidence of enlightened engineers. . . ." Thus Poncelet introduced a report on arch design read to the French Academy in 1852.[77]

In the design of arches, Coulomb was the first to apply fully both mathematical and physical factors. The 1773 memoir on statics contains a wealth of ideas. It seems that every topic covered in this essay solves some outstanding engineering problem: flexure in beams, masonry rupture, earth-pressure theory, and the design of arches. None of these problems began with Coulomb. All had submitted to empirical solutions for centuries and all had begun to be treated theoretically during the period of the growth of modern engineering after the late seventeenth century.

It is not exaggeration to treat Coulomb's brilliant memoir as fundamental. It would be unhistorical, however, to discuss it without reference to previous work in the theory of arch design. The study of these problems will begin with a discussion of work presented about 1690.[t] Historically, there were two avenues of ap-

---

[8] One source prior to Prony may have made use of Coulomb's work in earth-pressure theory—Reinhard Woltmann in 1794.[71] Woltmann never cited Coulomb, although he cited Bossut's earlier work on dikes (cited by Coulomb) and he employed Coulomb's nomenclature. Golder[72] speculated that Prussian-French politics in 1793 contributed to the omission of Coulomb's name. This would be difficult to prove, although this author has found that Woltmann cited French works published only before 1778.

[t] It is clear that a study of the formation of engineering in the period from Vauban and Bullet to Bélidor and Frézier could yield important results for the history of science.

proach to arch design. There was the inverted chain model suggested by Hooke and treated by numerous analysts.[78] There was also the rigid, static approach offered by the smooth voussoir theory of Philippe de La Hire. The latter was the one more developed in eighteenth-century engineering. Hooke's elastic approach was favored by mathematicians, but in either there was an unbridged gap between the recognition of the influence of flexure in arches and the possibility of treating this in design calculations.[79]

La Hire (1695)[80] was the first to investigate arch design as a problem of mathematical statics. It is probably due to the influence of his teacher, Desargues, that La Hire approached his mechanics geometrically.

La Hire solved the problem of the design of a circular arch using geometrical methods (see Fig. III.11).[81] He assumed the arch sec-

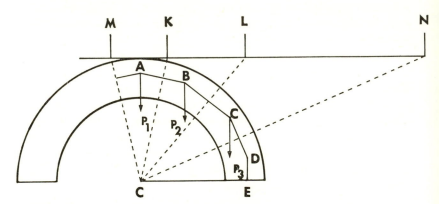

Fig. III.11. La Hire's theory of arch design

tions to be rigid and frictionless. Thus, pressure from one section to another could be transmitted only normal to the common arch surfaces. Each surface must therefore sustain its gravitational weight (P), plus the normal pressure of the arch sections above it. Upon the proposed arch (see Fig. III.11), he constructed radial lines through the joints inward to their common center (C) and outward to meet the horizontal line (MN) drawn tangent to the arch at its top center. This was the first use of the funicular polygon in the design of arches. La Hire found the weights P_n of the sections must be proportional to the line segments $(MK, KL, LN,$ etc.) of the tangent line for equilibrium to obtain. By the same polygon, the normal pressures are proportional to the radial lengths (*CK, CL, CN,* etc.).

La Hire realized that for this geometrical situation to be exact, the last section (the *naissance* of the arch) must have infinite weight to sustain the infinite pressure at the surface of the last joint. He accounted for this physical impossibility by stating that cement between the joints of an actual arch would permit stability at lesser pressures. In a later memoir[82] he modified this method. He assumed the joints nearest the crown of the arch to permit analysis by his smooth voussoir approach. He then assumed the voussoirs that were close to the springing (*CE* in Fig. III.11) to form part of the solid abutment. He finally treated the arch as having only three sections, supposing that the arch would rupture at the intrados (inside of the arch) at the crown, and at the extrados (outside of the arch) at the springing. La Hire's theory contained two major errors. First, arches do not always rupture at the crown—due to tilting they often rupture away from it. Second, he neglected the fact that due to friction and cohesion the forces between the sections are not perpendicular to the joint surfaces.

Bélidor developed La Hire's method of arch design in his famous work *La science des ingénieurs* (1729).[83] He assumed a virtual hinge would tend to produce rupture at a point 45° away from the crown. This theory is presented pictorially in Fig. III.12.[84] Bélidor's presentation of La Hire's theory was widely used in the eighteenth century, and Perronet and Chézy[85] later used it to construct extensive empirical tables for arch design.

One other engineering solution to the problem of arches deserves our attention. Couplet discussed this question in two memoirs presented to the French Academy in 1729 and 1730.[86] He attempted to extend La Hire's theory by considering the two extreme physical cases of zero friction and of infinite friction. This method produced cumbersome solutions theoretically no less faulty than those of La Hire.

None of these men were so naive as to believe that their idealistic solutions really explained the physical behavior of arch rupture. It may seem that they were rather ignorant to neglect, for example, friction and cohesion in arch design. Once again, though, I must stress the difficulty of these problems for the eighteenth-century engineer. What may seem rather clear and simple to the modern reader was beyond treatment for La Hire and Bélidor. In studying the evolution of the physics and engineering of this period it is

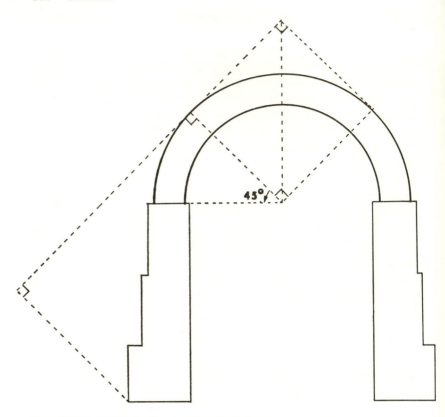

Fig. III.12. Bélidor's theory of arch design

sometimes too easy to say that these disciplines awaited only the proper method, or that engineering matured when it learned to join analysis to experiment.

Frézier aptly described the difficulties of this synthesis in his important work, *Traité de stéréotomie* (1737–1739).[87] He constantly called for an application of theory to practice in engineering but he realized the difficulties in this. The achievement of physically real solutions was more than just a question of plugging some constants into an equation. Speaking of problems in the design of arches, Frézier said: "I know of no one who has yet been able to order them, this determination being too mixed with physical causes . . ."[88] and again: "The theory of Arch Thrusts is very mixed up with physical causes. . . ."[89]

Coulomb's solution is valuable precisely because it considers two "real" affects in arch stability: (1) cohesion and friction, (2) rupture due to rotation or tilting.

Coulomb introduced his section on arches[90] by showing that the arch must take the shape of an inverted catenary if one neglects friction and cohesion. He cited David Gregory's essay in the *Philosophical Transactions* as the first demonstration that the inverted chain has the same form as an arch "formed by an infinite number of infinitely small elements having constant thickness." This method, however, "can be of no use in practice"[u,91] if one neglects friction and cohesion.

Coulomb noted the impossibility of meeting the condition of infinite weight at the last joints if one used the existent (La Hire) theory. To modify this ideal solution, he said, "In the following we will seek a method of including these new coercive forces (friction and cohesion) in the expression for arches," for the theory which neglects these effects "can be of only feeble utility."[94]

Coulomb's arch solution is presented in its full generality in Article XVIII of his 1773 statics memoir. There he constructed an arch with an interior curve (*aB*) and exterior curve (*Gb*), with joints (*Mm*) perpendicular to the surface of the interior curve (*aB*) (see Fig. III.13).[95] Given these data, he proposed to solve for the limits of the horizontal pressure applied at point *f* which would keep the arch in equilibrium, assuming the arch to be acted upon by its own weight ϕ and by the cohesion and friction of the joints (*Mm*, etc.).

He supposed an arch section (*GaMm*) to be solid and capable of sliding or tilting only along its surfaces (*Ga* and *Mm*). The horizontal thrust at *f* Coulomb called *A* for investigation of sliding conditions and *B* for tilting. Angle *GRm* is given as *h*. For the arch to be in equilibrium the horizontal thrust must lie within some maximum and minimum limits both of *A* and of *B* in order to prevent sliding and tilting.

Summing up horizontal and vertical forces:

$A \sin h =$ component of *A* along *Mm*,
$\phi \cos h =$ component of ϕ along *Mm*,
$A \cos h =$ component perpendicular to *Mm*,
$\phi \sin h =$ component perpendicular to *Mm*.

[u] For the complete solution of the inverted chain Coulomb mentioned Euler's memoir presented in 1732.[92] Except for the solution, he said, his method had nothing in common with Euler's. He also cited Jacques Bernoulli's solution for an arch composed of equal sections.[93]

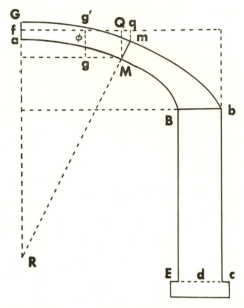

FIG. III.13. Coulomb's figure illustrating his theory of arch design

Therefore, for equilibrium against sliding either up or down along *Mm*, the thrust *A* must lie between values

$$A = \frac{\phi(\cos h - \dfrac{\sin h}{n}) - \delta Mm}{\sin h + \dfrac{\cos h}{n}}$$

and

$$A' = \frac{\varphi(\cos h + \dfrac{\sin h}{n}) + \delta Mm}{\sin h - \dfrac{\cos h}{n}}$$

where, as usual, $1/n$ = coefficient of friction and
δ = cohesion.

For all possible values of angle *h*, expression *A* must be a maximum and *A'* a minimum. Using the principles of maxima and minima, Coulomb solved for these by putting dA/dh and dA'/dh equal to zero.

Coulomb realized that for equilibrium in arches, one must satisfy not only conditions of sliding along joints but also relative rotation between the joints. This condition was first examined in 1732 by Augustin Danyzy,[96] a mathematician and member of the *Société des sciences* of Montpellier. Danyzy conducted experiments on model arches and noted that La Hire's considerations of rupture did not always hold and that arches often ruptured due to rotation around a point of the arch joints (see Fig. III.14).[97] Danyzy gave

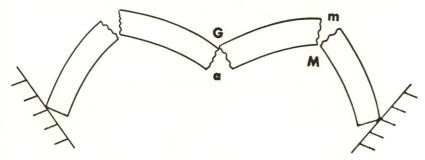

FIG. III.14. Arch rupture due to rotation around points of the arch joints

full details of his experiments to Frézier so the latter could publish them in his *Traité de stéréotomie*.[98] Poncelet[99] and other writers on the history of arch design claim that Coulomb probably included rotative effects due to the influence of Danyzy's experiments.[v]

Just as for the case of slipping, equilibrium against rotation also fell between two force limits (B and B'). If the moment $B[QM]$ failed to resist the moment $\phi[gM] - \delta'zz$ (see Fig. III.13), then the joint $GaMm$ would open at points a or m. If the moment $B'[qm]$ overcame the moment $\phi[g'q] + \delta'zz$, then the joint would open at points G or M. Where:

$\delta' =$ a constant times the "cohesion" (tensile strength) coefficient (*i.e.*, $k\delta$),

$zz =$ cross section of the arch (Coulomb neglected to indicate zz in Fig. III. 13),

[v] This is not proven, as Coulomb nowhere cites Danyzy. It is not an unlikely assumption, however, for two reasons. Danyzy's experiments were well known due to their presentation in Frézier's famous work. Also, Danyzy was a member of the society at Montpellier from 1729 until his death in 1777. Coulomb certainly knew Danyzy, because the society met at Danyzy's home[100] during the period when Coulomb was an adjoint member for mathematics.[101]

δ' zz = total resistance to shear along the plane (here, the plane Mm).

Coulomb thus sought to satisfy four conditions for the thrust at f for equilibrium of the arch:

Sliding
- (I) The Force (A) had to be great enough to prevent downward sliding along Mm.
- (II) The Force (A') had to be less than the value which would cause upward sliding along Mm.

Tilting
- (III) The Force (B) had to resist counterclockwise rotation about points a or m.
- (IV) The Force (B') had to resist clockwise rotation about points G or M.

In practice, the friction between the joints allowed one to neglect sliding motions, so Coulomb said that equilibrium Conditions (I) and (II) could usually be ignored. The main concern, then, was to prevent rotation about an opening of a joint. From his experiments on newly mortared joints, Coulomb noted that cohesion could be ignored in calculating the turning moments. Thus, Conditions (III) and (IV) reduce to:

(III')
$$B = \frac{\phi[gM]}{[QM]}$$

(IV')
$$B' = \frac{\phi[g'q]}{[qm]}.$$

Now, exact determination of the force values B and B' is very difficult. The curve for dB/dh however, is quite broad about the maximum and minimum points. This means that approximate values for the factors in Equations (III) and (IV) suffice to provide a workable solution. Therefore, Coulomb outlined an approximate method useful in practice.[102] First, one assumes a value for angle h, then B and B' are obtained. Next, if a smaller value of angle h produces a higher value for thrust B, then the maximum thrust will occur in an arch section nearer to the crown of the arch. Conversely, if a smaller value of angle h produces a lower value of thrust B, then the maximum thrust occurs farther away from the crown. Coulomb said it is easy to find this rather uncritical maximum or minimum after a few trial calculations.

Coulomb's method for arch design was not presented in a manner ready for application by artisans. He provided a method for determining conditions of stability in arches but he gave no definite rules of design. It is probably for this reason that it was largely ignored by civil engineers of his time. As I indicated above, most engineers preferred to use ready-made tables like those compiled by Perronet and Chézy. Coulomb *said* he was designing his method for artists and tradesmen. It is not clear whether he indicated this only to increase the value of the memoir in the eyes of the Academy or whether he actually overrated the abilities of the eighteenth-century engineer. Considering his long experience in Martinique, it is most probable that he realized his memoir would not gain immediate use. Poncelet accounted for the neglect of Coulomb's theory of arch stability in the following words: "The generality and the abstruseness to which Coulomb confined himself on this point and on that which concerns the position of thrust at the key, the simple lack of examples or of any application of the principles to special cases, suffices to explain how the beautiful and useful conceptions of this illustrious engineer remained completely forgotten until recent times, in spite of their scientific and practical value."[103] Other contemporary writers agree here with Poncelet.

Coulomb's theory of arch stability was resurrected by Audoy[104] in the early part of the nineteenth century. This was soon picked up by Navier[105] and others. Coulomb's arch theory as well as his earth-pressure theory was then discussed in numerous articles from 1820–1850 in the French engineering journal, *Mémorial de l'officier du génie.*[106]

The 1773 Statics Memoir
and the Later Physics Essays

Upon first examination the Coulomb statics memoir appears to be quite different in composition and in purpose from his later physics memoirs. In some ways the impression is correct, but this does not imply a transformation in his investigative method. Rather, it demonstrates the different purposes for which the memoirs were written and the alteration in his own professional status. If we compare this 1773 work with one of his famous electricity memoirs of the 1780s, the earlier memoir appears sparse, theoretical, and less specific in character. Unlike many eighteenth-century writers, Coulomb never wrote a memoir unless he had close first-hand knowledge of the subject. Never did he write a purely theoretical memoir—if by this one means a memoir produced in the Cartesian manner or one in pure mathematics. Each of his contributions was based on lengthy experimentation or long physical experience. The statics memoir is grounded upon years of engineering experience, but unlike the later works, this one contains few experimental data. Principles are expounded but are not supported by overwhelming physical proofs. In short, this was a model of the type of essay that one would present to the Academy of Sciences to apply for membership.

Coulomb followed an established path for entrance into the Academy. First one presented a concise, polished memoir. If it was good enough, the work would then enable the author to gain the position of correspondent to the Academy. One also entered the Academy's annual prize contests. Winning two or more of these almost certainly resulted in membership. If one examines the dozens of memoirs submitted to the Academy and if one considers that the judges for the Marly machine contests (1785–1787) had to work through some forty-five entries, the advantages of an important work presented concisely become clear.

In contrast, the electricity and magnetism memoirs were works of physics and physics alone. The 1773 statics memoir, in spite of its contributions to elasticity and strength of materials, was designed as a contribution to eighteenth-century civil engineering. It was a call to use the new method of a "mélange du calcul et de la physique" in engineering work. It showed the advantages of the calculus in providing general solutions for particular engineering problems and it laid open the way for similar treatment of specific problems. Coulomb was not proving a theory here, he was exposing principles of investigation. With cohesion and friction constants of soils and materials known only to an approximate degree, Coulomb was concerned with solutions to types of engineering problems and was not attempting to give exact numerical proofs. In his electricity and magnetism memoirs, Coulomb introduced new experimental means to prove an exactly quantitative problem —the precise determination of the magnetic and electrostatic force laws. The significance of these later memoirs rests on their precision and on Coulomb's beautiful experimental work. Yet, one cannot say that the statics memoir and his later work were different in method; they differed in purpose.

I stated above that page for page, this was the most brilliant engineering memoir read at the Academy during Coulomb's lifetime. This is not meant to belittle any of the many fundamental memoirs in physics and in analysis that were presented at the Academy. Coulomb's memoir stood above the scores of *engineering* memoirs presented there, and it is in that context that I make the statement.

His earth-pressure theory and the "Coulomb Equation" are the fundamental tenets of modern engineering texts in soil mechanics. From 1800 until about 1833, the majority of European bridge builders utilized his theory of design and evaluation of arches.[107] It was his considerations in studying the neutral line in rupture of beams and strength of materials that were to be used in the early nineteenth century. One is not surprised, after all, to know that much of this memoir remained unused for forty years. It required that group of *Polytechniciens*, teachers and students, to appreciate the importance of this work in the context of the new engineering mechanics.

Four · THEORIES OF FRICTION IN THE EIGHTEENTH CENTURY

Introduction

This chapter will examine theories of friction from 1699 to 1781 and will present an analysis of Coulomb's work in this area. His memoir, "Theory of Simple Machines,"[1] was presented in 1781 in response to one of the contests set by the Academy of Sciences. Unlike the theoretical 1773 memoir[2] on problems in strength of materials, soil mechanics, and arch design, Coulomb's friction study contained both a rational analysis of the problems and the results from extensive engineering tests. The "Théorie des machines simples" is closer to the tradition of eighteenth-century engineering than any of Coulomb's other studies. Perhaps for this reason alone it became his most celebrated engineering memoir. It does not show the brilliance of his 1773 statics memoir, but it dealt with a complicated phenomenon and one very difficult to examine.

Friction is the study of the surface interactions of bodies. The effects of this phenomenon have been observed since antiquity[a,3] but the tradition of quantitative study of its parameters began only at the end of the seventeenth century. There are three important phases in the early development of theories of friction: Amontons' initial experiments and theory (1699),[4] Desaguliers' addition of the idea of cohesion or molecular attraction (1725),[5] and Coulomb's work (1781).[6] Parent's[7] and Euler's[8] development of the Amontons theory in terms of rational mechanics contributed rather little to the knowledge of friction. Coulomb combined a

---

a Observations of friction and efforts to allay its effects have been ascribed to the Egyptians, Greeks, and Romans; and Leonardo da Vinci supposedly conducted experiments on friction and recorded observations of these in his notebooks. These references are interesting but of slight relevance here. Eighteenth-century authors were unanimous in according Amontons credit for the first studies of friction; none mentions any studies by the ancients or by Leonardo, whose notebooks were unknown until the nineteenth century.

generalized theory with the only extensive and satisfactory series of experiments performed until the mid-nineteenth century. In his 1773 statics memoir, Coulomb accepted Amontons' theory,[b] but following Bossut[9] he noted that the coefficient of friction could vary with the materials used. He found that it could be 3/4 in the case of clay bricks and that for granite and other building stones it varied with each individual stone. Friction was considered here only in relation to Coulomb's theoretical use of *maxima* and *minima* principles of calculus in design problems in applied mechanics.

In his prize-winning magnetism memoir of 1777[10] Coulomb investigated the design and mounting of small magnetic needles. He attempted to design an accurate compass suitable for practical use in the marine service. This involved studies of the pivot friction in compass needles. He stated that Amontons' Law did not seem to hold for small mechanisms. In compass needles the friction of the pivot varied approximately as the 3/2 power of the normal force. Though recognizing the practical worth of Amontons' work, Coulomb was aware of the fact that it was strictly applicable only to a narrow class of interacting material bodies. Before a comprehensive theory could be constructed it would be necessary to inaugurate a systematic series of experiments on friction phenomena. These experiments would entail investigation of the effects of all possible variables, and small scale-model experiments would not suffice.[11] The investigation would take considerable time and require the construction of numerous pieces of large test equipment.

Before analyzing Coulomb's studies in detail, I will discuss the evolution of theories of friction in the eighteenth century.

Early Theories of Friction

Friction studies were initiated in the late seventeenth century when animals began to be replaced by "engines." In a 1699 memoir on the design of turbine water wheels, Guillaume Amontons[12] remarked that the frictional force is proportional to the load, usually equals about 1/3 of the load, and is independent of the surface areas of contact. There was nothing to surprise one in the statement that the friction was proportional to the load and equal to about 1/3 of it. On the other hand, the statement that the frictional force was independent of the surface "caused some aston-

---

[b] Friction proportional to the normal force acting on the surfaces.

ishment at the Academy,"[13] so much in fact that Philippe de La Hire was asked to repeat Amontons' experiments.

Amontons began his article "On the Resistance Generated in Machines" with a rather elegant plea for the study of friction:

> The great use which all the arts are obliged to make of machines is convincing proof of their absolute necessity; thus, without losing further time to establish this truth, I will be content to say here that if the name "machine" is sometimes taken in a bad sense, and if it becomes sometimes a contemptible thing, this is in part because the few rules we have in mechanics do not always suffice to predict with certainty the effect that the machines which one envisions must achieve when they are put into operation; what happens very often is that many people who know nothing about machines believe themselves so well versed as to have nothing to learn about them and fall therefore into strange absurdities. Indeed, of all the authors who have written on motive forces, there is perhaps not one who has paid sufficient attention to the effect of friction in machines and to the resistance caused by the stiffness of ropes, or who has given us rules for knowing the effect of either one and for reducing them to mathematical formulas. Moreover, this knowledge is no less necessary in order to obtain a good judgment of the effect of a machine than is the knowledge of the relationships of the parts that compose it, and it is only too true that the lack of this knowledge of the resistance caused by friction and by the stiffness of ropes is almost always, in regard to machines, an obstacle all the more to be feared because, up to the present, its magnitude has been unknown.[14]

Amontons considered the study of friction requisite to a knowledge of the effect and proper use of machines. Along with their development had come a flood of ideas for perpetual-motion devices. Without proper consideration of friction, there was no way to deter a would-be inventor from presenting the Academy with yet another design for a perfect machine. A correct knowledge of the effect of machines could be obtained only through experiment. Amontons constructed a sliding device employing a leaf spring, a coil spring, and a variety of lubricated sliding surfaces (copper, iron, lead, and wood) coated with axle grease (see Fig. IV.1).[15] He would pull on the coil spring until the sliding block began to move. Noting the

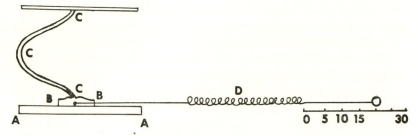

Fig. IV.1. Amontons' sliding friction device

extension which resulted in the movement of the sliding block and the known force exerted by the leaf spring, he could then calculate the force needed for horizontal movement. It is clear that he made use of Hooke's Law, although as is the case in nearly all eighteenth-century work with springs, he made no mention of Hooke or his work. After testing the various blocks in all possible orientations Amontons concluded that friction depends on the normal force only and not on the contact area of the surfaces. He stated that the coefficient of friction is about the same for all the materials tested and that the friction is about 1/3 the normal force. He added another fact: "That the resistances are mutually proportional to the weights or pressures [*poids ou pressions*] of the parts that rub, the times, and the velocities of their movements."[16] From this he concluded: "Now if we meditate carefully on the nature of friction we will find that it is nothing other than the action by which a body that is pressed against another is moved on the surface of that which it touches."[17]

Thus a conservation of *action* was the basis of his calculations, where *action* for Amontons was equal to a weight (*poids* or *pression*) moved through a distance.[c] He supposed that one could consider the nature of friction to be either that of a system of springs or of rigid asperities. In one case it amounts to depressing a spring through a given distance. The same amount of *action* is accounted for by pressing one spring through a distance X or two springs through a distance $X/2$ or N springs through a distance X/N. In

[c] Note that *action* for Amontons is equivalent dimensionally to work, though of course he never uses the term. *Action* for him is either a force moved through a distance ($F \cdot s$), or a force acting at a velocity for a given time ($F \cdot V \cdot t$), which has the same dimensions. This is true, however, only if *poids* or *pression* for Amontons actually meant a weight or force.

the case of rigid bodies with surface asperities the *action* is the same whether one lifts a body M through a distance X or if one lifts each of four bodies of weight $M/4$ through a distance X.

Throughout his discussion Amontons was never troubled by the question of energy loss. His systems of springs or rigid bodies explained why friction seemed to depend 1) only on the normal force and 2) not on the area of contact. In the case of two perfectly smooth plane bodies he gave the ingenious explanation that even this is equivalent to lifting one of the bodies over an asperity because when it slides it has to recede from the center of the earth and therefore is being lifted against gravity (see Fig. iv.2). Amon-

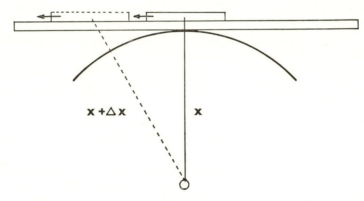

FIG. IV.2. Author's representation of Amontons' conception of action against gravity in sliding two infinitely plane surfaces

tons examined also the effect of friction in bending of cords. From experiments he determined that the coefficient of resistance to bending in cords is proportional to the diameter of the cord and approximately inversely proportional to the diameter of the pulley. He found, however, that as the pulley size increased, the relative resistance decreased. He closed his paper with impressive tables giving the coefficient of resistance for cords and pulleys loaded up to 100,000 pounds.

Amontons was interested in finding a practical value for the coefficient of friction in order that he might correctly calculate the effect of his heat engines. His experiments showed that friction is proportional to normal force (*pression*) and not the area, and that the coefficient of friction seemed to be roughly the same for numerous lubricated materials. These phenomena could be easily accounted for either with the theory of interaction of springs (*ressorts*) or the theory of lifting weights over surface asperities.

Amontons' work was important throughout the eighteenth century. The central weakness in his paper is that he drew his conclusions from extrapolations of his data. A good indication of this is in his lengthy tables for the calculation of resistance in bending of cords. Amontons used cords no more than 1/4 inch in diameter and weights no greater than 60 pounds, yet he gave data for hawsers up to 2½ inches in diameter and weights up to 100,000 pounds! Similarly, his experiments in sliding friction involved blocks of about a square foot in surface area and weighing only some tens of pounds. His work would be applied in shipyards and millhouses where ropes of several inches in diameter were used and where pressures between sliding surfaces reached several thousand pounds per foot[2]. Though many other experiments were performed and some authors questioned Amontons' data, no one until Smeaton[18] in 1759 noted the importance of full-size equipment for friction experiments.

Amontons established the quantitative study of friction phenomena. He sought a single coefficient of friction for all interacting surfaces and suggested a theory of bending springs or lifting rigid bodies. This limited concept was to be the basis of arguments for over seventy-five years. Some workers accepted his basic premises; others did so but held that the universal coefficient of friction was not 1/3, but rather 1/4 or 1/2 or some other average value.[19] Still others challenged his statement that friction was dependent only upon the normal force.[20]

Philippe de La Hire had written a lengthy text on the theory and operation of machines in 1695.[21] He was considered the best choice to repeat Amontons' experiments. He did so and reported before the Academy.[22] In general, La Hire verified Amontons' data, but in summing up the possible mechanism of friction he added two new factors. If the surface asperities were to wear away or break off, La Hire suggested that the broken particles would contribute to the friction in some proportion as the area of surface contact. One other factor, he said, could add to the surface-area effect. It was known that two extremely polished surfaces were very hard to separate once pressed together. La Hire explained that air particles are larger than oil or water particles. If two surfaces were polished so that they fit together closely or if they were coated with oil or water, the air particles would be driven out from between the body surfaces. The pressing bodies would then be deprived of the springy counterbalancing effect of the air! "The parts of lubricated machines carry, therefore, all the weight of the atmosphere, and they carry more as they have more surface, and their friction is proportional to the surface area, or very nearly so."[23] Thus La Hire suggested the possibility of variations from Amontons' Law[d] (that friction was proportional to the normal force and independent of the surface area).

Antoine Parent joined analysis to Amontons' conjecture and provided a more rigorous support for the hypothesis of friction due to lifting over rigid asperities. He accepted Amontons' value of 1/3 for the coefficient of friction but added little to Amontons' *theory*.[25]

Though various authors would differ over the value of the coefficient of friction, through most of the eighteenth century the accepted theory of friction was that of Amontons' mechanistic action. A challenge to this came from Jean Théophile Desaguliers. Writing in the *Philosophical Transactions*, Desaguliers and his followers produced a number of short notes of an experimental nature connecting Newtonian forces and cohesion to the phenomenon of friction. As early as 1719, a student, Paul Dawson, pirated Desaguliers' lecture notes and had them published as *Lectures of Experimental Philosophy*.[26] In this early work Desaguliers glorified Newton and attempted to destroy the Cartesian physics. He spoke little of friction here. He knew of its effects but probably preferred to keep silent out of distaste for the then current mechanistic explanation of it. He said: "Tho engines are imperfect we must suppose them perfect, that by such a supposition we may better find out what they'll do as that Bodies are perfectly hard, smooth and homogeneous, lines strait, without Weight, Thickness or Flexibility, and cords extremely pliable."[27] He attributed actions in bodies to their *mutual attraction*; "The same thing is true in all other attraction."[28]

In 1725 Desaguliers became acquainted with "some experiments with cohesion in two balls of lead made by Mr. Trievall at Newcastle and at Edinburgh."[29] He repeated Trievall's simple experiment of pressing together two lead balls. He claimed that if the balls were cleaned, then pushed together with a "twist," that an

---

[d] Euler[24] was the first to express Amontons' theory in algebraic form. Amontons' Law as expressed throughout this work is of the form $F = kP$, where F = friction force, P = normal force, k = coefficient of friction.

area of contact 1/10th of an inch in diameter required a force of 47 pounds to separate them. In the next several volumes of the *Philosophical Transactions* Desaguliers continued reporting his experiments in very short notes. He had translated Edme Mariotte's *Mouvement des eaux*[30] and from this was led to examine friction effects in running water.[31] A criticism of "Monsieur Perault's new-invented *axis in peritrochio* [axle in wheel]"[32] led him to study cords, pulleys, and machines. In 1731 he wrote that he was planning a work on the theory.[33] At that time he must have been well along in the writing of his two-volume *Course of Experimental Philosophy*, which was published in 1734.[34]

There is little original material in his friction experiments in that work. He based his writings on the studies of Peter Van Musschenbroek[35] and François Joseph de Camus.[36] Desaguliers criticized Camus for using very small models of pulleys and cords, but he persisted in this himself. His experiments with sliding friction employed weights of only a few pounds. After Amontons' first mention of a theory of friction and La Hire's suggestion that wear or adhesion of surfaces might cause the friction coefficient to vary, others challenged Amontons' statement that friction is independent of surface area. Desaguliers combined all these facts in a loose way and emphasized the contribution of cohesion to friction effects. According to this hypothesis, cohesive forces would be proportional to the surface area and not the normal force alone. Nowhere did Desaguliers clearly state a theory of friction, yet his book is important as being the only major challenge to Amontons' theory. Those Englishmen who were to continue to contribute notes to the *Philosophical Transactions* throughout the eighteenth century viewed Desaguliers' friction work with an admiring, if uncritical, regard.

As experiments in the field multiplied, values of the coefficient of friction obtained began to vary widely. These discrepancies from Amontons' Law ($F = kP$) seem due to several causes. First, many workers plainly based their writings on both scanty experimental data and poor experimental technique. Second, for those who worked at very low surface pressures (such as merely sliding one plank across another), the frictional force *did* seem to vary widely from Amontons' value of 1/3 the normal force.[e,37] Third, those who investigated in the regions of extrapolation in

---

[e] It seems, though, that few *carefully* read Amontons' own paper where he said that 1/3 was an approximate value. In the first part of his paper he gives an illustration where the friction coefficient is more than 2/3.

Amontons' tables could easily detect that the tables were extrapolated calculations and not experimental findings.

Generally, those who criticized Amontons did so on the basis of scattered experiments performed with little concern for all the possible parameters. Thus, only a proliferation of confusing answers resulted. Amontons' limited set of experiments was taken as law by some and blindly attacked by others. In many cases the attacks were based on continental versus English physical ideas— *M. des Cartes* versus *Mr. Newton*.

Bowden and Tabor, authors of the standard English-language work on the modern theories of friction, attribute a major conceptual role to Desaguliers.[38] I would not deny this but would agree rather more with Kragelsky and Schedrov that Desaguliers influenced mainly some English writers and that cohesion as a major factor in eighteenth century theories of friction was short-lived.[39] Desaguliers' work was of value as a widely read popular work of experimental physics. It was important as well in that it represented the statement that the phenomena of friction were varied and complex and it presented, as a possibility, the molecular origin of friction. I feel that Bowden and Tabor imply, though, that Coulomb *ignored* Desaguliers when they say: "French scientists were committed to the concept of surface roughnesses, a conviction which was sustained and strengthened by Coulomb's work almost 100 years after Amontons."[40] I will show that Coulomb fully considered the importance of cohesion as a parameter in his theory of friction. In fact, his theory was basically a series of two-term equations: 1) a constant term usually attributed to cohesion (*cohérence*) or a surface film (*duvet*) and 2) a variable term. Cohesion was a minor factor for Coulomb because he found that it accounted for less than 5% of the friction effect in most of his experiments. Amontons began the modern study of friction; it was Coulomb's work which established it as a science. In 1775 the state of friction studies was as follows: there were two general theories of cause. The first as proposed by Amontons was that friction was due to the action of one body on another in bending springy surface fibers or in lifting the upper body across rigid surface asperities. The second "theory," as suggested by Desaguliers, was not really a complete theory at all. It was rather a statement of the complex situation with regard to friction phenomena and a call for the inclusion of the effects of the mutual attractive force of cohesion. Intermixed with these two conceptions of the causes of friction were Parent's and Euler's analytical solutions based on Amontons' theory and then a host of experimental bits and pieces which, taken separately, made little sense at all. In studying numerous eighteenth-century papers on the subject, I have noted thirteen different parameters that were investigated.[f] Most authors considered only three or four of these, however. This confused picture prevailed when Coulomb entered the Paris Academy's prize contest for 1781.

The Academy of Sciences and Its Interest in Friction

During the period 1720-1793 the Academy offered numerous prizes in essay contests. Capturing one of the handsome awards was not always a guarantee of entrance into the Academy, but those who did win found themselves among an impressive group which included Pierre Bouguer, three Bernoullis (Johann, Johann II, and Daniel), Euler, Lagrange, Bossut, and Bailly.[41] The contests fell into two main categories, astronomy and maritime, accounting for twenty-six and twenty-three prizes respectively.[g] The Academy was greatly concerned in implementing Newton's celestial mechanics, and the astronomical contests stimulated much brilliant work in this field.

The improvement of the French navy was the general subject of the other major category of contests. At mid-century the British navy was almost three times the size of the French. The French sought to improve by design what the English produced through experience. This was a period when Britain and France were fighting for colonies, trade, and sea power.[42] France suffered both at the Treaty of Aix-la-Chapelle (1748) and at the Treaty of Paris (1763) and after this was especially concerned with coastal defense and the improvement of its fleet. By the last years of the eighteenth century French naval design had improved considerably. After 1781 the naval prize contests changed to questions of marine insurance or safety. I am not arguing a strictly causal rela-

---

[f] Of thirteen parameters noted by the author, Coulomb investigated twelve. These are listed below in the section entitled *Coulomb's Method of Investigation*. He did not consider the relationship of the friction coefficient to the electric or magnetic state of the material.

[g] The contests were not actually named "astronomy" and "maritime," but the questions proposed usually alternated between a theoretical question in celestial mechanics and a practical one concerned with interests of the Navy.

tionship here between the French naval situation up to 1781 and the announcement of the prizes at the Academy. However, the wording of the prize questions and the substance of the entries leaves no doubt that the navy was highly interested in some very practical problems related to shipbuilding and operation.

A study of some of the memoirs entered in the Academy's naval prize contests[43] will show that the substance of a good engineering research memoir was judged much the same in 1765 as it is today. Authors who diverged from the stated questions fared poorly no matter how brilliant their digressions. The questions were usually phrased to ask both experimental and mathematical contributions of the authors. The Academy recognized the value of field-tested devices and experimentation. For a century they had been presented with schemes for frictionless clocks and pulleys, designs constructed on mere scale-model tests and many technically useless devices.

The Academy had proposed for the prize for 1779 (and again for 1781), the solution of problems of friction of sliding and rolling surfaces, the resistance to bending in cords and the application of these solutions to simple machines used in the navy. There existed so many friction theories and experimentally determined constants that it was specifically indicated that the contestants must examine "the effects resulting from the stiffness of ropes, being determined after *new experiments made on the full scale*; it is required also, that the experiments be applicable to *machines utilized* in the Navy, such as the pulley, the capstan, and the inclined plane."[44] The solutions of some of these problems were of the highest priority. For example, the data on inclined planes would be used in constructing arrangements for ship launchings. Coulomb noted[45] that often when ships were launched by sliding down ways they would stick halfway down, the ways would catch fire from the generated heat or the ship would fall over and possibly suffer major damage. Even if it did not overturn, the tallow used for lubrication would fuse and act as a cement rather than a lubricant. It was difficult then to persuade laborers to work close in under the ship while attempting to reshore it for a new attempt. A tragic example of these difficulties concerned the British ship *Felicity*. During the launching the ship stuck halfway down, the ways broke and thus strained the hull. The captain noted in his logbook that it was then almost impossible to sign on a crew because of rumors that the hull had been sprung. Two months after launching, the

Felicity sank with loss of all hands. The ship's log was found float-ing inside a cask.[46]

Coulomb's Method of Investigation

From the appearance of his first memoir on statics,[47] Coulomb was in full possession of his investigative method. Many of his memoirs begin with the title "Theoretical and Experimental Investigations of. . . ." He proceeded by discussing general theories and describing his experimental apparatus. Next he gave detailed descriptions of his experiments and numerical data derived from them. He fol-lowed this with theoretical remarks inspired by the observed facts and then discussed new experiments suggested by these remarks. Finally, he presented his conclusions and considered the possible practical applications of his work.[48]

In the preface to "Theory of Simple Machines" Coulomb dis-cussed the existing work in friction—the original hypothesis of Amontons and the experimental variances found by Musschen-broek, Camus, and Desaguliers. He criticized the neglect of defor-mation considerations in previous work. Camus and Desaguliers had noted that friction varied with the time that the two static surfaces had remained together before motion, but neither had in-vestigated this relationship. As in his previous engineering mem-oirs, Coulomb acknowledged his debt to Bossut.[49]

The "Theory of Simple Machines" was composed in two parts: 1) the friction of sliding surfaces and 2) the bending of cords and movements of rotation. In each of these sections Coulomb gave numerous figures depicting his apparatus. He carefully described his materials and the reason for employing each particular piece. For instance he explained that in the investigations on sliding sur-faces he disregarded the friction of a small pulley in his friction table apparatus (see Fig. iv.3).[50] He did so because in separate experiments he examined the friction in the pulley and found it to be less than 1/150th of the total value in the experiments with the table. In other cases he noted the exact temperature of the air, and examined rope that had been weathered by sun, rain, or salt water. He found correction factors for these variables. In another case he considered the humidity of the air. He left this factor out of his published results only after it was found to have no differential effect on the various experiments.[51] By performing some tests many times, new variables became apparent to him. Thus it had been

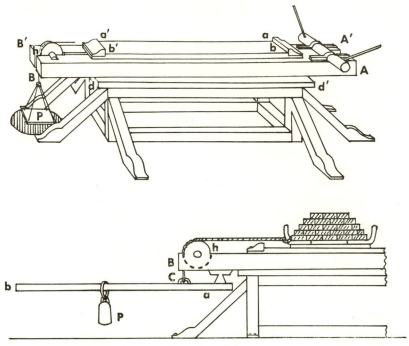

Fɪɢ. IV.3. Coulomb's table apparatus for sliding static and dynamic friction measurements

assumed that if a pulley or plane surface were polished to a high sheen that it could be considered smooth and as frictionless as possible. Desaguliers had stated that such surfaces would produce *higher* friction values due to cohesive forces. Coulomb discovered that one cannot determine directly by any human sense whether a plane surface, for instance, is perfectly smooth. Nevertheless, the friction coefficient can be decreased by "running-in" the object. For a plane surface this would entail passing a very heavy plane object back and forth over its surface.[52] A pulley could be "run-in" by drawing a rope over it for a number of hours. In each case the friction coefficient would be reduced after a period of time, even if the surface had formerly appeared absolutely smooth.

This patient, inquisitive, wide-ranging type of experimentation was unique in the history of friction studies. Coulomb's method produced physical answers expressed in analytical terms that could never arise out of the purely rational approach of an Euler, who said: "... I will show that one can produce simply by the action of gravity an effect entirely similar to that of friction, by which one could even discover the nature of friction, when it would not even yet be known by experiment."[53] And oppositely, Coulomb's use of analysis to frame his experimental laws and to guide him in searching for patterns of development could bring a myriad of facts into account. This was never accomplished by the rambling experimentation of a Bélidor or a Desaguliers. In his work on rolling and sliding friction Coulomb investigated many possible parameters:

1. materials constituting the reacting bodies
2. surface conditions (polished, rough)
3. lubricants (oil, tallow, tar, axle grease, water)
4. weight (normal force)
5. surface area of contact
6. deformation or cohesion effects due to time of repose
7. geometric orientation of interacting surfaces (whether wood grain parallel or perpendicular, etc.)
8. velocity of surface motion
9. deformation due to geometry of surfaces (shape of interacting surfaces—planar, pointed, curved)
10. temperature, humidity
11. state of motion (uniform or impulsive)
12. air pressure (extensive experiments in a vacuum were carried out by Coulomb only in later memoirs—1790).[54]

Coulomb used analytical methods evolved by Parent, Euler, Daniel Bernoulli, and Bossut. He extended and codified the experiments of Amontons, Desaguliers, and others. It was just this fruitful combination of analysis and of directed experiment that led him to his results.

Coulomb's Theory and Formulated Results

In nearly all of Coulomb's formulas for calculating friction effects he employed two-term equations. These contained a constant term and a term varying with time, normal force, velocity, or some other parameter. These formulas accounted for the small effect due to cohesion or surface films and the larger effect due to mechanical interaction. As mentioned earlier in this essay, I feel it would be inaccurate to contend that Coulomb ignored the theory of friction due to cohesive force. In Articles III and IV at the beginning of his memoir he noted the five most important parameters in static and dynamic friction:

1. the nature of materials and their surface coatings
2. the extent of surface area
3. normal force
4. the length of time that the surfaces remain in contact before motion begins (time of repose)
5. the relative velocity of the contact surfaces.

Coulomb then proceeded immediately to discuss the two major hypotheses for the cause of friction phenomena: first, the engagement or enmeshing of surface asperities; and second, the cohesion of the surface molecules.[55] Those, as Desaguliers, who held that friction depended on the area of surface contact, employed the cohesion theory to explain friction. Most others accounted for it by the use of Amontons' mechanical surface-asperity theory. The surface area coefficient would remain constant for a given friction surface unless wear altered the surface area. The constant term in Coulomb's formulas answered for this contact area or surface film effect. It was only because the constant term was usually very small in relation to the total friction (except in the case of very small normal forces with very large surface areas) that Coulomb said that Amontons' Law held for most practical cases of friction phenomena.[56] By this he meant that there was an approximately linear relationship between friction and normal forces but that this did not remain constant from one material to another. The formulas in Table IV.1, although for very different situations, illustrate Coulomb's basic two-term approach.[57]

As an example of the way in which Coulomb obtained his two-term formulas consider his Experiment No. XXX, for sliding friction of well-worn oak lubricated with old tallow. Here the friction is to be determined as a function of the length of time two oak surfaces remain together before one is set in motion. Following a given time of repose in each observation, Coulomb measured the force necessary to just barely keep in motion an oak sled loaded to a total weight of 5,810 pounds. He varied the time of repose from 0 to 960 minutes (see Table IV.2).[58] Since he observed that the force required at time $T = 0$ is 502 pounds, he proposed to analyze the data by the equation $F = A + kT^\rho$, where F is force in pounds,

TABLE IV.1

EXAMPLES OF COULOMB'S TWO-TERM FORMULAS FOR CALCULATION OF
SLIDING AND ROLLING FRICTION AND BENDING OF CORDS

1) $F = A + \dfrac{P}{\mu}$ *for friction between sliding surfaces;*[*]

2) $F = \dfrac{A\mu + P(\cos n + \mu \sin n)}{\mu \cos m + \sin m}$ *for friction between inclined sliding surfaces* (Note that this reduces to formula (1) for horizontal motion $(n, m = 0)$.

3) $F = A + kT^\rho$ *for friction between sliding surfaces after a given time of repose.* For the case where the time $T \to \infty$, $F \to \infty$: therefore Coulomb expressed this formula alternatively as:

$$F = \frac{A + kT^\rho}{C + T^\rho}$$

By letting $T = 0$, $F = A/C$. By letting $T \to \infty$, $F = k$. Therefore, using these two limit conditions and two experiments one can determine the four constants (A, C, k, ρ) of the formula.

[*] In the formulas above F = friction force; A = a constant force; P = normal force; μ = inverse of coefficient of friction; n, m = angles between the inclined plane and the horizontal, and the line of action of force F, respectively; T = time of repose; and k, ρ, C = experimentally determined constants.

T is time in minutes, k and ρ are constants to be determined, and A is the constant determined at time $T = 0$. Coulomb then solved for k and ρ from the several observations given in Table IV.2 and obtained k equal to about 2,700 and ρ equal to about 0.2.

TABLE IV.2

EXPERIMENTAL FRICTION DATA

Observation number	Time of repose T (minutes)	Force F (pounds)
1	0	502
2	2	790
3	4	866
4	9	925
5	26	1036
6	60	1186
7	960	1535

Within the memoir Coulomb gave constants for various situations:

1. surface materials—oak, green oak, guaiac wood, fir, elm, iron, "yellow copper"
2. surface condition—dry; lubricated with axle grease, tallow, water, or olive oil; polished or rough
3. velocities—up to three meters per second (this was more than velocities encountered in eighteenth-century marine usage)
4. surface areas and normal forces—pressures tested were up to and more than 3,000 pounds per square foot for sliding plane surfaces, and indefinitely large for angular sliding surfaces.

Thus his memoir provided not only many carefully detailed experiments useful to the scientific study of friction but also much data that made it a real engineering handbook for marine usage. This latter factor was a major reason that it was awarded the Academy prize.

Lazare Carnot had also studied at the *Ecole royale du génie* at Mézières.[59] Carnot submitted papers to both the 1779 and 1781 friction contests, but his memoirs were not really pointed toward the questions asked. They were concerned more with theoretical matters of continuity and effect in machine design. This is undoubtedly one reason why he did not obtain the prize. For instance, in the manuscript of his 1779 entry he only partially completed a table of coefficients. He explained that he did not have time to complete the calculations and that he would leave it to the reader to fill in the blank spaces![h]

Coulomb wrote for the practicing engineer who needed reliable data for various tasks in the marine. He also concerned himself with the theory of friction. Some years before he composed the memoir on simple machines, Coulomb became aware that Amontons' Law did not accurately reflect the situation in friction problems. Abbé Bossut had been the first to indicate clearly the difference between static and dynamic friction but he had not sufficiently examined the problem. Camus and Desaguliers[62] had noted that the friction of a body shocked or shaken (*ebranlé*) was less than

[h] Parts of the documentation of the 1779 and 1781 friction prize contests are missing from the Academy of Sciences Archives, Dossier Prix, for 1779 and 1781, but Coulomb won the prize in 1781 and three entrants, including Lazare Carnot, received honorable mention. All three of the entries receiving honorable mention had been submitted for the 1779 contest.[60] Kragelsky and Schedrov[61] indicate that two of the entrants were Paolo Delanges and (Père) Leonard Ximenes. The judges for both the 1779 and 1781 contests were d'Alembert, Etienne Mignot de Montigny (Voltaire's nephew), Etienne Bézout, the abbé Charles Bossut, and the marquis de Condorcet.

that of a body started from rest but they had not tried to determine the relation that exists between these two kinds of friction. Bossut had noted that the *longer* two surfaces remained in static contact the harder it was to start them in motion. Coulomb sought to explain these different aspects of friction as they were reflected in his formulas (see Table IV.1). Generally, the small constant effect had been attributed to cohesion (*cohérence*). Coulomb stated that this might be so but he also advanced the suggestion that the contacting surfaces might be covered with a small surface layer or film (*duvet*). Both of these hypotheses would explain a surface area effect in friction.[63]

Of greater import than the small cohesion contributions was the factor of normal force. According to Amontons' Law, the friction was approximately proportional *only* to the normal force exerted by the upper body. Amontons added further that the friction force was equal to about one-third of the normal force. Amontons had expressed both surface-asperity and surface-spring hypotheses to explain the behavior of friction. However, he considered the springs to deform instantaneously. Coulomb was faced with the following experimental facts: metals seemed to have approximately the same coefficient of friction for both static and dynamic conditions; friction in fibrous materials, on the other hand, varied depending upon the length of time the surfaces had remained in contact and upon the velocity of surface motion. Adopting the "brush bristle" analogy of Musschenbroek, Coulomb explained the variation of friction with time of repose and with velocity in fibrous matter in the following way: if wood fibers are considered as little springs capable of deformation, then as two substances remained pressed together, their asperities would interlock or enmesh more and more with time of repose. There was a definite time needed for this deformation to occur.[64] After increasing for a time the static friction seemed to reach a limit value. Coulomb assumed that this limit indicated the occurrence of full deformation. In dynamic friction, the surface asperities did not have time enough to enmesh, thus, the surface asperities could be regarded as almost rigid and the friction would be proportional to normal force alone.

Under "enormous" pressures the surface asperities or cavities became bent (see Fig. IV.4),[65] and with increasing velocity the asperities enmeshed less and less. This would explain the relative decrease of friction with increasing velocity at high pressures.[66] Metals did not seem to share this property. There was no effect of

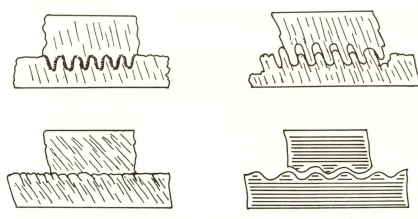

FIG. IV.4. Coulomb's diagrams of surface interactions

time of repose, nor of lessening of friction with velocity. This was easily explained by Coulomb. Wood was thought to be composed of flexible, elastic, elongated fibers. Metal, however, was composed of "angular, globular, hard, and inflexible parts, so that no degree of pressure nor of tension can change the shape of the parts which cover the surface of metals."[67]

Because metals acted as entirely rigid bodies, they conformed closely to the theory of lifting over surface asperities.

In all materials studied, the "coherence" was never quite zero, although it could be ignored if pressures exceeded "several hundred pounds per foot^2."[68] In the case of pulleys and ropes the deformation hypothesis used in describing the behavior of sliding in fibrous materials accounted well for the phenomena. In sum, Coulomb's hybrid two-term formulas and his composite theory gave a very good account of known frictional behavior.

Coulomb's Influence on Studies of Friction

Coulomb's work in friction was important for a century and a half. Kragelsky and Schedrov, authors of the only book on the history of friction, state: "Coulomb's contributions to the science of friction were exceptionally great. Without exaggeration, one can say that he *created* this science."[69] He was occupied with problems of friction and elasticity throughout his life. After his famous electricity and magnetism memoirs (written from 1785 to 1791) he returned to the study of friction and composed several shorter memoirs in the next two decades. In particular, he examined fluid friction, and friction and cohesion effects in a vacuum.[70] His friction and mechanics memoirs were so popular that after his death a collected edition was published, in 1821.

Coulomb's friction work was first presented to a wider audience by Prony in his *Nouvelle architecture hydraulique*, published in 1790. In the first years after the French Revolution, Prony published his famous course of mechanics in the Journal of the *Ecole polytechnique*. Prony gave credit to five men: Euler, Lagrange, Laplace, Bossut, and Coulomb (for his memoirs on machines).[71] In 1829, George Rennie confirmed Coulomb's work in his study of friction.[72] Shortly thereafter, Arthur Morin extended those results in a long series of experiments performed at the engineering school at Metz.[73] Morin was attacked both on theoretical grounds and for numerous algebraic errors by a young engineer, Arsène Dupuit. Whatever the merits of Dupuit's approach, Morin had the power of the *Institut de France* behind him, and Dupuit's work was not generally accepted.[74] Poncelet also used Coulomb's studies for his *Cours de mécanique*, and others of his texts.[75]

In discussing Coulomb's friction work, one must add that neither he nor any of his eighteenth-century contemporaries considered energy loss. It was known and often stated that friction resulted in heat or in loss of motion, but no one really introduced these considerations into a theory. John Leslie, in a study on the nature of heat (1804), first investigated these problems. Leslie introduced the idea of a deformation wave. This wave was produced by the interacting surfaces and traveled ahead of the contacting areas in the direction of propagation.[76] The resulting process was considered responsible for the generation of heat. Today, this is thought of in terms of "plowing," plastic deformation, and hysteresis loss.

Chapters III and IV of this book have been concerned with Coulomb's engineering studies. His 1773 statics memoir clearly shows how he joined rational analysis to traditional engineering problems. His friction studies, discussed above, illustrate especially the new use of experiment in engineering research.

Monographs that define a polarity in eighteenth-century physical sciences—rational mechanics versus natural philosophy—give insufficient basis for explaining the later development of the fields of heat, light, electricity, magnetism, and crystallography into the theoretical and experimental physics of the early nineteenth century. These did not emerge merely because analysis was joined to experiment. Perhaps *physique expérimentale* gave the curiosity, engineering the reality, and rational analysis the harmony that characterize physics.

I believe that these elements distinguish the development of Coulomb's career as well. It is natural then, both conceptually and chronologically, to consider Coulomb's turn away from engineering toward physics. Chapters v and vi will examine this transition.

Five · TORSION STUDIES

Introduction

In this chapter we shall consider Coulomb's work in torsion and its applications to mechanics. He presented his first researches in torsion in the memoir which shared first prize in the Academy of Science contest of 1777.[1] Following this he returned to his engineering duties and subsequently wrote memoirs on friction and the design of windmills. He returned to torsion studies after his election to the Academy in 1781 and read his major torsion memoir, "Theoretical and Experimental Investigations of the Force of Torsion and of Elasticity in Metal Wires,"[2] in 1784. He utilized these studies and his torsion balance later in his famous memoirs in electricity and magnetism and in lesser-known studies in fluid resistance.

The evolution of Coulomb's torsion studies from 1776 makes a fascinating story in the history of physics. As in the case of his friction studies, these investigations were initiated in response to a prize offered by the Paris Academy of Sciences. The adoption of his prize-winning method by the Paris Observatory and the Observatory's subsequent request for a solution to seemingly unresolvable problems with magnetic declination instruments caused Coulomb to undertake a series of experiments on torsion.

His major memoir on the theory of torsion, presented in 1784, emerged from this latter investigation. This in turn provided him with a means to investigate and determine quantitatively the force relationships in varied physical fields—electricity and magnetism, fluid resistance, and the elastic properties of matter.

The torsion balance and the theory of torsion aided Coulomb in constructing theories concerning the molecular interaction within fluids and solids and, as is widely known, provided the foundation for his work in electricity and magnetism. His torsion work in the early 1780s marked the turn in his career from engineering mechanics to physics. He never attacked the general problems of elasticity, but his simple, elegant solution to the problem of torsion in cylinders and his use of the torsion balance in physical applications were important to numerous physicists in succeeding years.

Coulomb's Introduction to Torsion: The 1777 Magnetism Contest

Coulomb's work in torsion and in magnetism began with his memoir "Investigations of the Best Method of Making Magnetic Needles"[3] submitted for the prize that the Paris Academy of Sciences had offered for 1777. Thus, as with his 1781 prize memoir on friction, Coulomb's interest was kindled or at least brought forth by the Academy's choice of a prize contest. In both of these contests the Academy offered the prize twice, and in both contests Coulomb entered on the second round and won. In 1773 the Academy announced that it would award a prize in 1775 for the question: "What is the best manner of constructing magnetic needles, of suspending them, of making sure that they are in the true magnetic meridian, and finally, of accounting for their regular diurnal variations."[4] No winner was chosen in 1775[a] and the contest was set again for 1777. Nine memoirs were submitted for this second round.[5] Some of these were trivial entries, but two stood out as excellent. The award was divided; Jan Hendrik Van Swinden and Coulomb were each awarded 1,600 *livres* as their share of the first prize. A Monsieur de Magny was given an honorable mention. Magny, an instrument maker, did not actually submit a memoir, but he received 800 *livres* for the entry of one of his magnetic compasses.

Van Swinden's entry for 1777 was an immense work of over 500 pages. This memoir, "Investigations of Magnetic Needles and of Their Regular Variations,"[6] summarized his considerable magnetic researches and included tables of over 40,000 observations of the diurnal magnetic variations. In spite of its bulk, Van Swinden's memoir offered no striking advance over current theory or design of magnetic compasses. It included a historical summary of observations of diurnal variation, comparisons of Van Swinden's own data with those of other workers, and considerable criticism of previous designs of pivot-supported magnetic compasses. It was an

[a] Van Swinden received an honorable mention but no money for his 1775 entry.

entry that obviously represented several years' hard work—a grand summary of the orthodox method of magnetic observations that corrected numerous small faults in compass design. In no way, however, was Van Swinden's work a major innovation in the science of magnetism.

Coulomb's entry was of moderate length and did not overly impress whoever wrote the summary of the contest that was entered in the introduction to the eight volume of the *Savans étrangers.*[7] The merit of Coulomb's work was recognized by those who were deeply concerned with the science of magnetism: the members of the Academy's prize committee and the men concerned with the development and use of magnetic compasses for science and navigation. The memoir discussed the current theories of magnetism and outlined and presented new methods of constructing both the traditional pivot-supported and the new thread-suspended magnetic compasses. The importance of this 1777 memoir for Coulomb's later work in electricity and magnetism will be discussed in Chapter VI. We will be concerned here mainly with his study of torsion.

In Chapter III of this memoir Coulomb developed the theory of torsion in thin silk and hair threads and the use of these in the suspension of magnetic needles. Here, he was the first to show how the torsion suspension could provide physicists with a method of accurately measuring extremely small forces, undisturbed by the effects of friction and air resistance.

There existed a tradition of careful experimental work with magnetic compasses that is best exemplified in the work of Musschenbroek. By analogy with the simple pendulum, Musschenbroek conducted experiments with the oscillation of compass needles.[8] The needle would be deflected, and then the resulting oscillations would be timed until complete damping occurred. In this way the relative strengths of various needles were compared. The thread-suspended compass is mentioned in the literature at least as early as 1686,[9] but this was never connected with the theory of torsion. Experiments were designed mainly to eliminate friction between the needle and its pivot. Difficulties in designing a practical suspended compass kept development work on the track of improving the traditional pivot-supported device. For example, though he knew of the early attempts at thread suspension, Van Swinden wrote that there were two methods of building regular compasses. The first involved a plane-surfaced needle which was made to rest carefully on a sharp-edged pivot. The second method was similar to the first except that a hole was drilled in the center of the needle so that it might rest more securely on a pointed pivot. Van Swinden said that even though this latter method of support was very poor, it was "almost universally adopted."[10]

The chief problems to be overcome in magnetic compass design were pivot friction, the general mechanical instability of the whole device, and the overall geometrical design of the needle itself.

There were excellent practical reasons for the Academy to announce a contest for the design of a magnetic compass. Condorcet, Borda, Le Roy, Le Monnier, and Bossut composed the 1775 (and 1777) Academy prize committee.[11] Of this group, Borda, Le Roy, and Le Monnier were directly concerned with the design and improvement of compasses. The main goals for the designer of marine compasses were to increase the magnetic strength of a given needle and to achieve a mounting design that would give good stability under shipboard motion. The requirements for terrestrial compasses used in scientific measurements included powerful needles and stable bases, but the major requirement was of another order. It was known that the earth's magnetic field suffered perturbations of a higher order and shorter period than the quasi steady-state changes over the years. Magnetic storms, accompanied by auroral displays, often produced wild, short-period fluctuations. In addition there seemed to be small diurnal and seasonal variations. Le Monnier, Père Cotte, and others had attempted for years to measure these, but their results were confusing. The force produced in the diurnal variation was so small that it was below the magnitude or of the same order as the force needed to overcome the friction of the compass pivot. There was no way to measure these small frictional effects and therefore no way to compute the smallest magnetic forces. Besides this, the frictional effects seemed to be erratic. A microscopic change in the positioning of the needle on the pivot would drastically change the observed fluctuations.

Until Coulomb's design was adopted in 1780, the Paris Observatory used Le Monnier's traditional pivot-supported needles for its magnetic observations.[12] Similar pivot-supported instruments were in use in other European observatories. Needless to say, there was no real standardization possible between a needle in London, for example, and one in Paris.

The Magnetic Torsion Balance

Coulomb's torsion suspension method changed the whole future of magnetic field measurement and brought forth possibilites for utilizing the torsion balance in the measurement of numerous other small-scale forces. His 1777 prize memoir discussed all the problems of compass design: air resistance, pivot friction, compass needle geometry, but the heart of his paper was the introduction of the magnetic torsion balance.

Coulomb first proved that there was negligible effect of the torsion in a silk thread or hair, and that this could be neglected, compared to the magnetic force tending to orient a compass needle in the field. Next he investigated these very small torsion forces and showed that through any moderate angle a deflected needle caused the torsion pendulum to oscillate in simple harmonic motion.[b] He examined the parameters relating the angle of twist to the length, diameter and elastic properties of the thread. The elasticity of the thread resulted in simple harmonic motion of the needle or cylinder attached to the end. Given this, Coulomb showed that the force of torsion was then proportional to the angle through which the thread was twisted.

He further experimented with threads (silk and hair) of different sizes and lengths and determined that the law of torsion in a thin cylindrical thread was[13]

$$M = \frac{\mu B D^3}{l}$$

where M = the torque (*momentum de la force de torsion*), μ = a constant coefficient depending on the material of the thread, B = the angle of twist, and D and l = diameter and length of the thread, respectively.

Coulomb was not absolutely certain of the D^3 parameter of the torsion equation, "because the difficulty of measuring the diameter of a hair or very fine silk thread and of assuring that it is homogeneous all along its length produced variations in the results."[14] In spite of this he proposed the hypothesis that the torsion was pro-

[b] Development of the equations of torsion will be presented later in this chapter. Within limits, I have retained Coulomb's original notation for the calculations of torsion and fluid resistance. I have done so to facilitate the reader's use of the original memoirs. Thus, I have used B and not ϕ for the angle, etc.

portional to the third power of the thread diameter. This was in error, and Coulomb corrected it in his 1784 torsion memoir. In the 1777 prize memoir he only indicated the use of his torsion balance for the investigation of fluid resistance problems but did not elaborate on this because, due to the requirements of the Academy contest, "the work has no relation to this Memoir."[15]

He wrote this memoir in 1776 while engaged in military engineering tasks at La Hougue, near Cherbourg. He built the first model of his magnetic compass himself and used it to make measurements of the diurnal magnetic variation in declination during five months—from March through July 1776. Coulomb's first model was not so elegant as he would have desired, for there were no instrument makers in La Hougue. As he said, "In the time when I worked on my Memoir . . . I found absolutely no help there."[16] Nevertheless, he was so confident of the potential of his new method as to state that his torsion balance made possible a precision "that one could never hope for using capped needles suspended upon pivots."[17]

The first magnetic compass using the principle of the torsion balance as constructed by Coulomb in 1776 is shown in Figure v.1.[18] Using his notation in Figure v.1, *AB* is a vertical shaft about 20 inches high. This shaft encloses and supports the silk torsion thread *CG*. The top of the enclosure *ALKQPMA* is covered with glass so that one may observe the interior. For this first balance Coulomb employed a magnetized steel bar 10 inches in length by 3½ *lignes* (about 1/4 inch) in width, weighing 250 grains. The bar was fitted with a small copper counterweight at one end and a very thin copper pointer at the other. Above the pointed end of the magnetic needle Coulomb installed a small magnifying lens. To simplify the balancing in this first model Coulomb joined the silk suspension thread to the magnetic needle at two points (*g* and *h* in Fig. v.1). A finely divided scale placed under the eyepiece at *K* completed this balance. It was relatively rigid; air currents within the device were eliminated. It could measure variation in magnetic declination to within a few minutes of arc.

Coulomb took magnetic measurements several times daily for five months to prove the device. He found the greatest declination to occur near 1 P.M. each day. This decreased until about 7 P.M. then remained steady throughout the night. From 8 A.M. it rapidly increased until the 1 P.M. maximum. The amplitude of variation was usually from 8 to 12 minutes of arc, though some variations

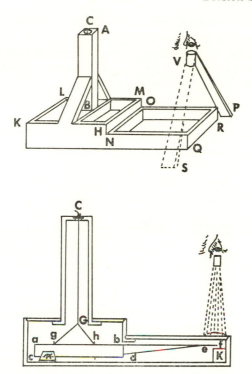

Fɪɢ. V.1. Artist's representation of Coulomb's first magnetic torsion balance, constructed in 1776

reached as much as 61 minutes. There was a clear correlation with auroral disturbances.[19]

Based on this limited data Coulomb offered a hypothesis for the diurnal variation. Others had suspected the sun to be the cause of the earth's diurnal magnetic variations. The heat of the sun was supposed to reduce the terrestrial magnetic field in the same way that the heating of a magnet was known to destroy its magnetism. Coulomb agreed that the sun was responsible but *not* the heat of the sun. If the mechanism were one of loss of terrestrial magnetism due to solar heat, then the earth's field should have been depleted long before. Rather, Coulomb saw the solar atmosphere as modulating the earth's magnetic field. The diurnal variations have an obvious correlation with the sun, he said, and "the sun acts on the terrestrial globe as a magnet acts on another magnet. . . . It is probable that the same cause which sustains the earth's magnetism produces the movements of magnetic material, seen in the declinations and in the annual and diurnal variations."[20]

Thus was the first torsion balance presented in Coulomb's prize memoir of 1777. The memoir was of moderate length but solved problems of the traditional pivot-supported compasses, provided a theory for the terrestrial diurnal magnetic variations, and most importantly, introduced a new instrument for precise, quantitative measurement—the torsion balance. Though the contest called only for the development of a better magnetic compass, Coulomb more than hinted at some of the applications of the torsion balance: the study of the elasticity and rigidity of materials, and its use to measure small magnetic forces and forces of fluid resistance. In his later memoirs Coulomb would extend considerably the applications of the torsion balance to physics.

The Paris Observatory and Coulomb's Return to Torsion Studies

During the eighteenth century the various academic prize contests advanced many careers and stimulated much fundamental work in science. The 1777 magnetism contest was indeed important for its winners, Van Swinden and Coulomb.[c] It was important as well for the Paris Observatory and for magnetic measurements in general. After the magnetism contest Coulomb was able to secure the help of an artisan to construct an improved version of his magnetic balance.[21] Until this time the Paris Observatory had relied on the traditional pivot-supported needles for its magnetic observations. In August of 1780 Jean Dominique Cassini, the actual director of the Observatory,[d] abandoned the use of Le Monnier's compasses and introduced Coulomb's improved model of the magnetic torsion balance.[22]

Once in daily use, the instrument showed great potential but certain flaws became evident. Irregular vibrations troubled the measurements and the cause of these was not known for certain. To attempt to correct these flaws, Cassini conducted three series of experiments with Coulomb's balance from August 1780 until Sep-

[c] See Chapter II.

[d] Jean Dominique Cassini (1748–1845), known as Cassini IV, did not officially become director of the Observatory until the death of his father, César François Cassini de Thury (1714–1784), known as Cassini III. It seems, though, that he may have filled the role of director near the end of his father's life.

tember 1781.[23] The problems seemed to arise from vibrations set up by carriages passing in the street, from winds blowing into the Observatory buildings, and from convection currents set up within the instrument due to heating and cooling of the apparatus and the surrounding room. Once elected to the Academy and resident in Paris, Coulomb could actively consult with Cassini on the improvement of the magnetic torsion balance.

In the spring of 1782 Coulomb suggested that two needles of the same weight and shape but magnetized to different strengths could be operated simultaneously.[24] In this way perhaps the effect of air resistance could be isolated. On March 18, 1782 two identical needles (twelve inches in length by about one-half inch in width) were installed at the Observatory.[25] One was magnetized to one-tenth the value of the other. These were placed in sealed enclosures, and the measurements were recommenced.

Coulomb suspected that the observations would never be successful on the main floor of the Observatory and that the equipment would have to be moved to the basement.[e]

Coulomb's suspicions proved correct. The measurements taken from March 18 until May 12, 1782 showed very irregular results, especially on the feebly magnetized needle. He decided that the needles would have to be moved into the basement where the temperature remained constant to within a fraction of a degree[f] and where street vibrations and wind currents were negligible. Cassini had commented that slamming the Observatory doors often had no effect on the motion of the needles. However, when he or his assistants touched the microscope eyepiece the needles always moved. This was the crucial clue for Coulomb:

> The cause can only be electricity in different portions of the atmosphere; electricity which varies perhaps, in a noticeable manner, for each cubic foot of air in the observation room. This electricity should differ in each portion of the air, according to

[e] Since there were 172 steps down to the basement it was decided to save Cassini the work of constantly descending and ascending by continuing the measurements for another few weeks on the ground floor. If the experiment persisted in failure, then "since Monsieur de Cassini has several intelligent assistants at the Observatory, he could spare himself the fatigue of climbing up and down several times each day."[26]

[f] The "basement" of the Paris Observatory was a well-known laboratory far underground, utilized for studies where constant temperature was necessary. Lavoisier, for example, visited there on July 7, 1783 in connection with some work in thermometry.[27]

the nature of the bodies between which air was able to rub in its movements. Moreover, this air, charged with electricity, communicates more or less electricity to the different bodies against which it passes according to whether they are more or less conductive.[28]

Thus it was the electrical isolation of the needle that was at the base of the problems of irregularity. Perhaps moving the balances to the basement would eliminate the problem of static induction, for: "It is probable that the considerable humidity of the basement destroys the electricity of the air; or, at least as far as the air currents are unable to penetrate, the degree of electricity must be everywhere uniform."[29]

For this method to succeed, Coulomb instructed Cassini and his assistants to remain for some time in the basement before making the magnetic measurements so that any static charge on their bodies would be discharged onto the damp floor and surroundings. He asked Cassini to move the instruments to the basement and to conduct the measurements there for five or six days. If this didn't work, he said, then the base and footings of the instrument would probably have to be fashioned out of a conducting material (copper) instead of wood.[30]

Again, the experiments went without success. Regardless of the precautions taken, the needles always moved at the approach of the investigator toward the balance.[31]

One might ask why Coulomb did not simply replace the insulating silk torsion thread with one of silver or brass. This would be an easy way to allow the induced charge to leak off the magnetic needle. It would certainly be a simpler operation than moving the whole apparatus to the basement, hermetically sealing it, and constructing the base and foundation out of copper. And if Coulomb had been mistaken and the street vibrations and convection currents had not been major problems after all, then one would suppose that substituting the metal torsion thread would have been the obvious solution. Coulomb had a very good reason for delaying the use of a metal thread; it might require too much torque to twist it, or it might not follow the laws of simple harmonic motion —torsion proportional to the angle of twist.

He indicated his hesitation in a note to Cassini written at the end of May 1782:

These thoughts lead us to propose trying suspension by means of a metal wire, which does not insulate the needle and which serves as a conductor in continuously discharging the electricity, although the torsion force of this kind of suspension would be much more considerable than that of silk threads. Considering that the torsion angle is null when the needle is located almost on its magnetic meridian, it is probable that this force would influence the variation very little; which is easy[g] to calculate. It is necessary, moreover, to give to this suspension wire the greatest possible length. If this metal wire does not succeed, we will come back to the silk thread.[32]

How beautifully this last passage shows us the state of Coulomb's thought on the matter of torsion! He really did not know whether his torsion law would hold for metals. He said that if the needle were very close to the magnetic meridian, then the wire would suffer practically no torsion at all: *in this case* the torsion force would not amount to much. Note how he sought further to reduce the probable torsion force by stating that the wire should be chosen to be as long as possible. And finally he left open the possibility of returning to the silk threads.

Clearly there was a break here in his conception of torsion in hairs or silk threads and torsion in other materials. It was not just a matter of the magnitude of the torsion force necessary to twist the metal threads through a certain angle, for he already knew that he could not obtain a metal thread with the small torsional rigidity of a silk thread. Hoping to keep the magnetic needle very close to the magnetic meridian position of equilibrium implied also the fear that perhaps the linear region for torsion in metals might be very small.

There are no more letters from Coulomb referring to Cassini's compasses. Some solution must have been found for Cassini continued testing the magnetic torsion balance throughout 1783, and in August one of Coulomb's magnetic compasses was sent to Père Cotte's observatory at Laone. From archival notes it appears though that the metal-threaded torsion balance was unsuccessful at this time.[33] Either the thread was too rigid to enable measurement of magnetic declination forces or perhaps Coulomb encountered

[g] It is interesting to note that Coulomb wrote first "very easy to calculate" and then crossed out the word "very."

the "imperfection" of elasticity that he describes in his 1784 torsion memoir. In any case it was from this theoretical and experimental challenge that Coulomb resumed his work. During the next two years he worked with the problems of torsional elasticity and extended the applications of the torsion balance to the measurement of forces of electricity and fluid resistance. Evidently, both the wire and silk-thread suspensions eventually proved satisfactory, for both were in use during Thomas Bugge's visit to the Observatory in 1798.[h]

The Torsion Memoir of 1784

PRELIMINARIES. Coulomb returned to torsion studies seeking not only to extend the experimental data to different materials but also to grapple with torsion as a problem within the theory of elasticity. On September 4, 1784, "M. Coulomb presented some experiments on the torsion force of brass wires" to the Paris Academy.[35] This was the first presentation of his complete memoir, "Theoretical and Experimental Investigations of the Force of Torsion and of the Elasticity of Metal Wires."[36] Coulomb sought to do two things in this memoir: 1) to discover the laws of torsion and to determine possible applications of them and 2) to investigate the laws of cohesion and elasticity of bodies by means of torsion. This program may be stated in another way, and Coulomb did so in Section IV of the memoir. His study is effectively in two regions of the torsion spectrum—the linear and the nonlinear. Within the first he proposed to determine the linear relationship of force to torsion and to advance practical applications of this phenomenon for use in measuring various types of small forces. In the second, nonlinear, region he proposed to investigate the mechanism of torsion itself "in order to determine the laws of cohesion and elasticity in metals and in all solid bodies."[37]

Of all his studies in physics and engineering, Coulomb's work

[h] On October 31, 1798 the Danish Astronomer Royal, Thomas Bugge, visited the Paris Observatory and viewed two thread suspension declination compasses. One, having a needle 24 inches in length, was suspended by a small wire and was described as "Coulomb's instrument." The other, having a needle 10 inches in length, was described as "Cassini's instrument . . . suspended by a silk filament, after the method of Coulomb."[34] Observation of the magnetic variation using the two instruments produced readings differing only by 15 seconds of arc (declination of 22° 12′ versus 22° 11′ 45″).

in torsion is perhaps most revealing of his scientific method; in the 1784 memoir one can finally understand his concern with the properties of matter. In the broad sense he participated in the articulation of the Newtonian theory. This is obvious in his extension of the inverse square law to forces in static electricity and magnetism. There were other areas, however, where (Newtonian) rational mechanics either ignored physics or treated it in an idealized manner. One of these areas was the constitution of forces in physical interaction. Coulomb approached this in his work on friction.[1] He studied the resistance to rolling and sliding in bodies and determined friction coefficients for these phenomena. But this resistance seemed to admit of another parameter in addition to friction—that of cohesion. Cohesion did not trouble Coulomb experimentally, for it always seemed to account for less than five percent of the total resistance, and in general his friction theory accorded well with experimental results. Theoretically, however, he was not able to understand cohesion. He finally came to grips with it in his work on torsion. He saw torsion both as an elastic *intra*molecular and as an inelastic *inter*molecular phenomenon. This is why he divided his study of torsion into two parts, linear and nonlinear, and why he saw the relevance of the first sort of investigation to the study of external forces and the second sort to the study of matter on the molecular level.

His work draws on both the traditions of the established eighteenth-century rational mechanics and the emergent experimental physics: Newton, Euler, and especially Daniel Bernoulli in the first instance; and Musschenbroek, 'sGravesande, and the better practitioners of *physique expérimentale* in the second. In an indirect, though very important, way Coulomb brought his engineering thoughts and experiences to bear on his work concerning torsion. His theory of stress rupture in soil mechanics and in compression of masonry piers will be shown as related to his theory of molecular slippage in nonlinear torsion phenonema.

Framing his work in the terms of rational mechanics, Coulomb drew upon his engineering experience and upon the best tradition of *physique expérimentale* to enter into a study of torsion. Perhaps this synthesis is an example of what Biot[38] meant when he said that it was to Borda and Coulomb that one owed the renaissance of exact physics in France.

[1] See Chapters III and IV.

PART I: THE LAWS. Coulomb's method for determining the force of torsion consisted in suspending a weight from a thread. When the thread was twisted and released the torsion reaction caused the thread to oscillate as it untwisted through the equilibrium point and then twisted in the other direction. Coulomb found that within a very wide range the torsion device oscillated in simple harmonic motion—that is, with constant period.[39]

If the metal suspension thread were perfectly elastic and if the torsion device operated in a vacuum, then the oscillations would continue undamped. Coulomb supposed that damping in the torsion balance was due to these two factors: the "imperfection" of elasticity, and air resistance. If air resistance was accounted for, then alterations in the elastic torsion force could be determined.[40]

Expressed in modern notation, Coulomb established that the torque of the equation of torsion is equal to $L = n\Theta$, where n is a constant and Θ is the angle of torsion. He also showed that the equation of motion is equivalent to $I \dfrac{d\Theta}{dt^2} = - n\Theta$, where I is the moment of inertia of the body.

In his 1784 torsion memoir and in his subsequent studies using the torsion balance Coulomb presented the analysis of the mechanics of the torsion reaction as follows:

Given a torsion balance as illustrated in Fig. v.2,[41] let the cylinder B be turned through angle $ACM = A$. After time t let this torsion angle A be reduced by the amount $MCm = S$ to the resultant ACm. Therefore,[42]

(1) $ACM - MCm = ACm = (A - S)$.

Preliminary experiments showed that the torsion balance oscillates with constant period. Therefore one can suppose the torque proportional to the torsion angle. The torque ("moment of the force") will then be

(2) $n(A - S)$

where n = a constant coefficient depending on the length, thickness and material of the wire under torsion. Let v equal the velocity of any mass point p^j at radius r from the center of the cylindrical disk suspended from the torsion balance in Fig. v.2. At time t,

---

[j] Note in Fig. v.2 that Coulomb's notation for the mass point is π rather than p. I have changed this to allow π to have its modern connotation.

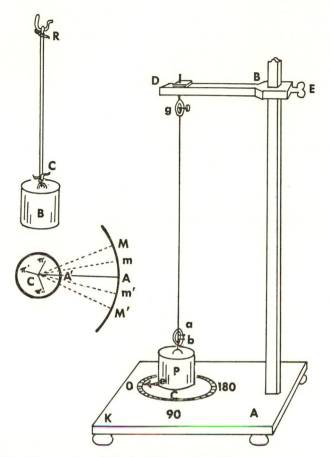

FIG. V.2. Illustration of Coulomb's torsion balance

when the torsion angle is $ACm = (A - S)$, one has, equating the angular momentum,[k]

(3) $$n(A - S)dt = \int p \, r \, dv.$$

Now, let $CA' = a$ equal the radius of the disk, and let the velocity of a point A' on the edge of the disk at time t be u. Then, $v = \dfrac{r u}{a}$, and

[k] In modern notation this is equivalent to $\int_m r \, dm \, dv$, where v (or Coulomb's dv) is a function of the mass points dm.

(4)
$$n(A - S)dt = du \int \frac{p\,r^2}{a}.$$

Now, $\dfrac{ds}{dt} = \dfrac{u}{a}$. Combining this with Equation (4) and integrating with respect to S gives

(5)
$$n(2AS - S^2) = \frac{u^2}{a^2} \int p\,r^2.$$

Coulomb then solved for dt and obtained

(6)
$$dt = ds \sqrt{\frac{\int p\,r^2}{n(2AS - S^2)}} = \frac{ds}{\sqrt{2AS - S^2}} \left(\frac{\int p\,r^2}{n} \right)^{\frac{1}{2}}.$$

Now the function $\dfrac{ds}{\sqrt{2AS - S^2}}$ is equal to 0 when $S = 0$; it is equal

to $\dfrac{\pi}{2}$ when $S = 2A$. Coulomb employs the French definition of the period equal to π radians (that is, equal to one-half the English period). Expressed in this way the period will be:

(7)
$$T = \pi \sqrt{\frac{\int p\,r^2}{n}}.$$

Coulomb wrote this as
$$T = \left(\frac{\int p\,r^2}{n} \right)^{\frac{1}{2}} 180°.$$

Coulomb then compared this period with the period of a simple pendulum where, if λ equals the pendulum length and g equals the gravity constant,[43]

(8)
$$T = \pi \sqrt{\frac{\lambda}{g}}.$$

For the case of a cylindrical disk as illustrated in Fig. v.2, the moment of inertia is equal to $\dfrac{M\,a^2}{2}$, where M equals the mass of the disk and a the radius. In this case the period equals[44]

(9)
$$T = \pi \sqrt{\frac{M\,a^2}{2n}}.$$

Therefore, Coulomb's constant n (dependent on the geometry and properties of the wire under torsion), may be determined experimentally from Equation (9). Coulomb ascertained it using his torsion balance. For these tests he used iron (harpsichord strings) and brass wires.[45] He related fully the details of each experiment and gave all dimensions, angles, and time measurements. Unlike many earlier reports of physical experiments, Coulomb's presentation would enable one to repeat the same procedures.

Since the experimental data showed the oscillations to be isochronous through a very wide range of angles, Coulomb was justified in assuming the correctness of Equation (9). In his experiments he sought to determine the effect of the length and diameter of the torsion thread and the tension imposed on it by the load. Varying tensile loads were found to have little or no effect on the torsion period. From this Coulomb concluded: "Finally, that the tension, of greater or lesser amount, does not sensibly influence the torsion reaction force."[1,46]

After determining that the tensile load has only a higher-order effect on the period of the torsion balance, he examined the effect of the length of the torsion wire. His experiments showed that the period of oscillation varied as the square root of the length of the wire. Therefore, the torsion varied inversely as the length of the suspending wire. Similarly, he determined the effect of the diameter of the suspending wire and found the torsion to be proportional to the fourth power of the wire diameter.[48]

Combining these above relations and including a constant coefficient μ, "which depends on the natural rigidity of each metal,"[49] Coulomb obtained the following general equation for the torsion reaction torque, or, as he termed it, *momentum de la force de torsion*:[50]

(10)[m]   "General result": $M = \dfrac{\mu B D^4}{l}$

[1] Coulomb noted, however, that under great tensile loads the force of torsion decreased a little. He ascribed this to a slight stretching and therefore decrease in the diameter of the thread. As Truesdell shows,[47] this is not sufficient as an explanation. Coulomb has observed an effect of nonlinear elasticity related to the Poynting effect.

[m] Coulomb obtained a numerical value for n for a given iron wire. Potier[51] notes that one may use this to obtain numerical values for Coulomb's rigidity coefficient μ (the Lamé coefficient of rigidity). For iron, Coulomb's data give $\mu = 7.63 \times 10^{11}$ dynes/centimeter^2 which compares to the accepted value[52] for wrought iron of 7.5 to 8.0 x 10[11]. For brass, however, Coulomb's data give a value for μ of 2.78×10^{11} dynes/centimeter^2; somewhat lower than the accepted value of 3.53 x 10[11].[53]

where again, M = the torque (*momentum de la force de torsion*), μ = a constant rigidity coefficient, B = the angle of torsion, and D and l = the wire diameter and length, respectively.

One will note that Coulomb has now corrected the error he made in his memoir of 1777. There he stated that the torsion equation was proportional to the third power of the thread diameter. In the correct equation as given in his 1784 memoir, the torque is seen as proportional to the fourth power of the diameter. In his earlier memoir he spoke of the difficulty of accurately measuring the diameter of the thread. He didn't mention the method used in his 1777 memoir to determine the thread diameter. However, from the descriptive data given in Section XIII of the 1784 memoir it seems that he obtained values for the average thread diameter by weighing long lengths of the thread and then calculating the diameter from that. In 1784 he accounted theoretically for the D^4 relationship in the following way:[54]

1. For two wires of the same material and length, in the wire of double diameter the cross-section ratios will go as D^2. ("There are four times as many parts under torsional strain.")
2. The mean extension of the wire particles will be proportional to the wire diameter D.
3. The lever arm of the couple relative to the axis of rotation will be proportional to D.

Summing up these three factors, Coulomb explained the D^4 relationship.

At the conclusion of the first part of his 1784 torsion memoir Coulomb compared the torsional rigidity of his iron and brass wire samples and found this to be[55]

$$\frac{\text{Rigidity of brass}}{\text{Rigidity of iron}} = 3.34.$$

Using Musschenbroek's data[56] for the ratio of the specific weights of iron and copper (77/83), Coulomb noted that the ratio is close enough to one so that the ratio of the torsional rigidity of iron to brass or copper must be about 3 1/3:1. This seemed to puzzle him, for he noted immediately that the behavior of metals under torsion is not the same as the response to tensile loads. Thus, for iron and brass wires of similar dimensions, the iron wire was found to rupture under 1.7 times the load needed to cause tensile rupture in the brass wire. Here Coulomb perceived that the elastic torsion reaction in metals differs from the inelastic region near rupture. At this point he could not draw general conclusions from this because he knew that hardening (*écrouissement*) and annealing (*recuit*) change the physical response of metals. The continuation of this investigation forms the second part of his 1784 memoir.

In the final sections of the first part Coulomb discussed several practical applications of the torsion balance. He described several experiments in fluid resistance and presented the experimental apparatus necessary for these tests but concluded that further studies must be undertaken.[n,57]

Additionally Coulomb noted that after the reading of the text of this memoir at the Academy he had constructed balances for studies in electricity and magnetism. "But, as these two instruments (as far as the results which they have given relative to electrical and magnetic laws), will be described in the following Volumes of our *Mémoires*, I believe that it suffices here to announce them."[58] The principle of the "electric balance" and "magnetic balance" is the same as those discussed in this chapter.

A further examination of Coulomb's use of the torsion balance in electricity and magnetism will appear in Chapter VI.

PART II: THE THEORY. Once Coulomb established his "general result," that the torsion reaction torque equals $\dfrac{\mu BD^4}{l}$, he turned to the study of the mechanical properties of materials.[59] Working with his brass and iron wires, he found their elastic limits (that beyond which permanent set occurs). This limit could be raised by working or twisting the material, thus hardening it. This could be changed by annealing (heating and then cooling slowly to avoid brittleness), and thus the limit could be lowered. Though the elastic limit could be changed, Coulomb found that the elasticity itself remained the same.

This indicated to him that cohesion and elasticity were different things. By definition, elasticity implies a perfect return to prior material conditions once a distorting force is removed. Above a certain angle in torsion, however, a thin cylinder, for example, either becomes noticeably inelastic or undergoes a shift in the range of elastic behavior (permanent set). Here Coulomb gave the theory that intramolecular strains are elastically restored up to a

---

[n] Coulomb continued his fluid-resistance studies in his 1800 fluids memoir, discussed below.

certain limit. Beyond this, the stresses become enough to break the intermolecular cohesive bonds; then the material fractures or flows along molecular planes. After strain beyond the elastic limit but below rupture, the material is rearranged, but the intramolecular elasticity remains the same.[60]

Hamilton remarks that Coulomb's theory of torsion "must be regarded as a brilliant suggestion rather than as a legitimate deduction from Coulomb's limited experiments."[61]

I believe that his theory was not only a "brilliant suggestion" but that it was created from a wider base of experimentation than the 1784 investigations alone would indicate. Coulomb's first attempts to describe cohesion occur in his 1773 memoir on statics, and Timoshenko[62] regards this as one of the more important papers of the eighteenth century. That work, however, was concerned with macromechanics, and Coulomb offered no theory for molecular behavior. His torsion theory as presented in the 1784 memoir was successful from a contemporary standpoint as it arose from his general studies in engineering mechanics in the 1770s. The torsion work stood at the focus of his experience in engineering and his work in the physics of materials.

From his studies of rupture in beams, soil banks, and masonry piers, Coulomb realized that beyond a certain point, stress was revealed in strain and resultant rupture often in a planar or quasi-planar section through the material. Fibrous materials such as wood could extend or compress, but the hard particulate structure of metals and stone admitted only of rupture. Coulomb's experiments on "Bordeaux stone" led him to believe that the values of tensile and shear rupture were nearly the same.[o,63] This indicated that metals and stone were probably composed of hard, homogeneous, globular particles. The results of friction tests upon wood and upon metals lent weight to this same hypothesis.

A strict rational mechanical solution to problems in friction and strength of materials did not fully account for the observed phenomena, but the discrepancies, especially with friction, were minor. They were explained by possible surface roughnesses, surface film, or by cohesion—possibly forces acting inversely as some high power of the distance—therefore, perceptible only over microscopic intervals. Desaguliers and others had championed this cause of cohesion in their studies of friction, but this was not a fruitful

---

o He based this conclusion, however, on very limited experimental data. See Chapter III.

area in which to investigate it. For Coulomb as for many others, cohesion was a "passive" force. Beyond a certain limit, *any* material subjected to stress would rupture due to exceeding the cohesive force limit.

For the first time, he could clearly see and deal with cohesion in his torsion work. Here, as in none of his previous studies, Coulomb saw two rather clearly defined forces. One could characterize a material by a coefficient of the elastic properties of the materials (μ) and by the limit of elasticity. These were different because the latter could be changed by quenching, annealing, or work-hardening. This is why Coulomb said: "It is clear that, in order to have an idea of what occurs in the flexion of metals, one must distinguish the elastic force of the individual particles (*parties inté-grantes*) from the force of adherence which mutually unites them. . . . What we have just explained for the case of metals seems to be applicable to all bodies. . . ."[64] Cohesion was seen as a constant quantity for a given molecular arrangement.[65] In the first portion of the torsion region, the elasticity is almost perfect. As Coulomb thought of it, the integral particles (*molécules intégrantes*) change shape under stress[66] without relative change of place. But when the force of torsion is equal to or above the force of cohesion, then the molecules must separate or slide over one another. Through a certain range, the sliding increases the area of mutual contact between the molecules, and, therefore, the range of elasticity is increased. Coulomb posited that, within limits, the molecules have a definite shape, and, thus, there is a maximum possible area of contact between the sides of the molecules. Beyond this point, the sliding stops and outright rupture occurs.[67] The author has attempted to present a pictorial interpretation of Coulomb's theory in Fig. v.3.

Another of his experiments seemed to confirm his theory. He magnetized an iron wire and measured it with the torsion balance. He then took the same wire, twisted it to the point of rupture, and again magnetized it. After measurement, it was found to exert nine times as much magnetic force as the wire in the untwisted state. Coulomb interpreted this as indicating that the fields of each magnetic molecule were less canceled in the state of maximum contact between molecules.[68]

Finally, to test his theory in metals deformed other than by torsion, Coulomb experimented with rectangular steel bars and obtained similar results. As with the torsion wires, bars with different

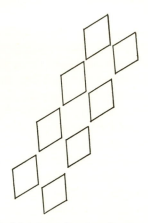

(1) Metal molecules in normal state

(2) Metal molecules in state of elastic *intra*molecular strain

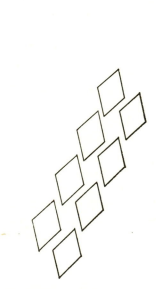

(3) Metal molecules in imperfectly elastic state of *inter*molecular strain, approaching the limit of cohesion—with sliding

(4) Metal molecules in state of strain greater than limit of cohesion—showing resultant rupture

FIG. V.3. The author's conception of Coulomb's torsion theory

heat-treatment[p] showed varying elastic limits but no change in the elastic rigidity constant (μ) of the material.

I believe that with torsion Coulomb first encountered a relatively "clean" experimental situation. He was able to eliminate or account for the perturbing factors that complicated other eighteenth-century materials experiments: air resistance, friction, non-homogeneity of the materials investigated, contaminated surfaces, and the difficulty of precise force measurements. With torsion, he could clearly see two forces at work, one perfectly elastic, the other inelastic. It is not just that he stumbled upon an easy experimental situation; his method of carefully separating all parameters finally paid off. It can be seen that his inelastic region of permanent set involves a supposed increase in the surface area of contact between molecules. I think Coulomb posited this for two reasons. First, influenced by his theories of soil mechanics and crushing of piers, he saw permanent set as an intermolecular sliding. If, as he believed, cohesion was a positive force acting between bodies, then the molecules would tend to increase their areas of contact. Second, Desaguliers and others had attributed friction phenomena to a cohesion effect proportional to the surface area of the materials in contact. Similarly, Coulomb attributed the range of permanent set to this sliding or realignment because it gave him definite points for the start of permanent set and of final rupture.

Coulomb's theory of the role of cohesion in elastic phenomena became important to others who succeeded him. In his *Traité analytique de la résistance des solides* . . . (1798), P. S. Girard spoke of Coulomb's "ingenious hypothesis of cohesion."[70] Eighty years after Coulomb's work Todhunter wrote: "The theoretical basis of the theory of elasticity and the strength of materials must be ultimately sought for in the law of molecular cohesion; the discovery of that law will revolutionize our subject as the discovery of gravitation revolutionized physical astronomy."[71]

No one in the eighteenth century attempted to form general equations for the motion or equilibrium of elastic solids. The real foundations of the theory of elastic mechanics occurred with the early nineteenth-century French mathematicians and physicists— Navier, Poisson, and Cauchy.[72] I make no claim for Coulomb's work in torsion as founding modern elasticity theory. His prob-

[p] "One of these bars had been tempered very rigid, the second had been brought to the consistency of an excellent spring, and the third had been annealed at white heat and cooled slowly."[69]

lems were simple and elegant, and, as Timoshenko shows,[73] his solutions were rigorous. One might ask, then, why Coulomb limited himself mainly to the investigation of torsion in thin cylinders. Perhaps Truesdell[74] is correct in positing that Coulomb was clever enough to realize the limits of his own mathematical talents. Probably, having explained the physics of torsion, he preferred to exploit the potentialities of the torsion balance in areas of physics in which he had previously shown interest.

However limited Coulomb's torsion studies, they were known to physicists in the generation following. Prony, Girard, Biot, Savart, and others[q] cited him. Poisson[76] extended Coulomb's torsion studies just as he progressed from Coulomb's work in magnetism. Perhaps most interesting for the development of science is the case of Thomas Young. Young first came to know Coulomb's work through studying the mechanics of the circulation of the blood. This led him to the memoir on the use of the torsion balance for fluid resistance studies. Subsequently, Young was responsible for much of the presentation of Coulomb's work in England. He summarized nineteen of his memoirs in his biographical sketch of Coulomb written for the *Encyclopædia Britannica*. Young was inspired by Coulomb's work in several areas of mechanics, and this is shown in his *Course of Lectures on Natural Philosophy* (1807).[77]

"Invention" of the Torsion Balance

Given the state of various secondary accounts of the invention of the torsion balance, it would be worthwhile here to discuss Coulomb's role in this episode. The *idea* of suspending a magnetic needle from a thread was by no means original with him. Previous investigators, however, had merely constructed a new sort of toy or had used the suspended thread only in a qualitative way. It was known that a fine thread or hair was very "flexible" and could support relatively large stresses. In 1686 Lana[78] mentioned supporting a compass needle by a thread. Lous[79] experimented with this in 1773. Musschenbroek talked of it, but all of his quantitative experiments of timing needle oscillations seem to have been with pivot-supported compasses. In 1778 Le Monnier[80] mentioned in an offhand way that Coulomb's idea wasn't new, that a naval officer (possibly Borda) had told him of some experiments on this

[q] Todhunter[75] cites many who were influenced by Coulomb, including Duleau, C. J. Hill, Avogadro, and Ignace Guilio.

in 1776. Le Monnier wrote of this after Coulomb's 1777 magnetism prize essay and it is possible that he was a little jealous of Coulomb's success with an idea that Le Monnier termed, after the fact, "so natural." Remember that Coulomb's magnetic torsion compasses were to replace Le Monnier's equipment at the Paris Observatory.[81]

It is quite possible that Borda did do something with the suspension thread needle. As a physicist and naval captain with encyclopedic interests, he was concerned with the development of marine compasses. Borda must have done very little though, for he never wrote about this nor does his biographer mention it.[82] An entrant in the 1777 magnetism contest submitted a thread-suspension compass; Monsieur de Magny was awarded an honorable mention for a complicated suspension needle supported by four threads.[83]

One is not at all surprised that a number of individuals were involved in some aspects of the early history of torsion devices. One is even less surprised that Coulomb's ideas in torsion were considered "so natural." Practically every problem that Coulomb considered had existed as just that—a problem—usually ill-defined and always misunderstood.[r] These predecessors were in a position very similar to that of Robert Hooke with respect to the Newtonian theory of gravity. It is to Coulomb's credit, absolutely, that he made all of these problems a part of exact physics, fitting them into the heart of the discipline, and suggesting new areas of investigation.

There is one more instance of a pretender to the title of inventor of the torsion balance. John Michell[84] published an 81-page pamphlet entitled *Treatise of Artificial Magnets* at Cambridge in 1750. This had a second English edition in 1751 and a French translation was contained in Père Rivoire's[85] *Traités sur les aimans artificiels*, published in 1752. In none of these editions nor in any of his articles in the *Philosophical Transactions* did Michell mention torsion.[s]

In spite of this, Wolf,[87] Hoppe,[88] Jammer,[89] Geikie,[90] and Whittaker[91] claim that Michell invented the torsion balance. Jammer[92] even cites a year (1768) but gives no references whatsoever. It is

[r] In Chapter VI one will see that I. B. Cohen and others list several investigators who speculated on the inverse square law with respect to electricity or magnetism.

[s] Clifford A. Truesdell, a scholar impeccable in his quotation of sources, concurs in this.[86]

possible that Michell did no more with this idea than had Lana, Lous, Musschenbroek, Magny, Borda, or any other before Coulomb. Michell was interested in questions of geology and in measuring the earth's density, and it was in this connection that Michell's balance was first mentioned by Henry Cavendish in 1798, in the *Philosophical Transactions*:

> Many years ago, the Rev. John Michell . . . contrived a method of determining the density of the Earth . . . but, as he was engaged in other pursuits, he did not complete the apparatus till a short time before his death, and did not live to make any experiments with it.
>
> Mr. Coulomb has, in a variety of cases, used a contrivance of this kind for trying small attractions; but Mr. Michell informed me of his intention of making this experiment, and of the method he intended to use, before the publication of any of Mr. Coulomb's experiments."[93]

Michell died in 1793. F.J.W. Wollaston obtained the device after his death and subsequently gave it to Cavendish. It is impossible to know what Cavendish, writing in 1798, meant by "many years ago," but it is clear that a "short" time before Michell's death would not be before 1776 (i.e., the date when Coulomb constructed his first torsion balance). Cavendish said that Michell informed him of his plans before Coulomb published on the torsion balance. This does not claim anything except that Michell may have spoken to Cavendish about the torsion balance before 1780, the year in which Coulomb's 1777 magnetism essay was published.

None of this *proves* that Michell invented the torsion balance nor that it was even built by him before Coulomb had published articles describing the use of this device. An obituary of Coulomb appeared in the *Journal de l'Empire* the week after his death. Commenting on his character, the author said: "Throughout his life, M. Coulomb was always modest, unaffected and kind. He never experienced the torment of envy; never did he stand in the way of anyone. An Englishman seized his idea for the suspension of needles, and he never deigned to complain. It was M. de Lalande [probably referring to Lalande's speech at Coulomb's funeral], who reclaimed his rights."[94] In his first remark on torsion (1777) Coulomb wrote: "We cannot cite here the experiments of any author,"[95] and in Barré de St. Venant's estimate, "torsion was . . . treated for the first time by Coulomb, with his usual superiority."[96]

The search for the moment of invention is usually not significant for the history of science[t] nor is the event often confined to a moment in time. The main point here is that Michell's experiments (if any were undertaken) and public knowledge of his ideas occurred long after Coulomb's balance was known. Musschenbroek, Magny, Borda, and the others conceived the thread-suspension method as a means of obtaining some comparison of forces by eliminating the inefficiency of the measuring instrument. They meant to eliminate pivot friction, not to attempt a study of the force laws of torsion. These various approaches centered the suspension device in the position of minimum torsion on the thread and, then, *assuming the torsion reaction could be neglected*, measured forces producing very small angle deviation. For Michell, there was no question of studying torsion in the nonlinear region of strain. Those who used a suspension device for magnetic measurements ignored torsion altogether. Essentially, they were seeking to allow a magnetic needle to align itself exactly with a given vector magnetic field. Their desire was to construct a device that could be considered frictionless, thus, the suspension method seemed to allow a needle to align itself with the smallest of magnetic fields. Without a knowledge of the laws of torsion, however, there could be no precise measurement of the strength of those fields.

Coulomb went far beyond this. In his 1777 essay, he employed a silk suspension thread because its relative friction and torsion reactions were negligible but he realized the use of the torsion principle in measuring forces of cohesion, fluid resistance, and electricity and magnetism. The full development of the torsion laws came in his 1784 memoir. The applications to measurement would occupy the rest of his life.

Applications of Torsion: Fluid Resistance

Coulomb had been interested in the question of complex forces in the interaction of bodies since the writing of his first memoir in 1773. There, the attempt to define and measure cohesion as different from friction caused him difficulty. In his 1777 magnetism prize essay, he was again faced with a type of retarding force due to several factors: the "imperfection" of elasticity and the friction and cohesion of the air. In his 1781 prize memoir on friction, he ex-

[t] See a discussion of this in Chapter VI of T. S. Kuhn's book, *The Structure of Scientific Revolutions*.[97]

plained most of the resistance to sliding and rolling of bodies as being due to a coefficient of friction, primarily dependent on the total weight acting on the friction surfaces. Another parameter dependent on the surface area of the interacting bodies was attributed to a surface film or to cohesion. None of these memoirs concerned cohesion as the central problem. He never ignored it, but it must have bothered him as an element that was never really elucidated. He finally began to explain this in his work in torsion, at least he was able to account for some of the ways cohesion reveals itself in physical phenomena. His suggestion that there were intramolecular elastic forces and intermolecular (cohesive) inelastic forces provided him with a plausible theory of stress-strain behavior in elastic and inelastic materials. In a way his work in fluid resistance was an extension of this. Coulomb's experimentation with the torsion balance applied to fluid studies resulted in a theory that partially explained the various parameters—velocity, molecular inertia, internal friction—in problems of fluid resistance. As a corollary to the study of fluid resistance with the torsion balance, Coulomb demonstrated[98] a simple way to determine experimentally the moment of inertia of any body.

His mathematical approach to the solution of these problems was familiar in rational mechanics. It was relatively new, however, to problems in physics and engineering.[u] Briefly, the method was to investigate a function in terms of a series—seeking to evaluate constant coefficients for each term of the series. Thus, in investigating the function of velocity as a parameter in some physical phenomenon, Coulomb would construct an equation of the form

$$F = K + Av + Bv^2 + Cv^3 + \ldots$$

Today this is a familiar approach to many problems in physics (the induction field versus the radiation field in an electromagnetic wave, etc.). In problems relatively free of complicating mechanisms, for example the force laws of gravity and of electrostatics, the eighteenth-century investigator usually phrased the question as "Does the force law vary as the inverse square power *or* the inverse cube?" That is, in certain problems it was assumed that a particular physical phenomenon was primarily a function of one or another

[u] The author has not determined the first applied use of this approach. It was probably taught at Mézières, for both Coulomb and Lazare Carnot utilized it in their memoirs submitted to the Paris Academy's friction contest. The most obvious source is Newton, in Book II of the *Principia*; Coulomb cites this frequently.

power of a given parameter. In problems concerning the resistance of fluids, however, it was recognized that either the resistance varied as a function of the velocity in more than one way or else that experimental difficulties prevented the determination of the true relationship.

Though Mariotte[99] and others had studied fluid resistance, the first major work on these problems was presented by Newton in the second book of the *Principia*.[100] Coulomb worked from Newton's studies as well as from the later works of Daniel Bernoulli,[101] 'sGravesande,[102] and Bossut.[103] He did not mention the memoirs of Borda[104] and Du Buat[105] but was undoubtedly familiar with their work. All of these previous studies had examined some part of the fluid resistance to solids, but none had examined all permutations of this: high viscosity or low viscosity fluids, high or low velocity flow, fluid in motion with solid body stationary (or vice versa), the effect of surface irregularities or of depth within the fluid. The results of these major eighteenth-century investigations of various fluid resistance parameters are presented in Table v.1. There it is seen that nearly all investigators found the resistance to fluid flow to be a function of the second power or approximately the second power of the velocity. Depending on circumstances, the resistance seemed also to be a function of other powers of the velocity or perhaps of a constant factor.

Coulomb had touched on the problem of fluid resistance in earlier papers. He mentioned the use of the torsion apparatus to study the resistance of air in his 1777 magnetism essay. In the 1784 torsion memoir, he described the use of his "balance for measuring the friction of fluids against solids."[106] In general he found that with very small velocities the resistance was proportional to the first power of the velocity and with large velocities proportional to the second power. He performed only one series of experiments, however, and that was limited to water as the fluid. In hesitating to draw general conclusions from this he said: "These experiments require a special study, and one to be performed with different fluids."[107]

Coulomb returned to the study of fluid resistance after the French Revolution. The results of this later work were presented in a paper that he read to the Institute in 1800, "Experiments Designed to Determine the Coherence of Fluids and the Laws of Their Resistance to Very Slow Movements."[108] The object of this memoir was 1) to utilize an instrument that could determine precisely the

TABLE V.1

SUMMARY OF EIGHTEENTH-CENTURY RESULTS
FOR FLUID RESISTANCE AS A
FUNCTION OF VELOCITY

Author	*Law of fluid resistance with respect to velocity*	*Specific case*
Newton	$F \propto AV + A'v^{3/2} + Bv^2$	Body moving through fluid
Newton	$F \propto K + Bv^2$	Body moving through fluid at low velocity
D. Bernoulli	$F \propto K + Bv^2$	
'sGravesande	$F \propto Av + Bv^2$	Fluid in motion; body stationary
'sGravesande	$F \propto K + Bv^2$	Body in motion; fluid stationary
Borda (1763)	$F \propto Bv^2$	Body moving in air
Borda (1767)	$F \propto Bv^2$	Body moving in fluids
Bossut, d'Alembert, Concorcet	$F \propto Bv^2$	Or more accurately as $F \propto Bv^x$ where $x > 2$
Du Buat	$F \propto Bv^2$	Or more accurately as $F \propto Bv^x$ where $x < 2$

smallest forces and 2) to produce accurately controlled very low
velocities. For this project Coulomb chose the torsion balance. It
could reliably measure forces as small as 1.6×10^{-5} grains (9×10^{-4}
dynes)[109] and produce relatively stable velocities on the order of
a fraction of a millimeter per second.[110]

Coulomb stressed that his method of determining the resistance
of fluids was similar to that of Newton and others; it was the *means*
employed that were new. To illustrate this, Coulomb enumerated
the difficulties encountered in using common pendulums or linearly
towed test objects in fluid resistance studies. If one uses a simple
pendulum suspended by a wire, then the only possible bob configuration is that of a sphere. Any other type of symmetry would not
admit of a fixed position during oscillation. If one seeks to avoid
this by employing a rigid-rod (*verge*) support, the rod does not
remain at a constant depth of immersion and "the uncertainty in

the evaluation of the friction and the resistance of the support does not permit one to measure the small quantity that one wishes to determine."[111] The use of the simple pendulum is possible, in general, only if an exact figure can be obtained for the ratio of the specific weight of the bob relative to the fluid. The least error here will invalidate the result. Other approximations necessary to the employment of the simple pendulum operating in simple harmonic motion limit the amplitude of swing to a very small arc, but with motion in such a small arc the least air currents or motions within the fluid make this procedure difficult. Also, with either a wire- or rod-supported simple pendulum, the fluid inevitably flows more or less up the wire, producing additional resistance. Finally, the only practical means of obtaining a very long period of oscillation in the simple pendulum is to make the bob of the same specific weight as the fluid. In this case, however, it is difficult to ascertain that the center of gravity of the bob is the same as its geometrical center. The slightest error here results in the bob oscillating around its center of gravity in a nonplanar motion.

Experimentally, the situation is almost as difficult with the method of producing linear motion through a fluid. This could be done (as did Bossut et al.) by towing a raft or boat through a fluid. Here, however, the experimental situation is vastly complicated by the generation of bow waves and stern turbulence.

In contrast to the difficulties inherent in the use of the above methods, Coulomb almost delighted in counting the advantages of the torsion pendulum method.[112] First, the body may be entirely submerged if desired. Since each part of the body is oscillating in a horizontal plane, the ratio of the specific weights of the body and the fluid is of no importance. If the body is lighter than the fluid it can be weighted down, for example, by inserting a lead plug in the center. Second, by changing the parameters of the torsion balance (lengthening the wire, decreasing its diameter, or increasing the moment of inertia of the body), the oscillation period may be chosen so as to be as long as desired. In practice, Coulomb found that the most reliable periods were between 20 and 30 seconds with amplitudes from 8 to 480 degrees. Coulomb noted finally that the laboratory investigation of fluid resistance using the torsion balance is limited to low velocities. This is because in a tank of finite extent (as in Coulomb's small tank), the outwardly traveling waves caused by the motions of the body are reflected by the walls of the tank and produce turbulence upon return to the body. In these cases of higher velocity, Bossut's method of linear towing has the advantage.[113]

Before presenting his experimental results and conclusions, Coulomb analyzed the mechanics of the problem. *Assuming* that the fluid resistance is a function of the velocity in the form[114]

$$F \propto Av + Bv^2.$$

Coulomb analyzed the fluid torsion balance in the same manner as the ordinary torsion balance[115] (see above). He obtained an equation for the differential change in amplitude as follows:[116]

$$(1) \qquad \frac{dA}{A} = m + pA$$

where m and p = constants, A = the amplitude, and dA = the change in amplitude per oscillation. When the velocity is very low, the second power of the velocity can be neglected[v] and Equation (1) becomes

$$\frac{dA}{A} = m = \text{constant.}$$

This is equivalent to $\dfrac{A - A'}{A} = m$, or[118]

$$(2) \qquad A_q = A(1 - m)^q$$

where A = the amplitude at swing A, A' = the amplitude at swing $A + 1$, and A_q = the amplitude at swing $A + q$. If this holds, then,

$$(3) \qquad \frac{\log A - \log A_q}{q} = - \log(1 - m) = \text{constant.}[119]$$

Following this analysis Coulomb presented experimental results to show that Equation (3) is indeed constant.[120]

His experimental method was similar to that used in his torsion studies described earlier. An illustration of his balance to measure fluid resistances in fluids having low velocity is given in Fig. v.4.[121] Coulomb obtained numerous closely spaced experimental values for the constant m and from this showed that the resistance for water against a cylindrical copper disk moving at a velocity of

---

[v] Coulomb later found the inertia constant p to be less than 1/100th the value of the constant m, for very low velocities.[117]

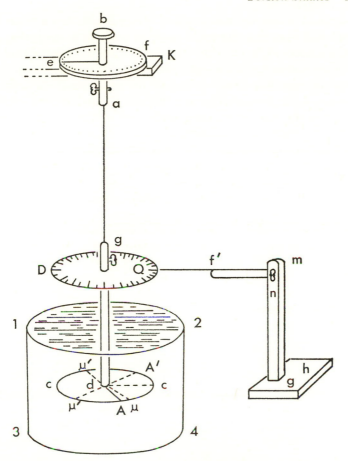

FIG. V.4. Coulomb's torsion balance for fluid resistance measurements

1 centimeter per second is equal to 0.703 grains (0.069 dynes/centimeter²).[122]

As a further investigation, Coulomb measured the relative "cohesion" of oil and water. He realized that oil viscosity changes markedly with temperature and thus conducted his experiments with oil in the region from 12° to 20° centigrade. Repeated trials always gave him a ratio of "cohesion" of oil to water as from 17:1 to 17.5:1.[w,123]

Previous studies[124] had indicated that perhaps surface roughness

---

[w] Although not strictly equivalent, the ratio of viscosities of common light oils to water at these temperatures range from about 50:1 to 1000:1.

or depth of immersion contributed to resistance between fluids and solids. Coulomb experimented with an iron disk measuring the fluid resistance with the iron suspended from his torsion balance. He then carefully coated the disk with wax and polished it. Tests with the wax-coated disk gave the same results as with the uncoated disk. He next sifted very fine grit through a sieve onto the surface of the wax-coated disk. Under test this procedure resulted in "a barely noticeable increase in the resistance."[125] From these last tests he drew this important conclusion: "It appears that one can conclude from this experiment that the portion of the resistance which we have found to be proportional to the simple speed is due to the mutual adhesion of the fluid molecules and not to the adherence of these molecules with the surface of the body."[126]

Coulomb would elaborate on the above statement later in this memoir. One should indicate, however, that here he is beginning to formulate his idea that there are two types of resistance in fluid-solid interactions: one due to the intermolecular condition of the fluid and the other due to the fluid in contact with the body.[x]

Benjamin Franklin and Bossut had posited that the fluid resistance to the motion of submerged bodies would vary in some way with the depth of immersion.[128] In testing this statement, Coulomb conducted fluid resistance tests with a disk submerged under water —2 centimeters at first, then 50. He could determine no difference in the resistance. Realizing that the addition of a pressure head of 50 centimeters of water was only a fraction of the atmospheric pressure, he decided to repeat the experiment in a vacuum. In the *cabinet* at the Institute, Coulomb and "citizen Lasuze"[y] measured the resistance to a copper disk rotating in water, the whole apparatus being enclosed within a *machine pneumatique* (vacuum chamber). A similar experiment using a small plane rotating perpendicularly to its surface was conducted by Coulomb and Jacques Charles in the latter's *cabinet de physique*. In neither case was Coulomb able to measure a difference between operation under atmospheric pressure and operation in a vacuum. From this, he concluded that the portion of the resistance to fluids under pressure proportional to the velocity was considerably less than the resistance due to friction, which was proportional to the normal force acting on the surfaces.[129]

[x] Dugas states, however, that "Coulomb was, before Stokes, the first to hold that the velocity of a viscous fluid relative to a solid was nothing at the surface of contact and that it then varied continuously in the fluid."[127]

[y] "Citizen Lasuze" is probably the academician Pierre Lassus (1741–1807).

Coulomb's tests with fluids of differing viscosities (oil and water) enabled him to distinguish two kinds of fluid resistance. When the same cylinder moved at the same velocity in oil and in water, the part of the resistance proportional to the second power of the velocity was almost the same. He saw this as due to something inherent in the fluids themselves and not in the fluid-body inter-action; due to the *quantity* of fluid molecules in motion and not their cohesion. This portion of the resistance, therefore, should be due to the inertia of the fluid molecules and proportional to the density of each fluid under test. If the immersed surface was con-sidered smooth, Coulomb distinguished then between the fluid re-sistance due to inertia alone and the resistance to internal friction within the liquid.[z,130]

Coulomb's Contribution to Fluid-Resistance Studies

Coulomb's fluids studies do not form a major part of the corpus of his work. They are, however, more than an illustration of the usefulness of his torsion balance. No doubt he was intrigued with the potential of this instrument (as where he says, "master of diminishing the speeds as much as I wish").[132] He saw these studies as more than an exercise in physical dexterity. The use of the torsion balance in fluid-resistance experiments offered a chance to investigate the nature of close-acting natural forces. After sur-veying the eighteenth-century work in fluid resistance, Coulomb posited a portion of this resistance to be a function of the first power of the velocity. This resistance was generally small as com-pared to the term proportional to the second power of the velocity. At low velocities (below a few millimeters per second), however, this latter resistance could dominate the portion due to the square of the velocity. Using his balance to conduct research towards this end, he determined resistances for fluid-solid interactions at low velocities and ratios of fluid resistance for bodies of differing vis-cosities.

He concluded that the relation of velocity to fluid resistance is of the form

$$F \propto K + Av + Bv^2.$$

The constant K was not conclusively determined by him, but he suspected it could appear only in fluids of very high viscosity. The

---

[z] Though Coulomb is correct in his distinction here, Potier[131] notes that his substantiation of this is not strictly accurate.

discovery of resistance proportional to the first power of the velocity led Coulomb to state that there must be two kinds of fluid resistance. One, dependent on the velocity, is due to the cohesion of the fluid. The other, dependent on the square of the velocity, is due to the simple inertia of the fluid molecules. These facts were not enough for the construction of a larger theory, and he planned further research in fluid-resistance problems.[133] He intended to determine quantitatively the values of fluid resistance dependent on the square of the velocity and to extend the whole series of researches into bodies of varying geometrical shape. Coulomb died before completing this work. Beyond his published memoirs, there are a few pages of notes on research concerning fluid resistance in his manuscript notebooks.[134] These few pages are undated and very difficult to decipher, but they are included with some magnetic researches he did about 1805.[aa]

[aa] References by Delambre[135] and Biot[136] indicate that some of Coulomb's papers have been lost. Perhaps further studies of fluid resistance are among these missing manuscripts; perhaps the position of inspector general of public instruction occupied most of Coulomb's time during the last four years of his life.

Six · COULOMB'S WORK IN ELECTRICITY AND MAGNETISM

Introduction

Charles Augustin Coulomb is best remembered for his researches in electricity and magnetism. The purpose of this chapter is to examine this work: his memoir that won the Academy's 1777 magnetism contest, the famous series of seven electricity and magnetism memoirs read at the Academy from 1785 to 1791, and several magnetism memoirs prepared after the Revolution. In his electrical studies, Coulomb determined the quantitative force law for electrostatics, gave the notion of electrical mass, and studied charge leakage and the surface distribution of charge on conducting bodies. In magnetism, he determined the quantitative force law, introduced the idea of the demagnetizing field, and created a theory of magnetism due to molecular polarization.

If this essay seems not to dwell on the labors of Franklin and other predecessors,[a] it is because there was a real break here indicating the emergence of a portion of physics from natural philosophy. In a sense, this break was initiated by Franz Aepinus' *Tentamen theoriae electricitatis et magnetismi.*[3]

Coulomb admired both Aepinus' efforts at subjecting the phenomenon of magnetism to analysis and Musschenbroek's experimental ability and inquisitive faculties. In the memoirs discussed here, Coulomb mentions few other men. I believe there are two reasons for the relative lack of author citations in Coulomb's physics researches. First, his work is tightly organized about the quantitative determination of the laws regarding force relationships, charge distributions, and spatial structure in electric and magnetic phenomena. In this work there was little from which to cite others. Of course, in the broadest sense, Coulomb attempted to extend

[a] For a history of this earlier period the reader is directed to Daujat, and to Cohen.[1] For analyses of Coulomb's work see Bauer, and Sharp.[2]

the Newtonian conception of attractive and repulsive forces to the physics of electricity and magnetism.

Second, Coulomb cited few predecessors because, I believe, he wanted to divorce his studies from the mass of traditional matter relating to electricity and magnetism. His generation may well represent the "knee" of the curve in the emergence of the empirical physical disciplines, for Coulomb is much closer to Biot and Poisson than to Franklin or Nollet. Coulomb knew Franklin and cooperated with him at the Academy of Sciences, yet he cited him only once in his memoirs.[4] This generational break is also indicated, for example, in the composition of the committee chosen in 1787 to report on Haüy's epitome of Aepinus' work.[5] It was Coulomb,[b] Laplace, Legendre, and Cousin who were directed to report. In the same way, it was the *géomètre-physicien* Laplace[6] and not the traditional natural philosopher who was excited by Coulomb's work. Such traditionalists as Sigaud de la Fond[7] (still talking of Franklin, Canton, and Nollet) belonged now to a different time.

Coulomb's concern was to establish electricity and magnetism on the basis of attractive and repulsive forces and to determine quantitative relations answering to their effects. The argument, for him, was not over a one- or two-fluid system. He said that either system could answer to the mathematics and that both theories at best have only a certain degree of probability.[8] Whatever became of the fluid theories, it was not Coulomb's intent to place this question at the center of his investigations.

From the following examination of his studies, I hope to show how it was that he led electricity and magnetism into physics. I will discuss his electrical and then his magnetic researches. As a prelude to both, however, it will be necessary to examine his 1777 magnetism memoir.

The 1777 Magnetism Memoir

Coulomb began his magnetism studies in 1775 when he was stationed at La Hogue, near Cherbourg. In the early months of 1776, he constructed a magnetic compass utilizing a torsion suspension, conducted measurements of the diurnal variation of the terrestrial magnetic declination, and then submitted these results in a memoir to the Academy of Sciences as an entry in the contest for 1777.

[b] Coulomb left for a tour of English hospitals soon after being named to the committee and was unable to join in the report.

"Investigations of the Best Method of Making Magnetic Needles,"[9] shared the first prize.

A large part of this paper was devoted to the design and testing of compasses. At the beginning, however, he attempted to refute the view that magnetism was somehow due to vortex motions. These neo-Cartesian views had gained acceptance due to an earlier Academy contest, in 1746, on the theory of magnetism. The three winning entries[10]—of Leonhard Euler, Daniel and Jean (II) Bernoulli, and Etienne François du Tour—had strengthened the idea that vortices entered magnetic materials at one end and exited at the other. The presence of pores in magnetic matter thus allowed the vortices to enter and exit easily. The alignment of magnets along a field line was attributed to the vortices pushing against the pores or channels in the magnet. Nonmagnetic matter either had no such pores, or they were constructed so as to prevent the passage of the vortices.

Coulomb wanted both to destroy the notions of vortices and to establish the Newtonian idea of attractive and repulsive forces. With this in mind he stated two fundamental principles:

FIRST FUNDAMENTAL PRINCIPLE.
    If, after having suspended a needle by its center of gravity, one moves it away from the direction that it takes naturally, it is always brought back by forces which act parallel to this direction and which are different for different points along the needle, but which are the same for each of these points in particular, in whichever direction the needle is placed in relation to its natural direction; so that a magnetized needle always experiences the same action, in any position, due to the magnetic forces of the Earth.

SECOND FUNDAMENTAL PRINCIPLE.
    The magnetic forces of the terrestrial globe that attract the different points of a compass needle act in two opposite ways. The north part of the needle is attracted towards the north pole of the magnetic meridian. The south part of the needle is attracted in the opposite direction. Whatever may be the law according to which these forces act, the sum of the forces which attract the needle towards the north pole is exactly equal to the sum of the forces which attract the south pole of the needle in the opposite direction.[11]

The first principle is a statement that the earth's magnetic field can be considered constant for a given spatial position.[c] The second principle states that the terrestrial magnetic forces acting on a magnet are equal and opposite, or as Coulomb developed it, that they reduce to a couple[d] proportional to the sine of the angle between the position of the magnet and the magnetic meridian. As his proofs for the first principle, Coulomb assumed that magnetic forces are attractive or repulsive in nature and that, therefore, the centers of the magnetic forces in the earth (the poles) may be considered as being at an infinite distance from the magnet so that the field lines can be considered parallel and rectilinear. He cited Musschenbroek's earlier experiments[12] on the oscillations of magnetic needles to show that the forces are proportional to the sine of the angle between the needle and the magnetic meridian. He conducted a modified version of this experiment himself, to ascertain further the correctness of the principle.[13]

As proof for the second principle, Coulomb presented Musschenbroek's results[14] that a magnet weighs the same both before and after magnetization. Thus, by principles of static mechanics, the forces remain in equilibrium. Coulomb also floated a small magnetic needle on a piece of cork. He observed that though the cork would turn to align the needle with the meridian, it underwent no movement in translation. Thus, he said, the austral and boreal forces must be the same, otherwise the needle and cork would have had other than a movement of rotation. Finally, he mounted a magnetic needle on a pivot at the end of a light wooden bar which was in turn mounted on a pivot at its center. The needle was found to align itself with the meridian without disturbing the position of the wooden bar. It must be admitted that all of the above "proofs" are rather crude and that Coulomb was really supporting the second principle mostly on faith in the system of attractive forces. He would return to these proofs later in his Seventh Memoir, on magnetism.

Based on the above two principles, Coulomb then offered a corollary:[15]

One can, it seems to me, conclude that the direction of a magnetized needle cannot depend on a torrent of fluid which, moving

[c] Coulomb is concerned here only with the steady-state main field component.

[d] Couple: two equal and opposite forces whose lines of action are parallel but not congruent.

rapidly along the magnetic meridian, forces the needle, by its impulsion, to direct itself along this meridian . . . one must necessarily resort to attractive and repulsive forces of the nature of those which one is obliged to make use of in order to explain the weight of bodies and celestial physics.

He assumed that any vortex torrents of fluid would follow laws analogous to those of known fluids; therefore, the impulsions of the fluids should act differently depending on the angle of the magnet with the fluid. But since the forces act equally on a needle in any position, this negated the vortex theory. In addition, some imagined that there were two vortex fluids entering the magnet from opposite ends. Since from Coulomb's second principle the forces acting upon the needle are equal and opposite, the vortex theory would require currents or torrents acting equally in opposite directions without suffering mutual destruction. This, said Coulomb, also negated the vortex theory.[16]

Thus his introduction to his memoir, by attacking the vortex theories, showed that a neo-Cartesianism was still evident in hypotheses —at least in magnetism. Coulomb was a careful writer and he rarely put something into a memoir without good reason. He would base all of his subsequent studies on this affirmation of the Newtonian principles of attractive and repulsive forces.

Following the two "fundamental principles" outlined in the introduction, Coulomb developed the mathematical analysis of the motion of magnets oscillating on pivots.[17] He compared the isochronous motions to those of a simple pendulum and obtained an equation expressing the magnetic momentum of an oscillating needle in terms of its physical dimensions:[18]

$$Ql = \frac{Pl^2}{3\lambda}.$$

That is, a weight Q acting at a lever arm l would have the same momentum as a magnetic needle of weight P, length l, with λ as a function of the horizontal component of the earth's field and of the pole-strength of the magnet. Coulomb then proceeded to determine the momentum law for magnets (relative to parameters of length, width, and thickness), in terms of the time of oscillation of the needle.[19] From numerous experimental studies he obtained the general formula[20]

$$T = (n\,L^{1/2}E + ml)$$

where T is the time of one oscillation through 180°,[e] and l, L, and E, respectively, represent the length, width, and thickness of the needle. The constants of the particular magnetic material are n and M.

Discussing the implications of his general formula, Coulomb stated that due to the demagnetizing effect of adjacent parts of a magnet, the best shape for magnetic needles would be long, thin parallelopipeds. This demagnetizing effect was also observed in tests with magnets composed of bundles of magnetized wires. The ratio of the total magnetic momentum to the number of component wires in the bundle was found to vary as less than the first power.[21]

The 1777 contest did not call for the development of a theory of magnetism, and Coulomb's statement of a molecular theory did not emerge until he read his Seventh Memoir on electricity and magnetism in 1791. In this earliest (1777) memoir, however, Coulomb questioned both prevailing theories of magnetism[22]—the two-fluid system of Brugman and Wilcke and the one-fluid system of Aepinus. Brugman, Wilcke, and others assumed that magnetic material in a neutral state contained equal amounts of two elastic fluids in equilibrium. In the magnetized state, the two fluids were separated into different parts of the magnet, and the particles or portions of each fluid attracted the opposite fluid and repulsed the fluid of the same nature. Aepinus, adopting Franklin's one-fluid system of electricity to magnetism, imagined that there was only a single fluid and that upon magnetization all or nearly all of it went to one end of the magnet, leaving the other end with a deficit. In Aepinus' theory the parts of the fluid were mutually repulsive but had an attractive force for matter. In this hypothesis the parts of matter itself were then required to be mutually repulsive.

Coulomb considered both of these theories to be in contradiction to the observations of magnetic phenomena. In the first place, he opposed the assumption of the one-fluid theory that particles of matter and magnetic fluid were repulsive among themselves yet had an attraction for each other.[23] He also criticized another assumption in both theories. If, upon magnetization, the fluids are removed to one or both ends of a magnet, then upon cutting the magnet into pieces, those parts in the middle should not be magnetizable. This Coulomb found contrary to observation, but trying to work within the confines of the existing theories, he suggested that perhaps only

e Note that in the French system used by Coulomb, the period of an oscillation is defined as π radians or 180°, rather than 360°.

a very small portion of the fluid was transferred. If this were so, then the other portions of the magnet might still have enough fluid to indicate magnetism after separation.[24] This macroscopic theory did not satisfy him, however, and there is evidence that he began thinking in molecular terms long before his Seventh Memoir for he said in the 1777 essay: "Each point of a magnet or of a magnetized bar can be regarded as the pole of a tiny magnet. . . ."[25]

It is clear that the 1777 magnetism contest memoir was important in Coulomb's career because the outlines of several of his further researches—torsion, fluid resistance, magnetism—are contained there. It is equally clear why he seemed to drop the study of magnetism after writing this first memoir. As an engineer in the *Corps du génie*, he had neither the opportunity nor the time for further study. One can not be sure, of course, that the engineering duty absolutely prevented further research. However this may have been, he was very desirous of obtaining a permanent post in Paris where he would be near the Academy of Sciences. After he obtained this in the autumn of 1781, his studies again turned to research in physics.

In Chapter v, I indicated that Jean Dominique Cassini had several examples of Coulomb's suspension-thread compass built for use at the Paris Observatory. When Coulomb was transferred to Paris, Cassini asked him to aid in modifying and improving the compass. It was in grappling with these problems that Coulomb returned both to the study of magnetism and of torsion. This renewed work resulted in his major torsion memoir,[26] read to the Academy in September 1784, and in the adaptation of the torsion balance to the study of force relationships in electricity, magnetism, and fluid resistance. From this he proceeded to his seven memoirs in electricity and magnetism.[f,27]

Most secondary sources present this great series as having been delivered in succession from 1785 to 1789. The actual situation was different. Coulomb realized what he wanted to do with the torsion balance, but his execution of the series of experiments and his development of the analysis came at irregular intervals. In addition to reading the seven electricity and magnetism memoirs, he presented several minor papers on magnetizing compass needles,[28] constructing electrometers,[29] calculating the magnetic meridian,[30] and developing improved models of his magnetic declination com-

---

f Coulomb himself named these his "seven" memoirs in electricity and magnetism, and they will be referred to as this below.

pass.[31] These papers were developed from secondary issues that result from any major research project.

Evidence indicates that Coulomb struggled with the seven memoirs, for his thoughts and direction change occasionally from one memoir to the other. He had certainly tried his torsion balance in electrical, magnetic, and fluid-resistance experiments by the beginning of 1785, but his memoirs were to be much more than a casual reporting of experimental data. A glance at the seven memoirs shows that only the Seventh (1791)[g] and part of the Second (1787) are concerned with magnetism while all the rest are devoted entirely to electricity. I cannot explain why he attacked the problems of electricity first, except that the phenomenon of magnetism was conceptually more difficult. That he did not neglect magnetism is shown by the minor magnetism papers he read from 1780 to 1787. The electricity memoirs presented many problems too. With the exception of the Second and Third Memoirs, there is an average interval of thirteen months between his presentation of each. In the First (1785), he presented the details of his electric torsion balance and proved the inverse square law of forces for repulsive electric charges. In the Second (1787), he extended these investigations to the proof of the inverse square laws for electricity and magnetism for both repulsive and attractive forces. In the Third (1787), he examined the losses due to leakage of electric charge. In the Fourth (1787), Fifth (1788), and Sixth (1790), he investigated the distribution of charge on conducting bodies. In the following sections I shall analyze these memoirs and discuss the evolution of Coulomb's research in electricity and magnetism.

Coulomb's First and Second Memoirs in Electricity and Magnetism: The Determination of the Force Laws

Coulomb opened the presentation of his First Memoir by recalling his work in torsion. He then described in detail the adaptation of the torsion balance to studies in electricity. He would later introduce further modifications in his balances, but the one described here[32] will serve well to illustrate the method of his experiments (see Fig. VI.1).[33] The balance is constructed on a cylinder of glass,

[g] The dates given in parentheses for the seven electricity and magnetism memoirs are the actual occasions when Coulomb first read each memoir at the Academy. For the citation of each memoir in the Academy's manuscript minutes, see Appendix A.

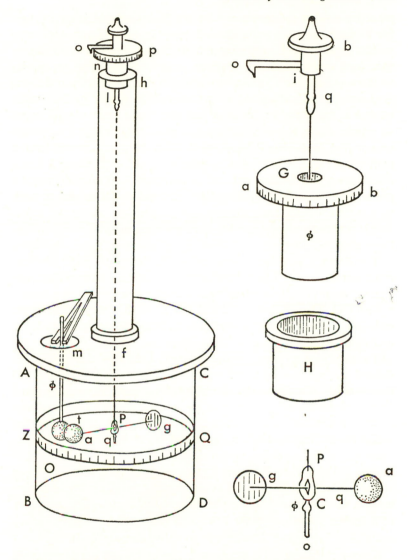

FIG. VI.1. Coulomb's torsion balance for electrical studies

ABCD, 12 inches in diameter by 12 inches high. This cylinder is covered by a glass plate having two holes 20 *lignes*[h] in diameter, one hole in the center, at *f*, and the other near the circumference, at *m*. In the center of the cover plate, at *f*, Coulomb cemented vertically a tube 24 inches in length. In the top of the tube he

[h] Recall that the *ligne* is equal to approximately one-twelfth of an inch.

placed a torsion micrometer. This contained several parts, including a circumferential scale divided into degrees, a knob with scale pointer, and a chuck or pincer to hold the torsion wire. The torsion wire used was either silver, copper, or silk. At the lower extremity of the torsion wire, Coulomb attached a thin metal pincer 1 *ligne* in diameter and suspended it vertically. This pincer had to weigh enough to keep the torsion wire taut and thus linear, yet not cause so much tensile stress that the torsion wire ruptured. The pincer held a thin, horizontally suspended straw or a silk thread coated with sealing wax. A tiny, gilded, elderwood pith-ball, about 2 *lignes* in diameter, was fixed at one end of the straw, and a small, vertical paper plane was fixed at the other. The paper plane served both as a counterweight and to damp out oscillations. A second scale, *ZOQ*, marked in degrees, was attached around the outside of the large glass cylinder.

The balance was then employed in the following way. The micrometer at the top was turned until the horizontal thread *ag* containing the pith-ball, lined up with the zero degree marking on the scale *ZOQ*. Then a thin, insulated rod *mt* with a second, identical pith-ball *t*, mounted at the end was inserted through the hole *m*, and made to touch the pith-ball *a*, mounted on *ag*.[i]

To introduce a charge to the balance, Coulomb charged an insulated pin by use of a Leyden jar or an electrostatic machine. He next touched the pin to the two pith-balls. These, having the same charge, were found to separate by a certain distance. Coulomb noted the separation in degrees on the lower scale *ZOQ*, and the initial micrometer setting on the upper scale. He then twisted the micrometer dial to different settings and noted the resultant separations of the pith-balls. In his 1784 torsion memoir, Coulomb had already calculated the torque necessary to turn the particular wire used in this balance. For the wire used here, and with a lever arm of 4 inches, a force of only $1/40,800$ grains (12.8×10^{-4} dynes) sufficed to turn the balance through three degrees.[j,34]

Two factors must be accounted for in measuring large-angle separation of the pith-balls. The first consideration is that the force between the balls goes not as the arc in degrees but as the chord

---

[i] It is clear from later passages that Coulomb neutralized both pith-balls by grounding them before beginning the experiment.

[j] Coulomb found that various errors made the balance unsuitable for use at less than about two or three degrees of separation.

of the arc. Also, the lever arm upon which the pith-ball *a* acts is not one-half the length of the horizontal support but actually the cosine of the half-angle between the balls. For a pith-ball separation of less than about 30°, however, Coulomb noted[35] that these two considerations tended to cancel and that the forces can be calculated simply from the torsion separation in degrees. In this First Memoir, he tabulated the results of three representative experiments to determine the force law for repulsive electric charges (see Table VI.1).[36]

TABLE VI.1

DETERMINATION OF THE FORCE LAW
FOR REPULSIVE CHARGES

Experiment	*#1*	*#2*	*#3*
Separation of pith-balls	36°	18°	8.5°
Micrometer setting	0°	126°	567°
Total torsion angle (equal to the sum of above)	36°	144°	575.5°

A study of Table VI.1 will show that the difference in torsion goes very closely as the inverse square power of the distance between the two pith-balls. From this Coulomb stated:[k,37]

Fundamental law of electricity.

The repulsive force between two small spheres electrified with the same type of electricity is inversely proportional to the square of the distance between the centers of the two spheres.

Here is his first partial statement of the inverse square law of forces. He noted that the presentation of only three readings was given merely as an example of the experimental method used, and he knew well that in this short memoir he had given evidence only for the force between *repulsive* charges. This memoir was published to establish the principles of investigation. There was good cause for Coulomb to withhold reporting further data and results for the force law for *attractive* charges. The major reason is that the force changes as the inverse square of the distance while the tor-

k Loi fondamental de l'électricité.
La force répulsive de deux petits globes électrisés de la même nature d'électricité est en raison inverse du carré de la distance du centre des deux globes.

sion changes as the simple distance. This presents a case of unstable equilibrium, and in most instances, the attractive pith-balls quickly come together, nullifying any results. Over a two-year period, from 1785 to 1787, Coulomb worked on this problem and sought to determine the force laws for magnetism as well. These experiments were conducted successfully, and in February 1787 Coulomb read his Second Memoir on electricity and magnetism.

In the Second Memoir, Coulomb noted that he had actually succeeded in utilizing the torsion balance to measure attractive forces but that because of the difficulties mentioned above "it is only after having failed at many attempts that one succeeds in preventing the mutually attractive balls from touching."[38] One method of measuring attractive forces consisted in placing an insulating plate between the balls to prevent their touching while the torsion micrometer was adjusted. This was not very satisfactory, however, for with small forces the "cohesion" of the pith-ball with the insulating plate masked the electrical forces, which "results in fumbling while a part of the electricity is lost."[39]

To ascertain the force law for attractive as well as repulsive charges, Coulomb returned to the method of timing oscillations that he had used in his 1777 magnetism memoir. Though this method is indirect and less simple, it presented fewer practical problems in the case of attractive forces. The applicability of the oscillation method rests on two assumptions: 1) that the electrical forces on a sphere act as if concentrated at a point in the center of the sphere, and 2) that the line of action between the two bodies is along the axis joining their centers, and that the electrical field lines are parallel and equal. The first assumption requires forces acting as the inverse square power of the distance, and the second assumption requires that the dimensions of the bodies be small compared to the distance between them.[1] If these conditions hold, the forces causing motion will be constant for a given distance and will act along the axis between the two body centers. Thus, the force, ϕ, will be proportional to the inverse square of the time of oscillation T, or[40]

$$\phi \propto \frac{1}{T^2}.$$

[1] In the experiments described here the least distance between the bodies was 9 inches whereas the diameter of the small body was only about ½ inch (7 *lignes*), or 6.5% of the distance between the bodies.

Similarly, if the inverse square law of forces is true, the time of oscillation T will be directly proportional to the distance d between the two bodies, or, if[41]

$$\phi \propto \frac{1}{d^2},$$

then

$$T \propto d.$$

To test this predicted relationship, Coulomb placed a large tin-plated globe several inches from a gilded paper disk attached to a shellac-thread needle which was suspended horizontally from a silk thread. After charging the large globe, he grounded the small disk and thereby induced a charge on it opposite to that of the globe. He then set the suspended needle and disk into motion and measured the oscillation frequency for various given distances between the centers of the globe and the disk. As an example of the procedure, he presented the results of three readings (see Table VI.2[42]) and corrected these for charge leakage. These data show that the time T varies very closely as the distance of separation d. This indicates, then, that the force is proportional to the inverse square of the distance.

TABLE VI.2

DETERMINATION OF THE FORCE LAW
FOR ATTRACTIVE CHARGES

Experiment	#1	#2	#3
Distance between centers (inches)	9	18	24
Time required for 15 oscillations (seconds)	20	41	60
Corrected time for 15 oscillations (seconds)	20	41	57
Results predicted by inverse square law (for 15 oscillations)	20	40	54

In this Second Memoir, Coulomb stated that corrections for charge leakage would be discussed in his Third Memoir and that he would also present a third method to determine the force law—a method where not only the total mass of the electric fluid could be measured but also "the electric density of each part of the body."[43]

He concluded from his investigations that he had proved the force law for attractive as well as for repulsive charges and had done so by a system "absolutely different"[44] from the direct torsion balance method. That is, he had proved these laws by utilizing both a direct (static) approach and an indirect (dynamic) approach.

In the latter half of his Second Memoir, Coulomb sought to determine the force laws for repulsive and attractive forces of *magnetism*. He noted that magnetism shares with electricity at least the analogy that the forces act over perceptible distances, in contrast to "all the other attractive or repulsive phenomena with which Nature presents us; whether in the cohesion of bodies, or in their elasticity, or in chemical affinities, where the forces of attraction and repulsion appear to act only over very small distances. . . ."[45] But this analogy is no more than that, he said, and does not necessarily prove any identity in the natures of electricity and magnetism.

As with his electrical experiments, Coulomb employed both his torsion balance and the method of oscillations to determine the magnetic force law. For a full description of the two experimental methods, he referred the reader to his 1777 magnetism memoir and to his First Memoir in electricity and magnetism. He found it necessary before determining the force law to locate the "center of action" (or pole) at each end of the magnet. In order to calculate the action, he needed to have magnets with clearly defined poles approximating point sources, thus he utilized thin needles. After correction for the force due to the terrestrial magnetic field, he found that in a long thin needle each pole could be assumed to act as if in a small region near the end of the needle. For a needle 25 inches in length, this region seemed to be "toward the last ten *lignes* of its extremity."[46]

Having shown that long needles do act as if their poles are point sources, Coulomb proceeded to state the law to be proven: "The magnetic fluid acts by attraction or repulsion according to the ratio compounded directly of the density of the fluid and inversely of the square of the distances between its molecules."[m,47]

To prove this experimentally,[48] he took a small needle 1 inch in length and suspended it horizontally from a single silk thread, aligning it with the magnetic meridian. Perpendicular to this, he hung the 25 inch needle so that its end was 10 *lignes* below the

---

m Le fluide magnétique agit par attraction ou répulsion suivant la raison composée directe de la densité du fluide et la raison inverse du carré des distances de ses molécules.

axis of the small one. In this way he could assume that the centers of force of the corresponding needles lay in the same horizontal plane. Next, he removed the long needle to a great distance and timed the oscillations of the small one. Then he moved the long needle gradually closer and timed the oscillations at distances of 4, 8, and 16 inches. If the inverse square law holds, the force should be as the square of the frequency of oscillation of the small needle. The terrestrial field component must also be accounted for in the calculations, and Coulomb did so by subtracting the force due to this (long needle at infinity) from the total force. The results of three measurements, corrected for the terrestrial field component, are presented in Table VI.3.[49] (Experiment 1 represents the measurement taken with the long needle assumed at infinity.)

TABLE VI.3

DETERMINATION OF THE MAGNETIC FORCE LAW

Experiment	#1	#2	#3	#4
Distance from end of long wire to center of needle (inches)	∞	4	8	16
Square of number of oscillations in 60 seconds (minus terrestrial field component)	$0 - (15)^2$	$(41)^2 - (15)^2 = 1456$	$(24)^2 - (15)^2 = 351$	$(17)^2 - (15)^2 = 64$
Corrected for pole effects		1456	351	79

Examination of the second and third experiments[50] shows good agreement with the hypothesis of the inverse square law, that is

$$\frac{(\frac{1}{4})^2}{(\frac{1}{8})^2} \approx \frac{1456}{351}$$

The fourth observation, however, differs somewhat. Coulomb noted[51] that in this case one must consider the effect of the upper pole of the long magnetized needle (at a distance of 28.1 inches from the end of the small needle). He calculated for this effect and adjusted the observed value of 64 up to 79. Though the ratios for these results still are not in exact agreement with the inverse square law,[n] Coulomb repeated the experiment with needles of differing lengths and concluded: "I have always found that, in making the necessary corrections that I have just described, the action of the magnetic fluid, whether repulsive or attractive, was as the inverse square of the distances."[52]

He then introduced the second method of determining the force law for magnetostatics—the use of his torsion balance. As mentioned above, the proofs given in the 1777 magnetism memoir for the uniformity and constancy of the terrestrial field were rather crude, or as Coulomb now said, "subject to some dispute."[53] Therefore he conducted a new set of experiments measuring the static deflection of a long magnetized wire suspended in the balance. As the torsion suspension was twisted through measured increments, Coulomb observed the position of equilibrium and found that the angular deflection due to torsion was almost exactly proportional to the sine of the angle between the axis of the magnetized wire and the magnetic meridian. In four experiments, he found the error between calculation and experiment to be only $- 1/210$, $+ 1/232$, $+ 1/169$, and $- 1/75$.[54] Further experiments with the balance reaffirmed that the force law for attractive or repulsive magnetic poles is as the inverse square of the distance between the poles.

At the end of his Second Memoir, Coulomb recapitulated the major propositions that resulted from his study:[o,55]

1. The electric action, whether repulsive or attractive, of two electrified spheres, and therefore of two electrified molecules,

---

[n] If 1456 is chosen as unity, the ratios of $1/1456:1/351:1/79$ are as $1:4.15:18.4$. If 79 is chosen as unity, the ratios of $79:351:1456$ are as $1:4.4:18.4$. For the inverse square law, the exact ratios should be as $1:4:16$.

[o] 1° Que l'action, soit répulsive, soit attractive de deux globes électrisés et, par conséquent, de deux molécules électrisés, est en raison composée des densités du fluide électrique des deux molécules électrisés et inverse du carré des distances;

2° Que dans une aiguille de 20 à 25 pouces de longueur, aimantée par la méthode de la double touche, le fluide magnétique peut être supposé concentré à 10 lignes des extremités de l'aiguille;

3° Que lorsqu'une aiguille est aimantée, dans quelque position où elle soit placée sur un plan horizontal, relativement à son méridien magnétique, elle est toujours ramenée à ce méridien par une force constante parallèle au méridien, et dont la résultant passe toujours par le même point de l'aiguille suspendue;

4° Que la force attractive et répulsive du fluide magnétique est exactement, ainsi que dans le fluide électrique, en raison composée de la direct des densités, et inverse du carré des distances des molécules magnétiques.

is in the ratio compounded of the densities of the electric fluid of the two electrified molecules and inversely as the square of the distances;

2. In a needle 20 to 25 inches in length, magnetized by the double-touch method, the magnetic fluid can be supposed to be concentrated at 10 *lignes* from the ends of the needle;

3. When a needle is magnetized, in whatever position it is placed, it is always attracted back to this meridian by a force, constant and parallel to the meridian, of which the resultant passes always through the same point of the suspended needle:

4. The attractive and repulsive force of the magnetic fluid, as of the electric fluid, is exactly in the ratio directly of the densities and inversely of the square of the distances between the magnetic molecules.

Points two and three above were fairly proven by Coulomb in this memoir, but it must be noted with regard to points one and four that nowhere did Coulomb specifically prove that the electric and magnetic force laws are proportional to the *product* of the charges or pole-strengths, or as he said, "en raison composée des densités." That is, Coulomb had proved

$$F \propto \frac{1}{d^2},$$

but had only implied

$$F \propto q_1q_2 \text{ or } F \propto m_1m_2$$

This might appear as an oversight on his part, unless one examines his first statement of the law of force for magnetism: "The magnetic fluid acts by attraction or repulsion according to the ratio compounded directly of the density of the fluid and inversely of the square of the distances between its molecules."[56] Immediately following this statement, he said: "The first part of this proposition does not need to be proved." Therefore, he intended that the statement regarding force components proportional directly to the density of the fluid should be accepted without proof. Earlier in the memoir he implied the same for the case of electric attraction or repulsion when in one formulation he introduced "$D =$ the product of the electrical masses of the two balls."[57] In the same section of the memoir he went on to say that in later memoirs he would show how one can determine the proportionate quantity of electricity on bodies.

Though Coulomb may have been careless here in omitting an *explicit* proof that the force is proportional to the charge or pole-strength, it seems he assumed this could be taken as given. The relative ease with which he could have proved this and his subsequent operational use of the general formula support this opinion.

There remains the question of why Coulomb would have thought that this portion of the general formula could be taken without explicit proof. This may be due to two factors. First, he had experimented with charge separation on identical bodies. This is indicated in his Second Memoir.[58] He would measure the force on a charged globe for a given distance, then touch the globe to an identical uncharged globe. By symmetry, he could take the two globes to divide the charge equally. After separation, he measured the charge remaining on the original globe and determined that the force had fallen by half. Second, he was following very closely the analogy with the Newtonian formulation of the law of gravitational attraction. This would explain his reference to the similarity between the simple gravity pendulum and the electrical torsion pendulum[59] and his inclusion of a footnote developing theoretically the analysis of forces acting over perceptible distances.[60] This footnote contains concepts similar to those in the famous passages in Propositions LXX and LXXI of the First Book of Newton's *Principia*.[61] Coulomb's introduction of the notion of "electric mass,"[62] the correspondence to certain analyses in the *Principia*, and the experiments that he discussed, explain, at least in part, why he neglected any explicit proof of the proportionality between the force and the product of the charges or pole-strengths.

Priority in the Establishment of the Force Laws

The question of priorities in the history of science was discussed briefly in Chapter V regarding the torsion balance. I presented the case for several inventors in the history of torsion and argued that it was Coulomb who developed the study of torsion and its applications and brought it into the discipline of physics. An even longer list of predecessors exists for the electric and magnetic force laws. I will not discuss this problem in detail, for it has been covered by Cohen,[63] Roller and Roller,[64] and others. I will attempt to show, however, that it was the researches of Coulomb that proved the validity of the inverse square laws of force to the benefit and satisfaction of the scientific community. If one searches the eighteenth-century literature to discover where, before Coulomb, the inverse square law was stated, hypothesized, or observed experimentally, one finds at least ten occasions. Nine of these statements or events have been discussed by others, but I will add one more to the list. In a memoir submitted to the Paris Academy of Science magnetism contest for 1746, Daniel and Jean (II) Bernoulli presented experimental evidence that the force law for magnetic attraction varied as the inverse square of the distance.[65]

Ten statements or observations on the inverse square law of forces for electricity or for magnetism were: *Electricity*—Franz Aepinus (1759),[66] Daniel Bernoulli (1760),[67] Joseph Priestley (1767),[68] John Robison (claimed, 1769),[69] Henry Cavendish (manuscript, 1771-1773),[70] and Lord Stanhope (1779);[71] *Magnetism*—Daniel and Jean (II) Bernoulli (1746),[72] John Michell (1750),[73] Tobias Mayer (1760),[74] and Johann Lambert (1766).[75] The first explicit statement of the proportionality of force to the inverse square of distance is due to Daniel Bernoulli (1760), for electricity, and to John Michell (1750), for magnetism. Coulomb knew of the work of at least several of these predecessors.[p] I would note, however, that though there existed enunciations of the correct form of the force relationships with respect to distance, there were many more incorrect statements. I. B. Cohen's *Franklin and Newton* contains a passage relevant to this question: "Often, once a theory has proved successful, jealous contemporaries (like later historians) can show how each part of the theory had already been stated; yet it is to be noted that such prior statements achieve at this later date a significance they never had before."[76] Cohen is referring to Franklin's discoveries in electricity but the statement holds as well, I think, for Coulomb.

The most important thing for Coulomb was not the tentative, halting, or partial statements regarding the inverse square law of force but the attack against electric atmospheres and effluvia and against magnetic vortices. It is this attack, begun by Michell and Aepinus and completed by Coulomb, that turned theories of electricity and magnetism towards action at a distance. Once the boundary conditions could be set for the physical extent of the electric and magnetic "fluids," once these fluids could be assumed

[p] Coulomb was probably aware of the work of Daniel and Jean (II) Bernoulli (1746), John Michell (1750), Franz Aepinus (1759), and Joseph Priestley (1767).

to act as point sources, then regardless of whether one employed the one- or the two-fluid system, the mechanics of the Newtonian central force system of action at a distance could be applied to electricity and magnetism.

As Thomas Kuhn remarks, "Coulomb's measurements need not, perhaps, have fitted an inverse square law."[77] Though Coulomb suspected that they would answer to this function, the ability to conduct the investigation depended on the assumption that all electric and magnetic particles (for Coulomb, the *molécules électrisés* and *molécules magnétiques*) acted on each other at a distance. This is why the destruction of the theories of electric atmospheres and magnetic vortices was important to the development of the quantitative theories of electricity and magnetism and why Coulomb moved against these in his first, 1777, memoir on magnetism. In his First and Second Memoirs in electricity and magnetism, Coulomb firmly established the force laws for electricity and magnetism. Along with this, he completed Aepinus' and Michell's attacks on the vortex and effluvia theories and wedded the physics of electricity and magnetism to the Newtonian idea of action at a distance.

The Third Memoir: Charge Leakage

Coulomb's Third Memoir in electricity and magnetism (1787) is illustrative of how he adjusted and focussed parts of his research in the course of his general investigation of electricity. In his first memoirs,[78] Coulomb noted that the force between two separated, charged bodies diminished with the passage of time and that this seemed to vary with the particular insulating supports utilized and with the humidity of the air. In these first experiments he accounted for the problem of charge diminution either by performing the experiment in a very short time or by obtaining an approximate value for the average charge leakage. These methods could satisfy experimental requirements for the determination of the force law. In studying the charge *distribution* over various bodies, however, it would be necessary to determine more exactly the laws governing charge leakage.

In the first paragraph of the Third Memoir, Coulomb defined this task:[79]

When an electrified conducting body is insulated by idio-electric [dielectric] supports, experiment shows that the electricity of this body decreases and is destroyed rather rapidly. The object of this memoir is to determine the law that this decrease follows: the knowledge of this law is absolutely necessary in order to be able to submit to calculation the other phenomena of electricity.

Coulomb posited two causes as responsible for this loss. First, he believed that in nature there is probably no perfect dielectric. That is, all bodies have a limit above which they can not resist the passage of electricity. Second, the relation between humidity and charge loss indicated to him that water molecules or conducting gas particles could lead to charge flow along the surface of bodies or into the air itself.

In Coulomb's view, charge could leak off to the air directly from conducting bodies in the following way. From his knowledge of contemporary gas chemistry, he believed that the atmosphere was composed of different elements "more or less idio-electric."[80] Thus the conducting molecules in the air adjacent to body surfaces could share the charge of the body. Then, charged with like sign, they would be repulsed. This repulsion would be followed by the replacement of the molecule with a new, uncharged one. The whole process would accelerate as the body was charged with a higher electric density or as the air contained proportionately more aqueous or conducting molecules.[q]

In the case of dielectric bodies, charge might leak off if the electric density exceeded the (dielectric) limit for a given material or it might flow along the surface if the dielectric were covered with a thin layer of water molecules. These aqueous conducting molecules did not permit continuous, smooth charge transfer. Though these particles, once electrified, would tend to be repelled by the dielectric body, the adhesion between the aqueous molecules and the body surface might prevent this. Then a charged aqueous molecule on the dielectric surface just next to the charged body would remain stationary but would transfer part of its charge "from molecule to molecule up to a certain distance from the body."[82] Coulomb believed each aqueous molecule on the surface of a dielectric body was separated from the next by a small, constant dielectric (*idioélectrique*) interval. The resistance offered by this interval, he posited, would be proportional to the length of the interval. Therefore, the resultant electric density would decrease along the surface of the electric body.

---

[q] Bauer[81] states that this theory remained classic until the end of the nineteenth century.

Coulomb was rather bold and speculative in this discussion of charge leakage even though he stated that his was only a probable theory. His primary concern was to determine the laws of this leakage, but the theoretical commitments he brought to this research influenced his hypothesis. Since he did not agree with the theory of electric atmospheres, he felt that the charge leakage must take place by direct contact on a molecular level—either through charge-sharing with adjacent air molecules or across the small *idio-électrique* interval he believed there to be around each molecule in the material. The resistance that each interval offered recalls his engineering experience with friction and strength of materials, for here is a coercive or passive force which must be overcome. The distribution of electricity was not a dynamic phenomenon for Coulomb; it was the establishment of a state of equilibrium. As with his engineering studies, he believed here that there is a limit to this establishment. Along the dielectric, at a certain distance from the charged conducting body, there is finally a point at which the electric force is not sufficient to overcome the coercive force between one molecule and the next.

Proceeding to the experimental determination of the *laws* of charge leakage, Coulomb proposed to examine first the charge leakage through contact with the air and then leakage along the surface of the dielectric supports. If the cross-sectional surface of the supporting dielectric were made infinitely small, then Coulomb supposed that all charge leakage would be due to leakage through the air. He experimented with threads of glass, wax, shellac, silk, and goat's hair to determine the best dielectric substance. For the leakage experiments he chose two gilded pith-balls attached to thin, rigid shellac threads. One pith-ball was mounted horizontally in the torsion balance; the other was inserted through the hole in the glass cover of the balance. Using the balance in a way similar to that described in his First Memoir, Coulomb conducted a series of experimental tests and determined that for a given degree of humidity, the ratio of the decrease in the torsion force in a unit of time to the mean of the total force was a constant.[83] He kept the two pith-balls separated at a constant distance by changing the torsion micrometer as the force decreased due to leakage. From these experiments, he concluded that the rate of charge loss was proportional to the charge, or[84]

$$\frac{-d\delta}{\delta} = m\, dt$$

where δ and $d\delta$ = charge and charge loss, dt = an element of time, and m = a constant factor dependent upon the humidity and other unknowns.

He found this equation to hold regardless of the initial charge or the sizes of the pith-balls. For days of exceptionally low humidity and for low charge density, he found that the ratio of the charge to the rate of charge loss was a constant.[85]

Coulomb next examined the charge leakage for conditions of different humidity. He compared the leakage rates with H. B. de Saussure's[86] hygrometric data and found that the charge leakage was approximately proportional to the cube of the weight of water contained in a given volume of air. Uncertain factors due to temperature change, rapid changes in humidity, and the method of construction of hygrometers led Coulomb to state that this whole question required extensive further investigation.[87]

Leakage along the surface of the dielectric support was his second cause of charge leakage. Theoretically, in order to determine this he should have sought to maximize the cross-sectional perimeter of the dielectric. In practice, however, this resulted in such rapid charge leakage that he was unable to take any measurements on the torsion balance before the charge had entirely leaked off the pith-ball.[88] Thus he was forced to adopt a compromise situation. In place of the shellac-coated, silk suspension thread, Coulomb used an uncoated thread; that way the loss rate was increased but was still small enough to permit measurement with the torsion balance. Under given conditions of temperature and humidity, he measured the charge leakage in the same manner as with the coated, "perfectly" insulated thread. He then subtracted the leakage rate due to contact with the air and obtained what he assumed to be the component due to leakage along the surface of the dielectric.

This procedure gave what Coulomb considered to be rather remarkable results. When the charge density (*densité électrique*) was considerable, the rate of leakage over the surface of the dielectric was much higher than that due to the air. But when the charge density was below a certain level, the total leakage rate seemed to be exactly the same as that due to leakage through the air and the dielectric support then appeared to insulate perfectly![89] For a given temperature and degree of humidity, Coulomb found that the limit at which a cylindrical dielectric body began to insulate "perfectly" varied as the square root of its length, "so that, for example, if a silk thread 1 foot in length begins to insulate the body perfectly when the density is D, a thread 4 feet in length will begin to insulate it when its density is $2D$."[90]

These experimental results and Coulomb's conceptions of the strength of materials led him to the theory that in electricity there are two classes of substance—perfect conductors and dielectrics. With perfect conductors, the electricity can flow freely over the surface of bodies. With dielectrics, conduction is resisted by the nature of the dielectric, but if there are "conductive molecules which enter into the composition of the imperfect idio-electric support, or which are distributed along its surface,"[91] then the electricity may flow over the dielectric, provided the intensity is more than the coercive force offered by each *idio-électrique* interval within it. Each interval opposes a constant resistance due to the assumed spatial homogeneity. If the charge on the conducting body and the length of the "imperfect" dielectric are so chosen that the resultant force along the dielectric is less than the limit of the coercive force, then there are "an infinity of density curves . . . which equally satisfy the state of stability of the electric fluid."[92] Coulomb analyzed this in terms of the inverse square law of force, but I believe he saw an analogy with his mechanics work—in earth pressure, say, or in torsion or static friction. There, each molecule resisted change of position until the active force overcame the resistive force. Once this limit was passed, the whole physical behavior changed, giving way to flow, rupture, or motion.

Coulomb spoke only once of the question of a *perfect* dielectric. This was in the second paragraph of his Third Memoir,[93] where he stated that there probably exists nothing in nature that will act as a perfect dielectric if the electric density be great enough. There were a number of factors unknown to Coulomb that affect charge leakage on dielectrics.[r] Nevertheless, the laws that he determined in the Third Memoir are exact, especially his exponential law of charge leakage. The work of this memoir provided him with an accurate law (if not an accurate theory) for use in his Fifth and Sixth Memoirs, dealing with charge distribution.

The Fourth Memoir: Affinities and Surface Distribution

In his Fourth Memoir (1787), Coulomb aimed to demonstrate two principles of electricity:

[r] One factor, for example, is the ionization of the air.

The first: that this fluid does not spread over any body by a chemical affinity or by an elective attraction, but that it distributes itself, between different bodies put in contact, solely by its repulsive action;

The second: that in conducting bodies, the fluid which has reached a state of stability is spread over the surface of the body and does not penetrate into the interior.[94]

In this paper, he recalled the researches presented in his first three memoirs and mentioned that afterwards he had constructed a number of electric balances differing (mainly in size) from the balance previously described. He had utilized these large devices to investigate bodies too large to be placed in his original balance but he noted that in order to keep both the experimental and theoretical manipulations simple it was preferable to use small bodies.[95] This would allow the assumption that the bodies used were much smaller than the distance between their centers.

In the first half of this Fourth Memoir Coulomb proceeded to show that electricity spreads over *conducting* bodies without regard for the particular conducting material. Utilizing copper, elderwood, iron, and paper formed into disks and balls of various sizes, Coulomb charged one body and measured its force in the torsion balance. He next placed an identical body of different material in contact with the first, then removed the second and again measured the force on the balance. In each instance he found them to share the charge equally. He was careful to state this only for the case of conducting bodies. With perfectly conducting bodies, "like all the metals,"[96] the charge was distributed in an imperceptibly short time. With an imperfect conductor (paper), he found that several seconds were needed for the charge to become equally divided and that the manner of placing the two bodies in contact seemed to affect this distribution.[97] Coulomb believed that the peculiar behavior of imperfect conductors in charging was explained by his theory of the limiting coercive force needed to be overcome in imperfect conductors. He did not announce the thicknesses of the paper used in this experiment and seemed not to notice that his coercive-force theory for imperfect conductors did not account for time. That is, though he calculated the degree of density that could result in flow for a given distance along an imperfect conductor, he made no attempt to consider the time necessary for this flow.

What he was primarily concerned with here was to show that

electricity distributes itself over conducting bodies regardless of the particular conducting material. In his view, this could only mean that electricity distributes itself according to the geometrical shape and positioning of the conducting bodies and not according to some unknown law of chemical attraction or affinity.

In the second part of his Fourth Memoir, Coulomb demonstrated that on a charged conducting body, electricity in a *stable state*[s] is distributed only on the surface of the body. In order to establish this principle, he constructed his famous proof-plane (*plan d'é-preuve*).[98] First, he constructed a very tiny balance consisting of a shellac thread 10 to 12 *lignes* in length, suspended from a single silk thread. On one end of the shellac thread he mounted a pin head and on the other end a tinsel (*clinquant*) disk 2 *lignes* in diameter. Placed within a glass cylinder, this balance was found to turn through more than 90° by a force of 9 x 10⁻⁴ dynes, or only ten millionths of a dyne per degree. To introduce charge onto this balance, he fashioned the actual proof-plane of a shellac thread with a gilded paper disk 1½ *lignes* in diameter and 1/18 *ligne* in thickness attached to the end. This apparatus, he said, could be used upon a solid body of any shape. In the experiment described below, Coulomb employed a solid wooden cylinder 4 inches in diameter pierced with several shallow holes 4 *lignes* in diameter and in depth.

After charging the wooden cylinder, he touched the proof-plane to points on the surface and then noted the resultant deflection of the balance by the proof-plane. If, however, he touched the proof-plane to the bottom of one of the holes in the wooden body and then presented it to the balance needle he found no signs of electricity. Coulomb believed the proof-plane to be thin enough so that upon contact with the body it could be considered to form part of the body surface and therefore to take a quantity of electricity equal to that contained on the part of the body equal in area to one side of the proof-plane.[t,99] Presented to the outside of the body, the proof-plane indicated the charge there, but on the inside it indicated no charge; this was in accord with the inverse square law of force. In spite of the predictable consequences of this force law,

[s] By making explicit that the electricity was in a state of stability, Coulomb avoided the then almost impossible problem of determining the laws of spatial distribution of charge flow *during* the process of charging.

[t] Later, in his Sixth E & M Memoir, Coulomb attempted to demonstrate[100] that the proof-plane took a charge equal to that on a body of double the surface area of one side of the proof-plane. This is incorrect.

Coulomb insisted that it was experiment and not theory that led him to this result.[101] To justify this, he announced a theorem and general proof:

> THEOREM. Whenever a fluid (enclosed in a body where it can move freely) acts by repulsion in all of its elementary parts with a force less than the inverse cube of the distances, as would be, for example, the inverse of the fourth power, then the action of all the masses of this fluid which are placed at a finite distance from one of its elements is null relative to the action of the points of contact. . . . Thus, the fluid which owes its electricity to this law of repulsion will spread itself uniformly in the body; but whenever the repulsive action of the fluid elements which produce its elasticity is greater than the inverse of the cube, as, for example, we have found for electricity, which is as the inverse square of the distances, then the action of the masses of electric fluid placed at a finite distance from one of the elements of this fluid being not infinitely small relative to the elementary action of the points in contact, all the fluid must move to the surface of the body and there must not remain any at all in its interior.[102]

Coulomb's interesting method of demonstrating this was the following[103] (see Fig. VI.2[104]). Given a body *AaB* of any shape filled

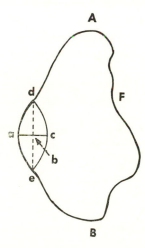

FIG. VI.2. Coulomb's figure for proof of surface distribution of charge on conductors

with a "fluid" whose particles act mutually as the inverse square of the distances between them, construct an infinitesimal element *ab*, normal to the surface. Through point *b* pass a normal plane through the body *AaB*, thus dividing it into two parts—an infinitesimal volume *daeb* and a finite volume *dAFBeb*. If the forces with which the infinitesimal volume *daeb* acts on point *b* are resolved along the normal *ab*, then these forces must be in equilibrium with the resultant along *ab* of all the forces in the finite volume *dAFBeb*.

Now imagine the infinitesimal volume *daeb* divided along the plane *dbe* into two identical volume elements, *dae* and *dce*. Construct the normal line *ab* to the point *c* so that *cb* equals *ab*. Now, said Coulomb, if the fluid were diffused throughout the body, "so that the law of continuity holds," it is necessary (since *ac* can be made infinitely small) that the fluid density at point *c* either be equal to, or differ only infinitesimally from, the density at point *a*. This requires that the fluid in the infinitesimal volume element *dceb* be in equilibrium with the fluid in element *daeb* and the action of the fluid in the rest of the volume (*AFBecd*) must be zero. Given the condition that each particle acts upon each other with a force proportional to the inverse square of the distance, this is possible only if the spatial density of the electricity everywhere inside the body is zero.[u]

Thus, in his Fourth Memoir, Coulomb proved experimentally and theoretically that charge distributes itself only on the surface of conducting bodies and is null within and also that charge on conducting bodies distributes itself according to geometrical shape and positioning and not chemical affinities.

The Fifth and Sixth Memoirs: Surface Distribution of Charge on Conducting Bodies

Coulomb's Fifth (1788) and Sixth (1790) Memoirs were devoted to the experimental investigation of charge distribution between conducting bodies of differing sizes and shapes—both in contact and after separation. Following the measurement of charge distribution, he attempted to develop analytical justification for his results using various approximative formulations. It was mostly from data presented in these two memoirs that Poisson composed his

---

[u] Bauer[105] notes that this demonstration is true only for a body charged with one polarity only. In certain complicated conditions involving both positive and negative charge, Coulomb's proof does not hold.

analytical theory of electrostatics some two decades later in the memoirs of the Institute (1811).[106] Coulomb's measurements were carried out on spheres, cylinders, and planes of different sizes. In the latter portion of the Sixth Memoir he extended his investigation to applications to the electric kite and the lightning rod. Finally, he promised to examine in a future study the distribution of charge on and under the surface of dielectrics, as well as conducting bodies, but this later memoir never appeared.

The aim of the Fifth Memoir was to determine in what ratios electric charge is shared between two bodies of similar shape but unequal size and also to determine the "density" of the electric fluid at each point of the body surfaces. Coulomb employed two experimental methods for this investigation. First, he measured the overall charge ratios directly by the use of the torsion balance. New, much larger balances were constructed for this purpose.[107] Second, to measure the charge at each point on a body, Coulomb employed the proof-plane introduced in his Fourth Memoir. By use of his smallest, most sensitive balance, Coulomb measured the charge introduced onto the proof-plane and took due consideration for charge loss through leakage off the bodies tested.

Coulomb conducted his first set of experiments[108] on spheres with radii from 1/12 to 12 inches. He placed the spheres in contact, charged them, and then separated them. After separation he measured the (mean) value of charge on each. Finally, after "many experiments," he compiled a table of ratios of charge on the separated spheres. These results as observed by Coulomb and as later calculated by Poisson[109] are presented in Table VI.4.[110] Coulomb's data for the limiting ratio tending to infinity were obtained using spheres with 1/12 and 4-inch radii.

TABLE VI.4

CHARGE DENSITY RATIOS FOR SPHERES

Ratio of the Spheres		Ratio of Charge Density on Small Sphere Compared to Large	
Radii	*Surface*	*Coulomb* (*observed*)	*Poisson* (*calculated*)
1	1	1	1
2	4	1.08	1.16
4	16	1.30	1.32
8	64	1.65	1.44
∞	∞	< 2.00	1.65 (i.e. $\frac{\pi^2}{6}$)

Coulomb knew that this first study gave only a mean value for charge on the body. Since he used spheres, he could assume that after separation the charge on each one distributed itself symmetrically over the surface, provided that the spheres were removed some distance from each other. In the second series of experiments[111] in the Fifth Memoir, Coulomb examined the charge distribution on bodies *during* contact. Using pairs of globes with diameters in the ratios 1:1, 1:2, 1:4, Coulomb placed them in contact, charged them, and then measured the charge density at various points on their surfaces. For two unequal spheres, the density gradient was found to vary on the small one in proportion as the ratio of the sphere diameters was increased. Thus, the density at point of contact was zero and increased rapidly up to the point 180° from the point of contact. On the larger sphere, the density was also zero at point of contact and remained so up to about 7° or 8° from the point of contact. Above about 30°, however, the density on a large sphere in contact with a small one remained about the same over the rest of the surface.[112] These results showed that when the figure ratio was high, the small sphere acted only as a minor perturbation of the field pattern on the large one, while the large sphere had a major effect on the distribution over the small one.

To show the influence of the large sphere on the charge distribution of the small sphere in contact with it, Coulomb compiled a table of the ratio of densities at a point on the small sphere 180° from the point of contact. The results of this are shown in Table VI.5,[113] where R and r are the radii of the large and small spheres respectively, δ is the charge density at the extremity of the small sphere, and D is the mean charge density on the large sphere. Poisson's calculated ratios are presented in the table for comparison.[114]

TABLE VI.5
CHARGE DENSITY RATIOS FOR
SPHERES IN CONTACT

Ratio of Radii of Spheres	Ratio of Charge Densities (δ/D)	
R/r	Coulomb (observed)	Poisson (calculated)
1	1.27	1.32
2	1.55	1.83
4	2.35	2.48
8	3.18	3.09
∞	>4.00	4.27

Many of these distribution studies were continued in Coulomb's Sixth Memoir, but one more item from the Fifth should be mentioned here. Coulomb felt that his experiments showed "that the electric fluid is almost entirely distributed on the surface of electrified conducting bodies, and that it does not form a very extended atmosphere around these bodies, as several authors have thought."[115] To prove this experimentally, he contrived an illustration[116] which would show that electricity on conducting bodies exists only on their surfaces. He took two copper wires and coated one of them (except for one end) with shellac to a thickness of one-half inch. Then the ends of the two wires were touched to a charged sphere which was suspended in the torsion balance. As measured on the balance, each wire was found to take the same amount of charge from the conducting sphere. Since shellac is an excellent dielectric, Coulomb interpreted these results as indicating that the electricity in each case was distributed only on the surface of the copper wire and therefore did not form an "electric atmosphere" around the wire.

Coulomb's Sixth Memoir continued the study of the surface distribution of charge and, in particular, extended the investigation to *groups* of conducting spheres, cylinders, planes, and variations of these groupings. He found the charge distribution on large numbers of spheres placed in contact along a line to vary most near the ends. For example, in the case of twenty-four spheres placed in this manner, the ratio of charge density at the center of the line to that at the sphere second from the end was only 1:1.12, while the ratio of the same center sphere to the end sphere was 1:1.75[117] Similar results were found for the cylinder;[118] in fact, Coulomb showed that the distribution along a series of spheres in contact, in a line, approximated the distribution along a cylinder.

He developed a practical application of these experiments for the case of the electric kite as follows. From his experiment with the various cylinders and spheres, he determined an empirical formula for the ratio of charge densities for a sphere in contact with the end of a cylinder to be[119]

$$\delta = \frac{mDR}{r^{4/5}},$$

or (if $R >> r$),

$$\delta = \frac{mDR}{r},$$

where δ and D = the surface densities on the cylinder and sphere, respectively, r and R = the radii of the cylinder and sphere, and M = a constant coefficient (determined here as 9/48).

Applying this formula to the imagined case of a cloud with a radius of 1,000 feet and a kite string with a thickness of 1/6 inch, Coulomb found that the mean density on the surface of the kite string was 27,000 times that of the cloud. Since he had already determined that the ratio of density at the ends of a cylinder to that of its mean was 2.3:1, this gave the charge density at the ends of the kite string as 62,000 times that of the cloud![120] Later in the memoir, he gave the analysis of a lightning rod with a cloud passing overhead.[121] (This was idealized as a grounded cylinder placed at a distance from an insulated charged sphere.)

In his Fourth and Fifth Memoirs, Coulomb had stated and proved to his satisfaction that the distribution of electricity on conducting bodies occurs only on their surfaces and that inside the body surface there is no charge. Several times in his Fifth and Sixth Memoirs, he noted that he planned to study the distribution of electricity within the body in the case of dielectric materials. This promised work was never published. In the Sixth Memoir (1790), however, Coulomb again set out to demonstrate experimentally that there is no charge inside a conducting body. A theoretical proof of this in his Second Electricity and Magnetism Memoir had been based on propositions similar to numbers LXX, LXXI and LXXIII in Book I of Newton's *Principia*,[122] and his previous experimental demonstration depended on measuring a null charge inside holes drilled in a solid body. Now Coulomb presented an indirect demonstration of nearly the same conception as that performed by Cavendish (1771–1773) and left by him only in manuscript form. Since Cavendish's method has been shown by Maxwell to have been unknown to the world until 1849,[123] it would be fruitful here to indicate Coulomb's demonstration. He introduced it as

> . . . a new experiment which appears decisive: Here is what it consists in. One insulates a conducting body that one has electrified; next, an envelope is fashioned and cut into two parts, so that a little space is left between when it is placed over the body. Whether or not this envelope has the same shape as the body has little importance for the success of the experiment. If one electrifies the body, which is placed on an insulator, and if

one covers it with the two parts of the envelope, supported by two idio-electric rods, upon withdrawing the two enveloping halves, one will find, by means of our small silk-suspension electrometers, that all the electricity of the body has passed to the envelopes and that the body either retains none of it or retains only an imperceptible part.[124]

This is an interesting citation, considering Maxwell's statement about Coulomb.

It is impossible to overestimate the delicacy and ingenuity of his apparatus, the accuracy of his observations, and the sound scientific method of his researches; but it is remarkable, that not one of his experiments coincides with any of those made by Cavendish.[125]

Here is *perhaps* an instance of the axiom that the exception proves the rule. Coulomb's experiment, with two enveloping halves surrounding an inner body, is very similar to that done by Cavendish. Cavendish's (unpublished) experiment allowed him to claim the force law for electricity as being proportional to the inverse square of the distance plus or minus 1/50th.[126] Coulomb had a very sensitive proof-plane and torsion balance. Therefore, when he found no electricity (or only an imperceptible amount) remaining on the inner globe, this was proof enough of the inverse square law. There is possibly some difference, however, between Cavendish's and Coulomb's experiment here. Unlike Cavendish, who clearly said that he provided a temporary wire connection between the inner and outer globes, Coulomb made no such statement. We are not told how the charge leaks from the inner body to the outer enveloping halves. This is not necessarily due to ignorance on his part. He casually inserted the description above (note 124) within a paragraph and quickly returned to the matters at hand. The key to the proof here for the inverse square law is that no charge could remain within a charged conducting sphere, for if the force followed any other law there would be a resultant force either toward or away from the walls of the sphere. Thus, it is the fact that the charge "has passed to the envelopes" from the inner globe that is critical and the proof in no way rests on the *means* by which the charge is transferred.

Since he doesn't tell us, one might speculate how Coulomb accounted for the transmission of the charge from the inner to the outer body. First, he might simply have short-circuited the inner and outer bodies while they were arranged concentrically, in the same manner as did Cavendish. Or, given Coulomb's theory of air leakage due to charge sharing with adjacent air molecules, he might have supposed the charge to leak to the outer body through the air. It would have been difficult to have avoided touching the enveloping halves to the insulating stand which supported the globe. In this case a globe of about the size Coulomb utilized, and its envelope, would have a capacitance of roughly 10^{-11} farads. The leakage resistance might be about 10^8 ohms. Therefore the time constant would be a fraction of a second. Thus, even if Coulomb accidentally touched the envelopes to the insulator support he could have obtained the result he stated. My surmise is that given his experimental sophistication, he probably brought the envelopes purposefully into contact with the inner globe while placing them around it. Whatever the actual situation, Coulomb states that there is no perceptible charge remaining on the inner body and that it has all passed to the outer envelopes, which is what he wished to show. Finally, in attempting to interpret Maxwell's statement that Coulomb and Cavendish never performed an identical experiment, one would have to contend that in performing this experiment Coulomb never assumed to be proving the inverse square law of forces but merely the fact that no charge exists within a conducting body. Given his knowledge of the *Principia*, I would hesitate to accept this contention.

Coulomb did not proceed further along this line as he was oriented toward a direct method of solution in his preoccupation with the torsion balance. Maxwell is basically correct in his statement that Coulomb's experiments did not coincide with those of Cavendish. Their work is correlative in that both were attempting to extend to electricity the Newtonian system of attractive and repulsive forces acting at a distance. Thus can be explained Bauer's remark[127] that Coulomb's mathematical proof for the attraction and repulsion of bodies following the law of distances is similar to Cavendish's proof as previously published in the *Philosophical Transactions* in 1772.[128] Considering the similarity in the two proofs, it is probable that Coulomb depended on Cavendish's paper. But the material in *both* proofs is based upon propositions in Book I of the *Principia*. I believe that Coulomb's debt here is more to Newton than to Cavendish.

Finally, in the latter part of the Sixth Memoir, Coulomb gave one of his rare discussions of the nature of electricity, and in a demonstration of his (incorrect) theory of the proof-plane he presented a rigorous demonstration of what is known today as "Coulomb's Theorem."[v,129]

In his short discussion of the question of one versus two electric fluids,[130] he said that whatever the cause of electricity, one could explain the phenomena by use of the two-fluid theory. For most of his experiments, the question was academic because he was studying force relationships between charge distributions and it mattered not at all whether he talked of one or of two fluids. Coulomb knew well, and he stated it here, that Aepinus' one-fluid theory answered to all *calculations*. He gave two reasons for utilizing the hypothesis of two fluids—one of these was philosophical and one was drawn from an analogy to contemporary gas chemistry.[w] The first reason follows:

It appears to me contradictory to admit at the same time in the parts of bodies an attractive force proportional inversely as the square of the distances, demonstrated by universal gravity, and a repulsive force in the same proportion of the inverse square of the distances, a force which would necessarily be infinitely large relative to the attractive action from which gravity [*pesanteur*] results.[132]

The second reason was:

The supposition of two fluids, moreover, conforms to all the modern discoveries of the chemists and physicists, who have made known to us different gases of which the mixture in certain proportions destroys suddenly and entirely their elasticity, an effect which cannot take place without something equivalent to a repulsion between the parts of the same gas which constitutes their elastic state and to an attraction between the parts of different gases which makes them suddenly lose their elasticity.[133]

I would not belabor the point, but it is important to indicate that Coulomb was, I believe, earnest in his denial of any essential truth inherent in the two-fluid system. Both systems, he said, had only

---

[v] "Coulomb's Theorem" establishes that the electric force near a conductor is proportional to the surface-density of electrification. The incorrect proof for the proof-plane in no way impairs the value of Coulomb's experimental measurements of charge density and surface distribution.

[w] I. B. Cohen[131] attributes this idea to the influence of the work of Stephen Hales.

a certain degree of probability and in using the two-fluid system he meant only to "present, with the fewest elements possible, the results of calculation and of experiment, and not to indicate the true causes of electricity."[134] It should be noted that Coulomb's assertion of the *hypothetical* nature of the two-fluid system was often ignored by those who abstracted his memoirs for periodicals like the *Journal de physique*.[135]

The Seventh Memoir: Magnetism

With the exception of a portion of his Second Memoir where he determined the force law for magnetic attraction and repulsion, all of Coulomb's first six memoirs in his famous series were devoted to electricity. He did not desert the study of magnetism during the 1780s.[x] but the majority of his published researches in this period were in electricity. The seventh and last in his series was the memoir "On Magnetism," which he read in three sessions at the Academy in July 1791. This was the last important paper he read before the Revolution. Most probably this series would have extended to more than seven if not for the political situation in France, for Coulomb mentioned studies in the Seventh Memoir that he planned to continue. Some of these later magnetism researches appeared after the Revolution in the memoirs of the Institute.[136]

As to the subject of this Seventh Memoir, Coulomb said quite simply: "The Memoir I present today is intended to determine, by experiment and by theoretical calculation, the laws of magnetism."[137] At the beginning of this study,[138] Coulomb recalled four principles that he had proved in earlier papers, notably in his 1777 magnetism memoir and in his Second Memoir on electricity and magnetism. 1) For a given spatial location the terrestrial magnetic field can be considered uniform. 2) A magnetic needle placed in this field will be acted on equally by oppositely directed forces (with a resultant couple proportional to the sine of the angle between the needle and the magnetic meridian). 3) There is a definite limit to the amount any given magnet may be magnetized. 4) The force law for attraction and repulsion between magnetic molecules (*molécules magnétiques*) is proportional to the magnetic intensity (*intensité magnétique*) and to the inverse square of the distance between the bodies.

---

[x] The essay for the 1777 magnetism contest was followed by several secondary magnetism memoirs read to the Academy from 1783–1787.

Given these principles and laws, Coulomb proposed to determine the following in this memoir: the dimensional parameters of magnetic needles as a function of their momenta, the magnetic intensity at each point along a magnetized needle, the limits within which experiment and theory agree in the hypothesis of attractive and repulsive forces, and finally, some practical means of magnetizing needles to saturation and of making strong artificial magnets.[139]

The magnetic balance used by him in this memoir was "absolutely similar" to his electrical torsion balance except that he added dash-pot damping[y] to simplify the experimental observations. As usual, he alternated between copper, silver, and silk torsion threads, depending upon the magnitude of the forces to be measured. Using test needles from ¼ to 18 inches in length but with constant diameter, he determined the momentum as a function of needle length. The results indicated an empirical formula describing the magnetic momentum in thin cylindrical needles as a function of the first power of the length for needles over 4½ inches in length and of the square of the length for needles less than this. In addition, he determined that the distances from the extremities of magnetic needles to their poles was in direct ratio to the diameters of the needles. Following this, he found for homologous needles of the same material and degree of magnetization that the magnetic momentum was proportional to the cube of the dimensions. That is, a cylindrical needle 6 inches in length and 1 *ligne* in diameter and a needle 12 inches in length and 2 *lignes* in diameter have homologous dimensions as $1:2$. In this case, if the needles are magnetized to saturation, their magnetic moments are as $(1)^3$: $(2)^3$, or $1:8$.[141]

Coulomb discovered that in practice it was almost impossible to obtain different samples of iron or steel having the same elastic characteristics.[142] He knew that the thermal and elastic history of the ferrous metals affected their magnetic characteristics because he had investigated this in his 1784 torsion memoir. Therefore, he made his magnets out of bundles of wires cut from the same long iron wire in order to ensure that all had the same elastic properties.

After determining at least an approximation for the magnetic momentum as a function of dimension, Coulomb experimented with

[y] Coulomb soldered a copper plane to the bottom of the needle support and then submerged this plane in a basin of water. He first described the principle of dash-pot damping in an instrumental memoir published in the Academy memoirs for 1785.[140]

the balance to determine the magnetic intensity at each point along the magnetic needle axis. From the momentum experiments described above and from the preliminary measurements reported in his Second Memoir, he observed that the centers of action on thin cylindrical needles are positioned near the extremities. It appeared that the region contributing to the magnetic momentum extended from each extremity inward to a distance equal to about 25 needle diameters.

Coulomb decided to verify this directly by measuring the momentum on a magnetized test needle placed at various positions along the axis of a long magnetized needle. In a first experiment,[143] he timed the vibrations of a tiny magnetized needle (2 *lignes* in length and ½ *ligne* in diameter) suspended at right angles to the long one. According to his analysis of momentum problems, the magnetic intensity at points along the long needle should have been proportional to the square of the number of oscillations of the test needle, after due correction for the terrestrial field effect. These first results varied from his predictions, and Coulomb posited that the test needle was so small as to undergo an increase in its magnetization due to the effect of the long needle. He changed the tiny test needle for another, larger one (6 *lignes* in length and 3 *lignes* in diameter) and repeated the experiments.[144] Again, taking the magnetic intensity at each point to be proportional to the square of the oscillations of the test needle, Coulomb constructed a graph of the magnetic intensity versus length for one-half of a thin, cylindrical needle 27 inches in length (see Fig. vi.3 A).[z,145] The results for the 27 inch needle showed that the magnetic intensity at a point *e*, 4½ inches from the end, was less than 1/18th the value at the end. The "center of gravity" under the curve was found to be 1.3 inches from the end.[aa]

From a comparison of all of the above experimental results, Coulomb was able to explain some of his findings.[147] He measured the intensity curve for various needles and concluded that the curve approximates a right triangle with the hypotenuse extending from

---

[z] The curve illustrated in Figure vi.3 A was not determined strictly from experiment. Coulomb altered the end portion *ab* so that the results shown in the figure represent an exponential extrapolation of the portion *bcd*.[146]

[aa] In Article xxi of this memoir, Coulomb calculated that for this particular needle the "center of gravity" should be 1.5 inches from the end.

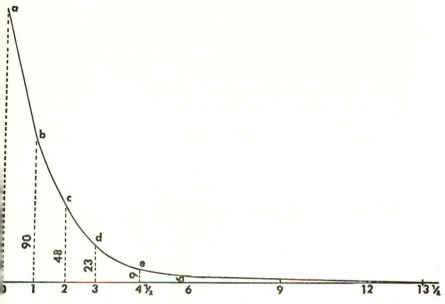

FIG. VI.3 A. Curve of magnetic intensity along the 13½ inch half-length of a thin magnetized needle. Point "0" is at the end of the needle

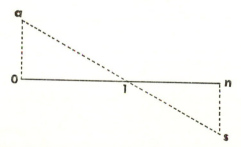

FIG. VI.3 B. Approximate magnetic intensity curve for needles with (length/diameter) ratios less than 25

a point above the end of the needle to a point along the axis at a distance of 25 diameters from the end. Thus, for any needle longer than about 50 times its diameter, the curve stays the same and moves outward as the needle lengthens. This means that the center of momentum moves linearly outward and explains why the magnetic momentum of long needles increased directly as the length.

If the overall length of a magnetic needle was less than about 50 times its diameter, the magnetic momentum seemed to go as the square of the length, but the intensity measured at the extremities remained the same. Coulomb explained this as follows (see Fig. VI.3 B).[148] For needles with a length-to-diameter ratio of less than 50, the intensity curve is a straight line from the end to the center of the needle. Let the magnetic intensity at the extremity of the needle *On* be *A* and let the half-length of the needle be *x*. Then the magnetic moment of the needle *On* will be[149]

$$M = (A) \ (x) \ \frac{2x}{3} = \frac{2Ax^2}{3}.$$

That is, the magnetic moment varies as the square of the length. Coulomb was not fully successful in interpreting his third discovery in a theoretical manner. The relationship of magnetic moment to volume was merely restated. In needles of the same material and homologous dimensions, the magnetic moments are proportional to the cube of their homology ratio. Thus, the magnetic moment in homologous bodies is proportional to the body volume.

"Essay on the Theory of Magnetism . . ."[150]

In the first half of the Seventh Memoir, Coulomb determined various parameters of the laws of magnetic momentum and provided several more or less empirical formulas. In the second half of the memoir, he examined the theories of magnetism. First, he again attacked the idea of magnetic vortices as he had done in his 1777 magnetism memoir and in the Second Memoir in electricity and magnetism. He clearly indicated that the major theoretical concern in magnetic researches is the basic question of the "system."

The Cartesian system of mechanics or modified versions of this had been present in a portion of the electrical and magnetic theories presented from the early seventeenth century through the mid-eighteenth century. Current monographs which present the great debate of eighteenth-century electricity and magnetism as being between theories of one or of two fluids ignore the fact that the fundamental question was one of *système*—whether the natural phenomena of electricity and magnetism could be explained by "simple suppositions of attractive and repulsive forces"[151] or whether these phenomena answered to vortices, effluvia, and electric atmospheres. Aepinus,[152] in 1759, wrote the first really quantitative work advocating the system of attraction and repulsion (or action at a distance), and Coulomb largely completed the overthrow of the Cartesian system. For these men the major questions were: first, the nature of the system (e.g., whether Cartesian or Newtonian); second, if Newtonian, the determination of the correct force laws; third, how to interpret these laws (i.e. whether one or two fluids, etc.). This is why Coulomb cited Aepinus, Musschenbroek, and Wilcke rather than Nollet, Canton, Watson, or Franklin. And this is why he prefaced each magnetism memoir with a discussion of the impossibility or improbability of the system of vortices. He gave evidence against the vortex system in his first (1777) memoir, but he could not provide a replacement for this system until he could prove the probability of the Newtonian system of central forces acting at a distance.

This proof had to rest not only on theoretical predictions verified by experiment but *also* on an exact experimental method which could accord some confidence in the results. Coulomb said it was impossible to replace the old hypothesis by the new

> . . . before knowing the law of attraction and repulsion for magnetic molecules in magnetized bodies, the law that we have found . . . to be proportional to the product of the density or of the magnetic intensity and proportional to the inverse square of the distances. It was equally impossible to verify any hypothesis before employing means that give exact measurements in experiments, such as we have tried to do.[153]

He stated repeatedly that it was the overall system of attractions and repulsions with which he was concerned and that the lesser question of the one- or two-fluid theory was moot in terms of answering to the phenomena. Coulomb is usually represented by his quasi-positivistic statements to the effect that though both the one- and two-fluid theories are mathematically the same, he preferred the two-fluid theory.[154] This was so because in the two-fluid theory particles of matter do not have to have simultaneously an attractive force for other matter (gravity) and a repulsive force for other matter (electricity or magnetism).

Few seem to have taken Coulomb's statements at face value. From the first popularized abstracts of his memoirs through their presentation in current secondary sources, his theories of electricity and magnetism are seen as responsible for the victory of the two-fluid theories. I would maintain that much of the credit for this "victory" belongs to those who reported for the *Journal de physique*[155] and other contemporary periodicals. There *is* some reason to interpret Coulomb in this way if one considers his electrical researches. In these memoirs, he often mentioned the *two* electric fluids.

The situation was somewhat different with magnetism. In his 1777 essay on magnetism, Coulomb did not even mention magnetic fluids until the last chapter.[156] There he discussed both the one- and the two-fluid theories in opposition to Cartesian vortices. He made no commitment to either but leaned toward Aepinus' one-fluid system. Nor did he comment upon either in the latter portion of his Second Memoir, concerning the law of force between magnetic poles. In fact, Coulomb never explicitly referred to his preference between the two theories until *after* his Seventh Memoir on magnetism. This choice first appeared in a memoir read in 1799, as a corollary to studies presented in his Seventh Memoir: "Whatever be the causes of magnetic phenomena, all these phenomena can be explained and submitted to calculation in supposing, in steel bars or in their molecules, two magnetic fluids."[157]

This discussion of the question of Coulomb's concern with the one- or two-fluid systems is to introduce the evolution of his own theory of magnetism. The concept of a coercive force ties his theories—both of electricity and of magnetism—to his work in torsion, friction, and strength of materials. This link to his earlier work is much firmer, however, with magnetism than with electricity because the physical analogies with gravitational matter seemed closer in the case of magnetism.

In his first essay (1777), Coulomb suggested that Aepinus' one-fluid system could be used to account for temporal magnetic variations. Both theories failed, though, in explaining why a magnet broken into pieces could result in each piece's acting as a little magnet. Either theory of macroscopic transfer of fluid(s) from one end to the other of a magnet would predict that a broken magnet would have either no fluid or an insufficient amount in some of the pieces. In this early essay Coulomb tried to stay within the fluid paradigm by positing that perhaps only a very small amount of the total fluid was transferred during magnetization and that the bulk remained.[158] He was considering a molecular theory even then, however, for he spoke of the demagnetizing effect among adjacent elementary magnetic parts (*parties aimantaires*)[159] and said that each point of a magnet could be considered as "the pole of a small magnet."[160]

In the portion of the Second Memoir where Coulomb treated magnetism, he utilized the fluid-transfer concept in determining the position of the poles in a magnet. Here he spoke of the magnetic fluid as being concentrated near the ends. The fluid analogy was necessary because he had to explain an apparent magnetic density gradient and saw no other way to do this than to assume the transfer of a "magnetic fluid." Coulomb had noted the effects of the demagnetizing field early in his researches, but at first this seemed only to result in the neutralization or cancellation of magnetism. He held that the magnetic fluid itself could not pass from one discrete body to another but he did not bring himself to confront the molecular situation. By the Seventh Memoir, however, he knew that magnets in proximity could demagnetize one another and that bundles of magnetic needles tied together could result in a more powerful magnet, though the interior of the bundle still suffered demagnetization. What he needed to break away from the theory of the macroscopic transfer of a magnetic fluid was a way for his magnetic molecules (*molécules aimantaires*) to combine so as to produce an increase in magnetic strength.

It was in the Seventh Memoir that Coulomb offered his theory. Here he reintroduced the one- and two-fluid theories and confronted them again with the paradox of the magnet broken into pieces. Neither theory could answer to this. However, Coulomb said:

I believe that one could reconcile the result of the experiments with calculation by making some changes in the hypotheses; here is one which appears able to explain all the magnetic phenomena of which the preceding experiments have given precise measurements. It consists in supposing in M. OEpinus' system that the magnetic fluid is contained in each molecule or integral part of the magnet or the steel; that the fluid can be transported from one extremity to the other of this molecule, which gives to each molecule two poles, but that this fluid cannot pass from one molecule to another. Thus, for example, if a magnetized needle was of a very small diameter, or if each molecule could be regarded as a small needle whose north end would be united to the south end of the preceding needle, there would be only the two ends *n* and *s* of this needle which would give signs of magnetism, because it would be only at the two ends where one of the poles of the molecules would not be in contact with the opposite pole of another molecule.[161]

To illustrate this (see Fig. VI.4),[162] Coulomb remarked[163] that if one took a long, very thin wire magnetized to saturation and then

FIG. VI.4. Coulomb's molecular magnetic polarization model

cut it into pieces, each piece was still found to be magnetized to saturation. He also cited the analogy with a series of glass plates charged oppositely on each side and then stacked together. In addition, one could take a thin straw or glass tube and fill it with steel filings. After magnetizing, the tube acted just as a magnet of the same dimensions, even though the filings were separable. The theory presented so far accounted only for an extremely thin magnet supposed to consist of single magnetic molecules joined end to end. Each end of the elements inside the line of molecules demagnetized the adjacent end so that only the extremities of the magnet showed poles.[164] In a later portion of the Seventh Memoir, Coulomb extended this molecular theory to magnets of macroscopic diameters.

Coulomb's molecular polarization model of magnetism was later important to Biot and Poisson,[bb] who based their conceptions of magnetism on this. It was important also to Ampère,[166] although he altered the magnetic polarization idea and suggested rather that magnetism consisted of molecular electric currents flowing normal to the axis of the molecule. Coulomb's model received general approval through the efforts of Haüy[167] and Biot, who wrote the official textbooks for the French Lycée system in the first few years of the nineteenth century. It was acceptable to supporters of both the one- and two-fluid theories, provided they were willing to limit the supposed transfer of magnetic fluid to within the molecule.

Thus far I have discussed several aspects of Coulomb's magnetic researches—the attack on the vortex theories, the support for the

bb Poisson said of it: "This opinion, very singular upon first glance, is, however, that which has generally prevailed."[165]

action-at-a-distance theory, the determination of the force law, and the consideration of magnetic fluid(s) and the molecular-polarization model. These alone would not account for Coulomb's further studies in magnetism. His magnetic researches after the Revolution centered on the effect of the previous thermal and elastic states[cc] of magnets on their properties, and on the extent of magnetic properties in all matter. These later researches were pointed toward further elucidation of the topics discussed above but, conceptually, they also took him back to his earlier studies in friction, torsion, and strength of materials. The reason for this was that once again Coulomb was faced with the problem of determining the effects, if not the nature, of forces of friction, cohesion and adhesion. These concerns were closely akin to problems considered, for example, by Haüy in crystallography[168] and Laplace in capillarity.[169]

In his torsion memoir of 1784, Coulomb discovered that the elastic history of ferrous metals affected not only their elastic properties but also their magnetic properties. In his electrical studies he saw all matter as being either a perfect conductor or a dielectric. He explained conduction over dielectrics as being due to surface contamination, but between the contaminating conductive particles, he postulated a dielectric interval with a given physical resistance. Electricity could pass across this only if the electric intensity were sufficient to overcome the coercive force offered by this dielectric interval. Though he only hinted at conduction across uncontaminated dielectrics, he supposed that *any* dielectric substance would break down under sufficient electric intensity.

In his Second and Seventh electricity and magnetism Memoirs, he saw this coercive force as responsible for the limiting value of magnetization that could be obtained in a material. Somehow, soft iron could easily be magnetized and it also easily lost its magnetism. Steel was difficult to magnetize but it afterwards held its magnetism. Perhaps these properties were due to a coercive force that, like friction in machines,[170] provided an upper limit to the stresses that a given material could withstand.

In his last magnetic researches, Coulomb was really investigating the nature and properties of this coercive force in matter. He began studies of temperature and magnetism in the Seventh Memoir and continued these later. These later results remain only in manuscripts, some of which are lost, one of which was utilized by Biot.[171]

cc Heating and subsequent tempering or work-hardening.

Not only did Coulomb want to know of heat, mechanical stress, and magnetization interactions in ferrous metals, he tried to determine if *all* matter might not be susceptible to magnetism. This was a natural extension of his work with iron and steel. By 1802, Klaproth, Tassaert, and Haüy[172] had found that nickel and cobalt also showed magnetic properties. If a coercive force limited magnetization in these materials, then perhaps this same type of force limited the degree of magnetizability in other materials to such an extent that no one had been able to measure their magnetism. With an extremely sensitive torsion balance, magnetism might be found in other forms of matter. At first, Coulomb thought that he had found this minuscule degree of magnetism in gold, silk, copper, lead, glass, chalk, bone, and wood.[173] Of course, it might be only that all his samples contained particles of iron. In collaboration with Balthazar Sage and Guyton de Morveau, and other chemists, Coulomb sought to obtain absolutely pure samples of various elements in which to look for magnetization. To investigate the smallest forces, he utilized his most sensitive torsion balance operating in a vacuum. With this apparatus he measured a sample of pure silver supplied by Sage and Guyton and found it to have a magnetic momentum equal to 1/133,119 that of an equivalent piece of iron.[174] This meant, he thought, that either the coercive force limiting magnetization in silver was immensely great, or that he had reached the limits of what could be done with eighteenth-century quantitative analysis in chemistry. Finally, it seemed that his silver, indeed, might only have contained a trace of iron.

The rest of Coulomb's researches in electricity and magnetism must remain unknown. His health, which had been poor ever since the tour of duty in Martinique, declined rapidly in the first month of 1806, and he died in August of that year. He read his last memoir at the Academy on July 30, 1804,[175] but the last paper that he published was read in the summer of 1802.[176] Coulomb's widow gave his manuscripts to Biot who made use of some of these in his *Traité de physique . . .* (1816).[177] Biot declined to cite most of the manuscripts, saying that it would be a disservice to Coulomb to present his incompleted researches.[178] Unfortunately, at least some of them must have been lost at Biot's death, for only two notebooks remain today.[179] A study of these has failed to reveal any material that would appreciably alter the results of Coulomb's earlier, published memoirs.

Coulomb's Contributions to Electricity and Magnetism

Coulomb's work has been presented here as more than merely a junction of experiment and analysis. His experimental work was much more sophisticated than was, say, Desaguliers'. At the same time, the tradition of experiment in the *cabinet de physique* merged with another type which developed largely from elements within the French engineering profession. The search for significance in experiment, contributed by a maturing engineering profession, was combined with the curiosity of the natural philosopher. Finally, analysis was joined to these studies. In the work of some men, Lavoisier, Haüy, and Charles for example, analysis was a way of thinking, a method more than a strict use of the calculus. For others, like Coulomb and Borda, formal analysis was employed to a considerable degree in their researches; but this analysis was closely tied to the purposes of physics.

It is true that Coulomb's studies were influenced partly by his limitations as a mathematician, yet Bochner[180] makes the extremely perceptive observation that in Coulomb's time it was not yet the fashion for *physicists* to "make up" mathematics to aid their work. Coulomb's mathematics is often crude, approximative, and in his electricity and magnetism studies, certainly not free from error. All of his work, however, was directed by its significance for physics. Neither experiment nor analysis controlled these studies; rather, they contributed in proportion to their relevancy to the physics at hand.

Coulomb's researches in electricity and magnetism form a magnificent contribution to the history of physics. His quantitative determination of the force laws in electrostatics and magnetism, his study of charge distribution and charge leakage, and his study of the parameters of magnetic interactions were of the first importance to the continental mathematical physicists of the first half of the nineteenth century. Finally, these studies contributed largely to the extension of Newtonian mechanics to the emerging disciplines in physics.

Epilogue

Coulomb's participation as a consultant to scientific and engineering projects declined after 1800. His health, which was damaged severely during the eight years in Martinique, deteriorated to an extent that though he continued his regular attendance at the Institute, he conducted most of his own research in an office at his home. In 1802, Napoleon named Coulomb to a commission organized to reestablish the French educational system. The first part of this Epilogue will discuss his role in this work—the last public service of his career. The second part will present what is known of Coulomb in his last years.

Coulomb's Role in French Education

Coulomb's appointment to a position of *Inspecteur-général de l'instruction publique* came indirectly as a result of Napoleon's desire to reorganize and to bring under control the chaotic system of education that had developed during the Revolution.[1] The free or "revolutionary" schools offering three-month courses were a product of the Revolution, but its best educational achievement was the system of *écoles centrales*, and, at the top, the *Ecole polytechnique*. The progress of the latter during its first decade of existence indicated the path that all of French education followed in the first years after the Revolution: liberality gave way to rigid, militarized control.[2] Free education according to capability shifted to education for the sons of the military, government bureaucrats, and the rich.

Napoleon appointed the chemist Jean Antoine Chaptal to be Minister of the Interior and in 1802 ordered him to produce a plan for the general reorganization of French education. Chaptal's liberal plan[3] omitted religion from the schools and doubled the educational budget by proposing a broad-based system of student subsidies. Napoleon flatly rejected this and asked another chemist,

Antoine François Fourcroy, to draft a new proposal.[4] Fourcroy's subsequent plan provided for education at four levels: *écoles primaires* and *secondaires*, administered by the towns, and *lycées* and *écoles spéciales*, administered and supported by the state. Fourcroy's plan lowered the total educational budget and it contained elements of militarization, religious authority, and strict state control.

Napoleon liked Fourcroy's proposal. He directed the *Corps legislatif* and the *Tribunat* to vote for it, and it became law on 11 *floréal, an* 9 (May 1, 1802).[5] In June 1802, Napoleon authorized the appointment of a six-man commission to enforce the "law of 11 *floréal*" with Fourcroy as *Directeur général de l'instruction publique*.[6] Coulomb served on this from its creation until his death in 1806.

The first commission included three *Inspecteurs-généreaux*: Joseph Delambre, the astronomer; François Noël, formerly an *abbé* and professor at the Collège Louis-le-Grand; and Despaulx, an ex-Benedictine and formerly director of the *Ecole de Sorèze*. The other three members were chosen by the Institute as *Commissaires pour l'organisation des études*. These were: Coulomb; Georges Cuvier, the naturalist; and Villard, former member of the National Convention during the Reign of Terror.[7] The commission soon became known as the *Inspecteurs-généraux de l'instruction publique*.

Although Fourcroy's proposal included education at four levels, the *lycées* were clearly indicated to be the privileged element in this system, and they received the most attention from the government. Chaplains were appointed by Bonaparte for each one. Rigorous religious training was intended not so much for the salvation of the students as for their control. The students were organized into military corps with student sergeants and corporals for each "company" of twenty-five boys, and punishment could involve imprisonment.[8]

The major subject in the *lycées* was Latin; the sciences did not receive the same emphasis as letters.[9] The course required three years and was divided into two divisions—"Latin" and "Mathematics." Latin included the Latin language, arithmetic, grammar, geography, ancient history, and the history and geography of France. Mathematics included natural history, basic geometry, elementary physics, astronomy, chemistry, and mineralogy. The best students in each division were allowed to have two additional years of advanced study. In Mathematics this amounted to the differential calculus applied to mechanics and fluids, geometrical cartography, and further studies in electricity and optics.

The commission's major task was the organization of the *lycées*, but they had responsibilities as well to the entire system. Thus, in the line of establishing the *lycées*, they were charged with visiting and examining a sampling of the *écoles primaires* to establish whether the various towns were generally following the law. They were ordered to investigate the *écoles secondaires* more closely, especially those which might be formed into *lycées*. At each school the commission was ordered to examine at least four students because, as Fourcroy said, the government feared the "titles and programs of these establishments are most often above the reality of their teaching."[10] They were responsible not only for examining the pupils and teachers but also for "the cleanliness of the rooms, the dormitories, the kitchens," and every aspect of the physical plant. The future actions of the government were to rest upon their reports. In particular, the group was charged with examining the *écoles centrales* to see how they could best evolve into the *lycées*. Also they were to determine which cities merited the establishment of *écoles spéciales*, and to report on the state of all other existing higher schools. Not only were state schools to be examined, but "even those which were founded by societies or private individuals must never escape your vigilance."[11]

It was Napoleon who directed the central effort of the state toward the new system of *lycées*, and the establishment of these was to be the primary concern of the commission. Immediate plans called for forty-five *lycées* in France and occupied Belgium. In each location the *Inspecteurs-généraux* were to examine the possible building sites. They were given exact plans as to the types of buildings and the number of dormitories and classrooms. Exercise yards were outlined; kitchens and common rooms had to be located on the ground floor. Dormitories (with no more than thirty beds per room), teachers' quarters, and classrooms were to be on the second floor. Bunk beds, *à la Rumford*, were to be used in place of ordinary beds in order to save space. Above the dormitories would be the servants' quarters and a chapel. Luxury "must be banished from educational facilities, but it must be replaced by space and salubrity."[12] Each *lycée* was to accommodate at least 150 students, and each library, 1,500 books.[a]

[a] Fontanes, Champagne, and Domairon from the Institute were named as commissioners to choose the books for the "Latin" division. Laplace,

The law of 11 *floréal* gave the commission the principal responsibility for choosing the faculty of the *lycées*. They would recommend two candidates for each position, and Bonaparte would then make the final choice. Students, also, were to be chosen by them from graduates of the *écoles secondaires* and from the *écoles centrales*. In effect, they were charged with "everything that will assure the success" of the *lycées*. Fourcroy recommended that the commission choose neither those students with an extensive knowledge, nor those with good memories, but those having "real abilities, a lively and penetrating turn of mind, and the first flashes of talent."[15]

From the record, it appears that the six commissioners had a considerable role in French education, and Fourcroy described the *Inspecteurs-généraux* as the "keystone" of the educational system.[16] Though they were presented with an immense task which required a great deal of work, it is not so clear that they played a major role in directing the *policy* of French education. As Aulard remarks, "What Fourcroy doesn't add is that only one man was the real head of public instruction . . ."[17]—that is, Napoleon himself.

Coulomb was more than a lackey, however. Both Delambre and Biot served in *l'instruction publique*, one as an *Inspecteur-général*, the other commissioned to write textbooks. In their memorials of Coulomb[18] both speak of his work as important. In fact, Biot[19] makes a mysterious allusion to the fact that Coulomb was to have been placed at the top of the educational reform work except for a "similarity of name."[b] Coulomb devoted a good part of his time to the position of *Inspecteur-général.* For example, his correspondence with a city official in Reims shows that he visited Reims, Amiens, and Metz in the spring of 1804.[20] He mentioned that his health was still a problem but that he planned further school visits. The argument that the commissioners' work had little effect on *policy*, however, is supported by his statement that he had practically no relations with or influence on the office of the Ministry of the Interior.[21]

What, then, were the accomplishments of Coulomb and the *Inspecteurs-généraux* in the development of French education?

Monge, and Lacroix were commissioners for the "Mathematics" division.[13] Certain other academicians (for instance Haüy and Biot) were instructed to prepare special texts.[14]

[b] Biot's remarks are not quite clear. Probably he meant by similarity of names the Coulomb (no relation to Charles Augustin Coulomb) who was head of Fourcroy's secretariat. He could, however, have been referring to the fact that Lucien Bonaparte was Minister of the Interior.

Many schools were organized. Fourcroy claimed that from 1804 to 1806, 370 *écoles secondaires*, 377 *écoles particulaires* (private schools), and 4,500 *écoles primaires* were organized. This represented a total student population of 75,000. The opening of the *lycées* was not so rapid. Forty-five were planned; twelve were opened in 1803, twenty in 1804, and thirteen in 1805—but only twenty-nine of these forty-five were fully operative by 1806.[22] A decree of 19 *vendemiaire, an* 7 (October 10, 1799) stated that for the *écoles secondaires*, only one scholarship in fifty would be given to sons of the military.[23] This soon changed; of 6,400 scholarships for middle and higher education in 1806, 2,400 went to sons of civil servants and the military.[24] For the *lycées*, of 3,923 scholarships awarded in 1806, 3,039 went to sons of military officers.[25]

The history of the *lycées* at Bordeaux and at Lyon indicates that they were soon considered military schools, or "irreligious" schools. There was a good deal of bourgeois sentiment against Napoleon, and partly for this reason the *lycées* were never too popular during Coulomb's lifetime.[26] It was this situation which induced Napoleon in 1806 to decree the founding of an Imperial University (though it did not become a reality until 1809). In his four years as *Inspecteur-général*, Charles Coulomb participated in the founding of the new system of French education; not one of revolutionary principles, nor a *Corps à talent*, but a semimilitarized system molded to the wishes of Napoleon.

The Last Years[27]

There is no collection of the personal letters of Coulomb. We can not peruse any of the widow's memoirs. Unlike the charming vignettes written by Madame Lavoisier, the Veuve Coulomb leaves us only a bitter letter asking the emperor for an additional pension.[28] Delambre and Biot tell us the usual story of the "good spouse, good brother, good father, and good friend." There remains no narrative of a typical day in Coulomb's life—no description of what he wore, what he may have read, what life was like in his family circle.

A biographer once wrote that a diarist should record everything about one given day to serve as an example. We can see that day for Coulomb, but only as one permitted into a house deprived of life, yet still filled with those appurtenances and objects amongst which Charles Augustin moved and worked and lived. The vagaries of history sometimes prescribe that we can know of a man's daily life only through the notary's balance sheets. Thus it is with Coulomb. We are allowed to follow the Commissaire Nicolas Jacinthe Philippe Bizet as he takes his ledger from room to room, pricing and summing. Bizet lifts a clock from a desk; how many memoirs did Coulomb compose at this desk? How many experiments were timed with this clock? We don't know. For Bizet this is only "an old rosewood desk appraised at six francs . . . an old wooden clock appraised at three francs." Still, the notary's cold examination has its uses for the historian. In his disinterest there is a certain objectivity. The whole story of the Breton canal commission comes a little more into focus when we see that in Bizet's eyes the commission's gift (the watch with the second hand mounted in a gilded box surrounded by thirty diamonds) would bring only 200 francs on the Paris market.

Sometime after 1803, Coulomb moved from 56, rue du Chantre on the Ile de la Cité, over to an apartment on the left bank, at the "quai et place de la Monnaie, no. 15." His previous address, on rue du Chantre, no longer exists, and the apartment on the quai is now filled with offices. One can only guess why he moved from his home into rented lodgings; perhaps to be closer to the Institute. Also his new landlord, Monsieur Duthail, was an old friend of Madame Coulomb. In June 1806, Coulomb contracted a fever which confined him to bed and prevented his taking nourishment. The effects of this fever finally caused his death, at eight in the morning on August 23, 1806.[29] His apartment and possessions were legally sealed the same day and the following week Monsieur Bizet brought his notary ledger. Most of what is known of Coulomb's laboratory, books, and possessions is recorded in Bizet's report to the probate court.

Coulomb lived in a six-room apartment on the fourth floor; and as was usual in those French apartments, he had use of the cellar below. The family used it for storage of goods and to keep numerous bottles of wine brought from the property near Blois. Of the six rooms upstairs, two rooms and the parlor looked out upon the quai, while the kitchen, anteroom and Coulomb's study faced an inner court. The rooms were not elegant. Madame Coulomb owned a piano, and there was a green felt game table. The family owned silver dinnerware and silver chandeliers, and Madame Coulomb employed a cook and a chambermaid. But the furniture was shabby, and the various taffeta and damask curtains were worth no more than nine francs each. One senses that the family ate more often from their earthenware plates than from silver.

Coulomb's bedroom held a double bed with bolster and damask canopy, a simple woolen blanket, and a copper candlestick. In his closet was a chair. His wardrobe was as simple as his furnishings: one coat of wool and another of green cloth, two suits—one black and one brown, his green brocaded costume (to wear to the Institute), three vests, some linen (he seemed fond of shirts, for he had eighteen), and his hat and boots.

We know more about his office, because it was here that he performed some of his last experiments in electricity and magnetism. He chose a room facing away from the Seine on an inner court. It was quieter, and the carriages in the street, he said, did not shake his torsion balance so much. Only part of his instruments were kept in this study (he must have done other experimental work with Jacques Charles at the Louvre), but it was here that he had his modest library. This room was more than just a study for Coulomb, for he kept a basin and red copper bathtub there alongside his books. The room was filled with furniture: his old rosewood writing desk and a little mahogany secretary desk, four chairs, and two worthless wooden tables for his instruments. On these tables were a quarter-circle magnetic needle, an electrostatic generator (*machine électrique*), several cardboard spheres covered with tin, a torsion balance, an ordinary pan balance, an insulating plate (*plateau électrique*), several barometers, pendulums and clocks, and a microscope and telescope.

Coulomb was accomplished in history but he was not a man of letters; his library reflects this. Except for a six-volume French edition of Polybius' *History* and Daniel's *Histoire de France*, his books were technical—Trevaux's *Dictionnaire*, a seventeen-volume atlas, Bossut's course in hydraulics, assorted texts in math and physics, and the publications of the Academy of Sciences. His largest collection consisted of 200 volumes of the *Mémoires* of the Academy in the Amsterdam edition. In all, he owned 307 volumes, of which 238 were books issuing from the Academy.

Coulomb owned little jewelry. There was the jeweled watch given him by the Breton canal commission, two small jeweled pins, a silver medal, a silver compass, and his *Croix de St. Louis* and *Médaille de la Légion d'Honneur*.

From this evidence one must try and define Coulomb's style of life. Little is known of his property near Luzarches or of his earlier residences in Paris. His house near Blois is a very simple farm-house of four large rooms. The tenant's houses on this property are of similar size. Certainly the six-room apartment on the quai de la Monnaie was a modest lodging. Coulomb must have been a man of moderate habits. His youth, spent with his penniless old soldier of a father, could not have been an extravagant one, and twenty years in various military posts would have accustomed him to at least a moderate, if not a frugal, living standard. He may have used his mother's inheritance to enter a more gracious life in the years from 1781 to 1793. His wife, and the authors of several short memorials, state that the Coulomb family suffered major financial losses during the Revolution. Neither Delambre nor Biot, however, was inclined to treat the Revolution favorably.

Delambre claims that Madame Coulomb was a wonderful wife and mother. One wonders if the young wife did more than tolerate the old physicist who was thirty years her senior. She auctioned all of his instruments six months after his death[30] and followed this by writing a tortured letter to Napoleon, asking for an additional pension. She claimed that Coulomb's 800-franc pension as a for-mer *Inspecteur-général de l'instruction publique* was the sole sup-port for herself, an aged mother, an aunt, two of Coulomb's octo-genarian sisters, and his two sons.[c,31]

It is true that his handsome salary as *Inspecteur-général*[d] stopped at his death but his estate was valued at over 43,000 francs, includ-ing nearly 16,000 in gold and banknotes and over 25,000 in mort-gages. Above this, Madame Coulomb had on hand at least 4,000 francs of her own in addition to her own possessions. If one con-siders that a military officer of field grade earned about 3,000 francs a year at this time and a professor of physics at the *Ecole poly-technique* earned about 6,000 francs, then the Coulomb family financial situation was quite good.

Finally, we reach the end of what we know of the life of Charles Augustin Coulomb. Some of the details must remain in shadow. It is hoped though that this biography has given an appreciation for Coulomb as public servant, engineer, and physicist, and some background of the development of physics and engineering in eighteenth-century France.

---

c Two weeks after Coulomb's death, his two sons were granted full tui-tion, Charles to *l'Ecole spéciale militaire de Fontainebleau*, and Henry to the *Lycée Napoléon*.[32]

d The salary as *Inspecteur-général de l'instruction publique* was 1,000 francs a month.

Perhaps in closing it may be fitting to recall three statements that define Coulomb's approach to his work. First, both in his view of the *Corps du génie* and in public service, Coulomb said that men should be judged on their ability, and that a public service body was a *Corps à talent*. Second, in his engineering work, he called for the use of rational analysis combined with reality in experiment—for the conduct of research in engineering through use of a "mélange du calcul et de la physique." Third, this use of rational analysis and engineering reality, coupled in the pursuit of *physique expérimentale*, led to Coulomb's work in physics and the evaluation of Biot that "it is to Borda and to Coulomb that one owes the renaissance of true physics in France, not a verbose and hypothetical physics, but that ingenious and exact physics which observes and compares all with rigor."[33]

Appendix A

COULOMB MEMOIRS PRESENTED TO THE ACADEMY OF SCIENCES

The following notations are taken from the manuscript *Procès-verbaux*[1] of the Académie des Sciences for the period, 1773–1793, and the published *Procès-verbaux*[2] of the *Première Classe* of the Institut de France for the period 1795–1806. Because of the difficulty of compiling a list of all of Coulomb's memoirs, the notations are given here in the original French.

Manuscript Volume	Date	Notation
92	10/III/73	M. Coulomb est entré et a commencé la lecture d'un mémoire intitulé: essai sur l'application des Règles de Maximis et Minimis à quelques problèmes d'architecture.
92	2/IV/73	M. Colomb [*sic*] est entré et a continué la lecture de son Mémoire commencé le 10 mars.
97	18/II/78	M. Coulomb a lû deux mémoires, l'un sur la manière la plus avantageuse d'appliquer la force aux mouvemens des machines, et l'autre sur les limites de la force des hommes et sur l'impossibilité d'imiter le vol des oiseaux.
98	5/V/79	M. Coulomb est entré et a lû l'ouvrage qu'il avait présenté la dernière séance, sur la manière d'executer sous l'eau differents ouvrages hydrauliques, sans épuisements.
98	8/V/79	M. Coulomb a présenté quelques notes à joindre à son mémoire sur les ouvrages sous l'eau.
99	19/IV/80	M. Coulomb est entré et a lû un mémoire sur les limites de la force des hommes et de la plus grande action qu'ils peuvent exercer pendant quelques sécondes, d'où il conclu l'impossibilité de voler en l'air comme les oiseaux.

Manuscript Volume	*Date*	*Notation*
99	26/iv/80	M. Coulomb est entré et a lû la description d'une nouvelle boussole pour observer les différences diurnes de la variation du compas.
100	20/vi/81	M. Coulomb a présenté un mémoire sur la manière de faire des observations magnétiques.
101	16/i/82	M. Coulomb a lû un mémoire sur la théorie des moulins, mûs par des fluides.
101	23/i/82	M. Coulomb a continué la lecture de son mémoire.
102	24/v/83	M. Coulomb a déposé une méthode d'aimanter les aiguilles des bossoles [*sic*].
103	4/ix/84	M. Coulomb a lû quelques expériences sur la force de torsion des fils de laiton.
104	6/iii/85	M. Coulomb a lû un mémoire sur l'action des rames.
104	4/v/85	M. Coulomb a lû un mémoire sur un nouvel électromètre.
104	8/vi/85	M. Coulomb a lû un mémoire sur l'électricité.
104	17/xii/85	M. Coulomb a lû un mémoire sur la manière de placer un méridien magnétique.
106	7/ii/87	M. Coulomb a lû son deuxième mémoire sur l'électricité et le magnétisme.
106	28/iii/87	M. Coulon [*sic*] a lû son troisième Mémoire sur l'électricité et le magnétisme.
106	21/xi/87	M. Coulomb a lû un 4e mémoire sur l'électricité.
106	5/xii/87	M. Coulomb a lû un Mémoire et fait des observations sur l'aimant.
107	13/xii/88	M. Coulomb a lû un 5e Mémoire sur l'électricité et fait des expériences.
107	11/vii/89	M. Coulomb a lû un Mémoire sur le frottement des pivots.
109	13/iii/90	M. Coulomb a commencé la lecture d'un sixième mémoire sur l'électricité et fait des expériences.
109	17/iii/90	M. Coulomb a fini la lecture de son mémoire sur l'électricité et fait des expériences.

Manu- script Volume	Date	Notation
109	19/vi/90	M. Coulomb a lû un supplement à son sixième mémoire sur l'électricité.
109	2/vii/91	M. Coulomb a commencé la lecture d'un 7e Mémoire sur l'électricité et le magnétisme.
109	6/vii/91	M. Coulomb a continué la lecture de son mémoire sur l'électricité et le magnétisme.
109	9/vii/91	M. Coulomb a fini la lecture de son mémoire sur l'électricité et le magnétisme.
109	5/v/92	M. Coulomb a présenté une boussole semblable à cette qu'il avait décrite dans le mémoires d l'Académie pour l'année 1785 avec quelques additions qui consistent 1e—dans la manière de centrer le fil de suspension. 2e—dans la plongeur que l'on fait descendre tout entier dans l'huile et qui rallentit le mouvement de manière qu'au bout de trois minutes, l'aiguille s'arrête dans tous les sens. 3e—dans une boite de suspension où l'aiguille peut se renverser. M. Coulomb estime qu'au moyen de cette aiguille, on aura la direction du méridien magnétique, à 20 secondes près, où même avec encore plus de précision. M. Coulomb ayant demandé des commissaires pour faire l'observation des declinations, M. le Directeur a nommé MM. Borda, Cassini et Méchain.

Published Volume	Date	Notation
I, p. 203	1 floréal an 5 (20/iv/97)	Le Cn Coulomb fait lecture d'un Mémoire intitulé *Expériences relatives à la circulation de la sève dans les plantes*; la Section de Botanique est chargée de suivre, avec le Cn Coulomb, les expériences rapportées dans ce Mémoire.
I, p. 353	6 ventôse an 6 (25/ii/98)	Le Cn Coulomb commence la lecture d'un Mémoire sur la quantité d'action que les hommes peuvent fournir dans le travail. Cette lecture sera continuée à la Séance suivante.
I, p. 357	11 ventôse an 6 (2/iii/98)	Le Cn Coulomb achève la lecture de son Mémoire sur la quantité d'action dont les hommes sont capables dans le travail.

Published Volume	Date	Notation
I, p. 587	26 prairial an 7 (14/VI/99)	Le Cⁿ Coulomb lit un Mémoire intitulé *Détermination théorique et expérimentale des forces qui ramènent différentes aiguilles aimantées à saturation à leur méridien magnétique.*
I, p. 625	26 fructidor an 7 (6/IX/99)	Le Cⁿ Coulomb lit un Mémoire intitulé *Exposé d'une nouvelle méthode de déterminer l'inclinaison des aiguilles aimantées.*
II, p. 172	6 prairial an 8 (26/V/00)	Le Cⁿ Coulomb lit un Mémoire intitulé *Expériences destinées à déterminer la cohérence des fluides et les lois de leur résistance dans les mouvemens très lens* [sic].
II, p. 401	26 fructidor an 9 (5/IX/01)	Le Cⁿ Coulomb donne lecture d'un second Mémoire sur les lois magnétiques.
II, p. 476	21 ventôse an 10 (12/III/02)	Le Cⁿ Coulomb lit un travail intitulé *Expériences qui prouvent que tous les corps sont susceptibles de magnétisme, et que même on peut en évaluer la force par des poids.*
*	13 prairial an 10 (2/VI/02)	[*"Résultat des différentes méthodes employées pour donner aux lames et aux barreaux d'acier le plus grand degré de magnétisme."*]
II, p. 588	28 vendémiaire an 11 (20/X/02)	Le Cⁿ Coulomb lit un Mémoire sur la meilleure manière d'aimanter à saturation.
III, p. 104	29 prairial an 12 (18/VI/04)	M. Coulomb lit un Mémoire sur le magnétisme.
III, p. 116	11 thermidor an 12 (30/VII/04)	M. Coulomb lit le résumé de son Mémoire sur le magnétisme.

* This date was given in the published memoir but not listed in the *Procès-verbaux* for 1802.

Appendix B

COULOMB'S ACTIVITIES AT THE ACADEMY OF SCIENCES

The following notations are taken from the manuscript *Procès-verbaux*[1] of the Académie des Sciences for the period, 1773–1793, and, in one instance each, from the Archives[2] of the Bibliothèque Nationale and the Archives Nationales.[3] Included here are summaries in English of *all* known references to Coulomb in the manuscript *Procès-verbaux*. An asterisk (*) indicates that the complete French language entry for a particular item is given in Appendix A. Entries for the period of Coulomb's membership in the Institut are not given here. These may be found through use of the indices of Volumes I-III of the published *Procès-verbaux*[4] of the *Institut*.

Manuscript Volume	Date	Subject of Notation
92*	10/III/73	Coulomb read his memoir "Essay on the application of rules of Maxima and Minima to some problems in architecture."
92*	2/IV/73	Coulomb continued reading his memoir of 10/III/73.
92	28/IV/73	Bossut and Borda named to examine Coulomb memoir of 10/III/73.
93	30/IV/74	Bossut and Borda reported on Coulomb memoir of 10/III/73.
93	6/VII/74	Bossut and Vandermonde recommended Coulomb as Correspondent to the Academy.
96a	9/IV/77	Condorcet announced that Van Swinden and Coulomb would share the [1777] magnet prize and that Magny earned honorable mention of 800 *livres*.

Manu- script Volume	Date	Subject of Notation
97*	18/ɪɪ/78	Coulomb read two memoirs, one on the most advantageous means to apply force to the movements of machines and the other on the limits of the force of men and on the impossibility of imitating the flight of birds. Bossut and Vandermonde named to examine these.
98	1/v/79	Tillet presented to the Academy Coulomb's memoir: "Researches on means to make all sorts of constructions underwater."
98*	5/v/79	Coulomb read the memoir presented 1/v/79. Bory, Le Monnier, Bossut, and Lavoisier named to examine this.
98*	8/v/79	Coulomb added some notes to his memoir read 5/v/79.
98	15/v/79	Le Monnier, Bory, Lavoisier, and Bossut reported on Coulomb's memoir of 5/v/79.
98	22/xɪɪ/79	Election to fill Bezout's chair of associate mechanician. Abbé Rochon elected, Coulomb received *deuxièmes voix*.
99*	19/ɪv/80	Coulomb read a memoir on the limits of men's force and on the greatest action that they can exercise during several seconds. He concluded the impossibility of flying in the air like birds. Bossut, Monge, and Condorcet named to examine this.
99*	26/ɪv/80	Coulomb read the description of a new needle for observing diurnal differences in the variation of the compass. The 1777 magnet prize commission named to examine this (Condorcet, Le Roy, Borda, Le Monnier, and Bossut).
99	10/v/80	Le Monnier, Borda, *Bory*, Le Roy, and Bossut reported on Coulomb's presentation of 26/ɪv/80.
99	24/v/80	Bossut, Monge, and Condorcet reported on Coulomb's memoir of 19/ɪv/80.
100*	20/vɪ/81	Coulomb presented a memoir on the means of making magnetic observations. Bory, Le Monnier, Cassini (IV), and Bossut named to examine this.
100	12/xɪɪ/81	Election to the place of adjunct mechanician. The members of the class for mechanics recommended Coulomb, Legendre, or Musnier (i.e., Meusnier de la Place). "Les Premières voix ont été pour M. Coulomb; les deuxièmes pour M. Musnier."

Manu-script Volume	*Date*	*Subject of Notation*
100	15/xii/81	Condorcet read a letter from Amelot at Versailles, naming Coulomb to the place of adjunct mechanician, replacing abbé Rochon.
100	15/xii/81	Coulomb and Bossut named to examine a memoir on a machine to clear rivers and ports, submitted by M. de Solignac.
101*	16/i/82	Coulomb read a memoir on the theory of mills, moved by fluids.
101	19/i/82	Le Roy, Bossut, and Coulomb named to examine M. Verra's machine.
101*	23/i/82	Coulomb continued the reading of his memoir of 16/i/82.
101	26/i/82	Le Roy, Bossut, and Coulomb named to examine machines of Gauthei and Verra.
101	2/iii/82	Bossut and Coulomb named to examine Campmal's memoir on capstans.
101	13/iv/82	Coulomb and Monge named to examine Leguin's machine to re-equip ships.
101	17/iv/82	Rochon and Coulomb named to examine an addition to Campmal's presentation. Bossut, Le Roy, and Coulomb named to examine a memoir on means to raise water, regarding M. Verra's machine, presented by M. Campmal.
101	24/iv/82	Campmal read a memoir on his different machines. Bossut and Coulomb named to examine this.
101	24/iv/82	Coulomb and Monge reported on Leguin's memoir of 13/iv/82.
101	8/v/82	Bossut and Coulomb reported on Campmal's memoir on capstans of 2/iii/82.
101	29/v/82	D'Alembert, Coulomb, and Condorcet named to examine Bossut's text "New Elements of Mathematics."
101	8/vi/82	D'Alembert, Coulomb, and Condorcet reported on Bossut's text.
101	12/vi/82	Bossut, Borda, Du Séjour, Coulomb, and Vandermonde named to examine Brumet's memoir on arch construction.

Manu-script Volume	Date	Subject of Notation
101	19/vi/82	D'Alembert, Bossut, Lalande, Le Roy, Coulomb, Tillet, and Condorcet named to examine Defer's memoir on bringing the Yvette river water to Paris.
101	17/vii/82	Bossut and Coulomb named to examine Bujot's memoir on windmills.
101	27/vii/82	Bossut and Coulomb report on an "arrêt du Parlement" to examine building arches.
101	17/viii/82	Bossut, Coulomb, and Condorcet named to examine Defer's memoir on draining the marshes of the Saone.
101	21/viii/82	Le Monnier, Bory, and Coulomb named to examine Deshayes' machine to clear ports.
101	7/ix/82	Tenon and Coulomb named to examine Barthez' memoir on theory of movements and equilibrium of men and of quadrupeds.
101	13/xi/82	Bossut and Coulomb named to examine Mathieu's machine to re-equip ships.
101	27/xi/82	Monge and Coulomb named to examine Renault's memoir on the Marly machine.
101	4/xii/82	Bossut and Coulomb named to examine Mathieu's memoir on re-equipping ships.†
101	14/xii/82	Delambre, Bossut, Coulomb, and Condorcet reported on Defer's memoir of 19/vi/82.
102	18/i/83	Coulomb and Bossut named to examine Leroux's machine to warn of floods.
102	1/ii/83	Bossut and Coulomb reported on Leroux's memoir of 18/i/83.
102	5/ii/83	Bézout, Monge, and Coulomb named to examine Defer's memoir on canals and bridges.
102	22/ii/83	Le Roy, Bossut, Cousin, and Coulomb named to examine Perrier's (Jacques-Constantin Périer) memoir on steam engines.
102	6/iii/83	Bory, Coulomb, and Condorcet named to examine Carret's hydraulic machine.

† Same as 13/xi/82 entry.

Manu- script Volume	Date	Subject of Notation
102	6/III/83	Le Roy and Coulomb reported on Campmal's unpublished work, "The Hydraulic Engineer."
102	19/III/83	Coulomb, Bossut, Le Roy, and Cousin reported on Périer's memoir on *pompes à feu* (steam engines) of 22/II/83. The report was written by Coulomb.
102	19/III/83	Desmarest, Tillet, Coulomb, and Monge reported on Duhamel's mining instrument.
102	22/III/83	Bossut and Coulomb gave a second report on a memoir of 27/VII/82.
102	26/III/83	Bossut and Coulomb demanded more committee members to examine the memoir and report of 27/VII/82 and 22/III/83.
102*	24/V/83	Coulomb presented a method for magnetizing compass needles.
102	3/XI/83	Le Roy, Coulomb, Monge, and Cousin named to examine Prom's memoir on theories of bridge arches.
102	15/XI/83	Bossut, Borda, Coulomb, Périer, and Monge named to examine comte d'Angiviller's plan for a Marly machine prize contest.
102	20/XII/83	Coulomb and Périer named to examine Vautrin's memoir on water-mills.
102	23/XII/83	Commissioners named to examine experiments on *machines aerostatiques*: duc de la Rochefoucauld, Bossut, Le Roy, Coulomb, Tillet, Lavoisier, Brisson, Berthollet, Condorcet, Fouchy named secretary for this work in case of Condorcet's absence.
103	10/I/84	Ségur, the Minister of War, asked for a report on lightning rods to protect powder magazines. (Benjamin) Franklin, Le Roy, Coulomb, Rochon, and Laplace named to examine this.
103	10/I/84	Comte de Maillebois, Bossut, Borda, and Coulomb named to examine a supplement to de Morbeck's memoir on forged cannon.
103	14/I/84	Election to replace Rochon in chair of associate mechanician. "On a lû le Réglement, Evangeliste, M. L'Abbé Rochon; Prémières voix, M. Coulomb, unanimité; Deuxièmes voix, M. Meunier [*sic*] (Meusnier de la Place)."

Manu-script Volume	*Date*	*Subject of Notation*
103	14/i/84	Borda and Coulomb named to examine Lalain's windmill model.
103	21/i/84	Condorcet read a letter of 19/i/84 from baron de Breteuil at Versailles naming Coulomb to the place of associate mechanician, replacing Rochon.
103	11/ii/84	Comte de Maillebois, Borda, Bossut, and Coulomb reported on supplementary memoir of 10/i/84.
103	14/ii/84	Borda, Coulomb, and Legendre named to examine vicomte de Roquefeuille's memoir on aerostatic machines.
103	18/ii/84	Coulomb elected to substitute for Bézout as member on the commission for mills.
103	25/ii/84	Tillet and Coulomb named to examine Jamard's memoir on guiding the flight of balloons.
103	3/iii/84	Coulomb and Meusnier named to examine a new pump.
103	6/iii/84	Bossut, Le Roy, and Coulomb named to examine Montgolfier's memoir on aerostatic machines.
103	10/iii/84	Bossut, Le Roy, and Coulomb named to examine Bertholet de Barbot's plan for a new carriage.
103	13/iii/84	Le Roy, Bossut, and Coulomb reported on Montgolfier's memoir of 6/iii/84 on the theory of oars applied to aerostatic machines.
103	13/iii/84	Borda, Coulomb, and Legendre reported on memoir of 14/ii/84.
103	20/iii/84	Bossut, Le Roy, and Coulomb reported on the plan of 10/iii/84.
103	24/iv/84	(Benjamin) Franklin, Le Roy, Coulomb, Laplace, and Rochon reported on memoir of 10/i/84, concerning lightning rods.
103	1/v/84	Borda, Coulomb, and Meusnier named to examine Paneton's memoir on means to direct the flight of balloons.
103	3/vii/84	(Benjamin) Franklin, Rochon, Laplace, and Coulomb reported further on a memoir of 10/i/84.
103	7/vii/84	Coulomb and Périer named to examine Châlet's machine for clearing ports.

Manu-script Volume	Date	Subject of Notation
103	10/vii/84	Coulomb and Périer named to examine Fourcroy's (de Ramecourt) memoir on maritime construction.
103	14/vii/84	Condorcet requested a report on his memoir on the application of analysis to decisions made by plurality of votes. Bossut and Coulomb named to examine this.
103	17/vii/84	Brisson and Coulomb named to examine Louis Gentil's model for re-equipping ships.
103	17/vii/84	Bossut and Coulomb reported on Condorcet's memoir of 14/vii/84.
103	4/viii/84	Coulomb and Périer reported on Fourcroy's memoir of 10/vii/84.
103	14/viii/84	De Gua, Coulomb, and Fougeroux named to examine St. Armand's memoir for providing water for Paris.
103*	4/ix/84	Coulomb read some experiments on the force of torsion in brass threads.
103	17/xi/84	Borda and Coulomb named to examine Stephano Catval's memoirs on measuring water currents.
103	17/xi/84	De Gua and Coulomb reported on a memoir of 14/viii/84.
103	27/xi/84	Election for position of *associé libre*. *Commissaires*: Vandermonde, Lalande, Coulomb, Daubenton, Lavoisier, and Lamarck. There were 13 candidates: Fourcroy (de Ramecourt) was elected; Montucla received second place.
103	27/xi/84	Bory, Borda, Rochon, Coulomb, and Meusnier named to examine Hofman and Marin's memoir on raising sunken ships.
104	8/i/85	Elections: Coulomb, Vicq d'Azyr, and Darcet elected to serve with Vandermonde "pour la Sécretairie."
104	8/i/85	Laplace, Borda, and Coulomb named to examine Bourgeois' model of a rifle.
104	26/i/85	Desmarest, Coulomb, and Sage named to examine abbé Mongez' memoir on use of forges.
104*	6/iii/85	Coulomb read a memoir on the action of oars.

Manu-script Volume	Date	Subject of Notation
104	20/IV/85	Borda, Bossut, Coulomb, and Condorcet named to examine Perez' memoir on modifications to a *pompe à feu*.
104*	4/V/85	Coulomb read a memoir on a new electrometer.
104	7/V/85	*Commissaires* above reported on a memoir of 20/IV/85.
104	13/V/85	Borda, Bossut, Bory, and Coulomb reported on Texier de Morbec's memoir on marine artillery.
104*	8/VI/85	Coulomb read a memoir on electricity.
104	15/VI/85	Tillet, Desmarest, Coulomb, and Condorcet reported on Grosbert's machine for manufacturing money.
104	3/VIII/85	Saron, Coulomb, and Méchain named to examine Le Monnier's magnetic inclination instrument.
104	6/VIII/85	Fourcroy (de Ramecourt), Coulomb, and Cadet named to examine St. Fav's memoir on using brick in constructing arches.
104	10/VIII/85	Le Roy and Coulomb named to examine Dausse's samples of polished steel.
104	17/VIII/85	Perronet, Coulomb, Vandermonde, and Fouchy named to examine a M. Legendre's plan for machines for milling sugar.
104	20/VIII/85	Coulomb named to "ad hoc" committee to recommend persons for corresponding membership.
104	3/IX/85	Laplace, Coulomb, and Monge named to examine Billiaux' plan for using sea tides to operate mills.
104	3/IX/85	Nominated to committee to examine general problems of drainage (*épuisements*): Le Roy, Bory, Borda, and Coulomb.
104	6/IX/85	Le Roy, Bory, Borda, and Coulomb named to examine Forbes' memoir on *épuisements* and on ship pumps.
104	6/IX/85	Le Roy and Coulomb reported on a presentation of 10/VIII/85.
104	6/IX/85	Fourcroy (de Ramecourt), Coulomb, and Cadet reported on a memoir of 6/VIII/85.

Manu-script Volume	Date	Subject of Notation
104	19/xi/85	Ségur, the Minister of War, asked for a report on a plan for river work in Alsace. Bossut, Laplace, and Coulomb named to report on this.
104	19/xi/85	Le Roy, Borda, and Coulomb named to examine Cordelle's report on the "machine de Compiégne."
104	23/xi/85	Borda, Rochon, and Condorcet added to the committee to report on Ségur's request of 19/xi/85.
104	7/xii/85	Fourcroy (de Ramecourt), Bossut, Laplace, Coulomb, Borda, Rochon, and Condorcet reported on Ségur's request of 19/xi/85.
104	10/xii/85	De Lassone, Daubenton, Le Roy, Tenon, Bailly, Lavoisier, Darcet, and Laplace named to examine Poyet's memoir for the Hôtel-Dieu (hospital). (See 14/xii/85)
104	14/xii/85	Le Roy asked that his memoir on the Hôtel-Dieu be printed. Coulomb, Darcet, and Tenon named to examine this request.
104	14/xii/85	Coulomb substituted for Le Roy on committee to examine Poyet's memoir of 10/xii/85.
104*	17/xii/85	Coulomb read a memoir on the method of placing a magnetic meridian. Le Monnier, Jeaurat, Cassini (IV), Legentil, and Méchain named to examine this.
105	7/i/86	Borda, Coulomb, and Bory named to examine Romme's memoir on the variation of magnetic compass needles.
105	7/i/86	Coulomb, Vicq d'Azyr, and Darcet elected to continue as _____ (blank, but on 8/i/85 these three were elected "pour la Sécretairie").
B.N., Fonds Libri N.A.F. 3258 fol. 129	25/i/86	Meusnier, Le Roy, Coulomb, Condorcet, and Lavoisier reported on Brun de Condamine's memoir of 17/xi/84 concerning aerostatics.
105	4/ii/86	Le Roy, Monge, and Coulomb named to examine Maastner's memoir on re-equipping ships.
105	22/ii/86	Le Roy and Coulomb named to examine the memoir of M. Jacquet.
105	1/iii/86	The Maréchal de Castries forwarded a plan to lessen friction in wagons used in ports. Bossut, Cousin, and Coulomb named to examine this.

Manu-script Volume	Date	Subject of Notation
105	18/III/86	Bossut, Cousin, and Coulomb reported on request of 1/III/86.
105	18/III/86	Coulomb and Meusnier named to examine Michel Missel's machine for boring-out cannon barrels.
105	29/III/86	Bossut and Coulomb named to examine Cerf's memoir on a *pompe à feu*.
105	29/III/86	Coulomb and Meusnier reported on memoir of 18/III/86.
105	1/IV/86	Bossut, Cousin, and Coulomb reported on Castries' proposal of 1/III/86.
105	5/IV/86	Bossut, Cassini,† and Coulomb continued their report of 1/IV/86.
105	3/V/86	Bossut, Tillet, and Coulomb named to examine a mill plan of G. B. Laurent.
105	31/V/86	Coulomb, Borda, and Bossut named to examine hydraulic work presented by Bernard.
105	21/VI/86	Bory, Le Roy, Coulomb, and Vicq d'Azyr named to examine d'Agobert's memoir on means to "plonger ou boucher les voies d'eau."
105	23/VI/86	Vandermonde, Coulomb, and Charles named to examine Margnet's new carriage.
105	12/VII/86	Coulomb, Bossut, Borda, and Condorcet elected as commissioners for the Yvette river project.
105	12/VII/86	Vandermonde, Coulomb, and Charles reported on presentation of 23/VI/86.
105	19/VII/86	Bossut and Coulomb named to examine Fleuri's memoir.
105	5/VIII/86	Darcet, Coulomb, Le Roy, and Tillet named to examine Irvine's invention.
105	12/VIII/86	Brisson, Le Roy, and Coulomb named to examine Muralt's hydraulic machine.
105	2/IX/86	Le Roy, Brisson, and Coulomb named to examine the report of lightning damage at Brest.

† *Cousin* listed above (1/IV/86), not Cassini.

Manu-script Volume	Date	Subject of Notation
A.N., K1024 No. 34	22/ɪx/86	De Lassone, Daubenton, Tenon, Bailly, Lavoisier, Laplace, Coulomb, and Darcet reported on the project for a new Hôtel-Dieu.
105	25/xɪ/86	Borda, Bossut, Coulomb, Le Roy, and Condorcet named to examine a proposal from baron de Breteuil at Fontainebleau concerning the establishment of a prize for the design of a hydraulic machine to replace those at Pont Neuf and Pont Notre Dame.
105	25/xɪ/86	The commission for the Hôtel-Dieu continued its report of 22/ɪx/86.
105	29/xɪ/86	The commission for the Hôtel-Dieu continued its report of 22/ɪx/86.
105	2/xɪɪ/86	The commission for the Hôtel-Dieu finished its report of 22/ɪx/86.
105	16/xɪɪ/86	Bossut and Coulomb named to examine Lebé's memoir on a machine to break stone.
105	20/xɪɪ/86	Cousin and Coulomb named to examine a memoir on carrying loads.
105	23/xɪɪ/86	Bossut and Coulomb named to examine Racine's machines for re-equipping ships.
106	1/ɪ/87	Berthollet and Coulomb elected to library committee.
106	17/ɪ/87	Le Roy, Lavoisier, Coulomb, and Berthollet named to examine Cadet's memoir on "méphitiques halaissons."
106	17/ɪ/87	Bossut, Coulomb, and Charles named to examine Baumé's memoir on pumps.
106	17/ɪ/87	Bossut, Coulomb, Cousin, and Périer named to examine Beauregard's machine.
106	27/ɪ/87	Borda, Coulomb, and Condorcet named to examine a letter from baron de Breteuil concerning a new station at Charenton.
106*	7/ɪɪ/87	Coulomb read his second memoir on electricity and magnetism.
106	14/ɪɪ/87	Périer and Coulomb named to examine Bonevot's machine to re-equip ships.

Manu-script Volume	Date	Subject of Notation
106	24/III/87	Abbé Haüy requested a committee to review his epitome of Aepinus on electricity. Named for this were Laplace, Cousin, Coulomb, and Legendre.
106*	28/III/87	Coulomb read his third memoir on electricity and magnetism.
106	25/IV/87	Borda, Coulomb, and Condorcet reported on a request of 27/I/87.
106	19/V/87	Condorcet was asked to write to "M. Le President" to indicate that Tenon and Coulomb were assigned by the Academy to make a trip to England.
106	13/VI/87	Tillet read a letter he had received from Coulomb and Tenon in London.
106	4/VII/87	Bailly read a letter from Tenon and Coulomb.
106	21/VII/87	Laplace, Cousin, and Legendre reported on Haüy's book, *Exposition de la théorie de l'Electricité et du Magnétisme suivant les principes d'Aepinus.*
106	1/VIII/87	Bailly read a letter from Tenon and one from Coulomb.
106	14/VIII/87	Bailly, Borda, Coulomb, Perronet, and Condorcet named to examine de Wailly's plan for a station for Paris.
106	14/VIII/87	Election of corresponding member. Commissioners: Borda, Le Monnier, Le Roy, Coulomb, Sabatier, Cadet, Desfontaines, Duhamel. The Commissioners proposed Banks, Aepinus, Black, Maskeline [*sic*], Thunberg, and Herschell. Banks was elected; Black received second place.
106	1/IX/87	Coulomb and Legendre named to examine Le Monnier's memoir on "La mesure de la base en Angleterre."
106	1/IX/87	Le Roy, Bossut, and Coulomb named to examine Dusaussoit's machine to re-equip ships.
106	17/XI/87	Perronet, Vandermonde, and Coulomb named to examine Mangin's memoir on a machine to cut stones.
106*	21/XI/87	Coulomb read a fourth memoir on electricity.

Manu- script Volume	Date	Subject of Notation
106*	5/xii/87	Coulomb read a memoir and made observations on the magnet.
106	12/xii/87	Le Roy and Coulomb named to examine Murat's memoir on hydraulic machines.
107	12/i/88	Elections: Coulomb continued on the library committee.
107	19/i/88	De Saron, Le Roy, and Coulomb named to examine Fol's memoir on time-keeping pendulum.
107	30/i/88	Le Roy, Bossut, and Coulomb named to examine Ango's model in iron.
107	9/ii/88	Vandermonde, Perronet, and Coulomb reported on memoir of 17/xi/87.
107	9/ii/88	Le Roy, Coulomb, and Cousin reported on memoir of 12/xii/87.
107	8/iii/88	Coulomb, Sage, and Monge named to examine Mesnier's machines for experiments on air.
107	28/v/88	Coulomb and Vandermonde added to Bailly, Lavoisier, and Périer as Commissioners to decide the priority argument between Thierri and Bergevin.
107	4/vi/88	Condorcet, Borda, Bailly, Perronet, and Coulomb named to report on de Wailly's project to beautify Paris.
107	4/vi/88	Bossut, Coulomb, Périer, and Condorcet named to examine Bellanger's project for a wooden bridge.
107	7/vi/88	Coulomb, Bossut, and Perronet named to report on proposal for a bridge near the Arsenal.
107	7/vi/88	Coulomb, Borda, Bailly, and Condorcet reported on a project presented 4/vi/88.
107	11/vi/88	Perronet, Bossut, and Coulomb named to examine Guyot's proposal for a 400 foot single-arch bridge.
107	14/vi/88	Bossut and Coulomb reported on the second edition of Perronet's work, *Description des projets et de la construction des Ponts. . . .*
107	5/vii/88	Le Monnier, Lavoisier, Le Roy, and Coulomb named to examine Le Roy's observations on lightning rods.

Manu-script Volume	*Date*	*Subject of Notation*
107	12/vii/88	Vandermonde, Coulomb, and Baumé named to examine Villet's machine to mix plaster.
107	30/vii/88	Condorcet and Coulomb named to examine abbé Rochon's memoirs on his voyage to the Indies.
107	30/vii/88	The hospital committee (de Lassone, Daubenton, Tillet, Tenon, Bailly, Lavoisier, Laplace, Coulomb, and Darcet), reported on Tenon's fifth hospital memoir.
107	2/viii/88	Condorcet announced that the contest for the design of a pump for Pont Notre Dame was closed and that there had been 45 entries. Borda, Le Roy, Bossut, Coulomb, and Condorcet were named as Commissioners.
107	5/ix/88	Coulomb and Le Roy reported on a memoir of 19/i/88.
107*	13/xii/88	Coulomb read a fifth memoir on electricity and conducted some experiments.
107	20/xii/88	Le Roy read some observations on electricity relative to Coulomb's memoir on the same subject.
108	24/i/89	Vandermonde and Coulomb added to the Commissioners to examine Michel's plan for a mill.
108	14/ii/89	Borda, Bailly, Desmarest, Vandermonde, Tillet, Coulomb, and Rochon named to report to the King on whether steam engines should be adapted to mills.
108	18/ii/89	Bossut, Laplace, Coulomb, Monge, Perronet, and Coulon [*sic*] (??) named to examine a project of de Villedeuil.
108	18/ii/89	Rochon, Desmarest, Coulomb, and Vandermonde reported on Missel's machine for grinding bark.
108	7/iii/89	Cousin and Coulomb named to examine Bougnon's memoir on a new principle of mechanics.
108	14/iii/89	Cousin and Coulomb reported on a memoir of 7/iii/89.
108	25/iv/89	Bossut, Coulomb, Le Roy, and Périer named to examine Rumsey's memoir on using steam engines to raise ships.

Manu-script Volume	*Date*	*Subject of Notation*
108	25/IV/89	Bory, Monge, and Coulomb named to examine Gari's new screw-plate for army rifles.
108	9/V/89	Bossut, Coulomb, and Charles named to examine a machine to raise water.
108	29/V/89	Bossut and Coulomb named to examine Girolet's hydraulic machine.
108	10/VI/89	Le Roy and Coulomb named to examine a memoir on re-equipping ships.
108	13/VI/89	Coulomb and Bossut reported on a memoir of 29/V/89.
108	13/VI/89	Coulomb, Bossut, and Charles reported on Guererot's machine to clarify and raise water.
108	27/VI/89	Darcet, Haüy, and Vandermonde reported on Volume Two of *Annales de Chimie* and Coulomb's memoirs extracted there.
108	27/VI/89	Lavoisier, Brisson, Laplace, Tillet, Coulomb, and Le Roy named as Commissioners for works on Weights and Measures.
108	27/VI/89	Bory, Coulomb, Monge, and Le Roy reported on memoir of 25/IV/89.
108*	11/VII/89	Coulomb read a memoir on pivot friction.
109	16/I/90	Legentil read Bailly's letter concerning examination of new trades. Bossut, Vandermonde, Coulomb, and Desmarest named to examine this.
109	10/III/90	Coulomb and Bossut named to examine a memoir on clearing the beds of rivers.
109*	13/III/90	Coulomb commenced the reading of a sixth memoir on electricity and conducted some experiments.
109*	17/III/90	Coulomb finished the reading of his memoir on electricity and conducted some experiments.
109	24/III/90	Giraud claimed that Barré de St. Venant's (*not* Adhemar-Jean Claude Barré de Saint-Venant) chain-suspension bridge was copied from him. Le Roy, Vandermonde, and Coulomb named to examine this matter.
109	17/IV/90	Bossut, Vandermonde, Coulomb, and Desmarest reported on Rivey's memoir on means to manufacture silk.

Manu- script Volume	Date	Subject of Notation
109	17/ɪv/90	Laplace, Coulomb, and Bossut reported on a memoir of 10/ɪɪɪ/90.
109	19/v/90	Tillet, Condorcet, Laplace, Lavoisier, Borda, Lagrange, and Coulomb named to consider a letter concerning future plans for money systems in Weights and Measures.
109*	19/vɪ/90	Coulomb read a supplement to his sixth memoir on electricity.
109	10/vɪ/90	Borda, Bory, Laplace, Bougainville, and Coulomb named to examine Augier's letter on a hydraulic machine for agriculture.
109	24/vɪɪ/90	Coulomb named among commissioners for the election to Franklin's place as *associé étranger*. Candidates: P. S. Pallas, Aepinus, Walter, Cavendish, and Lorgua. Elected—Pallas, second place—Cavendish.
109	24/vɪɪ/90	Vandermonde, Coulomb, and Le Roy began a report on a memoir of 24/ɪɪɪ/90.
109	31/vɪɪ/90	Vandermonde, Coulomb, and Le Roy continued with their report on the memoir of 24/ɪɪɪ/90.
109	7/vɪɪɪ/90	Tillet, Le Roy, Bossut, Coulomb, Saron, Vandermonde, and Legendre reported on a mill argument between Berthelot and Dransy. Desmarest and Coulomb charged to verify which of these mills are actually better.
109	7/vɪɪɪ/90	Coulomb, Vandermonde, and Le Roy finished their report on the memoir of 24/ɪɪɪ/90.
109	7/vɪɪɪ/90	Le Roy, Vandermonde, and Coulomb named to examine Henry Coq's safety locks.
109	27/x/90	Lavoisier, Borda, Lagrange, Tillet, Coulomb, Laplace, and Condorcet reported on a memoir of 19/v/90 concerning Weights and Measures. (Coulomb and Laplace did not sign the report.)
109	10/xɪ/90	Laplace, Lagrange, Vandermonde, Coulomb, and Condorcet named to examine a finance plan submitted by the National Assembly.
109	10/xɪ/90	Laplace, Coulomb, Borda, and Le Roy named to examine Le Blanc's method of manufacturing screwplates for rifles.

Manu-script Volume	Date	Subject of Notation
109	20/xɪ/90	Coulomb added to commission of Borda, Lalande, and Vandermonde to examine abbé de Maudre's machine, submitted by the National Assembly.
109	1/xɪɪ/90	Condorcet, Vandermonde, Lagrange, Laplace, and Coulomb reported on the National Assembly's memoir of 10/xɪ/90.
109	15/ɪ/91	Borda, Lavoisier, Darcet, Coulomb, and Tillet named to investigate the loss of metal due to friction in the manufacture of money.
109	15/ɪ/91	Vandermonde, Coulomb, and Borda reported on the plan of a machine presented 20/xɪ/90.
109	22/ɪ/91	Laplace, Coulomb, and Lavoisier named to examine Prony's memoir concerning the fall in the height of the Seine, 1788-90.
109	29/ɪ/91	Lavoisier, Laplace, and Coulomb reported on a memoir of 15/ɪ/91.
109	9/ɪɪɪ/91	Condorcet read Bailly's memoir concerning a commission to examine Périer's steam engines. Tillet, Vandermonde, Coulomb, Legendre, and Monge named for this.
109	16/ɪɪɪ/91	Le Roy, Borda, Bory, Bougainville, Coulomb, and Laplace named to report on a machine dispute between Augier and Schmidt.
109	16/ɪɪɪ/91	Borda, Laplace, Coulomb, and Le Roy reported on a presentation of 10/xɪ/90.
109	19/ɪɪɪ/91	Coulomb and Brisson added to Lavoisier and Méchain for Commission to examine memoirs concerning wood.
109	19/ɪɪɪ/91	Borda, Laplace, Coulomb, and Le Roy concluded their report on a memoir of 10/xɪ/90.
109	13/ɪv/91	Vote to know if the Academy would adopt the proposition of the Committee of Weights and Measures on the number of personnel who should comprise the five commissions. The Academy elected: "Cassini (IV), Méchain, Legengre—astronomie et mesure des triangles; Meusnier et Monge—mesure des bases; Borda et Coulomb—pour la longueur du pendule; Lavoisier et Haüy pour la mesure du poids de l'eau distillé; Tillet, Brisson et Vandermonde pour la comparaison des mesures anciennes."

Manu-script Volume	*Date*	*Subject of Notation*
109	7/v/91	Bossut, Meusnier, and Coulomb named to examine a memoir on canals.
109	7/v/91	Legentil and Coulomb named to go for the Academy to visit Cassini because of the death of his wife.
109	7/v/91	Bossut, Coulomb, and Meusnier named to examine a canal project presented by the National Assembly.
109	21/v/91	Bossut, Coulomb, and Meusnier reported on a a project presented 7/v/91.
109*	2/vii/91	Coulomb began the reading of a seventh memoir on electricity and magnetism.
109*	6/vii/91	Coulomb continued the reading of his memoir on electricity and magnetism.
109*	9/vii/91	Coulomb finished the reading of his memoir on electricity and magetism.
109	16/vii/91	Coulomb read a letter from M. Bell concerning plans for the St. Maur canal.
109	3/ix/91	Borda, Meusnier, and Coulomb named to examine plans for port work in Dunkerque.
109	3/ix/91	Coulomb, Meusnier, and Bossut reported on a letter of 16/vii/91.
109	14/ix/91	A letter from Schmidt concerning his dispute with Augier was referred to the committee of 16/iii/91.
109	2/xi/91	Conforming to the decree of the Constituent Assembly of the 27th of October and at the request of the Minister of the Interior, the Academy elected 15 of its members who would compose one section of the *Bureau des Consultation des Arts et Métiers*. The following were elected: Legentil—secretary, Lavoisier, Desmarest, Borda, Vandermonde, Coulomb, Berthollet, Meusnier, Brisson, Périer, Rochon, Duhamel, Lagrange, and Laplace. The next in order of votes (but not elected): Fourcroy, Messier, Darcet, Lalande, Jeaurat, La Rochefoucauld, Saron, Legentil, Cousin, and Vicq d'Azyr.
109	19/xi/91	M. Delessart, Minister of the Interior, invited the 15 Commissioners elected 1/xi/91 [*sic*] to meet with the other 15 (non-Academy) Commissioners.

Manu-script Volume	*Date*	*Subject of Notation*
109	23/xi/91	Borda, Bory, and Coulomb named to examine a memoir on navigation.
109	28/i/92	Bossut and Coulomb named to examine a memoir on mills.
109	8/ii/92	Bossut, Desmarest, and Coulomb reported on a plan for the Canal d'Argenteuil.
109	11/ii/92	Le Roy, Cousin, and Coulomb named to examine a memoir on mills.
109	5/v/92	Coulomb presented an improved magnetic compass and requested reporters. Borda, Cassini, and Méchain were named for this.
109	25/v/92	Le Roy, Vandermonde, and Coulomb named to examine Féron's clock inventions.
109	13/vi/92	Borda, Coulomb, and Bossut reported on Dillon's hydraulic machines.
109	27/vi/92	Lagrange, Laplace, Vicq d'Azyr, Coulomb, Fourcroy, Le Roy, and Lavoisier reported on Academy prizes.
109	4/vii/92	Le Roy, Coulomb, and Vandermonde named to examine Mercklein's memoir on "fabrication des assignats."
109	11/vii/92	Le Roy, Coulomb, and Vicq d'Azyr named to examine and repeat Valli's work on animal electricity.
109	13/vii/92	Vicq d'Azyr reported on the commission of 11/vii/92.
109	18/viii/92	Coulomb named among the commissioners for the election of a corresponding member for a place in the mechanics section.
109	1/ix/92	Bossut and Coulomb named to examine L'Objeoit's memoir on *machines à feu*.
109	13/ii/93	Le Roy and Coulomb reported on their experiments on the rifle presented by Le Faure.
109	9/iii/93	Bory and Coulomb reported on Duperron's plan concerning cannon.

Manu-script Volume	*Date*	*Subject of Notation*
109	9/III/93	Bory and Coulomb reported on Desros' plan concerning cannon.
109	17/v/93	Le Roy, Bory, and Coulomb reported on Levayer's plan concerning cannon.
109	31/VII/93	Coulomb, Borda, and Bory reported on Lalande's (Lalande—former professor of mathematics at the Ecole militaire) plan for a capstan designed to avoid shock.

End of *Procès-verbaux* anterior to the Revolution

Appendix C

COULOMB'S MEMOIR ON THE REORGANIZATION OF THE CORPS DU GENIE—1776

(Archives de l'Inspection du Génie, Article 3, Section 10, Carton 2, No. 5a.)

"Mémoire sur le service des officiers du Corps du Génie. Par M. Coulomb Cap^{tan}, Corps R^{al} du Génie"

Le Corps du Génie doit être considéré sous deux points de vue, comme corps à talent et comme corps militaire. Dans un corps à talent, si la marche des sujets est lente, l'espérance et l'émulation s'évanouissent par l'impossibilité de les satisfaire dans sa jeunesse et l'on se dégoute bientôt des études quand on n'était pas sur à tirer parti du temps qu'on y employe.

Si les ingénieurs sont instruits, si l'on exige d'eux autant de connaissance que de capacité pour les admettre dans les Ecoles, à quoi sert cet appareil, puis qu'ils doivent passer quarante années de service à faire remettre une porte ou un chassis ou à faire recrépir un mur? Un jeune sujet studieux qui sort de l'Ecole, n'a d'autre parti à prendre pour supporter l'ennui et la monotonie de ses occupations, que de se livrer à quelque branche de science ou de littérature absolument étrangère à son état. Ainsi l'homme qui par ses talents aurait pû rendre de très grands services à sa patrie, embarrassé par sa position devient oisif et inutil.

Cependant, s'il arrive qu'après 50 ans de service, une circonstance et son ancienneté le chargent d'un travail difficile d'où dépendra le salut d'une province, peut-on espérer que son esprit aussi vieux que son corps, ressérré par l'habitude de traiter en sous-ordre avec attention des objets minutieux, y portera l'énergie, l'étendue de lumière et les combinaisons qui lui seraient nécessaires dans cette occasion; l'exiger ce serait ne connaitre ni la marche de la nature, ni celle de l'esprit humain.

L'on se plaint que les ingénieurs sont trop minutieux, qu'ils ne savent plus mesurer leur dégré d'attention à l'utilité des objets qu'ils ont à traiter. Si ce reproche à été quelque fois fondé, à quoi doit-on s'en prendre? Les ingénieurs depuis nombre d'années ne sont chargés que de détails peu intéressants; ils s'abituent à y mettre de l'importance, parcequ'il est dans la nature de chaque homme de chercher à se persuader que ses occupations sont d'un grand prix.

Il en est des formes de l'esprit comme de celles du corps, l'un et l'autre ont besoin d'exercice pour leur conservation. Un corps à talent sans occupation perd son activité, l'émulation s'anéantit, et il arrivera peut-être qu'il remplira mal les petits objets dont il sera chargé. Mais qu'on y regarde de près, c'est une suite du vice de sa constitution.

Jetons un instant les yeux sur la position actuelle du Corps du Génie. Nous ne sommes pas toujours en guerre et toutes les guerres ne sont pas des guerres de sièges. En temps de paix à peine con-struit-on une place neuve tous les 50 ans; ainsi 400 ingénieurs ne sont occupés qu'à faire relever quelques vieux murs sur leurs an-ciennes fondations et qu'à l'entretien des bâtimens militaires, occu-pation précisément la même que celle d'un particulier qui fait couvrir sa maison ou relever le mur de son jardin. Comment veut-on qu'il se forme à un pareil travail.

Il semble que depuis quelques années l'on a résolu d'enlever aux fortifications tous les objets qui pourraient instruire les ingénieurs et les mettre à même de se faire connaitre. Citons un ou deux ar-ticles qui n'ont pas pû, sans danger, être soustraits de ce départe-ment.

Les Ponts et Chaussées sont actuellement chargés de la construc-tion de tous nos ports. Cependant les villes maritimes sont en même temps les places les plus intérressantes de nos frontières. Les écluses, le jeu des retenues et les innondations qui doivent servis au curement des ports et de leur chenal, doivent être com-binés de manière à faire la principale défense des places maritimes; les jetées et les môles qui les terminent sont des pièces de fortifica-tion intérressantes pour la sûrété des rades et pour la protection des côtes. Tous nos ports principaux doivent être fortifiés ou au moins mis à l'abri d'un coup de main, autrement l'ennemi détruira dans un jour cequi aura couté 20 années de travail et 20 millions de dépense. Peut-on espérer qu'un tracé de fortification puisse toujours s'accorder avec les travaux d'un port construit par un département civil? Ne-sera-t-on pas peut-être obligé, pour se mettre en sûrété, de détruire un jour des travaux qui auront épuisés les finances de l'état et de les rétablir sous de nouveau principes? L'architecture civile cherche toujours à élever et développer ses bâtiments pour faire spectacle; l'architecture militaire, au contraire, ne leur donne précisément que le degré d'élévation qui leur est nécessaire. Elle les enveloppe, les enterre et sait que, pour les conserver, il faut les soustraire au canon qui peut les détruire.

Passons au second article; il a encore un rapport plus direct avec le bien du service. La construction des places est divisée en deux étages; l'étage supérieur, formé par le tracé des pièces de la fortification, tire non seulement sa force de la position respective de ses parties, mais il la tire encore peut-être plus immédiatement des galeries et des mines qui forment l'étage inférieur. La combinaison respective des deux étages doit être dépendante l'une de l'autre et le rapport le plus intime de cette combinaison formera sans contredit la perfection de nos constructions. Cet étage inférieur est devenu depuis quelque temps, absolument indépendant du Corps des Ingénieurs et les officiers des mineurs, réunis avec l'artillerie, en sont chargés. Que peut-on attendre de cette division? Une opposition de sentiments et des contradictions continuelles que la rivalité excite entre deux corps qui seront rapprochés par les mêmes travaux. Ainsi au lieu de concourir aux mêmes objets, l'on doit craindre des embaras et des fausses dépenses, toujours funestes à l'état.

N'éprouve-t-on pas les mêmes inconveniens dans le moment d'un siège? La marche des tranchées, l'ordre des points qui doivent être attaqués et rompus les premiers, doivent être combinés avec l'emplacement des batteries et avec la marche du mineur. La charge, la quantité de mine, leurs positions, et leurs directions doivent être déterminées après les parties qu'on veut détruire et celles que l'on doit conserver. Tous ces objets réunis demandent le plus grand accord dans toutes les parties du projet, comme dans l'éxécution, et l'on se flatterait inutilement de l'obtenir en y faisant concourir deux corps différentes. L'on peut donc regarder comme indispensable au bien du service de réunir les compagnies des mineurs au Corps du Génie, de faire rouler ensemble les officiers de ces deux corps, et de prévenir d'avance des malheurs qui nous apprendront trop tard, la nécessité de cette réunion.

Il se présente des raisons, peut-être aussi fortes que les précédentes, pour attacher au Corps du Génie les compagnies de sapeurs, qui, par leur institution, sont destinés à travailler à la tête des tranchées, tous la conduite des ingénieurs. Ces compagnies actuellement réunies avec l'artillerie étant indépendantes des ingénieurs, ces derniers ne peuvent ni connaître ni conter, ni récompenser la valeur et l'intelligence du sergent et du soldat dont ils doivent diriger les opérations dans la moment le plus critique d'une siège.

Ajoutons que, si les compagnies de sapeurs ainsi que celles des mineurs étaient attachées au génie, elles seraient occupées pendant la paix, d'une manière aussi utile qu'économique, aux travaux des fortifications les plus relatifs à leur service. Elles s'y instruiraient mieux que dans les exercises d'une Ecole qui ne présente que des difficultés prévues et aucune variété.

Pendant la guerre, ces compagnies marcheraient avec l'avant garde de l'armée et seraient destinées à brasser et à charreter les retranchements les plus difficles et les plus importants du camp que l'on doit occuper.

L'on a déjà tenta de réunir le génie avec l'artillerie; cette opération n'a pas pu, n'a pas dû réussir, parce que la constitution fondamentale d'un corps dont le service exige autant d'émulation que d'étude, c'est d'être peu nombreux.

Le Ministre respectable, qui dirige le département de la guerre, cherche à soulager l'Etat, en en diminuant les dépenses. Toutes les autres parties du gouvernement doivent se prêter à des vues d'économie aussi sages et ce serait une erreur de soupçonner qu'aucun motif puisse arrêter, lorsqu'il s'agira de servir le meilleur des Rois, et de contribuer au bonheur de son peuple. Aussi on osera répéter, d'après tous les bond français, que le meilleur moyen d'augmenter nos richesses est de tirer le plus grand parti de tous les hommes. Nous sommes obligés d'entretenir des ingénieurs pour la sûreté, pour la conservation de nos places et pour faire la guerre. Nous avons 150 milles soldats choisis dans l'espèce la plus vigoreuse de la nation. Pourquoi les laisser inutiles dans nos garnisons, pendant la paix? L'esprit s'énerve, le corps s'affaibli, faute d'exercise et le courage du soldat se mesure presque toujours par la force de son corps.

Si les troupes étaient chargées de l'exécution de tous les travaux publics, sous la conduite des ingénieurs, elles rendraient à la France au lieu de l'épuiser, un fond nécessaire pour leur entretien. Il ne serait plus dit qu'un soldat n'est propre qu'à combatre et que, rendu à son village, il devient une charge, qu'il faut que sa famille nourisse. Le soldat fortifié par un exercice continuel, àmène par le gain de son travail de se procurer une meilleure nourriture, ne sera plus engourdi par l'oisiveté de nos garnisons; il supportera plus patiemment les fatigues de la guerre et nos hôpitaux ne contiendront plus, à la fin de chaque campagne, la moitié de nos armées; l'on verra cesser les désertions toujours occasionnées par l'oisiveté et la misère.

Dans un temps où l'on calcule si bien la richesse d'un Etat par la population, qui peut arrêter un établissement qui va faire refluer plus de cent milles citoyens dans l'agriculture et dans le commerce? N'avons nous pas ici l'exemple des Romains? Ce peuple belliqueux ne marchait à la conquête du monde qu'après avoir employé ses legions à des travaux publics. Le soldat de César, qui travaillait continuellement, était alerte et dispos. Il exécutait sous les yeux de l'ennemi les manoeuvres les plus hardies, avec autant de précision que de promptitude.

Qu'une partie de nos troupes soit occupée aux grands chemins et aux canaux de navigation, qu'une autre soit employée à la construction de nos portes, à l'entretien et à la garde de nos places; s'il nous reste encore des bras, déssécher les marais, et défricher les terres incultes du domaine. Le soldat s'habituera peu à peu à regarder le travail comme une partie essentielle de ses devoirs. Nos officiers sont déjà persuadés que tout ce qui peut être utile à leur patrie, honnore ceux qui en sont occupés.

Le nombre de quatre cent ingénieurs actuellement au service du Roi est plus que suffisant pour satisfaire à tous les objets. Leur instruction est portée à un point qui doit rassurer sur le danger qu'il y aurait de les leur confier. Plus ils seront occupés pendant la paix, plus ils acquéreront de moyens pour être utiles pendant la guerre. Et il y a cette circonstance où leur intelligence, qui ne peut se former que par un travail continu, peut-être intérressante pour le sort des frontières.

Mais s'il est utile pour le gouvernement de charger en temps de paix les ingénieurs militaires de tous les travaux publics, il est encore plus intérressant de ne confier l'emploi de ces finances, prise sur la subsistance du peuple, qu'à des mains sures qui sachent en disposer avec autant d'intelligence que d'économie. Ainsi comme il y a des genres de travaux qui exigent les plus grandes ressources de l'imagination, l'attention la plus suivie, autant d'étude que d'activité, faire dépendre l'avancement des sujets uniquement de l'ancienneté, ce serait risquer de ruiner l'Etat et de tout perdre!

Il faut d'un autre côté, que la protection, que des égards de soci-
eté, que des qualités seulement aimables ne s'emparent pas d'une
confiance qui n'est due qu'à la véritable capacité et qu'aux services
qu'elle peut rendre. Il faut donc que la constitution du Corps des
Ingénieurs soit telle que le Ministre puisse lui-même en connaître
les sujets par leur travail et par le jugement général de leurs Corps.
C'est à quoi il semble que l'on pourra parvenir en établissant dans
chaque direction un conseil de fortification, à peu près semblable à
ceux que la sagesse des ordonnances vient de former dans tous les
régiments. Esquissons le plan d'un pareil établissement.

Tous les ingénieurs de chaque direction seront assemblés pendant
le mois de décembre, après la clôture des travaux dans le lieu de
la résidence du Directeur. On tiendra dans le cabinet du dépôt des
papiers de la direction, trois assemblées par semaine et plus s'il est
nécessaire. Le Commandant de la province présidera à ces assemblées; dans son absence ce sera le Directeur. Chaque ingénieur y
rendra compte par écrit des travaux dont il aura été chargé pendant
le courant de l'année, des difficulties d'exécution qu'il a rencontré,
des differents moyens que les circonstances ont suggerés, soit à lui,
soit aux officiers à ses ordres. Il en sera fait un résumé général, qui
sera envoyé au Ministre.

Le Directeur exposera ensuite les travaux les plus urgents à faire
l'année suivante, dans chaque lieu de sa direction. Tous les dessins
nécessaires seront mis sous les yeux des ingénieurs, qui seront in-
vité de donner chacun par écrit leurs idées particulières. Le résumé
général qui en sera fait dans les dernières assemblées, sera envoyé
par le Directeur au Ministre, en même temps que les projets de
l'année suivante.

Outre ces comités provinciaux, il y aura tous les ans, à la suite
de la cour, un grand comité assemblé sous le nom de comité principal. Il sera composé de deux Directeurs, quatre Ingénieurs en
chef, quatre Ingénieurs ordinaires et d'un officier du même Corps,
qui fera les fonctions de secrétaire ou de rédacteur. Sa Majeste
nommera tous les ans un Lieutenant Général de ses troupes, pour
présider à ce comité.

L'on examinera dans ce comité, les résumés particuliers des
travaux de l'année envoyés de chaque direction. Ainsi que les projets de l'année suivante. On en rendra compte au Ministre, par des
notes que l'on joindra à ces résumés, et aux projets.

Tous les procédés nouveaux tendant à la solidité de la construction, à l'économie, toutes les épreuves nouvelles, tous les projets

relatifs aux travaux et qui pourront être de quelque utilité pour le service, seront aussi présentés à ce même comité, qui en rendra compte au Ministre.

Lorsque le gouvernement se déterminera à entamer quelqu'ouvrage de conséquence et dont l'éxécution présentera de grandes difficultés, l'on pourra destiner sur les fonds des fortifications un prix de cinq ou six cents livres à toute personne qui, au jugement de comité, donnera les moyens les plus surs et les moins couteux d'y réussir. L'auteur ne se fera connaître, que lorsque le comité principal chargé de l'examen des projets aura remis son avis signé au Ministre. Si le projet adopté était d'un Ingénieur ordinaire il paraitrait juste qu'il fut chargé de l'exécution.

Avec de pareils établissements, il semble que tous les officiers du Corps du Génie peuvent être parfaitement connus du Ministre, que leur avancement dependra véritablement de leur travail et de leur capacité. Chacun étant obligé de rendre compte tous les ans publiquement des ouvrages qui lui seront confiés, y portera la plus grande attention. Les projets seront examinés avec soin et tournés sous toutes les faces. Ils ne passeront que lorsqu'on verra des moyens surs de réussir et que leur dépense n'excédera pas l'utilité que l'on n'en peut espérer.

Le nombre des Ingénieurs en chef ne devra pas être borné comme il est actuellement à un nombre fixe; il pourra être augmenté suivant la quantité de travaux intérressant que le Roi ordonnera. L'ancienneté n'aura la préférence pour les chefferies qu'à mérite égal. Le titre de chef continuera à donner le rang de Major. Les dignités militaires supérieurs à ce grade seront principalement les récompenses des services de guerre. Mais des services intérressants rendus pendant la paix, seront un titre pour être employé de préférence en temps de guerre. Les directions ne seront accordées qu'à ceux qui auront également bien servis dans toutes les circonstances.

Si le Ministre croit que ces idées méritent son attention, il sera facile de former sur cette base, le plan de la nouvelle constitution du Corps du Génie, dont nous avons cherché seulement à faire connaitre les véritables principes.

A la Hougue ce 1er 7bre 1776. Signé
COULOMB. Ingr. Ordre du Roi.
(1 Septembre 1776)

Notes

CHAPTER ONE

1. Archives de la Guerre (Vincennes) (hereafter *A.G.*), Dossier Coulomb, "Extrait baptistaire." For a discussion of Coulomb's genealogy and a copy of his "Extrait," see Charles Stewart Gillmor, "Charles Augustin Coulomb: Physics and Engineering in Eighteenth Century France." Ph.D. dissertation (Princeton University, 1968), Appendix A.

2. Anonymous, *Journal de l'Empire* (Paris), 20 September 1806, pp. 3-4.

3. J.B.J. Delambre, "Eloge historique de M. Coulomb," *Mémoires de l'Institut national des sciences et arts—Sciences mathématiques et physiques*, VII (Paris, 1806), "Histoire," p. 206. (Hereafter this work is listed as Delambre éloge.)

4. Most of the details about the *Collège des quartre-nations* are drawn from Alfred Franklin, *Recherches historiques sur le Collège des quatre-nations* (Paris, 1862).

5. *Ibid.*, p. 167.

6. Archives Nationales (Paris) (hereafter *A.N.*), M258-M607, "Anciens cartons (généalogique) d'Hozier." A partial list of this material may be found in Louis de la Rogue and Edouard de Barthélemy, *Catalogue des preuves de noblesse reçues par d'Hozier pour les Ecoles Militaires, 1753–1789* (Paris, 1867).

7. Henry Lemonnier, *Le Collège Mazarin et le Palais de l'Institut: XVIIIe-XIXe siècle* (Paris, 1921), pp. 49-50.

8. Anonymous, *Journal de l'Empire* (Paris), 20 September 1806, pp. 3-4.

9. *Ibid.*

10. Pierre Vialles, *Etudes historiques sur la Cour des comptes, aides et finances de Montpellier d'après ses archives privées* (Montpellier, 1921), p. 173.

Dominique Donat, *Almanach historique et chronologique de la ville de Montpellier* (Montpellier, 1759), pp. 20, 51, 76.

11. J.M.F. Faucillon, *Le Collège de Jésuites de Montpellier, 1629–1762* (Montpellier, 1857), p. 150.

12. Archives Départmentales de l'Hérault, Montpellier (hereafter *A.D.H.*), Série D³200, fols. 39-42, 139-143.

Eugène Thomas, *Mémoire historique et biographique sur l'ancienne Société Royale des Sciences de Montpellier par Junius Castelnau, précédé de la vie de l'auteur et suivi d'une Notice historique sur la Société des Sciences et Belles-Lettres de la même ville* (Montpellier, 1858), p. 211.

13. *A.D.H.*, Série D, 120* (5), fol. 119; 121* (6), fol. 71.

14. Thomas, *Mémoire historique . . .* , pp. 153-155.

15. *A.D.H.* Série D, 121* (6), fols. 71-88.

16. Thomas, *Mémoire historique* . . . , pp. 153-155, 174-215.

17. Anonymous, *Histoire de la Société Royale des Sciences établies à Montpellier avec les Mémoires de mathématiques et de physique* . . . , I (Lyon, 1766), "Histoire," pp. 1-21.

Eugène Thomas, "Notice sur l'ancienne Société des Sciences . . . de Montpellier," *Annuaire de l'Hérault*, XLII (Montpellier, 1859), 70.

A.D.H., Série D, 121* (6), fol. 71.

18. *A.D.H.*, Série D, 120* (5), fol. 119.

19. *Ibid.*

20. *Ibid.*, 121* (6), fol. 71.

21. *Ibid.*, 120* (5), fol. 119.

22. *Ibid.*, fols. 119, 123, 125-128.

23. *Ibid.*, Série D, 204. Coulomb letter to de Ratte, Paris, 8 October 1758.

24. *Ibid.*, 121* (6), fol. 88.

25. *Ibid.*, Série D, 204. Coulomb letter.

26. *Ibid.*, 121* (6), fol. 117.

27. J.M.F. Faucillon, *La chaire de mathématique et d'hydrographie de Montpellier, 1682-1792* (Montpellier, 1855), pp. 3, 5-11.

28. *Ibid.*, pp. 3-5, 12.

29. Hans Straub, *A History of Civil Engineering*, trans. Erwin Rockwell (Cambridge, Mass., 1964), p. 120.

30. There exist many books on Vauban. See, for example, Alfred Rebelliau, *Vauban* (Paris, 1962).

31. Marcel Reinhard, *Le grand Carnot*, 2 vols. (Paris, 1950–1952), I, chaps. iii, vi, viii.

32. Antoine Marie Augoyat, *Aperçu historique sur les fortifications, les ingénieurs et sur le corps du génie en France*, 3 vols. (Paris, 1860–1864), I,

33. Théodore Le Puillon de Boblaye, *Notice sur les écoles du génie de Mézières et de Metz* (Metz, 1862), p. 7.

34. *Ibid.*, p. 9.

35. Pierre Bullet, *L'architecture pratique* (Paris, 1691).

36. Amédée François Frézier, *La théorie et la pratique de la coupe des pierres et des bois . . . ou Traité de stéréotomie,* 3 vols. (Strasbourg, 1737–1739).

37. Bernard Forest de Bélidor, *La science des ingénieurs dans la conduite des travaux de fortification et d'architecture civile* (Paris, 1729), and *L'architecture hydraulique*, 2 vols. (Paris, 1737–1739).

38. Antoine Marie Augoyat, "Notice sur les Chastillon, ingénieurs des Armées," *Spectateur militaire*, 15 August 1856 (Paris, 1856), p. 12.

39. Puillon de Boblaye, *Notice sur les écoles* . . . , p. 10.

40. Augoyat, *Spectateur militaire*, 15 August 1856, p. 12.

41. Puillon de Boblaye, *Notice sur les écoles* . . . , p. 27.

Augoyat, *Aperçu historique* . . . , II, 447.

René Taton, "L'école royal du génie de Mézières," *Enseignement et diffusion des sciences en France au XVIIIᵉ siècle*, ed. René Taton (Paris, 1964), p. 569.

42. Charles Etienne Louis Camus, *Cours de mathématique*, 4 vols. (Paris, 1749–1752).

43. Edme Mariotte, *Traité du mouvement des eaux* (Paris, 1686).

44. Pierre Varignon, *Traité du mouvement et de la mesure des eaux . . .*, ed. abbé Pujol (Paris, 1725).

45. René Robinet, "Un élève de l'école royale du génie de Mézières en 1756," *Etudes ardennaises*, no. 19 (October 1959), p. 37.

46. Augoyat, *Aperçu historique . . .*, II, 455.

47. *Ibid.*, pp. 444-446.

48. *Ibid.*, p. 445.

49. *Ibid.*, p. 551.

50. Most information regarding the Coulomb family has been obtained from the Archives Municipales de Montpellier, Paroisse Sainte Anne, GG158, 160, 162 and 164 and at the Archives de la Seine (Paris), DQ⁷1791, DQ⁸323, V4E¹560, V5E¹235, and V6E¹340.

51. *A.G.*, Dossier Coulomb.

52. Archives Communales, Archives Montpellier VI (1934), "Inventaire de Joffre," folio 455, Compoix de S. Mathieu.

Archives Municipales de Montpellier, Paroisse Sainte Anne, GG164, folio 69.

53. *A.N.*, M258-M607, "Anciens cartons (généalogique) d'Hozier." A partial list of this material may be found in Louis de la Rogue & Edouard de Barthélemy, *Catalogue des preuves de noblesse reçues par d'Hozier pour les Ecoles Militaires, 1753–1789* (Paris, 1867).

Bibliothèque Nationale, Paris (hereafter *B.N.*), Salle des manuscrits, Fr. 27363, Vol. 879, nos. 19875, 19876.

Louis de la Rogue, *Armorial de la noblesse de Languedoc*, 2 vols. (Paris, 1860), II, 16-17, 271, 308.

54. Puillon de Boblaye, *Notice sur les écoles . . .*, p. 28.

55. *Ibid.*

56. Archives de l'Inspection du Génie, Vincennes (hereafter *A.I.G.*), art. 18, sec. 1, #1, carton 1.

57. Reinhard, *Le grand Carnot*, I, chaps. ii, iii.

58. *A.I.G.*, art. 18, sec. 1, #1, carton, pièce 13.

59. *Ibid.*, pièce 8a.

Augoyat, *Aperçu historique . . .*, II, 446.

60. According to some archive reports from Mézières, the students received 720 *livres* salary each month. *A.G.*, Génie-"Ecole de Mézières," Xᵉ5, 14 April 1760.

61. Reinhard, *Le grand Carnot*, I, 34.

62. Robinet, *Etudes ardennaises*, no. 19 (October 1959), pp. 37-42.

63. *A.I.G.*, art. 18, sec. 1, #1, carton 1, pièce 14.

A.G., Dossier Coulomb, "Relevé de services," and Génie-Xᵉ 159, "Ecole de Mézières," 1760, 1761-1762.

64. Augoyat, *Aperçu historique*, II, 481.

65. *A.I.G.*, art. 18, sec. 1, #1, carton 1.

66. Taton, *Enseignement et diffusion . . .*, pp. 567-580.

67. Reinhard, *Le grand Carnot*, I, 39-40.

68. Jean Antoine Nollet, *Leçons de physique expérimentale*, 6 vols. (Paris, 1743–1748).

69. Charles Bossut, *Traité élémentaire de méchanique et de dinamique*

appliqué principalement aux mouvemens des machines (Charleville, 1763).

70. Charles Bossut, *Traité élémentaire d'hydrodynamique*, 2 vols. (Paris, 1771).

71. *A.I.G.*, art. 18, sec. 1, #1, carton 1, pièce 14.

A.G., Génie-"Ecole de Mézières," Xᵉ5, *"Mézières,"* 2 and 4 December 1761.

72. *Ibid.* Also, portions of Chastillon's report on Coulomb are reproduced in Lieutenant-colonel Metz and Capitaine Fadeuilhe, "Charles-Augustin de Coulomb," *Revue du génie militaire*, LXXVII (January-February 1938), 58-59.

73. *Ibid.*

74. Augoyat, *Aperçu historique . . .*, II, 477-478.

75. *A.G.*, Génie, Xᵉ6, 1763.

76. *Ibid.*, Dossier Coulomb.

A.I.G., art. 8, "Brest," carton 2, pièce 33b.

77. Archives Nationales, Section Outre-Mer, Paris (hereafter *O.M.*), Martinique, D.F.C., carton 1, no. 169.

78. *Ibid.*, no. 195.

79. *A.I.G.*, art. 3, sec. 2, carton 1, pièce 30; sec. 3, #1, carton 1, laisse 3, pièces 8, 42.

80. *Ibid.*, pièce 43.

81. *Ibid.*, pièces 43, 45bis.

82. *O.M.*, Martinique, D.F.C., carton 1, no. 218, 4 April 1764, "Procès verbal du conseil. . . ."

83. *Ibid.*, fols. 84-85.

84. *Ibid.*, no. 219, 4 April 1764, "Extrait du procès verbal . . . ," fols. 25-27.

85. *Ibid.*, carton 2, no. 234; no. 235, p. 5; no. 238; no. 272.

86. *Ibid.*, no. 237, p. 38.

87. *Ibid.*, carton 3, no. 330, pp. 1-10.

88. *Ibid.*, carton 1, no. 219, p. 29.

89. *Ibid.*, carton 2, nos. 244-246.

90. *Ibid.*, no. 246.

91. *Ibid.*, nos. 249, 275.

92. *Ibid.*, no. 249.

93. *Ibid.*, no. 252.

94. *Ibid.*, no. 274.

95. *A.G.*, Dossier Coulomb, memoir of July 1781.

96. Charles Augustin Coulomb, "Sur une application des règles de *maximis* et *minimis* à quelques problèmes de statique relatifs à l'architecture," *Mémoires de mathématique et de physique présentés à l'Académie Royale des Sciences, par divers savans*, VII (Paris, 1776), 343-382. This was later included in the 1821 edition of Coulomb's *Théorie des machines simples* (Bachelier, Paris). (Hereafter, this memoir is listed as Coulomb, 1773 statics memoir.)

97. Charles Augustin Coulomb, "Résultats de plusieurs expériences destinées à déterminer la quantité d'action que les hommes peuvent fournir par leur travail journalier, suivant les differentes manières dont ils employent leurs forces," *Mémoires de l'Institut*, première série, II (Paris, an 7:1799),

340-428. Also included in *Théorie des machines simples*. (Hereafter listed as Coulomb, Memoir on laboring men.)

98. *O.M.*, Martinique, D.F.C., Portefeuille XVI, pièce B331 (10 July 1773) Plan du Fort Bourbon.

99. *O.M.*, Martinique, D.F.C., carton 2, nos. 297, 300-301, 308.

100. *Ibid.*, no. 316.

101. *Ibid.*, no. 317.

102. *A.G.*, Dossier Coulomb, letter from Coulomb's widow to the Minister of War, 5 April 1807.

103. *Ibid.*, "Relevé de services."

104. *A.G.*, Dossier Coulomb, "Mémoire pour la croix de Saint Louis," 12 July 1781.

105. Académie des sciences de l'Institut de France (hereafter *A.S.*), *Procès-verbaux*, 10 March 1773. (For the published version of this, see Coulomb, 1773 statics memoir.)

106. *Ibid.*, 10 March and 2 April 1773.

107. *Ibid.*, 28 April 1773.

108. C. Stewart Gillmor, "Charles Bossut," *Dictionary of Scientific Biography*, ed. Charles Coulston Gillispie (1970–   ), II, 334-335.

109. C. Stewart Gillmor, "Jean-Charles Borda," *ibid.*, pp. 299-300.

110. Jean Mascart, *La vie et les travaux du chevalier Jean-Charles de Borda*, Annales de l'Université de Lyon, nouvelle série, II (Lyon, 1919), Fascicule 33.

111. [Jean Baptiste Biot and E.P.E. Rossel] B—t and R—l, "Jean Charles Borda," *Biographie universelle*, nouvelle édition (Paris, 1843), V, 58-60.

112. *A.S.*, *Procès-verbaux*, 30 April 1774.

113. *Ibid.*, 6 July 1774.

114. *A.I.G.*, art. 8, sec. 1, "Cherbourg," carton 1, pièce 29.

115. *Ibid.*, pièces 29, 29bis, 30, 30bis, and 32bis; and art. 3, sec. 8, carton 1, pièce 4.

116. Charles Augustin Coulomb, "Recherches sur la meilleure manière de fabriquer les aiguilles aimantées," *Mémoires de mathématique et de physique présentés à l'Académie Royale des Sciences, par divers savans*, IX (Paris, 1780), 166-264. *Portions* of this memoir are contained in *Mémoires de Coulomb*, ed. A. Potier, Collection de mémoires relatifs à la physique, publiés par la Société française de Physique (Paris: Gauthier-Villars, 1884), I. (Hereafter, this memoir is listed as Coulomb, 1777 magnetism memoir.)

117. *A.S.*, *Procès-verbaux*, 22 December 1779.

118. Reinhard, *Le grand Carnot*, I, 63.

Augoyat, *Aperçu historique . . .*, II, 585.

119. Reinhard, *Le grand Carnot*, I, 60-75.

120. The discussion of Coulomb's organizational memoir is based on *A.I.G.*, art. 3, sec. 10, carton 2, pièce 5a, which is a copy of the Coulomb memoir of 1 September 1776, "Mémoire sur le service des officiers du Corps du Génie." See Appendix C.

121. *Ibid.*, p. 4.

122. *Ibid.*

123. *Ibid.*

124. *Ibid.*

125. *Ibid.*, p. 1.

126. *Ibid.*

127. *A.G.*, Génie, X^{e}8, document of 20 January 1777.

128. *Ibid.*, Dossier Coulomb, memoir of July 1781, p. 2.

129. Charles Augustin Coulomb, *Recherches sur les moyens d'exécuter sous l'eau toutes sortes de travaux hydrauliques sans employer aucun épuisement.* This was published in Paris, with slightly varying titles, by Jombert, 1779; Du Pont, 1797; Bachelier, 1819 and 1846.

130. *A.S.*, *Procès-verbaux*, 5 May 1779.

131. *Ibid.*, 22 September 1786.

132. *Ibid.*, 15 May 1779.

133. *A.I.G.*, art. 3, sec. 4, carton 2, no. 35.

134. *A.S.*, *Procès-verbaux*, 18 February 1778.

135. This memoir was published in *Mémoires de l'Institut*, première série, II (Paris, an 7:1799), 340-428.

136. *A.I.G.*, art. 3, sec. 5, carton 1, pièce 25.

A.G., Dossier Coulomb, undated note from Montalembert to the prince de Montbarey, the Minister of War.

137. *A.I.G.*, art. 3, sec. 4, carton 2, pièce 39.

138. *A.S.*, *Procès-verbaux*, 1, 5, and 8 May 1779.

139. *A.I.G.*, art. 8, sec. 1, "Ile d'Aix," carton 1, no. 63^2.

140. *Ibid.*, art. 3, sec. 4, carton 2, pièce 36.

141. See for example, Augoyat, *Aperçu historique* . . . , II; Reinhard, *Le grand Carnot*, I; Prévost de Vernoi, *La fortification depuis Vauban*, 2 vols. (Paris, 1861); and Cosseron de Villenoisy, *Essai historique sur la fortification* (Paris, 1869). Augoyat and Cosseron de Villenoisy are very good on this; Prévost de Vernoi should be used with care.

142. *A.I.G.*, art. 8, sec. 1, "Ile d'Aix," carton 1, nos. 62, 66^1, 67.

143. *Ibid.*, no. 63^3, p. 2.

144. *Ibid.*, no. 59.

145. *Ibid.*, no. 60.

146. *Ibid.*, carton 2, nos. 10$^{1-2}$.

147. *Ibid.*, carton 1, no. 34^1.

148. *Ibid.*, art. 3, sec. 8, carton 1, no. 4.

149. *Ibid.*, art. 8, sec. 1, "Ile d'Aix," carton 1, no. 64^2.

150. *Ibid.*, nos. 63^1-63^3.

151. *Ibid.*, no. 64^1.

152. *Ibid.*, nos. 64$^{1-2}$, 67bis.

153. *Ibid.*, carton 2, no. 69.

154. *Ibid.*, art. 3, sec. 4, carton 2, no. 39, pièce 1.

155. *Ibid.*, sec. 5, carton 1, no. 25.

156. For example, Montalembert read a memoir at the Academy, 28 November 1783: *A.S.*, *Procès-verbaux*.

157. *A.S.*, *Procès-verbaux*, 4 August 1784.

158. Charles Augustin Coulomb, "Théorie des machines simples," *Mémoires de mathématique et de physique présentés à l'Académie Royale des Sciences, par divers savans*, X (Paris, 1785), 161-332; and later published as *Théorie des machines simples* (Paris: Bachelier, 1821). (Hereafter, this memoir is listed as Coulomb, 1781 friction memoir.)

159. *A.S.*, Dossier Prix, 1781.

160. *Ibid., Procès-verbaux*, 19 April 1780.

161. *Ibid.*, 26 April 1780.

162. This memoir was read 16 January 1782 (*A.S., Procès-verbaux*) and later published as "Observations théoriques et expérimentales sur l'effet des moulins à vent et sur la figure de leurs ailes," *Mémoires de l'Académie Royale des Sciences*, 1781 (Paris, 1784), pp. 65-81; and later included in the collection *Théorie des machines simples*.

163. Charles C. Gillispie, "Bernard Forest de Bélidor," *Dictionary of Scientific Biography*, ed. Charles Coulston Gillispie, ɪ, 581-582.

164. Augoyat, *Aperçu historique* . . . , ɪɪ, 188-189.

165. *A.G.*, Dossier Coulomb, memoir of July 1781, p. 3.

166. *Ibid.*

167. *Ibid.*

168. *Ibid.*

169. *Ibid.*

170. This list was compiled from use of *Index biographique des membres et correspondants de l'Académie des Sciences du 22 décembre 1666 au 15 novembre 1954* (Paris, 1954), and René Taton, "Structure et composition de l'Académie Royale des Sciences de sa réorganisation (26 janv. 1699) à sa suppression (8 août 1793)," unpublished article, 1966.

171. *A.G.*, Dossier Coulomb, memoir of July 1781, p. 3.

172. *Ibid.*, Génie, X^e8, 21 September 1775, "Etat actuel des Ingénieurs—Grades militaires."

173. *Ibid.*, Dossier Coulomb, "Mémoire pour la croix de Saint Louis," 12 July 1781.

174. *Ibid.*, letter from Pontleroy at Lille, 30 July 1781, and letter from Foulliac at Bordeaux, 30 August 1781.

175. *Ibid.*, copy of letter from Ségur to Coulomb, written at Versailles, 8 September 1781.

176. *Ibid.*, letter from Coulomb at Lille to Ségur, 13 September 1781.

177. *Ibid.*, Génie, X^e9, records for Coulomb for 30 September 1781.

178. *A.S.*, Dossier Coulomb, and *Procès-verbaux*, 12 December 1781. (Coulomb's election was made official by the king, 15 December 1781.)

CHAPTER TWO

1. This section of the book is based almost entirely on archival material deposited in the Archives of the *Académie des Sciences de l'Institut de France*. The statements below are drawn from study of the manuscript minutes (*Procès-verbaux*) of the Academy proceedings, volumes 92-109, and after the Revolution, from the published volumes: Institut de France, Académie des Sciences, *Procès-verbaux des séances de l'Académie tenues depuis la fondation de l'Institut jusqu'au mois d'août, 1835*, 10 vols. (Hendaye, 1910–1922). Materials from these sources concerning Coulomb's career are presented in Appendices A and B. Additional information has been obtained through study of the *plumatifs* of the *secrétaire perpétuel* and from the dossiers preserved from each *séance* of the Academy.

2. Bibliothèque de l'Institut de France (hereafter *B.I.F.*), MSS 1581–1582,

"Manuscrits de Charles Augustin de Coulomb: I. Recherches sur la théorie de l'aimant fondée sur l'expérience, II. Mémoires sur le magnétisme."

3. *A.G.*, Dossier Coulomb, memoir of July 1781, p. 3.

4. *A.S.*, *Procès-verbaux*, 19 March 1783.

5. *Ibid.*, 2 August 1788.

6. Institut de France, Académie des Sciences, *Procès-verbaux des séances* . . . , II, 1 germinal, an 9 (22 March 1801), p. 329.

7. Coulomb, 1777 magnetism memoir.

8. *A.G.*, Dossier Coulomb, memoir of July 1781, p. 3.

9. Charles Augustin Coulomb, "Recherches théoriques et expérimentales sur la force de torsion et sur l'élasticité des fils de métal," *Mémoires de l'Académie Royale des Sciences, 1784* (Paris, 1787), pp. 229-269. Portions of this memoir are contained in the collection, *Mémoires de Coulomb*, and the entire memoir in the volume *Théorie des machines simples*. (Hereafter, this memoir is listed as Coulomb, 1784 torsion memoir.)

10. *Ibid.*, art. 4.

11. See Paul Walden Banford, *Forests and French Sea Power, 1660–1789* (Toronto, 1956).

12. Bretagne, *Précis des opérations relatives à la navigation intérieure de Bretagne* . . . (Rennes, 1785). This is a collection of memoirs concerning canals in Britanny. Each memoir within is paged separately.

13. Bretagne, "Rapport de la Commission," p. 14, in *Précis des opérations.* . . .

14. *Ibid.*, p. 4.

15. *A.N.*, Marine D²22, pièces 296-297bis, letter from comte de Piré to Maréchal de Castries, c. June 1783.

16. Bretagne, "Rapport de la Commission," pp. 4-5, in *Précis des opérations.* . . .

17. *Ibid.*, p. 14.

18. *Ibid.*, "Rapport et Avis de M. Chézy."

19. *Ibid.*, "Rapport de M. de Coulomb."

20. *Ibid.*, "Rapport de la Commission," pp. 6-8, and "Rapport de M. Coulomb."

21. *A.N.*, Marine D²22, pièces 292, 292bis, 293, and B³742, pièce 106.

22. *Ibid.*, D²22, pièces 319-320. Coulomb letter to de Castries, 21 August 1783.

23. *A.G.*, Dossier Coulomb, Coulomb letter to Ségur, 23 August 1783.

24. Bretagne, "Procès-Verbal de vérifications indiquées entre les rivières de Villaine et de Mayenne par M. Coulomb, Capitaine au Corps royal du génie, Conseil de la Commission, et M. Robinet, Commissaire," in *Précis des opérations.* . . .

25. *A.G.*, Dossier Coulomb, Coulomb letter to Ségur, 3 November 1783.

26. *Ibid.*, letter from Breton canal commission to Maréchal d'Aubeterre, 27 September 1783.

27. *Ibid.*, Coulomb letter to Ségur, 3 November 1783.

28. *Ibid.*, "Corps royal du génie—Mémoire," 8 September 1783.

29. *Ibid.*, le Sancquer letter to Coulomb, 29 October 1783.

30. *A.N.*, Marine D²22, pièce 275, "Mémoire sur le projet de l'établisse-

ment d'un port de Roy à St. Malo présenté par M. le comte de Piré," 19
December 1783, signed by Borda, Bavre, Rochon, and Coulomb.

31. *Ibid.*, pp. 16-18.

32. *Ibid.*, pp. 21-22.

33. *Ibid.*, pp. 19-20.

34. *Ibid.*, pp. 19, 23-25.

35. *A.G.*, Dossier Coulomb, Coulomb letter to Ségur, 3 November 1783.

36. Bretagne, "Rapport de la Commission," p. 25, in *Précis des opérations.*

37. *A.I.G.*, art. 8, sec. 1, "Ile d'Aix," carton 1, no. 63[3], Coulomb letter
to Fourcroy, 20 October 1779. Coulomb refers to the incident with le
Sancquer on page four of this letter.

38. *A.G.*, Dossier Coulomb, le Sancquer letter to Coulomb, 29 October
1783.

39. *Ibid.*

40. *Ibid.*

41. *Ibid.*

42. *Ibid.*, Coulomb letter to d'Aubeterre, 3 November 1783.

43. *Ibid.*, Coulomb letter to Ségur, 3 November 1783.

44. *Ibid.*

45. *Ibid.*

46. *A.G.*, Dossier Coulomb, "Corps royal du génie—Mémoire," 6 November 1783.

47. *Ibid.*

48. *Ibid.*, Coulomb letter to Fourcroy de Ramecourt (?), 20 November
1783.

49. *Ibid.*

50. *Ibid.*

51. *Ibid.*

52. Bretagne, "Rapport de la Commission," pp. 25-26, in *Précis des opérations. . . .*

53. *Ibid.*

A.G., Dossier Coulomb, letter from Breton canal commission to Ségur,
24 January 1784; and Ségur's response, 9 February 1784.

54. *A.S.*, *Procès-verbaux*, May-July 1784.

55. Bretagne, "Rapport de la Commission," pp. 51-55, in *Précis des
opérations. . . .*

56. ———, *Rapport de M. l'abbé Bossut, de M. l'abbé Rochon, de M. de
Fourcroy [de Ramecourt], & de M. le marquis de Condorcet, membres de
l'Académie Royale des Sciences, sur la navigation intérieure de la Bretagne*
(Paris, 1786). Evidently this is the text of a report delivered at the Academy,
2 September 1786.

57. *Ibid.*, p. 20.

58. *A.G.*, X[e]10, Génie, 12 May 1785.

59. Jean Baptiste Biot, "Coulomb," *Mélanges scientifiques et littéraires*,
3 vols. (Paris, 1858), III, 100. The article entitled "Coulomb" appeared originally in the *Biographie universelle* for 1813. (Hereafter, this work is listed
as Biot éloge.)

60. Delambre éloge.

61. *A.N.*, Minutier Central, Etude XLVIII, notaire Louis François Robin,

laisse 475, 1 September 1806, "Inventaire après le décece [*sic*] de M. Charles Augustin Coulomb."

62. *Ibid.*, O¹1596, pièce 100, Report from comte d'Angiviller to the king, 1 July 1784, and O¹127, pièce 239, "Brevet d'Intendant des Eaux et fontaines . . . en faveur du Sr. Coulomb," July 1784.

63. The following paragraphs are drawn mainly from: Pierre Simon Girard, *Mémoires sur le canal de l'Ourcq* . . . 3 vols. (Paris, 1812–1831–1843), see especially Vol. II and the part entitled "Recherches sur les eaux publiques de Paris"; Eugène Beltrand, *Les travaux souterrains de Paris*, 3 vols. (Paris, 1872–1877); Nicolas de Lamare, *Traité de la police, où l'on trouvera l'histoire de son établissement* . . . 4 vols. 2nd ed. (Paris, 1722–1738), I, IV.

64. *A.N.*, O¹1599, pièce 250, Coulomb letter to d'Angiviller, 9 July 1784.

65. Bélidor *L'architecture hydraulique*, II, 215ff.

66. Jacques Payen, "Recherches sur les frères Périer et l'introduction en France de la machine à vapeur de Watt," Thèse—3ᵉ cycle, 2 Parts (Paris, 1966).

67. *A.S.*, *Procès-verbaux*, 22 February and 19 March 1783.

68. Girard, *Mémoires sur le canal.* . . .

Beltrand, *Les travaux souterains.* . . .

Jean Bouchary, *L'eau à Paris à la fin due XVIIIᵉ siècle, la Compagnie des eaux à Paris et l'entreprise de l'Yvette* (Paris, 1946).

69. *A.S.*, *Procès-verbaux*, 22 February and 19 March 1783.

70. Charles Claude de Flahault de la Billarderie, comte d'Angiviller, *Bâtiments du Roi, Notice sur l'arrière de ce département, son origine et ses causes (Paris, c. 1789)*, "Introduction."

71. Charles Claude de Flahault de la Billarderie, comte d'Angiviller, *Mémoires de Charles Claude Flahault, comte de la Billarderie d'Angiviller*, ed. Louis Bobé (Copenhagen and Paris, 1933), p. xi.

72. Girard, *Mémoires sur le canal* . . . , II, 58-59.

73. *A.N.*, Marine G108, pièce 15, fol. 157.

74. Girard, *Mémoires sur le canal* . . . , II, 70.

De Lamare, *Traité de la police* . . . , I, 581.

75. Girard, *Mémoires sur le canal* . . . , II, 74.

76. *Ibid.*

77. *Ibid.*, III, 198.

78. *Ibid.*, p. 384.

79. Beltrand, *Les travaux souterrains* . . . , III, 240.

80. *Ibid.*

81. De Lamare, *Traité de la police* . . . , IV, 386.

82. *Ibid.*

83. *A.N.*, O¹1599, pièce 250, Coulomb letter to d'Angiviller, 9 July 1784.

84. *Ibid.*, pièce 255, Coulomb letter to d'Angiviller, 26 July 1784.

85. *A.G.*, Dossier Coulomb, letter from Coulomb's widow to Minister of War, 5 April 1807.

86. D'Angiviller, *Bâtiments du Roi* . . . , p. 10.

Charles Claude de Flahault de la Billarderie, comte d'Angiviller, *Rapport au Roi fait par M. d'Angiviller en février 1790* (Paris, 1791), pp. 8-10.

87. D'Angiviller, *Bâtiments du Roi* . . . , p. 10.

88. *A.N.*, 0¹1596, pièce 104, Coulomb letter to d'Angiviller, 28 August 1784.

89. *Ibid.*, 0¹1599, pièce 282, Coulomb letter to d'Angiviller, 22 March 1786.

90. *Ibid.*, 0¹1596, pièce 140, Coulomb letter to d'Angiviller, 6 May 1790.

91. *Ibid.*, pièce 125, Coulomb letter to d'Angiviller, 25 February 1788.

92. Jacques Silvestre de Sacy, *Le comte d'Angiviller, dernier Général des Bâtiments du Roi* (Paris, 1953).

93. D'Angiviller, *Rapport au Roi . . .*, p. 7.

94. *A.N.*, 0¹1596, pièce 100, report from d'Angiviller to the king, 1 July 1784.

95. *Ibid.*, pièce 140, Coulomb letter to d'Angiviller, 6 May 1790.

96. Girard, *Mémoires sur le canal . . .*, II, iii-iv, 74.

97. Beltrand, *Les travaux souterrains . . .*, III, 389.

98. See Ernest Maindron, *Les fondations de prix à l'Académie des Sciences—Les lauréats de l'Académie, 1714–1880* (Paris, 1881).

99. Girard, *Mémoires sur le canal . . .*, II, 47.

100. *A.I.G.*, art. 8, sec. 1, "Cherbourg," no. 30bis, Coulomb memoir, "Mémoire sur l'histoire de Cherbourg, sur le nombre de ses habitans, son commerce et ses manufactures," 1 November 1775, p. 14.

101. *A.N.*, K1024, no. 34, "Rapport des Commissaires chargée par l'Académie des Sciences de l'examen du projet d'un nouvel Hôtel-Dieu. Extrait des Registres de l'Académie des Sciences du 22 septembre 1786." Details given in the text are from pages 21-22, 92-93, 125-135, and 157-158 of the report.

102. A. Maury, *L'ancienne Académie des Sciences* (Paris, 1864), p. 309.

103. *A.S., Procès-verbaux*, 19 May 1787.

104. *Ibid.*, entries for 13 June, 4 July, and 1 August 1787. See also, *The Banks Letters, A Calendar of the Manuscript Correspondence of Sir Joseph Banks Preserved in the British Museum, the British Museum (Natural History) and Other Collections in Great Britain*, ed. Warren R. Dawson (London, 1958), pp. 165, 227, 236, 431, 449, 481, 529, 806.

105. Service géographique de l'Armée, *Catalogue-guide du Musée des Plans-Reliefs* (Paris, 1928).

Archives du Musée des Plans-Reliefs (Paris).

106. Augoyat, *Aperçu historique*, II, 606.

107. *Ibid.*

108. Delambre éloge, p. 220.

109. Biot éloge, p. 100.

110. *A.G.*, Dossier Coulomb, "Relevé de Services."

111. *Ibid.*, Coulomb letter of resignation, 18 December 1790.

112. J.B.J. Delambre, *Base du système métrique décimal, ou Mesure de l'arc du méridien, par MM. P.-F.-A. Méchain et Delambre, rédigée par M. Delambre*, 3 vols. (Paris, 1806–1810), I, 13.

113. *A.S., Procès-verbaux*, 13 April 1791.

114. G. Bigourdan, *Le système métrique des poids et mesures* (Paris, 1901), p. 23.

115. Jean Dominique Cassini, *Mémoires pour servir à l'histoire des sciences et à celles de l'Observatoire Royale de Paris* (Paris, 1810), p. 214.

116. The history of this question may be found in Delambre, *Base du système métrique* . . . ; Bigourdan, *Le système métrique* . . . ; and C. Wolf, "Recherches historiques sur les étalons de poids et mesures de l'Observatoire et les appareils qui ont servi à les construire," *Annales de l'Observatoire (Impérial) de Paris—Mémoires,* XVII (Paris, 1883), c1-c78.

117. Cassini, *Mémoires* . . . , p. 214.

118. Mascart, *La vie . . . de Borda,* pp. 504-505.

Bigourdan, *Le système métrique* . . . , p. 24.

119. Mascart, *La vie . . . de Borda,* p. 672.

120. Bigourdan, *Le système métrique* . . . , p. 35.

121. *Ibid.*

122. *Ibid.,* pp. 51-52.

123. *Ibid.,* p. 8.

124. Mascart, *La vie . . . de Borda,* p. 511.

125. Bigourdan, *Le système métrique* . . . , pp. 51-53.

126. Delambre éloge, p. 220.

127. Bigourdan, *Le système métrique* . . . , p. 58.

128. *Ibid.,* pp. 75-77.

129. *Ibid.,* p. 146. See also Maurice Crosland, "The Congress on Definitive Metric Standards, 1798–1799: The First International Scientific Conference?" *Isis,* LX (1969), 226-231.

130. Bigourdan, *Le système métrique* . . . , pp. 147, 155. See also Institut de France, Académie des Sciences, *Procès-verbaux des séances de l'Académie,* I, 30, 218-219, 577-578: 6 floréal, an 4 (25 April 1796), 11 prairial an 5 (30 May 1797) and 26 floréal, an 7 (15 May 1799).

131. *A.S., Procès-verbaux,* 15 and 29 January 1791, and 4 July 1792.

132. *A.G.,* Dossier Coulomb, "Relevé de Services," and Xe10, "Travail du Roy le 23 mars 1786, Un Brevet de Major au S. Charles Augustin Coulomb. . . ."

133. Reinhard, *Le grand Carnot,* I, 166.

134. *A.G.,* Dossier Coulomb, Coulomb letter of resignation, 18 December 1790.

135. Reinhard, *Le grand Carnot,* I, 167.

136. *Ibid.,* I, 173.

137. *A.G.,* Dossier Coulomb, "Relevé de Services," and "Recompense Nationale en faveur de Charles Augustin Coulomb," Pension no. 216, 15 January 1792.

138. *Ibid.,* document of 1 vendémaire, an 8 (23 September 1799).

139. *Ibid.,* undated document, but evidently after 4 frimaire, an 12 (26 November 1803).

140. *A.S., Procès-verbaux,* 2 November 1791.

141. *Ibid.,* 31 July 1793.

142. *A.N.,* Minutier Central, Etude XLVIII, notaire Louis François Robin, laisse 475, 1 September 1806, "Inventaire après le décece de M. Charles Augustin Coulomb."

143. Bibliothèque Municipale et Universitaire de Clermont-Ferrand, MS 337, fols. 185-186. Letter from Coulomb to Lavoisier, 6 August 1793.

144. Edouard Grimaux, *Lavoisier, 1743–1794, d'après sa correspondance, ses manuscrits, ses papiers de famille et d'autres documents inédits* (Paris, 1888), pp. 368-369.

145. *A.N.*, Minutier Central, Etude XLVIII, notaire Louis François Robin, laisse 475, 1 September 1806, "Inventaire après le décece de M. Charles Augustin Coulomb."

146. Archives de la Seine (hereafter *A. Seine*), Mariages, V5E[1] 235 "Charles Augustin Coulomb—Louise Françoise Proust Desormeaux," 17 brumaire, an 11 (8 November 1802).

A.N., Minutier Central, Etude CXVIII, notaire Jean Baptiste Pierre Bévière, laisse 698, marriage contract between Charles Augustin Coulomb and Louise Françoise Proust Desormeaux, 17 brumaire, an 11 (8 November 1802).

147. *A. Seine*, Naissances, V4E[1] 560, "Charles Augustin Coulomb," 26 February 1790.

148. *B.I.F.*, MS 2041, nos. 85-86, fols. 535-561, Papiers de J.B.J. Delambre, "Notice sur la vie et les ouvrages de M. Coulomb." There are two versions of this; the first is fols. 535-544; the second 545-561.

149. Charles Augustin Coulomb, "Expériences relatives à la circulation de la sève dans les arbres," *Mémoires de l'Institut National des sciences et arts—Sciences mathématiques et physiques*, II (Paris, an 7:1799), 246-248.

150. *Ibid.*, p. 247.

151. Institut de France, Académie des Sciences, *Procès-verbaux des séances* . . . , III, 280 (18 frimaire, an 14: 8 December 1805), and 330-333 (7 April 1806).

152. *B.I.F.*, MS 2041, nos. 85-86, fols. 535-561, Papiers de J.B.J. Delambre, "Notice sur la vie et les ouvrages de M. Coulomb."

153. Institut de France, *Index biographique des membres et correspondants de l'Académie des Sciences du 22 décembre 1666 au 15 novembre 1954* (Paris, 1954), entry for Coulomb, p. 125.

154. *A. Seine*, Naissances, V4E[1] 560, "Henry Louis Coulomb," 30 July 1797.

155. Coulomb, Memoir on laboring men. References below are to article numbers in this memoir.

156. *Ibid.*, art. 4.

157. *Ibid.*, art. 3.

158. *Ibid.*, art. 2.

159. *Ibid.*

160. *Ibid.*, art. 29.

161. O. G. Edholm, *The Biology of Work* (New York, 1967), pp. 12-13.

162. Charles Augustin Coulomb, "Expériences destinées à déterminer la cohérence des fluides et les lois de leur résistance dans les mouvements très lents," *Mémoires de l'Institut National des sciences et arts—Sciences and mathématiques et physiques*, III (Paris, an 9:1801), 246-305. Reprinted in part in *Mémoires de Coulomb*. (Hereafter, this memoir is listed as Coulomb, 1800 fluids memoir.)

CHAPTER THREE

1. *A.S., Procès-verbaux*, 10 March 1773.

2. Coulomb, 1773 statics memoir.

3. *A.I.G.*, art. 18, sec. 1, #1, carton 1, and #2, carton 1.

4. *O.M.*, Martinique, D.F.C., carton 1, pièces 195, 201; carton 2, pièces 237, 251-252, 274, 280, 316-317.

A.I.G., art. 3, sec. 3, carton 1, laisse 3, pièce 43.

5. *A.I.G.*, art. 3, sec. 10, carton 2, pièce 5a, Coulomb, "Mémoire sur le service des officiers du Corps du Génie."

6. Bélidor, *La science des ingénieurs.*

7. Coulomb, 1773 statics memoir, "Introduction." To facilitate examination of Coulomb's original memoirs, article numbers and headings rather than page numbers are cited throughout. (Most of Coulomb's published memoirs are available in several editions, having varying pagination.)

8. Pierre Brunet, *Les physicians hollandais et la méthode expérimentale en France au XVIIIe siècle* (Paris, 1926).

9. *A.G.*, Dossier Coulomb, "Mémoire, 1781."

R. Prony, *Nouvelle architecture hydraulique* (Paris, 1790), i, "Avertissement de l'éditeur."

Bernard Forest de Bélidor, *L'architecture hydraulique, Nouvelle edition avec des notes et additions par M. Navier* (Paris, 1819), "Introduction" by Navier.

10. Charles Bossut, *A General History of Mathematics*, trans. J. Bonnycastle (London, 1803), p. 421.

11. *Ibid.*, p. 447.

12. Coulomb, 1773 statics memoir, "Introduction."

13. Bélidor, *La Science des ingénieurs.*

14. Frézier, *La Théorie . . . ou Traité de stéréotomie.*

15. Coulomb, 1773 statics memoir, art. i.

16. *Ibid.*, fig. 4.

17. Straub, *A History . . .* , p. 148.

18. Isaac Newton, *Opticks*, Query xxxi. Query xxxi first appeared in the 2nd English edition (London, 1717). I have used the Dover edition based on the 4th edition (London, 1730).

19. Guillaume Amontons, "De la résistance causée dans les machines," *Mémoires de l'Académie Royale des Sciences*, 1699 (Paris, 1718), pp. 206-227.

20. Coulomb, 1773 statics memoir, art. iv.

21. *Ibid.*, fig. 4.

22. Galileo Galilei, *Discorsi e dimostrazioni matematiche, intorno à due nuove scienze . . .* (Leida, 1638), English trans. Henry Crew and Alfonso de Salvio as *Dialogues Concerning Two New Sciences* (New York, 1914).

23. *Ibid.*, Second day, Prop. 1 (Crew and de Salvio ed., p. 116).

24. Robert Hooke, *De potentiva restitutiva* (London, 1678).

25. Mariotte, *Traité du mouvement des eaux.*

26. Gottfried Wilhelm Leibniz, "Demonstrationes novae de resistentia solidorum," *Acta Eruditorum*, July 1684 (Lipsiae, 1684), pp. 319-325.

27. James Jurin, "The Action of Springs," *Philosophical Transactions*, abridged ed. (London, 1756), x (1744–1750), 160-174.

28. Thomas Young, *Course of Lectures on Natural Philosophy*, 2 vols. (London, 1807).

29. Leonhard Euler, "De curvis elasticis" (1744), trans. W. Oldfather as "L. Euler's Elastic Curves," *Isis*, xx (1933), 72-160.

30. Antoine Parent, *Essais et recherches de mathématique et de physique*, 3 vols. (Paris, 1713), III, 187-188.

31. Stephen P. Timoshenko, *History of Strength of Materials* (New York, 1953), pp. 44-47.

32. Coulomb, 1773 statics memoir, art. VII.

33. *Ibid.*, fig. 6.

34. S. B. Hamilton, "Charles Auguste de Coulomb," *Transactions of the Newcomen Society*, XVII (1936–1937), 31.

35. Coulomb, 1773 statics memoir, art. VII.

36. *Ibid.*

37. Charles Bossut and Guillaume Viallet, *Recherches sur la construction la plus avantageuse des digues* (Paris, 1764).

38. Coulomb, 1773 statics memoir, art. X.

39. C.L.M.H. Navier, *Résumé des leçons données à l'Ecole des ponts et chaussées sur l'application de la mécanique . . . par Navier, Troisième édition avec des notes et des appendices par M. Barré de Saint-Venant* (Paris, 1864), p. 180.

40. *Ibid.*, p. c.

41. Coulomb, 1773 statics memoir, arts. VIII, IX.

42. Navier, *Résumé des leçons . . .* , p. 6.

43. Coulomb, 1773 statics memoir, fig. 5.

44. *Ibid.*, art. IX.

45. Peter van Musschenbroek, *Essai de physique*, 2 vols. French ed. (Leyden, 1739), I, 356.

46. Leonhard Euler, "Sur la force des colonnes," *Mémoires de l'Académie Royale des Sciences et Belles-Lettres*, 1757 (Berlin, 1759), pp. 252-282.

47. Coulomb, 1773 statics memoir, figs. 7, 5.

48. Musschenbroek, *Essai de physique*, I, 359.

49. Coulomb, 1773 statics memoir, art. IX.

50. *Ibid.*

51. Navier, *Résumé des leçons . . .* , pp. 7-8.

52. Sixteen eighteenth- and nineteenth-century sources are cited in Hugh Q. Golder, "The History of Earth Pressure Theory," *Archives internationales d'histoire des sciences*, XXXII (1953), 209-219. A good contemporary source is K. Mayniel, *Traité expérimental, analytique et pratique de la poussée des terres et des murs de revêtement* (Paris, 1808). See also Jean Victor Poncelet, "Mémoire sur la stabilité des revêtements et de leurs fondations," *Mémorial de l'officier du Génie*, XIII (1840), 7-270. Note also the relevant sections of Timoshenko, *History . . .* , Navier, *Résumé des leçons . . .* , and Hamilton, *Transactions of the Newcomen Society*, XVII (1936–1937).

53. Karl Terzaghi, *Theoretical Soil Mechanics* (New York, 1943), p. 1.

54. *Ibid.*, pp. 64-65.

55. Bélidor, *La science des ingénieurs*, 2nd ed., pp. 81, 88.

56. Bullet, *L'architecture pratique*, p. 171.

57. Golder, *Archives internationales d'histoire des sciences*, XXXII (1953), 217.

58. Mayniel, *Traité expérimental . . .* , pp. 75-82.

59. Fig. III.8 is based on Hamilton, *Transactions of the Newcomen Society*, XVII (1936–1937), 35, and on Pierre Couplet (de Tartreaux), "De la poussée des terres contre leurs revestmens, & la force des revestmens qu'on

leur doit opposer," *Mémoires de l'Académie Royale des Sciences*, 1726 (Paris, 1728), pl. IV, fig. 7.

60. Bélidor, *La science des ingénieurs*, 2nd ed., pp. 39-42.
61. Fig. III.9 is based on Timoshenko, *History* . . . , p. 60, and on Bélidor, *La science des ingénieurs*, 1st ed., Livre II, pl. 4.
62. Mayniel, *Traité expérimental* . . . , p. xvii.
63. Coulomb, 1773 statics memoir, "Introduction."
64. *Ibid.*, fig. 7.
65. Terzaghi, *Theoretical Soil Mechanics* . . . , p. 78.
66. Coulomb, 1773 statics memoir, art. IX.
67. R. Prony, *Nouvelle architecture hydraulique*, 2 vols. (Paris, 1790).
68. R. Prony, "Mécanique philosophique," *Journal de l'Ecole Polytechnique*, VIII (an 8:1800). (Also published separately.)
69. R. Prony, *Recherches sur la poussée des terres, et sur la forme et les dimensions à donner aux murs de revêtement* . . . (Paris, an 10:1802).
70. *Ibid.*

R. Prony, *Instruction pratique sur une méthode pour déterminer les dimensions des murs de revêtement, en se servant de la formule graphique de R. Prony* (Paris, an 10:1802).

71. Reinhard Woltmann, *Beiträge zur hydraulischen Architecture*, 3 vols. (Göttingen, 1791–1794), III.
72. Golder, *Archives internationales d'histoire des sciences*, XXXII (1953), 213.
73. Poncelet, *Mémorial de l'officier du Génie*, XIII (1840), 7-270.
74. Golder, *Archives internationales d'histoire des sciences*, XXXII (1953).
75. W.J.M. Rankine, "On the Stability of Loose Earth," *Philosophical Transactions*, CXLVII (1857), 9-27.
76. Terzaghi, *Theoretical Soil Mechanics*, p. 63.

Golder, *Archives internationales d'histoire des sciences*, XXXII (1953), 211.

77. Jean Victor Poncelet, "Examen critique et historique des principales théories ou solutions concernant l'équilibre des voûtes," *Comptes rendus hebdomadaires des séances de l'Académie des Sciences* . . . , XXXV (1832), 494-502.
78. Hamilton, *Transactions of the Newcomen Society*, XVII (1936–1937), 37.
79. Straub, *A History* . . . , p. 145.
80. Philippe de La Hire, *Traité de la mécanique* (Paris, 1695). Also published as, "Oeuvres diverses de M. de La Hire: Traité de mécanique," *Mémoires de l'Académie Royale des Sciences depuis 1666 jusqu'à 1699* (Paris, 1730), IX, 1-340.
81. Fig. III.11 is based on Timoshenko, *History* . . . , p. 63, and on La Hire, *Traité de mécanique*, fig. for Prop. CXXV.
82. Philippe de La Hire, "Sur la construction des voûtes dans les edifices," *Mémoires de l'Académie Royale des Sciences*, 1712 (Paris, 1714), pp. 70-78.
83. Bélidor, *La science des ingénieurs*, 2nd ed., pp. 100-186.
84. *Ibid.*, 1st ed., Livre II, pl. 5.
85. Pierre Charles Lesage, *Recueil de divers mémoires extraits de la Bibliothéque Impériale des Ponts et Chaussées*, 2 vols. (Paris, 1810), II, 246-273.
86. Pierre Couplet (de Tartreaux), "Mémoire sur les poussée de voûtes,"

Mémoires de l'Académie Royale des Sciences, 1729 (Paris, 1731), pp. 79-117, and 17-30 (Paris, 1732), pp. 117-141.

87. Frézier, *La théorie . . . ou Traité de stéréotomie.*

88. *Ibid.*, II, 92.

89. *Ibid.*, III, 354.

90. Coulomb, 1773 statics memoir, art. XVI.

91. *Ibid.*, "Introduction."

92. Leonhard Euler, "Solutio problematis de invenienda curva, quam format lamina utcunque elastica in singulis punctis a potentis quibuscunque sollicitatia," *Commentarii Academiae Scientiarum Imperialis Petropolitanae*, III (1728) (Petropoli, 1732), 70-84.

93. Jacques Bernoulli, *Opera*, 2 vols. (Genève, 1744), II, 1119.

94. Coulomb, 1773 statics memoir, art. XVII, 2e Remarque.

95. *Ibid.*, fig. 14.

96. Thomas, *Mémoire historique . . .* , pp. 153-155.

97. Fig. III.14 is based on Coulomb, 1773 statics memoir, fig. 9; and Timoshenko, *History . . .* , p. 65.

98. *A.D.H.*, Série D, 124* (9), fols. 13-19.

Frézier, *La théorie . . . ou Traité de stéréotomie*, III, 343-345, 381-385.

99. Poncelet, *Comptes rendus hebdomadaires des séances de l'Académie des Sciences . . .* , XXXV (1832), 496.

Timoshenko, *History . . .* , p. 65.

100. *A.D.H.*, Série D, 121* (6), fol. 71.

Thomas, *Mémoire historique . . .* , pp. 72-73.

101. *A.D.H.*, Série D, 120* (5); 121* (6); 128* (13).

Donat, *Almanach historique . . .* , p. 114.

102. Coulomb, 1773 statics memoir, art. XVIII, 2e Remarque.

103. Poncelet, *Comptes rendus hebdomadaires des séances de l'Académie des Sciences . . .* , XXXV (1832), 497.

104. ———— Audoy, "Mémoire sur la poussée des voûtes en berceau," *Mémorial de l'officier du Génie*, IV (1820), 1-96.

105. Navier, *Résumé des leçons . . .* , p. ci.

Straub, *A History . . .* , p. 155.

106. *Mémorial de l'officier du Génie*, I-XV (1803–1848).

107. Timoshenko, *History . . .* , p. 83.

CHAPTER FOUR

1. Coulomb, 1781 friction memoir.

2. Coulomb, 1773 statics memoir.

3. C. St. C. Davison, "Wear Prevention in Early History," *Wear*, I (1957), 155-159.

F. P. Bowden and D. Tabor, *The Friction and Lubrication of Solids*, 2 Parts (London, 1950–1964), II, 502-503.

I. V. Kragelsky and V. S. Schedrov, *Razvitia Nauki o Trenii—Sookoi Trenia (Development of the Science of Friction—Dry Friction)* (Moscow: Isdatelstvo Akademii Nauk, 1956), pp. 5-9.

R. Courtel and L. M. Tichvinsky, "A Brief History of Friction," *Mechanical Engineering* (September 1963), pp. 55-59.

C. Truesdell, *Essays in the History of Mechanics* (New York, 1968), pp. 7-12.

4. Amontons, *Mémoires de l'Académie Royale des Sciences*, 1699 (Paris 1718), pp. 206-227.

5. J. T. Desaguliers (elder), "Some experiments concerning the cohesion of lead," *Philosophical Transactions*, xxxiii (1725), 345-347; and in numerous other issues of this same journal.

J. T. Desaguliers, *A Course of Experimental Philosophy*, 2 vols. (London, 1734), i, Lectures i, iv.

6. Coulomb, 1781 friction memoir.

7. Antoine Parent, "Nouvelle statique avec frotemens et sans frotemens ou règles pour calculer les frotemens des machines dans l'état de l'équilibre," *Mémoires de l'Académie Royale des Sciences*, 1704 (Paris, 1706), pp. 173-197.

8. Leonhard Euler, "Sur le frottement des corps solides," and "Sur la diminution de la résistance du frottement," *Mémoires de l'Académie Royale des Sciences et Belles-Lettres*, 1748 (Berlin, 1750), pp. 122-132, 133-148.

9. Bossut, *Traité élémentaire de méchanique* . . . .

10. Coulomb, 1777 magnetism memoir.

11. Coulomb, 1781 friction memoir, arts. 1, 108. As in previous chapters of this book, references to Coulomb's memoirs list the article number rather than the page with either roman or arabic numerals chosen to follow Coulomb's original scheme. This is to facilitate use of the several editions of Coulomb's memoirs.

12. Amontons, *Mémoires de l'Académie Royale des Sciences*, 1699 (Paris, 1718), pp. 206-227.

13. Anonymous, *Histoire de l'Académie Royale des Sciences*, 1699 (Paris. 1718), p. 105.

14. Amontons, *Mémoires de l'Académie Royale des Sciences*, 1699 (Paris. 1718), pp. 206-207.

15. *Ibid.*, p. 208.

16. *Ibid.*

17. *Ibid.*, p. 211.

18. J. Smeaton, "An Experimental Inquiry Concerning the Natural Powers of Waters and Wind to Turn Mills, and Other Machines . . . ," *Philosophical Transactions*, li (part i, 1759), 100-174.

19. Among those who accepted Amontons' idea of a friction coefficient but questioned that it equaled 1/3 are:

Anonymous, *Histoire de l'Académie Royale des Sciences*, 1699, p. 105.

Parent, *Mémoires de l'Académie Royale des Sciences*, 1704 (Paris, 1706), pp. 173-197.

Jacob Leupold, *Theatrum machinarum generale* . . . (Lipsiae, 1724), pp. 78-90.

François Joseph de Camus, *Traité des forces mouvantes pour la pratique des arts & métiers* (Paris, 1722), pp. 304-325.

Georg Bernhard Bulfinger, "De frictionibus corporum solidorum," *Commentarii Academiae Scientiarum Imperialis Petropolitanae*, ii (1727) (Petropoli, 1729), 403-414.

Euler, *Mémoires de l'Académie Royale des Sciences et Belles-Lettres,* 1748 (Berlin, 1750), pp. 122-132, 133-148.

Bossut, *Traité élémentaire de méchanique* . . . .

Bélidor, *L'architecture hydraulique,* I, 70-125.

Keane Fitzgerald, "A Method of Lessening the Quantity of Friction in Nature," *Philosophical Transactions,* LIII (1763), 139-158.

S. K. Kotelnikov, *Kniga, soderzhaschia v sebye uchenia o ravnovesii i dvizhenii tel (A Book, Containing Instructions on the Equilibrium and Movement of Bodies)* (St. Petersburg, 1774), pp. 161-165; as quoted in N. A. Figurovskii, *Istoria Estestvoznania v Rossii (History of Natural Science in Russia)* (Moscow: Isdatelstvo Akademii Nauk, 1957), vol. I, part 1, pp. 287-290.

J. H. Lambert, "Sur le frottement entant qu'il rallentit le mouvement," *Nouveaux mémoires de l'Académie Royale des Sciences et Belles-Lettres,* XXVIII (1772) (Berlin, 1774), 9-32.

20. Among those who challenged Amontons are:

Desaguliers, *Philosophical Transactions,* XXXIII (1725), 345-347; and *A Course of Experimental Philosophy,* I, Lectures I and IV.

Peter van Musschenbroek, *The Elements of Natural Philosophy,* trans. John Colson, 2 vols. (London, 1744), pp. 124-125, 135-145, 174-175, 200-208, 234-235.

Nollet, *Leçons de physique expérimentale,* I, Leçon III, art. 2.

21. La Hire, *Traité de la mécanique.*

22. Anonymous, *Histoire de l'Académie Royale des Sciences,* 1699 (Paris, 1718), p. 105.

23. *Ibid.,* p. 106 (quoting La Hire).

24. Euler, *Mémoires de l'Académie Royale des Sciences et Belles-Lettres,* 1748 (1750), pp. 122-132, 133-148.

25. Parent, *Mémoires de l'Académie Royale des Sciences,* 1704 (Paris, 1706), pp. 173-197.

26. J. T. Desaguliers, *Lectures of Natural Philosophy* (London, 1719).

27. *Ibid.,* p. 23.

28. *Ibid.,* p. 63.

29. Desaguliers, *Philosophical Transactions,* XXXIII (1725), 345-347.

30. Mariotte, *Traité du mouvement des eaux.*

31. J. T. Desaguliers, "An Account of Several Experiments Concerning the Running of Water in Pipes, as it is Retarded by Friction," *Philosophical Transactions,* XXXIV (1726), 77-82.

32. J. T. Desaguliers, "An Examination of Monsieur Perault's New-Invented *Axis in peritrochio* Said to be Entirely Void of Friction," *Philosophical Transactions,* XXXVI (1730), 222-227.

33. J. T. Desaguliers, "An Experiment to Shew that the Friction . . . ," *Philosophical Transactions,* XXXVII (1732), 292-293.

34. Desaguliers, *A Course of Experimental Philosophy.*

35. Musschenbroek, *The Elements of Natural Philosophy.*

36. Camus, *Traité des forces mouvantes.* . . .

37. Amontons, *Mémoires de l'Académie Royale des Sciences,* 1699 (Paris, 1718), p. 207.

38. Bowden and Tabor, *The Friction and Lubrication* . . . , II, 507-509.

39. Kragelsky and Schedrov, *Razvitia nauki* . . . , p. 45.

40. Bowden and Tabor, *The Friction and Lubrication* . . . , II, 506.

41. Information about the contests was obtained in *Mémoires de l'Académie Royale des Sciences—Table générale des matières,* 10 vols. (Paris, 1734, 1729–1809); and from Ernest Maindron, *Les fondations de prix à l'Académie des Sciences—Les laureats de l'Académie, 1714–1880* (Paris, 1881).

42. G. Hanotaux and A. Martineau, eds., *Histoire des colonies française,* 6 vols. (Paris, 1929–1933), I, 478.

43. For example, see the memoirs in Volumes VII and VIII of the collection, *Recueil des pièces qui ont remporté les prix de l'Académie Royale des Sciences,* 9 vols. (Paris, 1721–1777).

44. Coulomb, 1781 friction memoir, art. 1.

45. *Ibid.,* art. 153.

46. Henry B. Culver, *The Book of Old Ships* (New York, 1935), p. 243.

47. Coulomb, 1773 statics memoir.

48. Edmond Bauer, *l'Electromagnétisme—hier et aujourd'hui* (Paris, 1949), pp. 215-216.

49. Coulomb, 1781 friction memoir, art. 1.

50. *Ibid.,* Plate I, figs. 1, 3.

51. *Ibid.,* art. 3.

52. *Ibid.,* art. 153.

53. Euler, *Mémoires de l'Académie Royale des Sciences et Belles-Lettres,* 1748 (1750), p. 125.

54. Charles Augustin Coulomb, "Mémoire sur les frottemens de la pointe des pivots," *Mémoires de l'Académie Royale des Sciences,* 1790 (Paris, 1797), pp. 448-471; and later included in Coulomb, *Théorie des machines simples* (Paris: Bachelier, 1821).

55. Coulomb, 1781 friction memoir, art. 3.

56. *Ibid.,* arts. 42, 44.

57. Formulas derived from *ibid.,* arts. 32, 151.

58. *Ibid.,* art. 32.

59. For an analysis of Carnot's work in mechanics and mathematics see the important, recently published study by Charles Coulston Gillispie, *Lazare Carnot Savant* (Princeton, 1971).

60. *A.S.,* Dossier Prix 1779, Lazare Carnot, "Mémoire sur la théorie des machines, pour concourir au prix de 1779 proposé par l'Académie Royale des Sciences de Paris," p. 12, and also, all documents contained in *A.S.,* Dossier Prix, 1779 and 1781.

61. Kragelsky and Schedrov, *Razvitia nauki* . . . , pp. 52, 69.

62. Cited by Coulomb, 1781 friction memoir, art. 1.

63. *Ibid.,* art. 44.

64. *Ibid.,* arts. 44, 69.

65. *Ibid.,* pl. II, figs. 8-11.

66. *Ibid.,* art. 44.

67. *Ibid.,* art. 97.

68. *Ibid.,* art. 96.

69. Kragelsky and Schedrov, *Razvitia nauki* . . . , p. 52.

70. Coulomb, 1800 fluids memoir.

71. Prony, *Nouvelle architecture hydraulique,* I, 427-515.

Prony, "Mécanique philosophique," *Journal de l'Ecole Polytechnique*, VIII (Paris, an 8: 1800), vii.

72. George Rennie, "Experiments on the Friction and Abrasion of the Surfaces of Solids," *Philosophical Transactions*, XXXIV (1829), 143-170.

73. A. J. Morin, "Nouvelles expériences sur le frottement . . . faites à Metz en 1833," *Mémoires présentés par divers savans à l'Académie Royale des Sciences de l'Institut de France*, VI (Paris, 1835), 631-783.

74. A. J. Dupuit, "Résumé du Mémoire sur le tirage des voitures et sur le frottement de seconde espèce," *Comptes rendus hebdomadaires des séances de l'Académie des Sciences*, IX (Paris, 1839), 698-700, 775.

75. Poncelet's *Cours* circulated in lithographed form as early as 1827. His relevant works are: Jean Victor Poncelet, *Traité de mécanique industrielle, physique ou expérimentale* (Bruges, 1st ed. 1829; 2nd ed. 1844); *Traité de mécanique appliquée aux machines* (Liège, 1845); and *Cours de mécanique appliquée aux machines* (Paris, 1874).

76. John Leslie, *An Experimental Inquiry Into the Nature and Propagation of Heat* (Edinburgh, 1804), pp. 299-303.

CHAPTER FIVE

1. Coulomb, 1777 magnetism memoir.
2. Coulomb, 1784 torsion memoir.
3. Coulomb, 1777 magnetism memoir.
4. The statement of the 1775 and 1777 magnetism prize contest is given variously in *Histoire de l'Académie Royale des Sciences*, 1775 (Paris, 1778) p. 40; and 1777 (Paris, 1780), p. 58.
5. *A.S.*, Dossier Prix, 1775, 1777.
6. Jan Hendrik Van Swinden, "Recherches sur les aiguilles aimantées, et sur leurs variations régulières," *Mémoires de mathèmatique et de physique présentés à l'Académie Royale des Sciences, par divers savans*, VIII (Paris, 1780), 1-576.
7. Anonymous, *Mémoires de mathématique et de physique présentés à l'Académie Royale des Sciences, par divers savans*, VIII (Paris, 1780), v-xi.
8. As cited by M. du Tour, "Discours sur l'aiman, présenté à l'Académie Royale des Sciences, pour concourir sur le sujet proposé, pour 1744," *Pièces qui ont remporté le prix de l'Académie Royale des Sciences . . . en 1741 sur la meilleure construction du cabestan & en 1743 et 1746 sur la meilleure construction des boussoles d'inclination; & sur l'attraction de l'aiman avec le fer* (Paris, 1748), pp. 67-69.
9. Francisco Lana, "Nova methodus construenda pyxidis magneticae, & observandi cum exacta praecisione gradus & minuta declinationum," *Acta Eruditorum*, November 1686 (Lipsiae, 1686), pp. 560-562.
10. Van Swinden, *Mémoires de mathématique et de physique . . .* , VIII, 239.
11. *A.S.*, Dossier Prix, 1775, 1777.
12. Archives de l'Observatoire de Paris (hereafter *O.P.*), AD5-33, folder II.
13. Coulomb, 1777 magnetism memoir, arts. 43-50. As in previous chapters of this book, references to Coulomb's memoirs list the article number

and not the page, with roman or arabic numerals chosen to follow Coulomb's original scheme. This is to facilitate use of the several editions of Coulomb's various memoirs.

14. *Ibid.*, art. 46.

15. *Ibid.*, art. 53.

16. *Ibid.*, "Addition," following art. 56.

17. *Ibid.*, art. 54.

18. *Ibid.*, pl. i, fig. 12, nos. 1 and 2.

19. *Ibid.*, art. 85.

20. *Ibid.*, art. 86.

21. *Ibid.*, "Addition," following art. 56.

22. *O.P.*, AD5-33, folder ii.

23. *Ibid.*, folder ix.

24. *Ibid.*, folder iii; Notes by Cassini, 18 March 1782.

25. *Ibid.*

26. *Ibid.*, folder iii; Coulomb, letter to Cassini, 14 May 1782.

27. *Ibid.*, folder x-xii.

28. *Ibid.*, folder iii; Coulomb, letter to Cassini 14 May 1782.

29. *Ibid.*

30. *Ibid.*

31. *Ibid.*, Coulomb, undated, unsigned letter to Cassini. The context places the letter about the last part of May 1782.

32. *Ibid.*

33. Louis Cotte, "Observations faites à Laone d'heure en heure sur la boussole de variation de M. Coulomb . . . ," *Observations sur la physique, sur l'histoire naturelle et sur les arts*, xxix, July 1786 (Paris, 1786), 189-193. Also see *O.P.*, AD5-33, folder iv.

34. Thomas Bugge, *Science in France in the Revolutionary Era, Described by Thomas Bugge, Danish Astronomer Royal and Member of the International Commission on the Metric System (1798–1799)*, ed. with Introduction and Commentary, Maurice P. Crosland (Cambridge, Mass., 1969), p. 114.

35. *A.S., Procès-verbaux*, 4 September 1784.

36. Coulomb, 1784 torsion memoir.

37. *Ibid.*, art. iv.

38. [Jean Baptiste Biot and E.P.E. Rossel] B—t and R—1, *Biographie universelle*, nouvelle édition, v (1843), 60.

39. Coulomb, 1784 torsion memoir, art. ii.

40. *Ibid.*, art. iii.

41. *Ibid.*, pl. iv, figs. 1, 2.

42. *Ibid.*, art. v. This article contains the material numbered as my equations 1 to 7.

43. *Ibid.*, art. vi.

44. *Ibid.*, art. vii.

45. *Ibid.*, arts. ix, x.

46. *Ibid.*, art. xi.

47. Clifford A. Truesdell, *The Rational Mechanics of Flexible or Elastic Bodies: 1638–1788*, "Leonhardi Euleri Opera Omnia," series secunda, Vol. xi, sectio secunda (Turici, 1960), p. 407.

48. Coulomb, 1784 torsion memoir, arts. XI-XIII.

49. *Ibid.*, art. XIV.

50. *Ibid.*

51. Potier, ed., *Mémoires de Coulomb*, p. 84.

52. E. U. Condon and Hugh Odishaw, eds., *Handbook of Physics* (New York, 1958), chap. 3, p. 12.

53. Charles D. Hodgman, ed., *Handbook of Chemistry and Physics*, 39th ed. (Cleveland, 1957), p. 2007.

54. Coulomb, 1784 torsion memoir, art. XIII.

55. *Ibid.*, art. XVI.

56. *Ibid.*

57. *Ibid.*, arts. XVII-XVIII.

58. *Ibid.*, art. XIX.

59. *Ibid.*, arts. XX-XXXIII.

60. *Ibid.*, art. XXXI.

61. Hamilton, *Transactions of the Newcomen Society*, XVII (1936–1937), 34.

62. Timoshenko, *History* . . . , p. 48.

63. Coulomb, 1773 statics memoir, arts. IV-V.

64. Coulomb, 1784 torsion memoir, art. XXXIII.

65. *Ibid.*, art. XXXI.

66. *Ibid.*, art. XXXIII.

67. *Ibid.*, art. XXXI.

68. *Ibid.*, art. XXXII.

69. *Ibid.*, art. XXXIII.

70. Pierre Simon Girard, *Traité analytique de la résistance des solides* . . . (Paris, 1798), p. xxxvi.

71. Isaac Todhunter and Karl Pearson, *A History of the Theory of Elasticity and of the Strength of Materials*, 2 vols. in 3, 2nd ed. (New York, 1960), vol. II, Part 1, p. 183.

72. *Ibid.*, I, 1, 77.

73. S. Timoshenko and J. N. Goodier, *Theory of Elasticity*, 2nd ed. (New York, 1951), pp. 249-250.

74. Truesdell, *The Rational Mechanics* . . . , p. 408.

75. Todhunter, *A History of the Theory of Elasticity* . . . , I, 70, 85, 101, 120, 123, 174, 201, 459, 658, 664.

76. Siméon Denis Poisson, "Mémoire sur l'équilibre et le mouvement des corps élastiques," *Annales de chimie*, XXXVII (1828), 337-355.

77. The *Encyclopædia Britannica* article by Young is contained in Thomas Young, *Miscellaneous Works of the Late Thomas Young*, ed. George Peacock and John Leitch, 3 vols. (London, 1855), II, 527-541. Coulomb's influence on Young is seen throughout Young's *Miscellaneous Works* . . . , especially, I, 491-498; II, 251-253 and 527-541; and also in Young, *Course of Lectures on Natural Philosophy*, 2 vols. (London, 1807).

78. Francisco Lana, *Acta Eruditorum* (November 1686 [Lipsiae, 1686]), pp. 560-562.

79. ———— Lous, as cited by Van Swinden, *Mémoires de mathématique et de physique présentés à l'Académie Royale des Sciences, par divers savans*, VIII (Paris, 1780), 22.

80. Pierre Charles Le Monnier, *Loix du magnétisme* (2 parts; Part I, Paris, 1776; Part II, Paris, 1778), Part II, xiii, 2.

81. *O.P.*, AD5-33, folder II.

82. Mascart, *La vie . . . de Borda*.

83. *A.S.*, Dossier Prix, 1777.

84. John Michell, *Treatise of Artificial Magnets, in which is shewn an easy . . . method of making them . . . & also a way of improving the natural ones, etc.* (Cambridge, 1750); 2nd "improved" edition, 1751.

85. (Père) Antoine Rivoire, *Traités sur les aimans artificiels . . . traduits de deux ouvrages Anglois de J. Michell et J. Canton, par le P. Rivoire . . . avec une préface historique du traducteur, où l'on expose les méthodes . . . de MM. Duhamel et Antheaume . . . pour perfectionner ces aimans* (Paris, 1752).

86. Truesdell, *The Rational Mechanics . . .*, p. 405.

87. A. Wolf, *A History of Science, Technology and Philosophy in the 18th Century*, 2 vols. paperback ed. (New York, 1961), I, 246.

88. Edmund Hoppe, *Geschichte der Physik* (Braunschweig, 1926), p. 50.

89. Max Jammer, *Concepts of Force* (Cambridge, Mass., 1957), p. 191.

90. Archibald Geikie, *Memoir of John Michell* (Cambridge, 1918), p. 84.

91. Edmund Whittaker, *A History of the Theories of Aether and Electricity*, 2 vols. 2nd ed. (London, 1951), I, 56.

92. Jammer, *Concepts of Force*, p. 191.

93. Henry Cavendish, "Experiments to Determine the Density of the Earth," *Philosophical Transactions*, LXXXVIII (1798), 469-470.

94. Anonymous, *Journal de l'Empire* (Paris), 20 September 1806, pp. 3-4.

95. Coulomb, 1777 magnetism memoir, art. 43.

96. Barré de Saint-Venant, in C.L.M.H. Navier, *Résumé des leçons . . .*, p. ccxciv.

97. Thomas S. Kuhn, *The Structure of Scientific Revolutions* (Chicago, 1962), chap. VI.

98. Coulomb, 1800 fluids memoir, arts. 8-10.

99. Mariotte, *Traité du mouvement des eaux*.

100. Isaac Newton, *Philosophiae Naturalis Principia Mathematica* (London, 1686); English trans. Andrew Motte, as *Sir Isaac Newton's Mathematical Principles of Natural Philosophy and His System of the World*, ed. Florian Cajori, 2 vols. (Berkeley, 1934), I, Book 2.

101. Daniel Bernoulli, "Dissertatio de actione fluidorum in corpora solida et motu solidorum in fluidis," *Commentarii Academiae Scientiarum Imperialis Petropolitanae*, II (1729), 304-342; III (1732), 214-229. "Theorema de motu curvilineo corporum, quae resistentiam patiuntur velocitatis suae quadrato proportionalem una cum solutione problematis in Act: Lips: M: Nov: 1728 proposui," *ibid.*, IV (1735), 136-143. "Experimenta coram societate instituta in confirmationem theoriae pressionum quas latera canalis ab aqua transfluente sustinent," *ibid.*, IV (1735), 194-201. "Dissertatio brevis de motibus corporum reciprocis seu oscillatoriis, quae ubique resistentiam patiuntur quadrato velocitatis suae proportionalem," "Additamentum ad theoremata," *ibid.*, V (1738), 106-125, 126-142.

102. Willem Jacob 'sGravesande, *Elémens de physique, ou Introduction à*

la philosophie de Newton, trans. C. F. Roland de Virloys, 2 vols. (Paris, 1747), arts. 1911, 1915.

103. Jean Le Rond d'Alembert; M.J.A.N. Capitat, marquis de Condorcet; and Charles Bossut, *Nouvelles expériences sur la résistance des fluides, par MM. d'Alembert, le marquis de Condorcet et l'abbé Bossut, membres de l'Académie royale des sciences, etc. M. l'abbé Bossut, rapporteur* (Paris, 1777).

104. Jean Charles de Borda, "Expériences sur la résistance des fluides," *Mémoires de l'Académie Royale des Sciences*, 1763 (Paris, 1766), pp. 358-376; and 1767 (Paris, 1770), pp. 495-503.

105. Pierre Louis Georges Dubuat, *Principles d'hydraulique* . . . (Paris, 1st ed., 1779; 2nd ed., 1786).

106. Coulomb, 1784 torsion memoir, art. xviii.

107. *Ibid.*

108. Coulomb, 1800 fluids memoir.

109. Charles Augustin Coulomb, "Construction et usage d'une balance électrique, fondée sur la propriété qu'ont les fils de métal d'avoir une force de torsion proportionnelle à l'angle de torsion," *Mémoires de l'Académie Royale des Sciences*, 1785 (Paris, 1788), 4e Remarque. Hereafter, this memoir is listed as Coulomb, First E & M Memoir.)

110. Coulomb, 1800 fluids memoir, art. 1.

111. *Ibid.*, art. 4.

112. *Ibid.*, art. 5.

113. *Ibid.*, art. 6.

114. *Ibid.*, art. 12.

115. *Ibid.*, arts. 7-14.

116. *Ibid.*, art. 14.

117. *Ibid.*, arts. 42-46.

118. *Ibid.*, art. 16.

119. *Ibid.*

120. *Ibid.*, arts. 16-23.

121. *Ibid.*, pl. ii, figs. 1, 2.

122. *Ibid.*, art. 31.

123. *Ibid.*, arts. 32-37.

124. René Dugas, *A History of Mechanics*, trans. J. R. Maddox (Neuchatel, 1955), pp. 314-315.

125. *Coulomb*, 1800 fluids memoir, art. 38.

126. *Ibid.*

127. Dugas, *A History of Mechanics*, p. 317.

128. *Ibid.*, pp. 314-315.

129. Coulomb, 1800 fluids memoir, art. 39.

130. *Ibid.*, arts. 51, 53.

131. A. Potier, ed., *Mémoires de Coulomb*, p. 357.

132. Coulomb, 1800 fluids memoir, art. 1.

133. *Ibid.*, art. 53.

134. *B.I.F.*, MSS 1581–1582, "Manuscrits de Charles-Augustin de Coulomb."

135. *B.I.F.*, MS 2041, Delambre's MS drafts of his *éloge* of Coulomb. The remarks concerning unpublished Coulomb MSS occur on folios 542-544.

136. Biot's references to unpublished Coulomb MSS occur frequently in all four volumes of Jean Baptiste Biot, *Traité de physique expérimentale et mathématique*, 4 vols. (Paris, 1816).

CHAPTER SIX

1. Jean Daujat, *Origines et formation de la théorie des phénomènes électriques et magnétiques* (Paris, 1945).

I. Bernard Cohen, *Franklin and Newton* (Philadelphia, 1956).

2. Edmond Bauer, *L'électromagnétisme—hier et aujourd'hui* (Paris, 1949).

G. R. Sharp, "The Physical Work of Charles Auguste de Coulomb and Its Influence Upon the Development of Natural Philosophy," M.Sc. dissertation (University of London, 1936).

3. Franz Ulrich Theodor Aepinus, *Tentamen theoriae electricitatis et magnetismi* (St. Petersburg, 1759 ? and Rostock, 1759).

4. Coulomb, 1777 magnetism memoir, art. 8.

5. For the selection of the committee, see *A.S., Procès-verbaux*, 28 March 1787. The report was to be made on the volume, René-Just Haüy, *Exposition raisonnée de la théorie de l'électricité et du magnétisme d'après les principes de M. Æpinus* . . . (Paris, 1787).

6. For example see Laplace's report, *A.S., Procès-verbaux*, 21 July 1787, or the extract from this in Haüy, *Exposition raisonnée* . . . , "Extrait de Review."

7. For example, see Sigaud de la Fond, *Précis historique et expérimental des phénomènes électriques* . . . , 2nd ed. (Paris, 1785).

8. Charles Augustin Coulomb, Sixth E & M Memoir, art. XL. For the full citation of this memoir, see reference 27 below.

9. Coulomb, 1777 magnetism memoir.

10. The contest for 1746 had previously been set for 1744, but no winners were declared. The winners in 1746 and their essays were: Leonhard Euler, "Dissertatio de magnete"; Etienne François du Tour, "Discours sur l'aiman"; and Daniel and Jean (II) Bernoulli, "Nouveaux principes de méchanique & de physique, tendans à expliquer la nature & les propriétés de l'aiman." All three of these are contained in Académie des Sciences (Paris), *Recueil des piéces qui ont remporté les prix de l'Académie Royale des Sciences, depuis leur fondation jusqu'à présent . . . Tome v, contenant les pièces depuis 1741 jusqu'en 1744* (Paris, 1752).

11. Coulomb, 1777 magnetism memoir, arts. 2, 3.

12. *Ibid.*, arts., 2, 3.

13. *Ibid.*, art. 2.

14. *Ibid.*, art. 3.

15. *Ibid.*, art. 4.

16. *Ibid.*

17. *Ibid.*, arts. 5-13.

18. *Ibid.*, art. 13.

19. *Ibid.*, arts. 27-31.

20. *Ibid.*, art. 31.

21. *Ibid.*, arts. 32-36, 79.

22. *Ibid.*, art. 84.

23. *Ibid.*

24. *Ibid.*

25. *Ibid.*, art. 23.

26. Coulomb, 1784 torsion memoir.

27. Coulomb's "seven" electricity and magnetism memoirs were published in the *Mémoires de l'Académie Royale des Sciences* from 1788-1793. In addition, *portions* of all seven were reprinted in the volume *Mémoires de Coulomb*, cited above. The memoirs are:

1) "Sur l'électricité et le magnétisme, premier mémoire, construction et usage d'une balance électrique, fondée sur la propriété qu'ont les fils de métal d'avoir une force de torsion proportionnelle à l'angle de torsion," 1785 (Paris, 1788), pp. 569-577.

2) "Sur l'électricité et le magnétisme, deuxième mémoire, où l'on détermine suivant quelles lois le fluide magnétique ainsi que le fluide électrique agissent soit par repulsion, soit par attraction," 1785 (Paris, 1788), pp. 578-611.

3) "Sur l'électricité et le magnétisme, troisième mémoire, de la quantité d'électricité qu'un corps isolé perd dans un temps donné, soit par le contact de l'air plus ou moins humide, soit le long des soutiens plus ou moins idioélectriques," 1785 (Paris, 1788), pp. 612-638.

4) "Sur l'électricité et le magnétisme, quatrième mémoire, où l'on démontre deux principales propriétés du fluide électrique . . . ," 1786 (Paris, 1788), pp. 67-77.

5) "Sur l'électricité et le magnétisme, cinquième mémoire, sur la manière dont le fluide électrique se partage entre deux corps conducteurs mis en contact, et de la distribution de ce fluide sur les différentes parties de la surface de ces corps," 1787 (Paris, 1789), pp. 421-467.

6) "Sur l'électricité et le magnétisme, sixième mémoire, suite des recherches sur la distribution du fluide électrique entre plusieurs corps conducteurs.—Détermination de la densité électrique dans les différents points de la surface de ces corps," 1788 (Paris, 1791), pp. 617-705.

7) "Sur l'électricité et le magnétisme, septième mémoire, du magnétisme," 1789 (Paris, 1793), pp. 455-505. To facilitate use of various editions and collections of these seven memoirs, they are referred to in this book by article numbers rather than pages (with the exception of the First, Second, and Third E & M Memoirs which are referred to by the original page numbers because Coulomb did not use article numbers in composing these first three memoirs.) (Hereafter, these memoirs are listed as First E & M Memoir, Second E & M Memoir, etc.)

28. *A.S., Procès-verbaux*, 24 May 1783, and 5 December 1787. (See Appendix A.)

29. *Ibid., Procès-verbaux*, 4 May 1785. (See Appendix A.)

30. *Ibid., Procès-verbaux*, 17 December 1785. (See Appendix A.) Portions of this memoir probably appeared in "Description d'une boussole dont l'aiguille est suspendue par un fil de soie," *Mémoires de l'Académie Royale des Sciences*, 1785 (Paris, 1788), pp. 560-568.

31. *Ibid., Procès-verbaux*, 26 April 1780, and 20 June 1781. (See Appendix

290 · *Notes to pages 182-193*

A.) Portions of the first of these probably appeared in *Mémoires de l'Académie Royale des Sciences*, 1785 (Paris, 1788), pp. 560-568.

32. Coulomb, First E & M Memoir, pp. 569-572.
33. *Ibid.*, pl. XIII.
34. *Ibid.*, p. 574.
35. *Ibid.*, pp. 575-576.
36. *Ibid.*, p. 573.
37. *Ibid.*, p. 572.
38. Coulomb, Second E & M Memoir, p. 578.
39. *Ibid.*, p. 579.
40. *Ibid.*, p. 584.
41. *Ibid.*
42. *Ibid.*, pp. 584-585.
43. *Ibid.*, p. 581.
44. *Ibid.*, p. 585.
45. *Ibid.*, p. 587.
46. *Ibid.*, p. 592.
47. *Ibid.*, p. 593.
48. *Ibid.*, pp. 593-595.
49. *Ibid.*, p. 596.
50. *Ibid.*
51. *Ibid.*, pp. 596-597.
52. *Ibid.*, p. 597.
53. *Ibid.*, p. 603.
54. *Ibid.*, p. 605.
55. *Ibid.*, p. 611.
56. *Ibid.*, p. 593.
57. *Ibid.*, p. 579.
58. *Ibid.*, p. 586.
59. *Ibid.*, p. 581.
60. *Ibid.*, 587-588.
61. Newton, *Principia*, ed. Cajori, I, 193-195.
62. Coulomb, Second E & M Memoir, p. 579.
63. Cohen, *Franklin and Newton*.
64. Duane Roller and Duane H. D. Roller, "The Development of the Concept of Electric Charge: Electricity From the Greeks to Coulomb," *Harvard Case Histories in Experimental Science,* ed. James Bryant Conant, 2 vols. (Cambridge, Mass., 1948), II, 541-639.
65. Académie des Sciences (Paris), Daniel and Jean (II) Bernoulli, "Nouveaux principes de méchanique & de physique . . . ," *Recueil des pièces . . . ,* V (Paris, 1752), 140.
66. Cohen, *Franklin and Newton*, p. 546.
67. Edmund Whittaker, *A History of the Theories of Aether and Electricity*, 2 vols. 2nd ed. (London, 1951), I, 53.
Roller and Roller, *Harvard Case Histories . . . ,* II, 610-611.
68. Cohen, *Franklin and Newton*, p. 546.
69. Whittaker, *A History . . . ,* I, 53.
Cohen, *Franklin and Newton*, p. 551.
70. Henry Cavendish, *The Electrical Researches of the Honourable Henry*

Cavendish, *F.R.S.*, ed. J. Clerk Maxwell (Cambridge, 1879), pp. 110-111.

71. *Ibid.*, p. xlvii.

72. Académie des Sciences (Paris), Daniel and Jean (II) Bernoulli, "Nouveaux principes de méchanique & de physique . . . ," v, 140.

73. John Michell, *Treatise of Artificial Magnets, in which is shewn an easy . . . method of making them . . . & also a way of improving the natural ones, etc.* 1st ed. (Cambridge, 1750).

74. Whittaker, *A History* . . . , I, 57.

75. *Ibid.*

76. Cohen, *Franklin and Newton*, pp. 298-299.

77. Kuhn, *The Structure of Scientific Revolutions*, p. 35.

78. Coulomb, First E & M Memoir, p. 575, and Second E & M Memoir, pp. 584-585.

79. Coulomb, Third E & M Memoir, p. 612.

80. *Ibid.*, p. 613.

81. Bauer, *L'électromagnétisme* . . . , p. 228.

82. Coulomb, Third E & M Memoir, p. 614.

83. *Ibid.*, p. 621.

84. *Ibid.*, p. 619.

85. *Ibid.*, p. 621.

86. *Ibid.*, p. 623. Coulomb refers to Horace-Bénédict de Saussure, *Essais sur l'hygrométrie* (Neufchatel, 1783), p. 173.

87. Coulomb, Third E & M Memoir, p. 627.

88. *Ibid.*, p. 628.

89. *Ibid.*, p. 629.

90. *Ibid.*, p. 632.

91. *Ibid.*, p. 633.

92. *Ibid.*, p. 636.

93. *Ibid.*, p. 612.

94. Coulomb, Fourth E & M Memoir, Preface, and arts. III, VII.

95. *Ibid.*, art. II.

96. *Ibid.*, art. V.

97. *Ibid.*, arts. V-VI.

98. *Ibid.*, art. VIII.

99. *Ibid.*, art. IX.

100. Coulomb, Sixth E & M Memoir, art. XLV.

101. Coulomb, Fourth E & M Memoir, art. X.

102. *Ibid.*, art. XI.

103. *Ibid.*

104. *Ibid.*, p. 76.

105. Bauer, *L'électromagnétisme* . . . , p. 231.

106. Siméon Denis Poisson, "Mémoire sur la distribution de l'électricité à la surface des corps conducteurs," and "Second Mémoire sur la distribution de l'électricité à la surface des corps conducteurs," *Mémoires de la classe des sciences mathématiques et physiques de l'Institut Impérial de France,* 1811, première partie (Paris, 1812), pp. 1-92; and 1811, seconde partie (Paris, 1814), pp. 163-274.

107. Coulomb, Fifth E & M Memoir, art. I.

108. *Ibid.*, arts. IV-IX.

109. Poisson, *Mémoires de la classe* . . . , première partie, p. 60.

110. Coulomb, Fifth E & M Memoir, art. xi.

111. *Ibid.*, arts. xii-xv.

112. *Ibid.*, art. xvii.

113. *Ibid.*, art. xvi.

114. Poisson, *Mémoires de la classe* . . . , première partie, p. 66.

115. Coulomb, Fifth E & M Memoir, art. xxvii.

116. *Ibid.*

117. Coulomb, Sixth E & M Memoir, art. vi.

118. *Ibid.*, arts. vii-viii.

119. *Ibid.*, art. xxvi.

120. *Ibid.*, art. xxvii.

121. *Ibid.*, arts. lvii-lix.

122. Newton, *Principia*, ed. Cajori, i, 193-195.

123. Cavendish, ed. Maxwell, *The Electrical Researches* . . . , pp. xxxix, xlvi-xlviii.

124. Coulomb, Sixth E & M Memoir, art. iv.

125. Cavendish, ed. Maxwell, *The Electrical Researches* . . . , p. xlix.

126. *Ibid.*, p. 111.

127. Bauer, *L'électromagnétisme* . . . , p. 226.

128. Henry Cavendish, "An Attempt to Explain Some of the Principle Phoenomena of Electricity, by Means of an Elastic Fluid," *Philosophical Transactions*, lxi (London, 1772), pp. 586-588. For Coulomb's proof, see his Second E & M Memoir, pp. 587-88.

129. Coulomb, Sixth E & M Memoir, art. xlv.

130. *Ibid.*, art. xl.

131. Cohen, *Franklin and Newton*, p. 548.

132. Coulomb, Sixth E & M Memoir, art. xl.

133. *Ibid.*

134. *Ibid.*

135. Anonymous, "Exposition succinte de quelques notions élémentaires sur l'électricité & le magnétisme, pour servir d'introduction à la théorie de Coulomb, relative à ces deux sciences," *Journal de physique, de chimie, d'histoire naturelle et des arts* . . . , ii (an 2: 1794) [listed as Vol. xlv], 448-453.

136. Three of these were published in the *Mémoires de l'Institut national des sciences et arts—Sciences mathématiques et physiques*. They are: "Détermination théorique et expérimentale des forces qui ramènent différentes aiguilles aimantées à saturation à leur méridien magnétique," first series, iii (Paris, an 9: 1801), 176-197. Reprinted *in part* in *Mémoires de Coulomb*. (Hereafter Coulomb, 1799 memoir on magnets.) Nouvelle méthode de déterminer l'inclinaison d'une aiguille aimantée," première série, iv (Paris, an 11: 1803), 565-584. "Résultat des différentes méthodes employées pour donner aux lames et aux barreaux d'acier le plus grand degré de magnétisme," première série, vi (Paris, 1806), 399-422. Reprinted *in part* in *Mémoires de Coulomb*. (Hereafter Coulomb, 1802 memoir on magnets.)

137. Coulomb, Seventh E & M Memoir, art. i.

138. *Ibid.*

139. *Ibid.*

140. Charles Augustin Coulomb, *Mémoires de l'Académie Royale des Sciences*, 1785 (Paris, 1788), pp. 560-568.

141. Coulomb, Seventh E & M Memoir, arts. VI-VII.

142. *Ibid.*, art. VII.

143. *Ibid.*, arts. XIII-XVIII.

144. *Ibid.*, art. XXIII.

145. *Ibid.*, pl. VIII.

146. *Ibid.*, art. XXIII.

147. *Ibid.*, art. XXIV.

148. *Ibid.*, pl. VIII.

149. *Ibid.*, art. XXIV.

150. *Ibid.*, art. XXV.

151. *Ibid.*

152. Aepinus, *Tentamen theoriae.* . . .

153. Coulomb, Seventh E & M Memoir, art. XXV.

154. *Ibid.*, and also Coulomb, Sixth E & M Memoir, art. XL.

155. Anonymous, *Journal de physique, de chimie, d'histoire naturelle et des arts* . . . , II [listed as Vol. XVL] (Paris, an 2: 1794), 453-456.

156. Coulomb, 1777 magnetism memoir, arts. 83-86.

157. Coulomb, 1799 memoir on magnets, art. 2.

158. Coulomb, 1777 magnetism memoir, art. 84.

159. *Ibid.*, art. 24.

160. *Ibid.*, art. 23.

161. Coulomb, Seventh E & M Memoir, art. XXX.

162. *Ibid.*, pl. IX.

163. *Ibid.*, art. XXX.

164. *Ibid.*

165. Siméon Denis Poisson, "Mémoire sur la théorie du magnétisme," pp. 247-338, and "Second mémoire sur la théorie du magnétisme," pp. 488-533, *Mémoires de l'Académie Royale des Sciences de l'Institut de France*, V (Paris, 1826). The quote is taken from p. 250.

166. Material relevant to Ampère's molecular current element is presented in *Mémoires sur l'électrodynamique*, première partie, "Collection de mémoires relatifs à la physique, publiés par la Société française de Physique" (Paris: Gauthier-Villars, 1885), II, 136-147.

167. René Just Haüy, *An Elementary Treatise on Natural Philosophy*, trans. Olinthus Gregory, 2 vols. (London, 1807), I, vi. Haüy composed this for use in the French lycées. Biot also wrote for the lycées, see his *Traité élémentaire d'astronomie physique* (Paris, 1805).

168. For a study of Haüy's work in crystallography see Seymour Harold Mauskopf, "Molecular Structure and Composition: The Interaction of Crystallography, Chemistry and Optics in the Early Nineteenth Century," Ph.D. dissertation (Princeton University, 1966).

169. For example, see the Laplace papers on capillarity which originally appeared in the *Journal de physique*, collected in Pierre Simon de Laplace, *Oeuvres complètes de Laplace*, 14 vols. (Paris: Gauthier-Villars, 1843–1912), XIV, 217-253, 259-264.

170. Coulomb, Second E & M Memoir, p. 611.

171. This had been published as "Influence de la température sur le mag-

nétisme de l'acier. Extrait d'après Biot, d'un Mémoire inédit," *Mémoires de Coulomb*, ed. A. Potier, "Collection de mémoires relatifs à la physique publiés par la Société française de Physique" (Paris: Gauthier-Villars, 1884), I, 373-375.

172. Anonymous, "Extrait des observations lues à l'Institut national par G. B. Sage," *Journal de physique, de chimie, d'histoire naturelle et des arts* . . . , LIV (Paris, an 10: 1802), 355.

173. J.B.J. Delambre, report on Coulomb's memoir, "Expériences qui prouvent que tous les corps, de quelque nature qu'ils soient, obéissent à l'action magnétique, et que l'on peut même mesurer l'influence de cette action sur la différentes espèces de corps," *Journal de physique, de chimie, d'histoire naturelle et des arts* . . . , LIV (Paris, an 10: 1802), 368.

174. Anonymous, report on Coulomb's memoir, "Recherches relatives à l'action que les barreaux aimantés exercent sur tous les corps," *Journal de physique, de chimie, d'histoire naturelle et des arts* . . . , LIV (Paris, an 10: 1802), 461.

175. Coulomb read his last scientific memoir 11 thermidor, an 12 (30 July 1804); it was a *résumé* of a "Mémoire sur le magnétisme." See Appendix A of this book.

176. The last memoir actually published by Coulomb himself was the 1802 memoir on magnets.

177. Jean Baptiste Biot, *Traité de physique expérimentale et mathématique*, 4 vols. (Paris, 1816).

178. *Ibid.*, I, viii-ix.

179. *B.I.F.*, MSS 1581-1582, "Manuscrits de Charles-Augustin de Coulomb."

180. Salomon Bochner, *The Role of Mathematics in the Rise of Science* (Princeton, 1966), p. 179.

EPILOGUE

1. For a general history of French education at this time see: Eugène Dubarle, *Histoire de l'Université depuis son origine jusqu'à nos jours*, 2 vols. (Paris, 1829); Victor Chauvin, *Histoire des lycées et collèges de Paris* (Paris, 1866); and Charles Dejob, *L'instruction publique en France et en Italie au dix-neuvième siècle* (Paris, 1894).

2. See A. Fourcy, *Histoire de l'Ecole polytechnique* (Paris, 1828).

3. Dubarle, *Histoire* . . . , II, 352-354.

A. Aulard, *Napoléon 1er et le monopole universitaire* (Paris, 1911), pp. 47-48.

4. Dubarle, *Histoire* . . . , II, 354.

5. Aulard, *Napoléon* . . . , pp. 48-49. Hereafter, textual reference to laws and decrees relating to education will be taken from *Recueil de lois et règlemens concernant l'instruction publique depuis l'édit de Henri IV, en 1598 jusqu'à ce jour*, première série; 8 vols. (Paris, 1814). Decrees from March 1800 to September 1803 are published in Volume II; decrees from October 1803 to March 1807 are in Volume III. The "Loi générale sur l'instruction publique" of 11 floréal, an 10 (1 May 1802) is presented in III, 43-54.

6. *A.N.*, AF^IV 64, pl. 367, "Minutes des Arrêtés," 22 prairial, an 10 (11 June 1802).

7. See *Almanach Royal* for 1803–1809 (Paris, 1803–1809).

8. Aulard, *Napoléon . . .* , pp. 94-95.

9. *Ibid.*, pp. 95-97.

10. *Recueil de lois . . .* , II, 289-304; "Instruction du conseiller d'état chargé de la direction et surveillance de l'instruction publique, aux inspecteurs-généraux des études, et aux commissaires de l'Institut, chargés de l'organisation des lycées," speech delivered 13 brumaire, an 11 (4 November 1804) by Antoine François Fourcroy. Reference here is to p. 292.

11. *Ibid.*, p. 304.

12. *Ibid.*, pp. 297-303.

13. A list of the 1,500 books recommended for use in the *lycées* is given in *Manuel de l'instruction publique pour l'an XIII ou, Recueil complet des lois, arrêtés, decisions et instructions . . . publié avec l'autorisation de M. le Conseiller* (an 13: 1805). Fourcroy was "Conseiller d'Etat, etc."

14. Aulard, *Napoléon . . .* , pp. 97-103.

15. *Recueil de lois . . .* , II, 302.

16. Aulard, *Napoléon. . . .*

17. *Ibid.*, p. 81.

18. J.B.J. Delambre, "Eloge historique de M. Coulomb," *Mémoires de l'Institut national des sciences et arts—Sciences mathématiques et physiques*, VII (Paris, 1806), "Histoire," 206-223.

Jean Baptiste Biot, "Coulomb," *Mélanges scientifiques et littéraires de Biot*, 3 vols. (Paris, 1858), III, 99-104.

19. Biot, *Mélanges . . .* , III, p. 103.

20. Bibliothèque Municipale (Reims), Item 2101, N. Fonds, "Papiers de M. Tronsson-Lecomte," Letters from Coulomb to Tronsson-Lecomte, 26 ventôse, an 12 (17 March 1804) and 22 germinal, an 12 (12 April 1804).

21. *Ibid.*

22. Aulard, *Napoléon . . .* , pp. 69, 84-85.

23. *Ibid.*, p. 69.

24. *Recueil de lois . . .* , II, 79.

25. Aulard, *Napoléon . . .* , p. 89.

26. *Ibid.*, pp. 103-116.

27. Unless otherwise noted, the material concerning Coulomb's apartment and personal effects is taken from *A.N.*, Minutier Central, Etude XLVIII, notaire Louis François Robin, laisse 475, 1 September 1806, "Inventaire après le décece de M. Charles Augustin Coulomb."

28. *A.G.*, Dossier Coulomb Letters from Coulomb's widow to Napoléon and to the Minister of War, 5 April 1807.

29. *A. Seine*, Décès V6E¹340, "Charles Augustin Coulomb," 23 August 1806.

30. *B.I.F.*, HR5* (T. 19, no. 15), "Notice des machines de physique du cabinet de sr. M. Coulomb, membre de l'Institut, etc., dont la vente se fera . . . le 11 Févr. 1807." This is a two-page printed auction list of Coulomb's instruments.

31. *A.G.*, Dossier Coulomb, Letter from Coulomb's widow to Napoléon, 5 April 1807.

32. *Ibid.*, "Extrait des Minutes de la Secretaire d'Etat," 5 September 1806.

33. [J. B. Biot and E.P.E. Rossel], B—t and R—l, "Jean Charles Borda," *Biographie universelle*, nouvelle édition (1843), v, 60.

APPENDIX A

1. *A.S., Procès-verbaux*, vols. 92-109.

2. Institut de France, Académie des Sciences, *Procès-verbaux des séances de l'Académie tenues depuis la fondation de l'Institut jusqu'au mois d'août 1835*, 10 vols. (Hendaye, 1910–1922), I-III.

APPENDIX B

1. *A.S., Procès-verbaux*, vols. 92-109.

2. *B.N., Fonds Libri*, N.A.F. 3528, fol. 129.

3. *A.N.*, K1024, no. 34.

4. Institut de France, Academie des Sciences, *Procès-verbaux.* . . .

Bibliography

The following Bibliography is arranged in five sections:
Coulomb's Published Memoirs
Archives
Published Works
Articles and Periodicals
Unpublished Articles and Dissertations

Coulomb's Published Memoirs

Coulomb published nearly all of his memoirs in the publications of the Académie des Sciences (Paris), either in the *Mémoires de l'Académie Royale des Sciences* and the continuation of these, the *Mémoires de l'Institut national des sciences et arts—Sciences mathématiques et physiques,* or in the supplementary series for memoirs of nonmembers, *Mémoires de mathématique et de physique présentés à l'Académie Royale des Sciences, par divers savans.* His later memoirs were often extracted by others in various physical journals. One paper, written in 1779 on the subject of underwater dredging, was published separately.

There exist collections of Coulomb's major memoirs. These are cited fully below. The collection of his mechanics memoirs, *Théorie des machines simples* . . . , is rather rare. *Mémoirs de Coulomb,* the collection of his memoirs in electricity and magnetism published by the Société française de Physique, is more easily located.

When a memoir is cited more than once in this book I give a short title for the memoir in addition to the full citation and utilize this short title for subsequent references. For example, citations subsequent to the first for Coulomb's memoir on mechanics of statics read at the Academy in 1773 and published in 1776 I entitle "Coulomb, 1773 statics memoir." Note that I cite the memoir by the date of recitation at the Academy rather than the year of publication. In the listings below, the full citation of any given memoir is preceded by its short title, if one has been used in this book.

MÉMOIRES DE L'ACADÉMIE ROYALE DES SCIENCES

"Observations théoriques et expérimentales sur l'effet des moulins à vent et sur la figure de leurs ailes," 1781 (Paris, 1785), pp. 65-81. (Reprinted in *Théorie des machines simples.* . . .)

1784 torsion memoir. "Recherches théoriques et expérimentales sur la force de torsion et sur l'élasticité des fils de métal," 1784 (Paris, 1787), pp. 229-269. (Reprinted in *Théorie des machines simples . . .* , and in *Mémoires de Coulomb*.)

"Description d'une boussole dont l'aiguille est suspendue par un fil de soie," 1785 (Paris, 1788), pp. 560-568.

First E & M Memoir. "Sur l'électricité et le magnétisme, premier mémoire, construction et usage d'une balance électrique, fondée sur la propriété qu'ont les fils de métal d'avoir une force de torsion proportionnelle à l'angle de torsion," 1785 (Paris, 1788), pp. 569-577. (Reprinted in *Mémoires de Coulomb*.)

Second E & M Memoir. "Sur l'électricité et le magnétisme, deuxième mémoire, où l'on détermine suivant quelles lois le fluide magnétique ainsi que le fluide électrique agissent soit par répulsion, soit par attraction," 1785 (Paris, 1788), pp. 578-611. (Reprinted in *Mémoires de Coulomb*.)

Third E & M Memoir. "Sur l'électricité et le magnétisme, troisième mémoire, de la quantité d'électricité qu'un corps isolé perd dans un temps donné, soit par le contact de l'air plus ou moins humide, soit le long des soutiens plus ou moins idioélectriques," 1785 (Paris, 1788), pp. 616-638. (Reprinted in *Mémoires de Coulomb*.)

Fourth E & M Memoir. "Sur l'électricité et le magnétisme, quatrième mémoire, où l'on démontre deux principales propriétés du fluide électrique . . . ," 1786 (Paris, 1788), pp. 67-77. (Reprinted in *Mémoires de Coulomb*.)

Fifth E & M Memoir. "Sur l'électricité et le magnétisme, cinquième mémoire, sur la manière dont le fluide électrique se partage entre deux corps conductors mis en contact, et de la distribution de ce fluide sur les différentes parties de la surface de ces corps," 1787 (Paris, 1789), pp. 421-467. (Reprinted in *Mémoires de Coulomb*.)

Sixth E & M Memoir. "Sur l'électricité et le magnétisme, sixième mémoire, suite des recherches sur la distribution du fluide électrique entre plusieurs corps conducteurs.—Détermination de la densité électrique dans les différents points de la surface de ce corps," 1788 (Paris, 1791), pp. 617-705. (Reprinted *in part* in *Mémoires de Coulomb*.)

Seventh E & M Memoir. "Sur l'électricité et le magnétisme, septième mémoire, du magnétisme," 1789 (Paris, 1793), pp. 455-505. (Reprinted in *Mémoirs de Coulomb*.)

"Mémoire sur les frottemens de la pointe des pivots," 1790 (Paris, 1797), pp. 448-471. (Reprinted in *Théorie des machines simples. . . .*)

MÉMOIRES DE L'INSTITUT NATIONAL DES SCIENCES ET ARTS—
SCIENCES MATHÉMATIQUES ET PHYSIQUES (first series)

"Expériences relatives à la circulation de la sève dans les arbres," II (Paris, 1799), 246-248.

Memoir on laboring men. "Résultats de plusieurs expériences destinées à déterminer la quantité d'action que les hommes peuvent fournir par leur travail journalier, suivant les differentes manières dont ils employent leurs forces," II (Paris, 1799), 380-428. (Reprinted in *Théorie des machines simples. . . .*)

1799 memoir on magnets. "Détermination théorique et expérimentale des forces qui ramènent différentes aiguelles aimantées à saturation à leur méridien magnétique," III (Paris, 1801), 176-197. (Reprinted *in part* in *Mémoires de Coulomb.*)

1800 fluids memoir. "Expériences destinées à déterminer la cohérence des fluides et les lois de leur résistance dans les mouvements très lents," III (Paris, 1801), 246-305. (Reprinted *in part* in *Mémoires de Coulomb.*)

"Nouvelle Méthode de déterminer l'inclinaison d'une aiguille aimantée," IV (Paris, 1803), pp. 565-584.

1802 memoir on magnets. "Résultat des différentes méthodes employées pour donner aux lames et aux barreaux d'acier le plus grand degré de magnétisme," VI (Paris, 1806), pp. 399-422. (Reprinted *in part* in *Mémoires de Coulomb.*)

MÉMOIRES DE MATHÉMATIQUE ET DE PHYSIQUE PRÉSENTÉS À L'ACADÉMIE ROYALE DES SCIENCES, PAR DIVERS SAVANS

1773 statics memoir. "Essai sur une application des règles de *maximis* et *minimis* à quelques problèmes de statique, relatifs à l'architecture," VII (Paris, 1776), 343-382. (Reprinted in *Théorie des machines simples. . . .*)

1777 magnetism memoir. "Recherches sur la meilleure manière de fabriquer les aiguilles aimantées," IX (Paris, 1780), pp. 166-264. (Reprinted *in part* in *Mémoires de Coulomb.*)

1781 friction memoir. "Théorie des machines simples en ayant égard au frottement de leurs parties et à la roideur des cordages . . . ," X (Paris, 1785), pp. 161-332. (Reprinted in *Théorie des machines simples. . . .*)

COULOMB'S MEMOIRS PUBLISHED SEPARATELY OR IN OTHER JOURNALS

Recherches sur les moyens d'exécuter sous l'eau toutes sortes de travaux hydrauliques sans employer aucun épuisement, published under slightly varying titles by C. A. Jombert: Paris, 1779; Du Pont: Paris, 1797; and Bachelier: Paris, 1819 and 1846.

"Moyen simple de condenser l'air dans un grand récipient avec toute espèce de pompe," *Observations sur la physique, sur l'histoire naturelle et sur les arts*, XVII (Paris, 1781), 301-303.

"Expériences qui prouvent que tous les corps de quelque nature qu'ils soient, obéissent à l'action magnétique, et que l'on peut même mesurer l'influence de cette action sur les différentes espèces de corps," *Journal de physique, de chimie, d'histoire naturelle et des arts* . . . , LIV (Paris, 1802), 367-369. (This note was actually contributed by J.B.J. Delambre, based on a memoir that Coulomb read at the Institute.)

"Recherches relatives à l'action que les barreaux aimantés exercent sur tous les corps," *Journal de physique, de chimie, d'histoire naturelle et des arts* . . . , LIV (Paris, 1802), 454-462. (This note was actually contributed anonymously by a reporter, based on a memoir that Coulomb read at the Institute.)

NOTE: Other short memoirs appearing in contemporary journals under the author "Coulomb" are usually *extracts* of his memoirs published by the Academy or the Institute.

COLLECTIONS OF COULOMB'S MEMOIRS

Théorie des machines simples, en ayant égard au frottement de leurs parties et à la roideur des cordages; . . . *à laquelle on à ajouté les Mémoires du même auteur, 1° sur le frottement de la pointe des pivots; 2° sur la force de torsion et sur l'élasticité des fils de métal; 3° sur la force des hommes, ou les quantités d'action qu'ils peuvent fournir; 4° sur l'effet des moulins à vent et la figure de leurs ailes; 5° sur les murs de revêtemens et l'équilibre des voûtes.* Paris: Bachelier, 1821.

Mémoires de Coulomb. Ed. A. Potier. (Collection des mémoires relatifs à la physique, publiés par la Société française de Physique. 5 vols. Paris: Gauthier-Villars, 1884–1891), I.

A German translation of Coulomb's first four memoirs on electricity and magnetism is *Vier Abhandlungen über die Elektricität und den Magnetismus* . . . *Uebersetzt und herausgegeben von Walter König.* Leipzig, 1890. (Ostwald's "Klassiker der exakten Wissenschaften," no. 13.)

Archives

Listed below are materials drawn from various archives in France. At least one piece concerning Coulomb was found in each of twenty-two public and private archives in France and in the United States. The lists below, however, are limited to those archive materials actually cited in this biography. Code letters have been used in the references for those sources quoted frequently. These codes, where used, precede the listing of each archival source.

A.D.H.—Archives Départementales de l'Hérault, 40, rue Proudhon, Montpellier (Hérault).

Série D 120*(5), fols. 117, 119, 123, 125-128.

    D 121*(6), fols. 71-88.

    D 124*(9), fols. 13-19.

    D 128*(13).

    D 204.

    D^3 200, fols. 39-42, 139-143.

A.G.—(Archives de la Guerre), Service historique de l'Armée, Chateau de Vincennes, Vincennes (Seine).

Dossier Coulomb.

Génie—X^{e}5, "Ecole de Mézières," 1760–1761.

    X^{e}6, 1763.

    X^{e}8, 1775, 1777.

    X^{e}9, 1781.

    X^{e}10, 1785–1786.

    X^{e}159, "Ecole de Mézières," 1760–1762.

A.I.G.—Archives de l'Inspection du Génie, 39, rue de Bellechasse, Paris 7e. (The archives are actually deposited at the Chateau de Vincennes.)

Art. 3, sec. 2, carton 1, pièce 30.

Art. 3, sec. 3, #1, carton 1, laisse 3, pièces 8, 42, 43, 45bis.

Art. 3, sec. 4, carton 2, nos. 35, 36, 39.

Art. 3, sec. 5, carton 1, pièce 25.

Art. 3, sec. 8, carton 1, pièce 4.

Art. 3, sec. 10, carton 2, pièce 5a.

Art. 8, sec. 1, "Brest," carton 2, pièce 33b.

Art. 8, sec. 1, "Cherbourg," carton 1, pièces 29, 29bis, 30, 30bis, 32bis.

Art. 8, sec. 1, "Ile d'Aix," carton 1, nos. 34^1, 59, 60, 62, 63$^{1-3}$, 64$^{1-2}$, 66, 67, 67bis; carton 2, nos. 10$^{1-2}$, 69.

Art. 18, sec. 1, #1, carton 1, pièces 8a, 13, 14; #2, carton 1.

A.N.—Archives Nationales, 60, rue des Francs-Bourgeois, Paris 3e.

AF^{IV} 64, pl. 367.

K 1024, no. 34.

M 258-607.

O^1 127, pièce 239.

O^1 1596, pièces 100, 104, 125, 140.

O^1 1599, pièces 250, 255, 282.

Marine B^3 742, pièce 106.

Marine D^2 22, pièces 275, 292, 292bis, 293, 319-320, 296-297bis.

Marine G 108, pièce 15, fol. 157.

Minutier Central, Etude XLVIII, notaire Louis François Robin, laisse 475.

Minutier Central, Etude CXVIII, notaire Jean Baptiste Pierre Bévière, laisse 698.

A.S.—Archives de l'Académie des Sciences de l'Institut de France, 23, quai Conti, Paris 6e.

Dossiers Prix, 1775, 1777, 1779, 1781.

Dossier Coulomb.

Procès-verbaux. (For a listing of *all Procès-verbaux* entries concerning Coulomb, see Appendices A and B of this book.)

A. Seine—Archives du Département de la Seine et de la Ville de Paris, 30, quai Henri-IV, Paris 4e.

Naissances, V4E¹ 560, "Charles Augustin Coulomb" (II), "Henry Louis Coulomb."

Mariages, V5E¹ 235, "Charles Augustin Coulomb—Louise Françoise Proust Desormeaux."

Décès, V6E¹ 340, "Charles Augustin Coulomb."

B.I.F.—Bibliothèque de l'Institut de France, 23, quai Conti, Paris 6e.

HR5* (T. 19, no. 15).

MS 1581–1582, "Manuscrits de Charles Augustin de Coulomb . . . , I. Recherches sur la théorie de l'aimant fondée sur l'expérience. II. Mémoires sur le magnétisme."

MS 2041, nos. 85-86, fols. 535-561. Papiers de J.B.J. Delambre. "Notice sur la vie et les ouvrages de M. Coulomb."

B.N.—Bibliothèque Nationale, rue de Richelieu, Paris 2e.

Salle des manuscrits:

Fr. 27363, vol. 879, nos. 19785-19786.

Fonds Libri, N.A.F. 3258, fol. 129.

Archives Municipales de Montpellier, Tour des Pins, Montpellier (Hérault).

Paroisse Sainte Anne, GG 158, 160, 162, 164.

O.M.—Service des Archives du Ministère de la France D'Outre-Mer, 27, rue Oudinot, Paris 7e.

Martinique, D.F.C.:

Carton 1, nos. 169, 195, 201, 218-219.

Carton 2, nos. 234-235, 237-238, 244-246, 249, 251-252, 272, 274-275, 280, 297, 300-301, 308, 316-317.

Carton 3, no. 330.

Portefeuille XVI, B331, Plan du Fort Bourbon (10 July 1773).

O.P.—Bibliothèque et Archives de l'Observatoire de Paris, 61, avenue de l'Observatoire, Paris 14e.

AD5-33, folders II-IV, IX-XII.

Archives du Musée des Plans-Reliefs, 6, bd. des Invalides, Paris 7e. (The relatively few archives here are uncatalogued.)

Reims—Bibliothèque Municipale (Bibliothèque Carnegie), 2, place Carnegie, Reims (Marne).

Item 2101, N. Fonds, Papiers de M. Tronsson-Lecomte.

Clermont-Ferrand—Bibliothèque Municipale et Universitaire de Clermont-Ferrand, 1, bd. LaFayette, Clermont-Ferrand (Puy-de-Dome). MS 337, fols. 185-186.

Published Works

Académie des Sciences (Paris). *Mémoires de l'Académie Royale des Sciences—Table alphabétique des matières.* 10 vols. Paris, 1729–1809.

———. *Recueil des pièces qui ont remporté les prix de l'Académie Royale des Sciences.* 9 vols. Paris, 1721–1777.

Æpinus, Franz Ulrich Theodor. *Tentamen theoriae electricitatis et magnetismi.* St. Petersburg, 1759(?), and Rostock, 1759.

d'Alembert, Jean Le Rond, et al. *Nouvelles expériences sur la résistance des fluides, par MM. d'Alembert, le marquis de Condorcet et l'abbé Bossut, membres de l'Académie royale des sciences, etc. M. l'abbé Bossut, rapporteur.* Paris, 1777.

Almanach royal (Paris). Volumes for 1782–1809. Paris, 1782–1809.

d'Angiviller, Charles Claude de Flahault de la Billarderie, comte. *Batiments du Roi, Notice sur l'arrière de ce départment, son origine et ses causes. Paris,* c. 1789.

———. *Mémoires de Charles Claude Flahault, comte de la Billarderie d'Angiviller.* Ed. Louis Bobé. Copenhagen and Paris, 1933.

———. *Rapport au Roi fait par M. d'Angiviller en février 1790.* . . . Paris, 1791.

Archives Communales. Archives Montpellier VI (1934). Montpellier, 1934.

Augoyat, Antoine Marie. *Aperçu historique sur les fortifications, les ingénieurs et sur le corps du génie en France.* 3 vols. Paris, 1860–1864.

Aulard, A. *Napoléon 1er et le monopole universitaire.* Paris, 1911.

Banford, Paul Walden. *Forests and French Sea Power, 1660–1789.* Toronto, 1956.

[Banks, Sir Joseph.] *The Banks Letters, A Calendar of the Manuscript Correspondence of Sir Joseph Banks Preserved in the British Museum, British Museum (Natural History) and Other Collections in Great Britain.* Ed. Warren R. Dawson. London, 1958.

Bauer, Edmond. *L'électromagnétisme—hier et aujourd'hui.* Paris, 1949.

Bélidor, Bernard Forest de. *L'architecture hydraulique.* 2 vols. Paris, 1737–1739.

———. *La science des ingénieurs.* 1st ed. Paris, 1729.

———. *La science des ingénieurs, Nouvelle édition, avec des notes, par M. Navier.* Ed. C.L.M.H. Navier. Paris, 1813.

Beltrand, Eugène. *Les travaux souterrains de Paris.* 3 vols. Paris, 1872–1877.

Bernoulli, Jacques. *Opera.* 2 vols. Genève, 1744.

Bigourdan, G. *Le système métrique des poids et mesures.* Paris, 1901.

Biot, Jean Baptiste. *Mélanges scientifiques et littéraires.* 3 vols. Paris, 1858.

———. *Traité élémentaire d'astronomie physique.* Paris, 1805.

———. *Traité de physique expérimentale et mathématique.* 4 vols. Paris, 1816.

Bochner, Salomon. *The Role of Mathematics in the Rise of Science.* Princeton, 1966.

Bossut, Charles. *A General History of Mathematics.* Trans. J. Bonnycastle. London, 1803.

———. *Traité élémentaire d'hydrodynamique.* 2 vols. Paris, 1771.

———. *Traité élémentaire de méchanique et de dinamique appliqué principalement aux mouvemens des machines.* Charleville, 1763.

———. See Jean Le Rond d'Alembert et al., *Nouvelles expériences sur la résistance des fluides.* . . .

———. See marquis de Condorcet et al., *Rapport.* . . .

———, and Guillaume Viallet. *Recherches sur la construction la plus avantageuse des digues.* Paris, 1764.

Bouchary, Jean. *L'eau à Paris à la fin du XVIIIᵉ siècle, la Compagnie des eaux à Paris et l'enterprise de l'Yvette.* Paris, 1946.

Bowden, F. P., and D. Tabor. *The Friction and Lubrication of Solids.* 2 parts. London, 1950–1964.

Bretagne. *Précis des opérations relatives à la navigation intérieure de Bretagne.* . . . Rennes, 1785. Each memoir within this collection is paged separately. The General Catalogue of the Bibliothèque Nationale lists *Bretagne* as the main entry for this volume, but I could find it only under the entry for Charles Augustin Coulomb.

Brunet, Pierre. *Les physiciens hollandais et la méthode expérimentale en France au XVIIIᵉ siècle.* Paris, 1926.

Bugge, Thomas. *Science in France in the Revolutionary Era, Described by Thomas Bugge, Danish Astronomer Royal and Member of the International Commission on the Metric System (1798–1799),* ed. with Introduction and Commentary, Maurice P. Crosland. Cambridge, Mass., 1969.

Bullet, Pierre. *L'architecture pratique.* Paris, 1691.

Camus, Charles Etienne Louis. *Cours de mathématique.* 4 vols. Paris, 1749–1752.

Camus, François Joseph de. *Traité des forces mouvantes pour la pratique des arts & métiers.* Paris, 1722.

Cassini, Jean Dominique. *Mémoires pour servir à l'histoire des sciences et à celles de l'Observatoire Royale de Paris.* Paris, 1810.

Castelnau, Junius. See Eugène Thomas, *Mémoire historique.* . . .

Cavendish, Henry. *The Electrical Researches of the Honourable Henry Cavendish, F.R.S.* Ed. J. Clerk Maxwell. Cambridge, 1879.

Chauvin, Victor. *Histoire des lycées et collèges de Paris.* Paris, 1866.

Cohen, I. Bernard, *Franklin and Newton.* Philadelphia, 1956.

Condon, E. U., and Hugh Odishaw (eds.). *Handbook of Physics.* New York, 1958.

Condorcet, M.J.A.N. Capitat, marquis de. See Jean Le Rond d'Alembert et al., *Nouvelles expériences sur la résistance des fluides.* . . .

Condorcet, M.J.A.N. Capitat, marquis de., et al. *Rapport de m. l'abbé Bossut, de M. l'abbé Rochon, de M. de Fourcroy de Ramecourt, & de M. le marquis de Condorcet, membres de l'Académie royale des sciences, sur la navigation intérieure de la Bretagne.* Paris, 1786.

Cosseron de Villenoisy, Louis Pierre Jean Mammès. *Essai historique sur la fortification.* Paris, 1869.

Culver, Henry B. *The Book of Old Ships.* New York, 1935.

Daujat, Jean. *Origines et formation de la théorie des phénomènes électriques et magnétiques.* Paris, 1945.

Dejob, Charles. *L'instruction publique en France et en Italie au dix-neuvième siècle.* Paris, 1894.

Delambre, J.B.J. *Base du système métrique décimal, ou Mesure de l'arc du méridien, par MM. P.-F.-A. Méchain et Delambre. Rédigée par M. Delambre.* 3 vols. Paris, 1806–1810.

Desaguliers, J. T. *A Course of Experimental Philosophy.* 2 vols. 2nd ed. London, 1744–1745.

————. *Lectures of Experimental Philosophy.* London, 1719.

Donat, Dominique. *Almanach historique et chronologique de la ville de Montpellier.* Montpellier, 1759.

Dubarle, Eugène. *Histoire de l'Université depuis son origine jusqu'à nos jours.* 2 vols. Paris, 1829.

Dubuat, Pierre Louis Georges. *Principes d'hydraulique.* . . . 2 vols. 2nd ed. Paris, 1786.

Dugas, René. *A History of Mechanics.* Trans. J. R. Maddox. Neuchatel, 1955.

Edholm, O. G., *The Biology of Work.* New York, 1967.

Faucillon, J.M.F. *La chaire de mathématique et d'hydrographie de Montpellier (1682–1792).* Montpellier, 1855.

————. *Le Collège de Jésuites de Montpellier (1629–1762).* Montpellier, 1857.

Figurovskii, N. A. (ed.). *Istoria Estestvoznania v Rossii (History of Naural Science in Russia.)* 2 vols. in 3. Moscow, 1957–1960.

Fond, Sigaud de la. *Précis historique et expérimental des phénomènes électriques.* . . . 2nd ed. Paris, 1785.

Fourcroy, Charles René de (alias Fourcroy de Ramecourt). See marquis de Condorcet et al., *Rapport.* . . .

Fourcy, A. *Histoire de l'Ecole polytechnique.* Paris, 1828.

Franklin, Alfred. *Recherches historiques sur le Collège des quatre-nations*. Paris, 1862.

Frézier, Amédée François. *La théorie et la pratique de la coupe des pierres et des bois . . . ou, Traité de stéréotomie*. 3 vols. Strasbourg, 1737–1739.

Galilei, Galileo. *Discorsi e dimostrazioni matematiche, intorno à due nouve scienze*. . . . Leida, 1638. Trans. Henry Crew and Alfonso de Salvio as *Dialogues Concerning Two New Sciences*. New York, 1914.

Geikie, Archibald. *Memoir of John Michell*. Cambridge, 1918.

Gillispie, Charles Coulston. *Lazare Carnot Savant*. Princeton, 1971.

Girard, Pierre Simon. *Mémoires sur le canal de l'Ourcq*. . . . 3 vols. Paris, 1812–1831–1843.

————. *Traité analytique de la résistance des solides et des solides d'égale résistance*. Paris, 1798.

'sGravesande, Willem Jacob. *Elémens de physique, ou Introduction à la philosophie de Newton*. Trans. C. F. Roland de Virloys. 2 vols. Paris, 1747.

Grimaux, Edouard. *Lavoisier, 1743–1794, d'après sa correspondance, ses manuscrits, ses papiers de famille et d'autres documents inédits*. Paris, 1888.

Hanotaux, G. and A. Martineau (eds.). *Histoire des colonies française*. 6 vols. Paris, 1929–1933.

Haüy, René Just. *An Elementary Treatise on Natural Philosophy*. Trans. Olinthus Gregory. 2 vols. London, 1807.

————. *Exposition raisonnée de la théorie de l'électricité et du magnétisme d'après les principes de M. Æpinus*. . . . Paris, 1787.

Hodgman, Charles D. (ed.). *Handbook of Chemistry and Physics*. 39th ed. Cleveland, 1957.

Hooke, Robert. *De potentiva restitutiva*. London, 1678.

Hoppe, Edmund. *Geschichte der Physik*. Braunschweig, 1926.

Institut de France. *Index biographique des membres et correspondants de l'Académie des Sciences du 22 décembre 1666 au 15 novembre 1954*. Paris, 1954.

————. Académie des Sciences. *Procès-verbaux des séances de l'Académie tenues depuis la fondation de l'Institut jusqu'au mois d'août, 1835*. 10 vols. Hendaye, 1910–1922.

Jammer, Max. *Concepts of Force*. Cambridge, Mass., 1957.

Kragelsky, I. V., and V. S. Schedrov. *Razvitia Nauki o Trenii—Sookoi Trenia (Development of the Science of Friction—Dry Friction)*. Moscow, 1956.

Kuhn, Thomas S. *The Structure of Scientific Revolutions*. Chicago, 1962.

Lagrange, Joseph-Louis de. *Oeuvres de Lagrange*. Ed. J. A. Serret. 14 vols. Paris, 1867–1892.

La Hire, Philippe de. *Traité de mécanique*. Paris, 1695. Later published as "Oeuvres diverses de M. de La Hire: Traité de mécanique," *Mémoires de l'Académie Royale des Sciences depuis 1666 jusqu'a 1699* (Paris, 1730), pp. 1-340.

Lamare, Nicolas de. *Traité de la police, où l'on trouvera l'histoire de son établissement.* . . . 4 vols. 2nd ed. Paris, 1772–1738.

Laplace, Pierre Simon de. *Oeuvres complètes de Laplace*. 14 vols. Paris, 1843–1912.

Lemonnier, Henry. *Le Collège Mazarin et le Palais de l'Institut: XVIIIᵉ-XIXᵉ siècle*. Paris, 1921.

Le Monnier, Pierre Charles. *Loix du magnétisme*. 2 parts. Paris, 1776–1778.

Le Puillon de Boblaye, Théodore de. *Notice sur les écoles du génie de Mézières et de Metz*. Metz, 1862.

Lesage, Pierre Charles. *Recueil de divers mémoires extraits de la Bibliothèque Impérial des Ponts et Chaussées*. 2 vols. Paris, 1810.

Leslie, John. *An Experimental Inquiry into the Nature and Propagation of Heat*. Edinburgh, 1804.

Leupold, Jacob. *Theatrum Machinarum Generale*. . . . Leipzig, 1724.

Maindron, Ernest. *Les fondations de prix à l'Académie des Sciences—Les lauréats de l'Académie, 1714–1880*. Paris, 1881.

Manuel de l'Instruction publique pour l'an XIII ou, Recueil complet des lois, arrêtés, decisions et instructions . . . publie avec l'autorisation de M. le Conseiller d'Etat, Directeur Général de l'Instruction publique. Paris, an 13 (1805).

Mariotte, Edme. *Traité du mouvement des eaux*. Paris, 1686.

Mascart, Jean. *La vie et les travaux du chevalier Jean-Charles de Borda* (Annales de l'Université de Lyon: nouvelle série), II, Lyon, 1919, Fascicule 33.

Maury, A. *L'ancienne Académie des Sciences*. Paris, 1864.

Maxwell, J. Clerk. See Henry Cavendish, *The Electrical Researches*. . . .

Mayniel, K. *Traité expérimental, analytique et pratique de la poussée des terres et des murs de revêtement*. Paris, 1808.

Michell, John. *Treatise of Artificial Magnets, in Which is Shewn . . . Method of Making Them . . . & Also a Way of Improving the Natural Ones, etc*. 1st ed. Cambridge, 1750. 2nd "improved" ed. Cambridge, 1751.

———. Trans. of his *Treatise of Artificial Magnets* in Antoine Rivoire, *Traités sur les aimans artificiels; . . . traduits de deux ouvrages Anglois de J. Michell et J. Canton, par le P. Rivoire . . . avec une préface historique du traducteur où l'on expose les méthodes . . . de MM. Duhamel et Antheaume . . . pour perfectionner ces aimans*. Paris, 1752.

Musschenbroek, Peter van. *Essai de physique*. 2 vols. Leyden, 1739.

Musschenbroek, Peter van. *The Elements of Natural Philosophy.* Trans. John Colson. 2 vols. London, 1744.

Navier, C.L.M.H. (ed.). Bernard Forest de Bélidor, *La science des ingénieurs, nouvelle édition, avec des notes, par M. Navier.* Paris, 1813.

————. *Résumé des leçons données à l'Ecole des ponts et chaussées sur l'application de la mécanique . . . par Navier, Troisième édition avec des notes et des appendices par M. Barré de Saint-Venant.* Paris, 1864.

Newton, Isaac. *Opticks* (based on the 4th ed., London, 1730). New York, 1952.

————. *Philosophiae Naturalis Principia Mathematica.* London, 1686. Trans. Andrew Motte as *Sir Isaac Newton's Mathematical Principles of Natural Philosophy and his System of the World.* Ed. Florian Cajori. 2 vols. Berkeley, 1934.

Nollet, Jean Antoine. *Leçons de physique expérimentale.* 6 vols. Paris, 1743–1748.

Parent, Antoine. *Essais et recherches de mathématique et de physique.* 3 vols. Paris, 1713.

Poncelet, Jean Victor. *Cours de mécanique appliquée aux machines.* Paris, 1874.

————. *Traité de mécanique appliquée aux machines.* Liège, 1845.

————. *Traité de mécanique industrielle, physique ou expérimentale.* 1st ed. Bruges, 1829.

Potier, Alfred (ed.). *Mémoires de Coulomb.* Collection des mémoires relatifs à la physique, publiés par la Société française de Physique. 5 vols. Paris: Gauthier-Villars, 1884–1891, I.

Prévost de Vernoi. *La fortification depuis Vauban.* 2 vols. Paris, 1861.

Prony, G.C.F.M. Riche, comte de. *Instruction pratique sur une méthode pour déterminer les dimensions des murs de revêtement, en se servant de la formule graphique de R. Prony.* Paris, an 10 (1802).

————. *Nouvelle architecture hydraulique.* . . . 2 vols. Paris, 1790.

————. *Recherches sur la poussée des terres, et sur la forme et les dimensions à donner aux murs de revêtement.* . . . Paris, an 10 (1802).

Rebelliau, Alfred. *Vauban.* Paris, 1962.

Recueil de lois et règlemens concernant l'instruction publique depuis l'édit de Henri IV, en 1598 jusqu'à ce jour. 8 vols., première série. Paris, 1814.

Reinhard, Marcel. *Le grand Carnot.* 2 vols. Paris, 1950–1952.

Rivoire, Antoine. See John Michell, *Traité sur les aimans.* . . .

Rochon, Alexis Marie de. See marquis de Condorcet et al., *Rapport.* . . .

Rogue, Louis de la. *Armorial de la noblesse de Languedoc.* 2 vols. Paris, 1860.

————, and Edouard de Barthélemy. *Catalogue des preuves de noblesse reçues par d'Hozier pour les Ecoles Militaires, 1753–1789.* Paris, 1867.

Royal Society of London. *Catalogue of Scientific Papers (1800–1863).* 6 vols. London, 1868.

Saint-Venant, Adhémar Jean Claude Barré de (ed.). C.L.M.H. Navier, *Résumé des leçons données à l'Ecole des ponts et chaussées sur l'application de la mécanique . . . par Navier, Troisième édition avec des notes et des appendices par M. Barré de Saint-Venant.* Paris, 1864.

Saussure, Horace Bénédict de. *Essais sur l'hygrométrie.* Neufchatel, 1783.

Service géographique de l'Armée. *Catalogue-guide du Musée des Plans-Reliefs.* Paris, 1928.

Silvestre de Sacy, Jacques. *Le comte d'Angiviller, dernier Général des Bâtiments du Roi.* Paris, 1953.

Straub, Hans. *A History of Civil Engineering.* Trans. Erwin Rockwell. Cambridge, Mass., 1964.

Taton, René (ed.). *Enseignement et diffusion des sciences en France au XVIIIe siècle.* Paris, 1964.

Terzaghi, Karl. *Theoretical Soil Mechanics.* New York, 1943.

Thomas, Eugène. *Mémoire historique et biographique sur l'ancienne Société Royale des Sciences de Montpellier par Junius Castelnau, précédé de la vie de l'auteur et suivi d'une Notice historique sur la Société des Sciences et Belles-Lettres de la même ville.* Montpellier, 1858.

Timoshenko, Stephen P. *History of Strength of Materials.* New York, 1953.

————, and J. N. Goodier. *Theory of Elasticity.* 2nd ed. New York, 1951.

Todhunter, Isaac, and Karl Pearson. *A History of the Theory of Elasticity and of the Strength of Materials.* 2 vols. in 3. 1st ed. Cambridge. 1886–1893. 2nd ed. New York, 1960.

Truesdell, Clifford A. *The Rational Mechanics of Flexible or Elastic Bodies: 1638–1788.* ("Leonhardi Euleri Opera Omnia"), series secunda, Vol. XI, sectio secunda. Turici, 1960.

————. *Essays in the History of Mechanics.* New York, 1968.

Varignon, Pierre. *Traité du mouvement et de la mesure des eaux. . . .* Ed. abbé Pujol. Paris, 1725.

Vialles, Pierre. *Etudes historiques sur la Cour des comptes, aides et finances de Montpellier d'après ses archives privées.* Montpellier, 1921.

Whittaker, Edmund. *A History of the Theories of Aether and Electricity.* 2 vols. 2nd ed. London, 1951.

Wolf, A. *A History of Science, Technology and Philosophy in the 18th Century.* 2 vols. paperback ed. New York, 1961.

Woltmann, Reinhold. *Beiträge zur hydraulischen Architecture.* 3 vols. Gottingen, 1791–1794.

Young, Thomas. *A Course of Lectures on Natural Philosophy.* 2 vols. London, 1807.

————. *Miscellaneous Works of the Late Thomas Young.* Vols. 1-2, ed. George Peacock; Vol. 3, ed. John Leitch. 3 vols. London, 1855.

Articles and Periodicals

Amontons, Guillaume. "De la résistance causée dans les machines," *Mémoires de l'Académie Royale des Sciences,* 1699 (Paris, 1718), pp. 206-227.

Ampère, André Marie. Material relevant to Ampère's molecular current element is presented in *Mémoires sur l'electrodynamique.* Collection des mémoires relatifs à la physique, publiés par la Société française de Physique. 5 vols. Paris: Gauthier-Villars, 1884–1891, II, première partie (Paris, 1885), 136-147.

Anonymous, "Exposition succinte de quelques notions élémentaires sur l'électricité & le magnétisme, pour servir d'introduction à la théorie de Coulomb, relative à ces deux sciences," *Journal de physique, de chimie, d'histoire naturelle et des arts* . . . , II (listed as Vol. XLV) (Paris, an 2: 1794), 448-456.

Anonymous, report on Coulomb's memoir, "Recherches relatives à l'action que les barreaux aimantés exercent sur tous les corps," *Journal de physique, de chimie, d'histoire naturelle et des arts* . . . , LIV (Paris, an 10: 1802), 454-462.

Audoy. "Mémoire sur la poussée des voûtes en berceau," *Mémorial de l'officier du Génie,* IV (Paris, 1820), 1-96.

Augoyat, Antoine Marie. "Notice sur les Chastillon, ingénieurs des Armées," *Spectateur militaire,* 15 August 1856 (Paris, 1856), pp. 11-14.

Bernoulli, Daniel. "Dissertatio de actione fluidorum in corpora solida et motu solidorum in fluidis," *Commentarii Academiae Scientiarum Imperialis Petropolitanae,* II (Petropoli, 1729), 304-342; and III (Petropoli, 1732), 214-229.

————. "Theorema de motu curvilineo corporum, quae resistentiam patiuntur velocitatis suae quadrato proportionalem una cum solutione problematis in Act: Lips: M: Nov: 1728 propositi," *Commentarii Academiae Scientiarum Imperialis Petropolitanae,* IV (Petropoli, 1735), 136-143.

————. "Experimenta coram societate instituta in confirmationem theoriae pressionum quas latera canalis ab aqua transfluente sustinent,"

Commentarii Academiae Scientiarum Imperialis Petropolitanae, IV (Petropoli, 1735), 194-201.

————. "Dissertatio brevis de notibus corporum reciprocis seu oscillatoriis, quae ubique resistentiam patiuntur quadrato velocitatis suae proportionalem," and "Additamentum ad theoremata," *Commentarii Academiae Scientiarum Imperialis Petropolitanae*, V (Petropoli, 1738), 106-125, 126-142.

————, and Jean (II) Bernoulli. "Nouveaux principes de méchanique & de physique, tendans à expliquer la nature & les propriétés de l'aiman," *Recueil des pièces qui ont remporté les prix de l'Académie Royale des Sciences, depuis leur foundation jusqu'à présent* . . . , *Tome V, contenant les pièces depuis jusqu'en 1744.* (Paris, 1752).

[Biot, Jean Baptiste and E.P.E. Rossel] B—t and R—l, "Jean Charles Borda," *Biographie universelle*, nouvelle édition, V (Paris, 1843), 58-60.

Borda, Jean Charles de. "Expériences sur la résistance des fluides," *Mémoires de l'Académie Royale des Sciences*, 1763 (Paris, 1766), pp. 358-376; and 1767 (Paris, 1770), pp. 495-503.

Bulfinger, Georg Bernhard. "De frictionibus corporum solidorum," *Commentarii Academiae Scientiarum Imperialis Petropolitanae*, II (Petropoli, 1729), 403-414.

Cavendish, Henry. "An Attempt to Explain Some of the Principle Phenomena of Electricity, by Means of an Elastic Fluid," *Philosophical Transactions*, LXI (London, 1772), 584-677.

————. "Experiments to Determine the Density of the Earth," *Philosophical Transactions*, LXXXVIII (London, 1798), 469-526.

Cotte, Louis. "Observations faites à Laon d'heure en heure sur la boussole de variation de M. Coulomb . . . ," *Observations sur la physique, sur l'histoire naturelle et sur les arts*, XXIX (Paris, 1786), 189-193.

Couplet (de Tartreaux), Pierre. "De la poussée des terres contre leurs revestemens, & la force des revestemens qu'on leur doit opposer," *Mémoires de l'Académie Royale des Sciences*, 1726 (Paris, 1728), pp. 106-164; 1727 (Paris, 1729), pp. 139-178; 1728 (Paris, 1730), pp. 113-138.

————. "Mémoire sur les poussée des voûtes," *Mémoires de l'Académie Royale des Sciences*, 1729 (Paris, 1731), pp. 79-117; and 1730 (Paris, 1732), pp. 117-141.

Courtel, R., and L. M. Tichvinsky. "A Brief History of Friction," *Mechanical Engineering* (September 1963), pp. 55-59.

Crosland, Maurice. "The Congress on Definitive Metric Standards, 1798–1799: The First International Scientific Conference?" *Isis*, LX (1969), 226-231.

Davison, C. St. C. "Wear Prevention in Early History," *Wear*, I (1957), 155-159.

Delambre, J.B.J. report on Coulomb's memoir, "Expériences qui prouvent que tous les corps, de quelque nature qu'ils soient, obéissent à l'action magnétique, et que l'on peut même mesurer l'influence de cette action sur la différentes espèces de corps," *Journal de physique, de chimie, d'histoire naturelle et des arts* . . . , LIV (Paris, an 10: 1802), 367-369.

————. "Eloge historique de M. Coulomb," *Mémoires de l'Institut national des sciences et arts—Sciences mathématiques et physiques,* VII (Paris, 1806), "Histoire," 206-223.

Desaguliers, J. T. "Some Experiments Concerning the Cohesion of Lead," *Philosophical Transactions,* XXXIII (London, 1725), 345-347.

————. "An Account of Several Experiments Concerning the Running of Water in Pipes, as it is Retarded by Friction . . . ," *Philosophical Transactions,* XXXIV (London, 1726), 77-82.

————. "An Examination of Monsieur Perault's New-Invented *Axis in Peritrochio* Said to Be Entirely Void of Friction . . . ," *Philosophical Transactions,* XXXVI (London, 1730), 222-227.

————. "An Experiment to Shew That the Friction . . . ," *Philosophical Transactions,* XXXVII (London, 1732), 292-293.

Dupuit, A. J. "Résumé du Mémoire sur le tirage des voitures et sur le frottement de seconde espèce," *Comptes rendus hebdomadaires des séances de l'Académie des Sciences,* IX (Paris, 1839), 698-700, 775.

Euler, Leonhard. "Solutio problematis de invenienda curva, quam format lamina utcunque elastica in singulis punctis a potentis quibuscunque sollicitatia," *Commentarii Academiae Scientiarum Imperialis Petropolitanae,* III (Petropoli, 1732), 70-84.

————. "De curvis elasticis" (1744), trans. with notes by W. Oldfather as "L. Euler's Elastic Curves," *Isis,* XX (1933), 72-160.

————. "Dissertatio de magnete," *Recueil des pièces qui ont remporté les prix de l'Académie Royale des Sciences, depuis leur fondation jusqu'à présent . . . , Tome V, contenant les pièces depuis 1741 jusqu'en 1744.* Paris, 1752.

————. "Sur le frottement des corps solides," and "Sur la diminution de la résistance du frottement," *Mémoires de l'Académie Royale des Sciences et Belles-Lettres,* 1748 (Berlin, 1750), pp. 122-132, 133-148.

————. "Sur la force des colonnes," *Mémoires de l'Académie Royale des Sciences et Belles-Lettres,* 1757 (Berlin, 1759), pp. 252-82.

Fitzgerald, Keane. "A Method of Lessening the Quantity of Friction in Engines," *Philosophical Transactions,* LIII (London, 1763), pp. 139-158.

Gillispie, Charles C. "Bernard Forest de Bélidor," *Dictionary of*

Scientific Biography, ed. Charles Coulston Gillispie, I (New York, 1970–   ), 581-582.

Gillmor, C. Stewart. "Jean-Charles Borda," *Dictionary of Scientific Biography*, ed. Charles Coulston Gillispie, II (New York, 1970–   ), 299-300.

————. "Charles Bossut," *Dictionary of Scientific Biography*, ed. Charles Coulston Gillispie, II (New York, 1970–   ), 334-335.

Golder, Hugh Q. "The History of Earth Pressure Theory," *Archives internationales d'histoire des sciences*, XXXII (Paris, 1953), 209-219.

Hamilton, S. B. "Charles Auguste de Coulomb," *Transactions of the Newcomen Society*, XVII (London, 1938), 27-49.

Histoire de la Société Royale des Sciences établies à Montpellier avec les Mémoires de mathématiques et de physique . . . , I (Lyon, 1766), "Histoire," 1-21.

Journal de l'Empire (Paris), 20 September, 1806, pp. 3-4.

Jurin, James. "The Action of Springs," *Philosophical Transactions, Abridged*, X (1744–1750, [London, 1756]), 160-174.

La Hire, Philippe de. "Oeuvres diverses de M. de La Hire: Traité de mécanique," *Mémoires de l'Académie Royale des Sciences depuis 1666 jusqu'à 1699*, IX (Paris, 1730), 1-340. (Published separately as *Traité de mécanique*. Paris, 1695.)

————. "Sur la construction des voûtes dans les edifices," *Mémoires de l'Académie Royale des Sciences*, 1712 (Paris, 1714), pp. 70-78.

Lambert, J. H. "Sur le frottement entant qu'il rallentit le mouvement," *Nouveaux mémoires de l'Académie Royale des Sciences et Belles-Lettres*, XXVIII, 1772 (Berlin, 1774), 9-32.

Lana, Francisco. "Nova methodus construenda pyxidis magneticae, & observandi cum exacta praecisione gradus & minuta declinationum," *Acta Eruditorum*, November 1686 (Lipsiae, 1686), pp. 560-562.

Leibniz, Gottfried Wilhelm. "Demonstrationes novae de resistentia solidorum," *Acta Eruditorum*, July 1684 (Lipsiae, 1684), pp. 319-325.

Mémoires de l'Académie Royale des Sciences, 1699 (Paris, 1718), "Histoire," p. 105.

Mémoires de mathématique et de physique présentés à l'Académie Royale des Sciences, par divers savans, VIII (Paris, 1780), v-xi.

Mémorial de l'officier du Génie, nos. 1-15 (Paris, 1803–1848).

Metz, Lieutenant-colonel, and Capitaine Fadeuilhe. "Charles-Augustin de Coulomb," *Revue du génie militaire*, LXXVII (January-February 1938), 58-72.

Morin, A. J. "Nouvelles expériences sur le frottement . . . faites à Metz en 1833," *Mémoires présentés par divers savans à l'Académie Royale des Sciences de l'Institut de France*, VI (Paris, 1835), 641-783.

Oldfather, W. "L. Euler's Elastic Curves," *Isis*, XX (1933), 72-160.

Parent, Antoine. "Nouvelle statique avec frotemens et sans frotemens ou règles pour calculer les frotemens des machines dans l'état de l'équilibre," *Mémoires de l'Académie Royale des Sciences*, 1704 (Paris, 1706), pp. 173-197.

Poisson, Siméon Denis. "Mémoire sur la distribution de l'électricité à la surface des corps conducteurs," and "Second Mémoire sur la distribution de l'électricité à la surface des corps conducteurs," *Mémoires de la classe des sciences mathématiques et physiques de l'Institut Impérial de France*, année 1811, première partie (Paris, 1812), pp. 1-92; and année 1811, seconde partie (Paris, 1814), pp. 163-274.

———. "Mémoire sur la théorie du magnétisme," *Mémoires de l'Académie Royale des Sciences de l'Institut de France*, v (Paris, 1826), 247-338, 488-533.

———. "Mémoire sur l'équilibre et le mouvement des corps élastiques," *Annales de chimie*, xxxvii (Paris, 1828), 337-355.

Poncelet, Jean Victor, "Examen critique et historique des principales théories ou solutions concernant l'équilibre des voûtes," *Comptes rendus hebdomadaires des séances de l'Académie des Sciences*, xxxv (Paris, 1832), 494-502.

———. "Mémoire sur la stabilité des revêtements et de leurs fondations," *Mémorial de l'officier du Génie*, xiii (Paris, 1840), 7-270.

"Prix," *Mémoires de l'Académie Royale des Sciences*, 1775 (Paris, 1778), "Histoire," p. 40; and 1777 (Paris, 1780), "Histoire," p. 58.

Prony, G.C.F.M. Riche, comte de. "Mécanique philosophique," *Journal de l'Ecole polytechnique*, viii (Paris, an 8: 1800). (Also published separately.)

Rankine, W.J.M. "On the Stability of Loose Earth," *Philosophical Transactions*, cxlvii (London, 1857), 9-27.

Rennie, G. "Experiments on the Friction and Abrasion of the Surfaces of Solids," *Philosophical Transactions*, xxxiv (London, 1829), 143-170.

Robinet, René. "Un élève de l'école royale du génie de Mézières en 1756," *Etudes ardennaises*, no. 19 (October 1959), pp. 37-42.

Roller, Duane and Duane H. D. Roller. "The Development of the Concept of Electric Charge: Electricity From the Greeks to Coulomb," *Harvard Case Histories in Experimental Science*, ed. James Bryant Conant. 2 vols. (Cambridge, Mass., 1948), ii, 541-639.

Sage, G. B. "Extrait des observations lues à l'Institut national par G. B. Sage," *Journal de physique, de chimie, d'histoire naturelle et des arts . . .*, liv (Paris, an 10: 1802), 355-356.

Smeaton, J. "An Experimental Inquiry Concerning the Natural Powers of Waters and Wind to Turn Mills, and Other Machines . . . ," *Philosophical Transactions*, li (1759), 100-174.

Taton, René. "L'école royale du génie de Mézières," *Enseignement et diffusion des sciences en France au XVIIIe siècle*, ed. René Taton (Paris, 1964), 559-615.

Thomas, Eugène. "Notice sur l'ancienne Société des Sciences . . . de Montpellier," *Annuaire de l'Hérault,* XLII (Montpellier, 1859), 52-92.

Tour, Etienne François du. "Discours sur l'aiman," *Pièces qui ont remporté le prix de l'Académie Royale des Sciences . . . en 1741 sur la meilleure construction du cabestan & en 1743 et 1746 sur la meilleure construction des boussoles d'inclination; & sur l'attraction de l'aiman avec le fer.* Paris, 1748.

Van Swinden, Jan Hendrik. "Recherches sur les aiguilles aimantées, et sur leurs variations régulières," *Mémoires de mathématique et de physique présentés à l'Académie Royale des Sciences, par divers savans,* VIII (Paris, 1780), 1-576.

Wolf, C. "Recherches historique sur les étalons de poids et mesures de l'Observatoire et les appareils qui ont servi à les construire," *Annales de l'Observatoire (Impérial) de Paris—Mémoires,* XVII (Paris, 1883), c1-c78.

Unpublished Articles and Dissertations

Gillmor, Charles Stewart. "Charles Augustin Coulomb: Physics and Engineering in Eighteenth Century France." Ph.D. dissertation (Princeton University, 1968).

Mauskopf, Seymour Harold. "Molecular Structure and Composition: The Interaction of Crystallography, Chemistry and Optics in the Early Nineteenth Century." Ph.D. dissertation (Princeton University, 1966).

Payen, Jacques. "Recherches sur les frères Périer et l'introduction en France de la machine à vapeur de Watt," Thèse—3ᵉ cycle, 2 parts (Paris: Ecole Pratique des Hautes Etudes, 1966).

Sharp, G. R. "The Physical Work of Charles Auguste de Coulomb and Its Influence Upon the Development of Natural Philosophy." M.Sc. dissertation (University of London, 1936).

Taton, René. "Structure et composition de l'Académie Royale des Sciences de sa réorganisation (26 janv. 1699) à sa suppression (8 août 1793)," unpublished article, 1966.

Index

An asterisk (*) preceding a name designates a seventeenth- or eighteenth-century person for whom little information is available. The asterisk is used to distinguish the names of these persons from other single names, which indicate geographical places.